Knowledge Policy for the 21st Century:
A Legal Perspective

Knowledge Policy for the 21st Century:

A Legal Perspective

Mark Perry & Brian Fitzgerald

EDITORS

Knowledge Policy for the 21st Century: A Legal Perspective
© Irwin Law Inc., 2011

Published in 2011 by

Irwin Law Inc.
14 Duncan Street
Suite 206
Toronto, ON
M5H 3G8

www.irwinlaw.com

ISBN: 978-1-55221-172-4

Cataloguing in Publication available from Library and Archives Canada

The publisher acknowledges the financial support of the Government of Canada through the Book Publishing Industry Development Program (BPIDP) for its publishing activities.

We acknowledge the assistance of the OMDC Book Fund, an initiative of Ontario Media Development Corporation.

Printed and bound in Canada.

1 2 3 4 5   13 12 11 10 09

Table of Contents

Considerations for a 21st-century Knowledge Policy

Mark Perry & Brian Fitzgerald

This book arose out of the Knowledge Policy for the 21st Century (KP 21) Conference that we organized in April 2007 at The University of Western Ontario Faculty of Law. The conference was a collaborative research exercise between our respective universities: The University of Western Ontario (UWO) and The Queensland University of Technology (QUT). The KP 21 Conference aimed to examine key copyright issues facing contemporary society. In doing so the conference was run over two days and focused on free and open source software on day one and copyright in the digital age on day two.

We owe thanks to all of the speakers: on the first day, "FLOSS as Democratic Principle," in addition to the editors, Professor Brian Fitzgerald, QUT Faculty of Law, and Professor Mark Perry, the UWO Faculty of Law, we had Stacie LeGrow, Red Hat; Matt Norwood, Software Freedom Law Centre; Professor Peter Swire, Ohio State University; Richard Stallman, founder of the GNU Project and Free Software Foundation; and Joseph Potvin, Senior Economic Analyst, Enterprise Technology & Application Strategies, Chief Information Officer Branch, Treasury Board of Canada, Secretariat. On the second day, in addition to the editors, we had Peter Black, QUT Faculty of Law; Scott Kiel-Chisholm, Open Access to Knowledge (OAK) Law Project; Jason Shultz, Electronic Frontier Foundation; Professor Susy Frankel, Victoria University Wellington; Professor Sam Trosow, UWO Faculty of Law; David Moorman, SSHRC; Professor M.A. Wilkinson, UWO Faculty of Law; and Marcus Bornfreund, CC Canada. These conference contributors have either directly or indirectly contributed to this book. We thank our administrative and research teams that include

Michelle Bothwell, Tanya Butkovsky, Amy Barker, Nidhi Kanika Suri, Anju Sharma, and Alex Lacko — the latter two in particular have extended great efforts in going through the text several times. We also acknowledge our respective Law Schools and the Australian Research Council Centre of Excellence for Creative Industries and Innovation (CCi), and Jeffrey Miller, Alisa Posesorski, Dan Wiley, and Heather Raven of Irwin Law for sponsoring the conference and assisting with the publication of this book.

Undoubtedly this century started with a bang, at least from the perspective of the widespread adoption of information technologies and market hype for overvalued technology stock. There was a second bang shortly afterwards, when the bubble burst. We are now entering a period of greater stability for the appreciation of information technology in society, as well as sustained development, albeit in a financial environment that has become uncertain. In this collection of essays we address some of the issues that face our society in deciding how best to handle access to and monopolies over knowledge.

We begin this book with a chapter from Richard Stallman, who addresses the issue of free software, something he has been working on for over twenty-five years. This is a revised version of the transcript of the talk he gave during the KP 21 Conference. He addresses many of the issues surrounding the use of proprietary software, which he calls "just-trust-me" programs, and the four essential freedoms that a user should have. As a torchbearer to freedom in an IT-driven world, Richard has a voice that should be heard.

The following paper, from Nic Suzor and the editors, takes a look at the use of computer systems by government, and the steps the governments should take in order to make them more open and responsive to their acclaimed democratic aspirations. Here it is argued that free software gives governments greater return on their investments, not only from a financial perspective, but also in terms of the basis of the code that runs the computers that function for government operations. It takes the example of electronic voting systems, which leads us to the next chapter, "A Theory of Disclosure for Security and Competitive Reasons: Open Source, Proprietary Software, and Government Systems" by Peter Swire.

Joseph Potvin gives us a Canadian perspective on Free/Libre Open Works (FLOW), and introduces FLOW licensing models tailored for an intellectual resource community, as well as an experimental "proof of concept" project in the Canadian government administration. Matt Norwood then brings us an analysis of the United States Federal Communication Commission rules governing the use of free and open source software in software-defined radio devices. He says the rules give mixed messages for developers and manufacturers. Brian Fitzgerald and Rami Olwan take a look at *Jacobsen v. Katzer*,[1] a landmark decision in the enforcement of Free/ Libre Open Source Software (FLOSS) licensing. Marcus Bornfreund and Phil Surette show how the development of access tools, described in the paper, can practically aid usability of Canadian legislation.

Another theme addressed in this first part of the book concerns one of the key influences of this century—social networks that can be seen as an instance of the evolution of Web 2.0. We take a look at the world of blogs, starting with an introduction to the issues from Damien O'Brien with a review of some of the problems and challenges to law in the blogosphere. Emma Carroll and Jessica Coates look at the use of images online and the content licensing problems that can arise with such contributor-built interactive sites and issues of control of the materials uploaded. For Dilan Thampapillai the concept of the Google Digital Library offers a fascinating tension between the potential good of such a project, and the problems it inevitably faces under copyright.

The second part of the book addresses recent developments in copyright. Brian Fitzgerald and Benedict Atkinson take a look at *Copyright Agency Limited (CAL) v. New South Wales*,[2] a case that questions whether the owner of copyright material in a public register can charge the government each time the material is reproduced. Anthony Austin, Maree Heffernan, and Nikki David present some of the results of a survey on academic authors' perceptions of open access, copyright, online repositories and open access journals and publishing agreements. Sampsung Shi and Brian Fitzgerald argue that the notion of the romantic author does not fit with the net-work world, but should rather recognize the cultural/collaborative nature of authorship. Margaret Ann Wilkinson analyzes the theoretical underpin-nings to different approaches to open access and compares the dislocation in the international environment when examining the detail of copyright in Canada and the US. In the penultimate chapter, the editors, along with Anne Fitzgerald, Scott Kiel-Chisholm, Erin Driscoll, Dilan Thampapillai, and Jessica Coates aim to show that best-practice copyright management can lead to greater exploitation of the power of networked digital technolo-gies. Finally Susy Frankel examines recent developments in a small-market economy, New Zealand, that has interests in common with both the devel-

---

1 535 F.3d 1373 (Fed. Cir. 2008).

2 [2008] HCA 35.

oped and the developing world, and has created an "own-interest approach" to digital copyright protection.

In this collection we have aimed at piercing through the shroud that obfuscates clear directions for societal management of knowledge in the coming years. These chapters can be seen as pinholes that may shed some light on the issues that are crucial for development in the next few decades. You will draw your own conclusions, but hopefully with more analysis of the challenges, more light will be thrown.

Professor Mark Perry (UWO) and Professor Brian Fitzgerald (QUT)
30 June 2008
Sapporo Japan

Professor Mark Perry
LL.B. (Hons.) (Man.), BCSA (NCC), M.Jur. (Distinction) (Auckland).
Faculty of Law and Faculty of Science, The University of Western Ontario
Barrister and Solicitor of the Law Society of Upper Canada

Professor Brian Fitzgerald
B.A. (Griff.), LL.B. (Hons.) (QUT), B.C.L. (Oxon.), LL.M. (Harv.), Ph.D. (Griff.).
Professor of Intellectual Property and Innovation, Faculty of Law,
The Queensland University of Technology
Chief Investigator, Australian Research Council Centre of Excellence for
Creative Industries and Innovation
Barrister of the Supreme Court of Queensland and High Court of Australia

Publisher's note:
The publication of Knowledge Policy in the 21st Century was delayed through no responsibility of the Editors or Contributors to this volume. The Publisher apologizes for the delay in bringing the book to press. However, we feel that the contents remain both timely and vital to our understanding of information management in both domestic and international contexts.

CHAPTER I

Free Software

*Richard Stallman**

A. INTRODUCTION

"Free software" means the software that respects the user's freedom, re-spects your freedom. Software that's not free is proprietary software; that is, software that tramples the user's freedom. Proprietary software keeps the users divided and helpless: divided because everyone is forbidden to share with anybody else, and helpless because the users don't have the source code, so they can't change anything. They can't even tell independently what the program is really doing to them.

But free software respects the user's freedom. What does that mean? There are four essential freedoms that the users of software should have. They are:

Freedom 0: The freedom to run the program as you wish;

Freedom 1: The freedom to study the source code of the program and change it to do what you wish;

Freedom 2: The freedom to help your neighbour. That's the freedom to redistribute copies of the program to others when you wish; and

---

* This is a revised transcript of the presentation given at the Knowledge Policy for the 21st Century Conference. Richard Stallman launched the development of the GNU operating system (see online: www.gnu.org) in 1984. GNU is free software: everyone has the freedom to copy it and redistribute it, as well as to make changes, either large or small. The GNU/Linux system (basically the GNU operating system with Linux added) is used on tens of millions of computers today.

Freedom 3: The freedom to contribute to your community. That's the freedom to distribute copies of your modified versions when you wish

If you have all four of these freedoms, then the program is free software. That means that the social system of the program's distribution and use is an ethical system. If one of these freedoms is substantially missing, then the program is proprietary software which means that the social system of its distribution and use is unethical. That software's distribution is not a contribution to society; it's an attack on society.

Now this is not a question of what the program does; it's not a technical question. It's a social and ethical question. Any program could be distributed as proprietary software and then it's unethical. The same program could be distributed as free software and then, at least in regards to its distribution, it's ethical. Of course, there may be other ethical issues in the use of some particular program. All sorts of things. But they are different issues, so we have to think about them separately in the specific case that raises them.

B.   FREEDOM TWO

But why define free software this way? What makes these four freedoms essential? Freedom number two—the freedom to help your neighbour, the freedom to distribute copies to others when you wish—is essential on basic moral grounds so that you can live an ethical upright life as a good member of your community. If you use a program that doesn't give you freedom two, then you're in danger of falling into a moral dilemma at any moment, whenever your friend says, "That program's nice, can I have a copy?"

At that moment you will have to choose between two evils. One evil is to give your friend a copy and violate the licence of the program. The other is to deny your friend a copy and comply with the licence of the program. Once you're in the dilemma, you ought to choose the lesser evil, which is to give your friend a copy and violate the licence of the program.

What makes this evil the lesser evil? Well, if you can't help doing wrong to somebody, it's better to do wrong to somebody who has behaved badly rather than to somebody who has behaved well. We can assume your friend is a good friend, a good member of your community. The reason we can assume this is: the other case is also possible, but it's easy. If a person who is nasty and not helpful asks you for your cooperation, you can simply say, "Why should I help you?" So that means the hard case is where it is a good person, who normally deserves your cooperation.

By contrast, the developer of the proprietary program has deliberately attacked the social solidarity of your community, so he is culpable. And therefore, if you've got to wrong one or the other, pick him. However, to be the lesser evil does not mean it is good. It is never good to make an agreement and break it. Some agreements are inherently evil, and it is better to break them than to keep them. But breaking them is still not good. Additionally, if you do give your friend a copy, what will your friend have? Your friend will have an unauthorized copy of a proprietary program, and that's a pretty bad thing. It's almost as bad as an authorized copy.

So, what you should really do, once you've understood this dilemma, is to make sure you are never in it. There are two ways to do that. One is, don't have any friends. That's the method recommended by the proprietary software developers.

The other method is, don't use proprietary software. If you don't use a program that doesn't give you freedom two then you'll never be in this dilemma. That's the solution I have chosen. If somebody offers me a program on the condition that I promise not to share it with you, I will reject it. No matter how attractive and useful that program will be for me, I will say, "My conscience does not allow me to accept that program, so take it away."

So that's the reason for freedom number two, the freedom to help your neighbour, the freedom to distribute copies to others when you wish. I should emphasize that each of these four freedoms is the freedom to do something if you wish, as you wish. It's not an obligation. You're never required to run the program in any particular way. You're never required to study and change the source code. You're never required to redistribute copies. And, if you've made modified versions, you're never required to publish them. But the point is that you should be free to do that if you wish. And so, I've explained the reason for freedom two.

C. FREEDOM ZERO AND FREEDOM ONE

Freedom zero is essential for a different reason: so you can have control of your computer. There are proprietary programs that actually restrict how people can use authorized copies, and that's obviously not having control of your own computing. So freedom zero is essential.

But it's not enough, because that's just the freedom to either do or not do whatever the developer has already decided and programmed into it. The developer decides what you can do, not through a licence, if you have freedom zero, but rather through deciding what's in the code. So you're still under the developer's power. Therefore, we need freedom one: the freedom to study the source code and then change it to do what you want. With this freedom you decide, instead of having the developer decide for you.

If you don't have this freedom, then you can't even check what the program is doing.

Many non-free programs contain malicious features designed to spy on the user, restrict the user, and even attack the user. For instance, spyware is common. One proprietary program that you may have heard of that spies on the user is called Microsoft Windows.[1] When the user of Windows—and I won't say "you," because I'm sure you wouldn't use a program like this—uses the feature to search throughout his files for a word, Windows sends a message saying what was searched for.

That's one spy feature, but there's another: when Windows XP asks for an upgrade, it sends a list of all programs installed on the machine. That's another spy feature. But Microsoft didn't announce these spy features. People had to figure them out, and it wasn't easy. For instance, the list of installed programs is sent encrypted. So it was hard work to figure out what information is actually in that message. There may be other spy features that we don't know about yet. It's always possible for there to be more.

But spying is not limited to Windows. Windows Media Player also spies on the user. It reports everything that the user looks at: total surveillance. But please don't think that this is because Microsoft is somehow uniquely evil. Spyware is common. For instance, Real Player spies on the user the same way Windows Media Player does.

Spyware is nasty enough, but it gets worse. There is also the functionality of refusing to function; where a program says, "I don't want to let you look at this file. I don't want to let you copy part of this file. I don't want to print this file for you—because I don't like you."

I'm not talking about "bugs" here. These are deliberately implemented features, designed to stop you from doing the natural things you might want to do with the files on your computer. They're also known as DRM, or Digital Restrictions Management. They are deliberately implemented functionality of refusing to function.

Now, one of the reasons why Apple switched to the Intel computer architecture is so that it could implement more powerful Digital Restrictions Management.[2] And the main advance in Windows Vista is not an

---

1   Michael Horowitz, "Windows is Spyware" (13 September 2007), online: CNET
     News, Defensive Computing, news.cnet.com/8301-13554_3-9778389-33.html.
2   JD Lasica, "Apple's Move to Intel: A DRM Gambit?" (8 June 2005), online: Darknet
     www.darknet.com/2005/06/apples_move_to_.html.

advance in serving the user, it's an advance in restricting the user. Take a look at badvista.org for more information about why people should avoid migrating to Vista even if they are Windows users. And to take a look more generally at our campaign against Digital Restrictions Management, look at defectivebydesign.org.

But malicious features can get worse than that. There's also the malicious features designed to attack the user: back doors. One proprietary program that you may have heard of that contains a back door is called Microsoft Windows.

You see, when Windows asks for an upgrade, Microsoft more or less knows the user's identity and therefore Microsoft can deliver to that user an upgrade designed specifically for him. In other words, Microsoft can take total control of his computer.

Well, this is the back door we can deduce from known facts. But it's not the only one that has been attempted. A few years ago in India, I was told they had arrested several programmers working on developing Microsoft Windows and accused them of working simultaneously for Al-Qaeda trying to install a back door that Microsoft wasn't supposed to know about. This attempt apparently failed. We don't know if another group tried the same thing and succeeded. But we do know that in 1999, Microsoft was caught having installed a back door for the United States government. Specifically, for the use of the National Security Agency.[3]

So, what this shows us is that you can't trust a proprietary program. You can divide proprietary programs into two big categories: those in which we have discovered malicious features, and those in which we have not discovered any. Those may not have any, or they may have some that we haven't discovered. There is no way we can be sure that any program does not have malicious features. The only way we can ever be sure of the answer is when we find some. The result is that you can never trust a non-free program, and yet every non-free program demands blind faith. They're all "just trust me" programs, demanding of a faith that they do not — by virtue of their own attacks on your freedom — that they *cannot* ever justify.

However, let's consider those non-free programs which do not have malicious features. We can be sure that they exist even though we can't be sure which ones they are. Their developers did not decide to abuse their power in this particular way. But they are human. They make mistakes. Their code is full of errors. And a user of a program without freedom number one is

---

3   "Crypto Expert: Microsoft Products Leave Door Open to NSA" (3 September 1999), online: CNN www.cnn.com/TECH/computing/9909/03/windows.nsa/.

just as helpless facing an accidental error as she is facing a deliberate malicious feature. If you use a program without freedom number one, you're a prisoner of your software.

We free software developers are also human, so we also make mistakes and our code is also full of errors (although there are some arguments that on the average it has fewer of them). But if you come across an error in our program that bothers you, you can fix it, or pay someone else to fix it. And that's the difference. We can't make ourselves perfect but we can respect your freedom. We, the free-software developers, are the ones who have chosen not to keep you helpless, to respect your freedom instead.

D. FREEDOM THREE

But freedom number one is not enough. Because that's the freedom to [personally] study and change the source code. That's not enough because there are millions of users who don't know how to program and they are not in a position to, they don't know how to exercise freedom number one. But even for programmers like me it's not enough. And the reason is, we're all busy and there's just too much software. There's too much free software for any one person to study all of the software that she uses and master it all and make all the changes that she might want. This is more than one person could do.

So, in order to fully take control of our computing, we need to do it working together, cooperating. And for that we need freedom three: the freedom to distribute copies of the modified version, the freedom to contribute to your community. With this freedom we can work together. Because it only takes one person to make any given change and publish the modified version, for everyone else to get to use it without having to write.

So if there are a million users of a free program who want some change, we can expect that there will be a few thousand who know how to program. And one day a few of those people will do it—make that change, publish their modified version—and then all of those users can switch to it. So they all get what they wanted and almost all of them didn't have to do the work. And that includes the ones who don't know how to program. So the result is that all the users get the benefit of the four freedoms.

E. THE FOUR FREEDOMS AND DEMOCRACY

Every user can exercise freedom zero and two, the freedom to run the program as you wish, and to distribute copies to others when you wish. These don't require programming. But any given user can only exercise freedoms one and three—the freedom to study and change the source code, and the freedom to distribute the modified versions—to the extent that he knows how to program.

Now this is not a zero-or-one question. Many people who don't learn enough to be professional programmers learn some programming, and they can make small changes which can be useful. Just as many people who don't know how to be professional car mechanics learn to do some maintenance on their cars and that's useful also. But in any case, any given person can exercise these two freedoms to their extents. But when programmers do exercise them and publish their modified versions, everyone else gets to use their results, so we all get the benefit. And together these four freedoms give us democracy. Because a free program develops democratically under the control of its users.

Every user, individually, can control what his copy is going to do if he wants to take the trouble to do it himself or hire someone else to do it. And together, collectively, the users make the decisions about what the program will do. The users are in control, so the users generally get what they want, because nobody is in a position to impose on the users something they don't want: malicious features such as spying on the user, restricting the user, or attacking the user. Or even mere incompatibility, which some proprietary software developers impose on the user because they think the user is captive, and that by making their software incompatible they can make sure the users never switch to anything else.

Now, one interesting thing about free software is that it brings with it a free market for all kinds of support and service. By contrast, the support of proprietary programs is strictly a monopoly. You see, only the developer has the source code, so only the developer can make a change. If the user wants a change, the user has to beg and pray, "Oh almighty developer, please make this change for me." Sometimes a developer says, "Pay us and we'll listen to your problem." If the user does, the developer says, "In six months there will be an upgrade. Buy the upgrade and you'll see if we've fixed your problem and you'll see what new problems we have in store for you." But with free software, anyone who has a copy can study the source code, master it, and begin offering support. So, free software support is a competitive market.

This is interesting because many people who are in favour of proprietary software, and who like to mislead the public, say that we're Communist. And yet they are the ones who operate a command-based, monopoly-based economy, where they just give the orders and all the users have to do what they say or escape.

And they don't respect private property, either. You see, if you have a copy of some proprietary program, typically it comes with an end user licence which says that that copy's not your property. All you get to do is use it under licence if you obey whatever orders they want to give you. So, they are the ones who should be compared to a Stalinist system, whereas with free software, your copy really is yours. It's your property and you can do all the things with it that contribute to society.

Now, the competitive market for free software [support] means . . . all businesses and agencies think that competition is desirable when they buy things. They want to have competition and they value good support for the software they use. They ought to be, if they are rational, running as fast as they can towards free software to make sure that they can buy their support through a competitive market and therefore that they can expect to get good support for their money.

And it's important to know that merely having a choice between proprietary software products does not give the same result. Usually, when there is a choice between two products to do a job, we say there is no monopoly. But when it's a choice between proprietary software products, that's still monopoly. Because if the user chooses this proprietary program then he falls backward into this monopoly for support. But if he uses this other proprietary program then he falls into this other proprietary monopoly for support. So it's a choice between monopolies, but no way to escape from monopolies. The only way to escape from monopoly is to escape from proprietary software.

And that is what you should do if you value your freedom. If you use a non-free program, then it has taken away your freedom. It has put a chain on you. If you want to live in freedom and use computers, it is necessary to reject non-free software and use only free software. And that's the goal of the free software movement: to help you and all users escape from non-free software. Escape to the free world.

And as you can see, this reference to the cold war is entirely intentional.

We have built a new world in cyberspace, because it is impossible to be free in the old world of cyberspace where every computer had its lord who dominates the users and pushes them around. So if you want to be free, you have to escape, you have to come to the new world, which is a new continent that we have built in cyberspace. Because it is a virtual continent, it has room for everyone. And because there are no indigenous people in cyberspace—and the closest thing to an indigenous people there ever was, was the community of free software that I belonged to in the seventies—we didn't displace any indigenous peoples, and everybody is entitled, everyone is welcome to be in the new world; everyone is welcome to escape and join us. And that's what you have got to do. And that's what all computer users have got to do.

To have a choice between proprietary programs is being able to choose your master. Freedom means not having a master. And when you use software, freedom means not using proprietary programs.

F.   THE HISTORICAL CONTEXT

I reached these ethical conclusions more or less—of course not in their current form—in the year 1983. I had spent the 1970s as part of a community of programmers who shared software. I used entirely free software, with occasional exceptions which showed me how evil and ugly proprietary software was. And so when my community died, I was in a position to make the moral contrast and recognize that the proprietary software way of life was an evil way of life. And I decided I wanted to use computers in freedom and make it possible for others to do so. But how?

I didn't think I'd be able to convince governments to change their laws, or companies to change their practices, because I was just one man with no particular political experience or talents and no particular fame except as the developer of the editor Emacs. So I didn't try that road. But I came up with another method, a way I could solve this social problem through technical work. I just had to develop an operating system and make it free. And that would give everybody a way to use computers in freedom.

You see, the computer won't run without an operating system, and all the operating systems in 1983 were proprietary. So it was impossible to use computers in freedom. But if I developed a free operating system, that would make it possible.

So I was aware of a social problem that was important in my field and that was growing because the use of computers was growing. And most people didn't recognize it as a problem. I had the skills necessary to try to solve this problem and chances are, nobody was going to solve it if I did not. That meant that I had been elected by circumstances to solve this problem.

Just as if you see somebody drowning, and you know how to swim, and no one else is around, then you have a moral duty to save that person.

So, I decided to make the system Unix compatible, so that it would be portable and so that it would be easy for Unix users to migrate. And I gave it the name GNU which is a recursive acronym for GNU's Not Unix. It's a humorous way of giving credit. And then in January 1984, I quit my job at MIT to launch the development of this system.

By the early 1990s, the GNU system was almost finished, but one important component was missing. That was the kernel, which is the program that allocates the computer's resources to all of the other programs you run. And then somebody else developed a kernel named Linux. And then in 1992, he made it free software by changing the licence and adopting the GNU General Public Licence (or GNU GPL), which is the licence I had written to use on the components of the GNU system. And at that point, the combination of the almost complete GNU system plus Linux made a complete pre-operating system: the "GNU plus Linux" system. And thus for the first time, it was possible to use a PC without giving up your freedom to proprietary software developers. And the goal that we set out to achieve when I founded the free software movement in 1983 had been reached.

The development of Linux was the last step, the step that carried us across the finish line. It was able to do so because of all of the steps that we had taken to get so close. So I'd like to ask you to please give us an equal mention. Give us a share of the credit for the work that we started and that we are still the biggest contributor to. Please call the system "GNU plus Linux." You'll find many people call it Linux which means they are giving all the credit to Linus Torvalds, and worst of all they think that the system flowed from *his* vision and *his* ideals. But in fact, he doesn't have ideals that are relevant to this. He describes himself as "apolitical," and his vision is an engineer's vision. He says that he wants powerful, reliable software. That is a viewpoint that today goes by the name "open source."

G. FREE SOFTWARE v OPEN SOURCE

Open source is a way that people who want to talk about free software—but cover up the ethical issues that are the base of the free software movement—talk about the software that is free and some other software which is almost free. They think it's acceptable; their criteria are different. So that's why I don't use the term "open source," that's why I haven't mentioned it, because that's not what I'm interested in, what I'm in favour of. I'm in favour of freedom of the users. Freedom for everyone who uses computers, whereas *they* say they are aiming only for powerful, reliable software.

Open source actually refers to a development methodology. They say that if you let everybody have more or less the same four freedoms, then that will make software more powerful and reliable. Well, I think that's a nice bonus, and if you're going to develop good software it's wise to take a look at good and bad software development methodologies. But that's the secondary issue when compared with freedom and social solidarity. That is to say, when compared with ethics and politics.

So open source misses the main point, and not by accident. That term was promoted with a rhetoric designed to miss that point, and that's why if you talk about open source, you're helping other people miss that point. So I never describe my work that way.

People motivated by those values have made contributions to our community. If you develop a program and it's free, well, your actions are good regardless of what your motives might be. But nonetheless, it's important to teach the rest of society about freedom and social solidarity. And it's important to teach the users of this operating system that it was developed for the sake of those ideals. Because if we want to keep our freedom, we have to value our freedom. And most people in our community have never even heard of these freedoms.

H. HUMAN RIGHTS AND SOFTWARE

Now, in other areas of life, people have been talking about human rights for centuries, so there have been centuries for people to address the questions of which human rights people are entitled to, and centuries to spread these ideas around the world. That doesn't mean it's easy to defend these human rights. The US has abolished the right to a trial following norms of justice before someone is imprisoned: a fundamental right. The United States has abolished freedom of association by administratively declaring organizations to be "terrorist." And many other freedoms are under great pressure in the US. Freedom of speech has not been officially abolished, but people have been put under a lot of pressure for criticizing the government.

And other countries that we think of as bastions of freedom have done similar things. In the UK, it is now a crime to be suspect. Literally. The offense consists of having possessed an object which gives rise to a suspicion which is judged to be reasonable. So they have adopted, officially in their laws, the practice of imprisoning people on suspicion. And this is not even to count the imprisonment without trial which fortunately in the UK was banned by judges. So defending freedom can be hard, even when these freedoms are understood.

But computing is a new area of life and there hasn't been much time for having a debate about which human rights belong to the person who is using software. And to the extent that there has been a debate, it has been mostly dominated by the proprietary software companies. They dominated it in two ways.

First of all, they set up a status quo so they get the advantage that they're not calling for a change. They're just saying that what everybody is used to, or just about everybody is used to, is right. And secondly, they have a lot of money, and they can use that for influence in getting the support of a lot of influential people and institutions. And even in the community of users of free software, most have never heard of the ideas I've told you because they've only heard the "open source" ideas. If we are to establish a community of freedom and make it last, the most important thing to do is to teach the people who are using free software to value the freedoms *as freedoms*, so they'll be ready to defend these freedoms.

I. LEGAL PROHIBITION AND FREE PROGRAMS

Freedoms are frequently threatened. The US has two different laws that can prohibit free software, and many other countries have adopted them also under US influence and pressure. One of these two laws in the US is the *Digital Millennium Copyright Act*,[4] which has been used to censor the free software for playing a DVD. You see, the movie on a DVD is often in encrypted format. The encryption format was secret so that all the authorized DVD players restricted the user. (They imposed digital restrictions management.) Then somebody figured out the format and wrote a free program to play the movie on a DVD. And then they published a free program to do the job.

Well, that free program is censored in the US. Even making a link to a foreign site that distributes it is illegal in the US. So how are we going to serve the public when it's illegal to serve the public? This law expresses— takes to the extreme—the corruption of democracy, which replaces government of the people, by the people, for the people, with government of the people, by the cronies, for the corporations. This law says that the people exist to be the market or the prey of business. And that for people to help each other is illegal.

But this law can only prohibit programs in a particular narrow range of jobs, that is, access to encrypted works. By contrast, patent law can prohibit any kind of free program no matter what job it does. Of course it can also prohibit proprietary programs too. In fact, any software developer is in danger of getting sued, probably dozens or hundreds of times, because in

---

4 *Digital Millennium Copyright Act of 1998*, Pub. L. No. 105–34.

the US, any software idea, any method, technique, algorithm, feature, even some aspect of a feature, some aspect of a technique can be patented. And in a large program, there are thousands of these. So a large program is likely to be covered by hundreds of different patents at once.

One study was done, about three years ago, by a lawyer who checked one particular large component—namely Linux, which is the kernel of the GNU/Linux system—and he found 283 different US software patents, each of which prohibited some computation done somewhere in Linux. Around the same time, I read an estimate that Linux was 0.25 percent of the entire system. So by multiplication, we can estimate that there are some 100,000 software patents prohibiting something somewhere in the system (rough estimate). That shows you how bad the patent system is. If you look at it as a distribution of GNU/Linux, you could expect around 100,000 patents covering that one CD-ROM worth of software. So we now face political battles just to be free to continue serving the public.

J. GOVERNMENT AND FREE SOFTWARE

Meanwhile, one secondary question is why government agencies should use free software. Now, there is a general reason: because the government's mission is to assure freedom and a good society for its citizens. Therefore, in regards to computer use, governments should try to direct society away, out of the propriety software path, and onto the free software path. Now this takes some effort, because there is inertia which keeps society, at least most of it, going down the proprietary software path. Society is essentially stuck in a rut. And the proprietary software developers know this, so every year they make the rut a little deeper, figuring that the more society uses computers, the more they can get away with squeezing society; thus, the deeper the rut, the more money they can make.

So, governments should make the investment of pulling society out of this path and onto the path that leads to freedom. Every government agency has its own particular mission, but all government agencies should participate in carrying out the overall mission for society of defending freedom, and not let their own narrow, specific missions blind them to the overall purpose of the government.

However, there is also a more direct reason. You see, a government agency does its computing on behalf of the public and it has a responsibility to assure its control over its own computing. It is wrong, it is a dereliction, for any government agency to allow computing to fall into private hands—any private hands. However, using a non-free program is doing exactly that.

It is allowing the agency's computing to fall into the hands of the software's developer. Thus, using proprietary software is a dereliction on the part of the agency.

When agencies migrate to free software, they not only regain their sovereign control over the work they do on behalf of the public, they also encourage free software use among private entities. For instance, these agencies want support, so when they use free software they then get the benefit of the free market of support so they can decide who to hire. But the point is, they are hiring somebody, so they are contributing to the growth of the free market that free software support. And the bigger that market is, the easier it is for private companies and NGOs to buy support for free software, the more choices they have. So that makes it easier for them to migrate as well.

K. GOVERNMENT SCHOOLS AND FREE SOFTWARE

Now, I've been talking about government agencies. One kind of government agency which you might not think of is actually the most important of all, and that is the school, the government-supported school, which, like all schools, should teach exclusively with free-software. There are four reasons for this.

The first reason is to save money. Schools in all countries are limited by their budgets. There are things they want to do but can't do, so they should not be wasting money paying for permission to run proprietary software. That reason is obvious and superficial, and some proprietary software companies get rid of it by donating *gratis* copies of their non-free software to the schools. And why do they do that? Is it because they are idealistic and want to promote education?

I don't think so. Rather, they want to use the school as an instrument to impose dependency on their software onto society. The idea is that the students in the school will learn to use that software and become dependent on it just as if they had been given an addictive drug. And then after they graduate, you can be sure that the same company is not going to donate *gratis* copies to them nor to the companies that they work for. And the result is that the schools push all of society into the path of dependency and helplessness and division which is the path of using proprietary software.

This is counter to the schools' mission in society which is to prepare people to be citizens of a free society in which people treat each other well. Therefore schools should refuse these poisonous gifts; actually you might say addictive gifts. For the school to teach the students dependency on the software is like teaching the students to be addicts to an addictive drug. And of course, the companies that make the drug would be glad to donate the first dose. The first dose is *gratis*. Afterwards, when you're hooked, you've got to pay.

Schools should refuse to participate in this. Schools should refuse to teach non-free software. They should teach exclusively free software. That's the second reason.

But there is an even deeper reason for the sake of computing, of computer science education. You see, at the age of thirteen, some people who are natural born programmers want to learn everything about the software, the computer and the system. So if they are using a program, they want to know how it works. But when the student says, "Teacher, how does this work?", if it's proprietary, the teacher can only say, "I'm sorry, it's a secret." So education cannot begin. But if the program is free, the teacher can explain what he knows and then say, "Here's the source code. Read it and you'll understand everything." And that student will read it because she wants to understand everything, she's fascinated by software. And this is the way these born programmers can fully realize their skills.

You see, they're supposed to teach them to program, because to them programming is obvious. But learning to program "well" is something else. You learn to program well by reading lots of code and writing lots of code. You can only do that with free software. First you read the program, and if there is anything you don't understand, you ask the teacher or an older student, "What does this do?" and from that experience you learn something very important: that is the wrong way to write it because it's not clear enough. You have to see lots of ways of doing things wrong to learn not to do them. Then, you can try something else that's useful for learning, which is, to write a small change in the big program you just read. This is before you are at the stage where you could do a good job of writing a large, useful program yourself, but you could try writing a small change in an existing large program. That's a small job.

So you could write one change, and another, and then change another big program. And after writing thousands of changes in large programs, you get very good at writing changes in large programs. This is the big job of the software field: writing changes into existing large programs. And now and then, of course, we write a new large program. But once you've written lots of changes, you could probably also write a new program because you've come to understand the right way to write each piece.

In 1971, I had to go to the artificial intelligence lab (at MIT) to have an opportunity to learn this way and realize my skill. Today, any school can provide this opportunity, but only with free software, not with proprietary software.

There's even a deeper reason: for the sake of moral education. You see, schools are supposed to teach not just facts and not just skills and techniques, but above all, how to be a good citizen: the spirit of goodwill, the habit of helping your neighbour. So, every class should have a rule: "students, if you bring a program to class, you can't keep it for yourself. You must share it with the rest of the class. If you won't share it, you can't bring it." However, the school has to follow its own rule to set a good example. So the school must only bring free software to class. This applies to all levels from elementary school to the university. The university you are in must use exclusively free software. And if that's not the case already, you ought to be working to make it so.

L. CONCLUSION

I'd like to urge you to look at the website for gnu.org for more information about the GNU system and free software movement, and please look at fsf.org for information about the Free Software Foundation and to join. We need your support.

Governments above all should call for free software because protecting the public's freedom is the mission of the government. If we have governments that don't want to talk about protecting the freedom of their citizens, we're in deep trouble.

As well, the universities ought to listen to you and start teaching students how [to work on free software]. And the best way is to set up programs where students who are interested in programming, work through the whole period of time that they are in the university on free software projects.

CHAPTER 2

Free Software as a Democratic Principle

Nic Suzor, Brian Fitzgerald, & Mark Perry

A. INTRODUCTION

Software forms an important part of the interface between citizens and their government. An increasing amount of government functions are being performed, controlled, or delivered electronically.[1] This software, like all language, is never value-neutral, but must, to some extent, reflect the values of the coder and proprietor.[2] The move that many governments are making towards e-governance,[3] and the increasing reliance that is being placed upon software in government, necessitates a rethinking of the relationships of power and control that are embodied in software.

It is important for software that directly influences administrative, legislative, and judicial decisions to be examinable by the citizenry, just as the decisions themselves are open and transparent. Without this safeguard, there can be no guarantee that the decisions made by government are legitimate. If the software that is relied upon to provide either the inputs or the

---

1   For example, see US, General Accounting Office, *Critical Infrastructure Protection: Challenges in Securing Control Systems* (GAO-04-140T) (2003), online: www.gao.gov/new.items/d04140t.pdf.

2   Brian Fitzgerald, "Software as Discourse: The Power of Intellectual Property in Digital Architecture" (2000) 18 Cardozo Arts & Ent. L.J. 337.

3   For a discussion of e-governance, see: Thomas Riley, "E-Government vs. E-Governance: Examining the Differences in a Changing Public Sector Climate" Commonwealth Centre for E-Governance (2003), online: www.rileyis.com/publications/research_papers/tracking03/IntlTrackRptMay03n04.pdf.

evaluation in a decision-making process cannot be trusted, there can be no trust in either the process or the final decision.[4]

A responsible government must be accountable for the decisions it makes, for and on the behalf of its people. Transparency is one of the most important factors of a representative democracy.[5] The entire system rests upon the proposition that if the government is not acting in a way that is supported by the majority of the people, then the people have the ability and the obligation to force a change in the government. If the people do not have the power to understand what the government is doing, and the basis upon which it is making decisions, there can be no question of an informed democratic process.

When the processes of a government are embodied in software, it is critical that the inner workings of that software be available for examination, discussion, and critique. Without access to the human, readable source code, it is practically impossible to be sure exactly how a piece of software functions, to assure oneself that it is not biased against or for any particular individuals or sectors of society, or to ensure that there are no critical bugs or vulnerabilities that may enable others to exploit the software for their own personal benefit. The investigation of these issues in code is no less important than the investigation of bias and corruption in government offices by traditional reporters.

This chapter will argue that use of free software in governments is an ideal way to foster trust and informed discussion in a democratic society.[6] Free software provides its users with the ability to examine and understand the source code of key software applications. The use of free software would increase the transparency of government decisions, and thus also the degree to which citizens can trust those decisions, or work for change in the decision-making process.

---

4   Rana Tassabehji & Tony Elliman, "Generating Citizen Trust in E-Government Using a Trust Verification Agent: A Research Note" (Paper presented to the European and Mediterranean Conference on Information Systems, Costa Blanca, Alicante, Spain, 6–7 July 2006), online: www.iseing.org/emcis/EMCIS2006/Proceedings/Contributions/EGISE/eGISE4.pdf.

5   See Onuora Awunor, "Transparency in Government" (29 July 2007), online: http://onuoraawunor.blogspot.com/2007/07/transparency-in-government.html.

6   For a look at how free software expresses democratic ideals of citizenship engaged with the affirmation of information of individual rights and freedom in North America and Brazil, see Alexandra Pinheiro & Henrique Cukierman, "Free Software: Some Brazilian Translations," online: www.csi.ensmp.fr/WebCSI/4S/download_paper/download_paper.php?paper=pinheiro_cukierman.pdf.

It is important to note that free software is not a strict requirement for transparency. While all free software is, by definition, transparent to the user, source code can also be made available for examination of non-free software.[7] There are, however, significant benefits to the use of free software in governments beyond transparency. The four freedoms encompassed in the term "free software" include: [8]

- The freedom to run the program, for any purpose (freedom 0).
- The freedom to study how the program works, and adapt it to your needs (freedom 1).
- The freedom to redistribute copies so you can help your neighbour (freedom 2).
- The freedom to improve the program, and release your improvements to the public, so that the whole community benefits (freedom 3).

While access to the source code of software is strictly necessary for transparency in governments, the other freedoms guaranteed by free software are also beneficial in the public sector. The use of free software allows for citizens to become involved in their governance by participating in the software-development process.[9] Free software also ensures that the benefits of publicly funded development and acquisition are returned to the public. In this chapter we will examine each of these propositions, and argue that there is a compelling case for the use of free software in governments.

B. "JUSTICE MUST BE SEEN TO BE DONE"

One of the most important aspects of democracy is that government must be accountable to its citizens. Decisions made by the executive, judicial, and legislative arms of government must, as far as possible, be transparent. Without transparency in the decision-making process, there can be no trust that a government is acting on behalf of its people. Accountability in government is a continual prerequisite for a functional democracy. The processes through

---

7   See, for example, Microsoft Shared Source, online: www.microsoft.com/resources/ sharedsource/default.mspx.

8   Free Software Foundation, "The Free Software Definition," online: www.gnu.org/ philosophy/free-sw.html.

9   For discussion of the political rights and participation of the citizenry in the information society, see: Hans Klein, "The Right to Political Participation and the Information Society" (Paper presented to the Global Democracy Conference, Montreal, 29 May–1 June 2005), online: www.ip3.gatech.edu/research/Right_to_Political_Participation.pdf.

which decisions are made in government must be both accountable and transparent, and the workings of critical software systems employed by the government to aid in that decision-making process are no exception.

1)   Electronic Voting Machines

One of the most important instances of accountability in a democratic society is that of the voting process. Citizens need to be able to trust that the voting process is not either (a) being deliberately manipulated, or (b) significantly flawed and susceptible to error. Without trust in the process through which our representatives are elected, there must be significant doubts as to the legitimacy of a democratic government.

Many governments are moving towards using electronic voting machines (EVMs) to assist in the voting process. While there are certainly concerns about electronic voting as a whole,[10] there are significant advantages that make it attractive to governments. Electronic voting makes accurate vote counting nearly instantaneous, eliminating many hours of tedious, error-prone work.[11] Computer assisted interfaces can be easily adapted to assist voters who have difficulty in reading and marking a paper ballot—the information can be presented and recorded in a number of ways to account for the individual needs of the voter.[12]

If electronic voting systems are going to be used, they must be able to be trusted. A key component of this trust is the availability of the source code that controls electronic voting software.[13]

Without being able to study and understand the source code of EVM software, citizens must rely on the assurances of the vendor or government

---

10   Security problems abound. See Dave Jefferson *et al.*, "A Security Analysis of the Secure Electronic Registration and Voting Experiment (SERVE)" (20 January 2004), online: http://servesecurityreport.org/. There are also significant issues with implementation, such as in the 13th District November 2006 elections where there were 18,000 "no vote for candidate" votes on ES&S machines. See Kim Zetter, "Did Florida Foul Another Ballot?" (17 November 2006), online: www.wired.com/politics/security/news/2006/11/72130?currentPage=all.

11   For a look at some of the issues surrounding electronic voting, see: Institute of Governmental Studies, University of California, "Electronic Voting: Overview and Issues" (November 2005), online: http://igs.berkeley.edu/library/htElectronicVoting2004.html.

12   For example, the Victoria Electoral Commission recently introduced electronic voting for people with vision impairment, online: www.vec.vic.gov.au/electronicvoting.html.

13   See, for example, Jason Kitcat, "Why Electronic Voting Software Should Be Free Software" (1 March 2001), online: www.inmyarea.org/h/n/WRITING/evoting/ALL/53/.

that there are no bugs (or "features") in the software that may affect the result of a vote.[14] In a representative democracy, however, these assurances are simply not good enough. The extent to which an accident or a malicious actor can influence an electronic vote far exceeds that of a paper-based ballot. Vote tampering in a paper system would involve substituting or removing a very large amount of ballots. In an electronic system, on the other hand, a few lines of code could substantially, and nearly imperceptibly, alter the results of a whole election.[15]

If electronic voting is to be used and trusted, it is clear that the source code must be able to be scrutinized.[16] The guarantees of a private company providing the electronic equipment are not sufficient in a field as critical to the practice of democracy as voting.

While it is obvious that not every voter will have the skills or time required to evaluate the trustworthiness of any given EVM software, public accessibility increases the probability that malicious or insecure code will be identified. This review function could conceivably be performed by a core group of independent auditors, but without public review there are no checks placed upon the evaluation of those auditors. The availability of the code for public review, even if the code is not actually reviewed by a large portion of the public, engenders trust in the review process.[17]

---

14   For an overview of the electronic voting process, see: Tadayoshi Kohno *et al.*, *Analysis of an Electronic Voting System: Proceedings of the IEEE Symposium on Security and Privacy, Berkeley, 2004* (Los Alamitos, CA: IEEE Computer Society Press, 2004).

15   See, for example, a report that ES&S machines are vulnerable to numerous exploits using a magnet and a PDA with an infrared port, potentially allowing an attacker to "exercise complete control over the results reported by the entire county election system" with no more access to the system than that typically provided to voters. See *EVEREST: Evaluation and Validation of Election-Related Equipment, Standards and Testing, Final Report* (December 2007), online: www.sos.state.oh.us/sos/upload/everest/00-SecretarysEVERESTExecutiveReport.pdf at 53, quoted in Kim Zetter, "Report: Magnet and PDA Sufficient to Change Votes on Voting Machine" (17 December 2007), online: http://blog.wired.com/27bstroke6/2007/12/report-magnet-a.html.

16   Additionally, in a discussion about the role of source code disclosure and transparency of voting systems, Joseph Lorenzo Hall concludes that disclosure of full system source code will promote technical improvements in voting systems: Joseph Lorenzo Hall, *Tranparency and Access to Source Code in Electronic Voting* (2006), online: http://josephhall.org/papers/jhall_evt06.pdf.

17   For a more in-depth discussion of the dangers of closed-source EVM systems, see Mark Perry & Brian Fitzgerald, "FLOSS as Democratic Principle: Free Software as

There are a number of reasons for which manufacturers of EVM systems are reluctant to make their code available to the public. The first, termed "security through obscurity," rests upon the assumption that it is undesirable to provide would-be attackers with a blueprint of the software, which could be used to make exploitation easier. Unfortunately, relying on the secrecy of the code is a very brittle security mechanism. Once an exploit has been found by a malicious attacker, it remains open until an attack is detected, analyzed, and the breach repaired. The better approach is to design a system that is secure even if everything about the system is public knowledge. This is known as Kerckhoffs' principle, named after Dr. Auguste Kerckhoffs, a nineteenth-century cryptographer. Kerckhoffs' principle was extended by Eric Raymond, in relation to open source software, who claims that "[a]ny security software design that doesn't assume the enemy possesses the source code is already untrustworthy."[18]

The argument follows that open source software can be more secure because it allows weaknesses to be found through widespread continuous testing, and does not rely on the secrecy of potential vulnerabilities.[19] On this basis, Bruce Schneier argues that in the long term, "public scrutiny is the only reliable way to improve security."[20]

Another argument against public disclosure rests upon the commercial exploitation of electronic voting software. Providers of EVMs argue that the code which runs their systems provides their competitive advantage over other providers. These providers claim protection of their code not only as copyright works, but also as trade secrets, and are reluctant to allow any public access that could lessen their competitive advantage.[21] This argument simply cannot be accepted. If it is true that public access to the

---

Democratic Principle" (2006) 2(3) The International Journal of Technology, Knowledge & Society 155, online: http://eprints.qut.edu.au/archive/00004425.

18   Eric S. Raymond, "If Cisco Ignored Kerckhoffs's Law, Users Will Pay the Price" (17 May 2004), online: http://lwn.net/Articles/85958.

19   See Bill Caelli, "Security with Free and Open Source Software" in Brian Fitzgerald & Graham Bassett, eds., Legal Issues Relating to Free and Open Source Software (Brisbane: Queensland University of Technology, 2003). See, further, Peter Swire, "A Theory of Disclosure for Security and Competitive Reasons: Open Source, Proprietary Software, and Government Systems" (2006) 42 Hous. L. Rev. 1333.

20   Bruce Schneier, "Internet Shield: Secrecy and Security" San Francisco Chronicle (2 March 2003), online: www.schneier.com/essay-033.html.

21   See, generally, Andrew Massey, "'But We Have To Protect Our Source!': How Electronic Voting Companies' Proprietary Code Ruins Elections" (2004) 27 Hastings Comm.& Ent. L.J. 233.

source code is a requirement for public trust in the voting system, then the interests of a private provider cannot be put above the needs of the public. If it is not possible for a private developer to create an EVM solution that adheres to the standard of trust needed for democratic elections, then the development must be carried out by the government. The integrity of voting infrastructure is not something that can be compromised for the benefit of private actors.

One other criticism of publicly disclosed source code rests in the proposition that there is no assurance that the code examined is the code that is actually running on the EVM systems on the date of the election. Examination in this case may not provide any greater level of security. While this criticism has some merit, it goes more deeply to a criticism of EVM itself, not of disclosure. There is much more to software security than the integrity of the source code. If the machines in question cannot be reasonably secured from interference, then they should not be used. If no electronic machine can provide a satisfactory level of security, then electronic voting should not be seen as a satisfactory replacement for paper-based ballots. If, on the other hand, electronic voting machines are used, then the code that is assumed to be running must be available for scrutiny.

The argument in this section does not rely on making a recommendation for whether or not electronic voting systems should be deployed. Put simply, if a government does decide to implement EVM, among the large number of other security concerns that must be considered, the source code of the machines must be available for public scrutiny. The use of free software is one, but not the only, way in which the source code may be made available.[22]

2) E-governance, Online Delivery, and Electronic Control

The basis for preferring publicly accessible source code is not limited to electronic voting. As more core government services move towards online delivery, and more of citizen interaction with government becomes mediated through software, there exists a greater need for that software to be accountable to the citizenry.

There is a very real possibility that the software that controls access to government services may contain errors or omissions that make it more diffi-

---

22   Open source solutions are available for development; see, for example, Halina Kaminski & Mark Perry, "Verifiable Electronic Voting System: An Open Source Solution," online: www.csd.uwo.ca/~markp/htmls/vev.pdf.

cult for individuals, or groups of individuals, to access those services. Whatever the software, be it related to tax collection, welfare, medical funds, or education, individuals can benefit from the ability of any (sufficiently trained and resourced) member of the public to examine the logic behind the software, and to expose and report on any hidden biases or flaws.

As more of the core functions of government are being fulfilled by the citizenry using electronic interfaces, with a gradual removal of human bureaucratic intervention, greater reliance is being placed on the efficacy and correctness of the electronic systems. Recovery from software errors can be a long and tedious process, and there is always a temptation to assume that the software is correct, and that the citizen-user must therefore be incorrect. It can be very difficult, especially when dealing with such important matters as taxation, health, welfare, and education, for a citizen to have these errors corrected before serious hardship is caused.

The ramifications of such errors are decidedly non-trivial. Faulty logic in a welfare system may result in a family missing vital income for a number of weeks; an incorrect calculation of tax rules may result in undetected increases in taxation liability. Faulty input validation or broken logic rules may prevent families from accessing healthcare benefits or rebates. The public availability of the source code for these systems is vital to offer some protection from hidden bias, bugs, and resulting inequity.

The use of free software in the public sector is also important to ensure that the public retains control of public resources and information. By guaranteeing the freedoms to use, modify, adapt, and share software, governments are able to avoid vendor lock-in and third-party control of important public information. For example, the use of free software guarantees the ability to switch back-end data storage formats without changing user interfaces, and without losing existing data. Without the ability to port user interface and data standards, governments and citizens face very high switching costs, both financially, and as a function of education and retraining.

3)   The Public Should Be Involved in Their Own Governance

Most of the discussion so far has centred on the availability of source code for public infrastructure software. Free software, however, can provide more benefits to the public than just accountability. Using free software has the opportunity to allow individuals to participate in the meaning-making process, as well as working to help improve software to better suit individual needs.

One of the features of market-based software development is that only profitable features are implemented, which leaves many applications without features that would be very useful to a minority of users, but for which demand cannot be adequately manifested.[23] These types of features can extend from multilingual language support, to alternative input and output modes for people with disabilities, or to support for niche market or non-profit applications. Through the use of free software, individuals or groups desiring such features can "scratch an itch," and add code (or employ someone to add code) for which they can see a benefit. This iterative production lowers the barrier to entry to production of niche features, and hence increases the utility of software to minority groups.

Even where demand for new features can be manifested, it is often not a simple process for a vendor to provide customized additions to existing software. After the initial roll-out of a system, a government may be tied to the original vendor for upgrades, and the process of negotiating and implementing new features can be extremely difficult. The inability to make changes independently means that feature requests must be made in accordance with extremely complicated contractual relationships. As the needs of government and citizens change and evolve over time, being tied to the original vendor, either contractually or through copyright, may become a very onerous limitation. The use of free software eliminates any strict tie to a particular vendor, and greatly reduces the barriers for the implementation of new features.[24]

To the extent that a functioning democracy needs to keep its software up to date with the ever-changing needs of its citizens, free software can be immensely beneficial in reducing the role of the vendor as a bar to the updating process. Free software has a direct advantage in that free software vendors may of course still provide support and additional development, but in those cases where vendors are not willing or able to do so, there are much smaller barriers to obtaining the same services from other vendors.[25] Free

---

23   See Jay P. Kesan & Rajiv C. Shah, "Deconstructing Code" (2004) 6 Yale Journal of Law & Technology 277 at 378–82.

24   For other benefits of free software, see Jason Kitcat, "Why Electronic Voting Software Should be Free Software" (9 July 2001), online: www.kuro5hin.org/?op=display story;sid=2001/7/9/81531/16879.

25   See Brian Fitzgerald & Nicolas Suzor, "Legal Issues for the Use of Free and Open Source Software in Government" (2005) 29(2) Melbourne U.L. Rev. 412.

software also gives citizens an opportunity to participate in the development of the software that controls their interaction with their government.[26]

4) Returns of Public Investment Should Benefit the Public

When a government develops or pays for the development of software, there are three broad options for the future of that software. It could remain locked up within the government, and never be released to the public. It could be commodified and commercialized and sold as a closed product in order to recoup the costs of development and perhaps become profitable. Alternatively, the government could release the software as free software, in order to return the benefits of the publicly funded development to the community.[27]

The advantages of this last option are numerous. The benefit to the public may be, in many cases, much greater when the availability of high-quality software commons is increased, rather than through the sale of a limited number of licences. Where exactly this line will be drawn will of course depend on the software, the market for the software, and its utility in potential derivative applications if it were made freely available. In assessing the balance, however, governments should be very clear that the benefits of a software commons increase exponentially with the amount of software that is made available, as the software can be used in any number of unexpected ways in combination with other available software.

There is a very significant advantage in allowing the private sector to repurpose high-quality government software for its own use. In many cases, this potential downstream increase in innovation will outweigh the immediate benefit of a limited number of software licences. The release of government-produced software as free software means that investment in software infrastructure has not only immediate payoffs for the purpose for which it was designed, but also long term benefits to sustained innovation

---

26   Eben Moglen notes that the choices we make in structuring copyright licences are of fundamental importance in structuring the community which develops around use of that material: see, for example, Eben Moglen, transcript of lecture given at the 3rd International GPLv3 Conference, Barcelona, 22 June 2006, online: www.fsfeurope. org/projects/gplv3/barcelona-moglen-transcript.en.html.

27   It is important to note that releasing government-developed software as free software does not remove the ability to commercialize the software, for example, by providing custom support or integration services, and realizing other benefits such as improved code, nor, indeed, from securing intellectual property rights.

in the private sector, where the code may be reused for seemingly unrelated purposes.

C. CONCLUSION: A CASE FOR FREE SOFTWARE IN GOVERNMENT

In a democratic society, there is a requirement that government resources are used in the interests and for the benefit of the public. As governments move towards adopting electronic approaches to automate vital functions and interface with their citizens, the use of free software ought to be carefully considered. The benefits of using free software include:

- increased accountability, in that citizens are able to examine the basis on which decisions are made;
- necessarily open standards, which extend data longevity and access far beyond that of any given technology or format;
- lower barriers to customization of software for minority groups and niche markets;
- the value of investment in software development is returned to the public for future reuse — allowing public, private, and non-profit organizations access to high quality software from which they can innovate and generate further value;
- less waste involved in the continual redeveloping of standard architectures; and
- citizens are given the opportunity to participate in the meaning-making process by directly soliciting inputs to the code that increasingly governs their lives.

The use of FLOSS in governments is growing, particularly in Europe. To date the adoption has primarily been for back-end operating systems (e.g., Apache and Linux) and common desktop applications (OpenOffice). There are policy pressures in the EU for adoption of FLOSS that range from community directives to municipal mandates.[28] Unfortunately, such moves have yet to take root in North America or Australia. We believe, however,

---

28 There is good data on EU government adoption, see Free/Libre/Open Source Software: Policy Support (FLOSSPOLS), online: http://flosspols.org and UNU-MERIT, *Study on the Economic Impact of Open Source Software on Innovation and the Competitiveness of the Information and Communication Technologies (ICT) Sector in the EU*, Final Report (20 November 2006), online: ec.europa.eu/enterprise/ict/policy/doc/2006-11-20-flossimpact.pdf [UNU-MERIT].

that there exists a strong argument that democratic governments ought to prefer free software to closed source software, in the best interests of their citizenry. It is critical, in our minds, that publicly funded software development, like publicly funded research, be conducted as much as possible in an open manner, with the results being shared with the community and made available for future innovation. In the future, we hope to see governments acting in accordance with this democratic principle by requiring vendors of software they acquire to release the developed code under free software licenses.

In each case where governments are procuring software development, the cost-benefit analysis should include a detailed examination of the lower development costs of free software and the public benefit of releasing the software, weighed against any increased costs caused by loss of the developer's ability to extract monopoly rents on closed-source applications.[29] To date, this analysis has largely ignored the public benefit arguments, and governments have focused on the fear expressed by private software development companies. We are hopeful that with recognition of the public benefits attainable through the use of free software, governments will be able to make more informed software procurement choices that will provide not only greater returns on investment, but also greater trust and participation in the democratic process.

---

29   See, for example, UNU-MERIT, *ibid.* at 11, which concluded that "FLOSS potentially saves industry over 36% in software R&D investment that can result in increased profits or be more usefully spent in further innovation."

CHAPTER 3

A Theory of Disclosure for Security and Competitive Reasons:
Open Source, Proprietary Software, and Government Systems

*Peter P. Swire**

A. INTRODUCTION

A previous article, "A Model for When Disclosure Helps Security: What is Different about Computer and Network Security?" proposed a model for when disclosure helps or hurts security and provided reasons why computer security is often different in this respect than physical security.[1] This chapter provides a general approach for describing the incentives of actors to disclose information about their software or systems. A chief point of this chapter is that the incentives of disclosure depend on two largely independent assessments: (i) the degree to which disclosure helps or hurts security,

---

*   This chapter draws on discussions with numerous people over the past five years. I appreciate comments I received during the drafting of the chapter from Jon Callas, Whitfield Diffie, William Kovacic, David Ladd, Mark Lemley, David McGowan, and Adam Shostack, participants at the 2005 IPIL/Houston Santa Fe Conference "Transactions, Information and Emerging Law," the ACM Conference on Computer and Communications Security, and George Washington Law School IP Workshop. Chris Palmer of the Electronic Frontier Foundation has been an especially thorough and helpful commentator on the project.

1   Peter P. Swire, "A Model for When Disclosure Helps Security: What is Different about Computer and Network Security?" (2004) 3 J. on Telecomm. & High Tech. L. 163 ["Security Model"], online: http://ssrn.com/abstract=531782. A slightly updated version of the material was published as Peter P. Swire, "A Model for When Disclosure Helps Security: What is Different about Computer and Network Security?" in Mark F. Grady & Francesco Parisi, eds., *The Law and Economics of Cybersecurity* (New York: Cambridge University Press, 2006) 29.

and (ii) the degree to which disclosure creates competitive advantages or disadvantages for the organization.

Table 1 presents a 2 × 3 matrix in which disclosure for security and competition are assessed for three types of systems or software: open source; proprietary software; and government systems. The matrix indicates that there is a greater convergence on disclosure between open source and proprietary software than most commentators have believed. For instance, open source security experts use secrecy in "stealth firewalls" and in other ways. Open-source programmers also often rely on gaps in open source licences to gain a competitive advantage by keeping key information secret. Meanwhile, proprietary software often uses more disclosure than assumed. For security reasons, large purchasers and market forces often lead to disclosure about proprietary software. For competitive reasons, proprietary software companies often disclose a great deal when seeking to become the standard in an area or for other reasons.

Table 1

	Security	Competition
Open Source	Ideologically open; some "secret sauce" (Case 1)	Ideologically open; significant use of secrecy in practice (Case 2)
Proprietary Software	Monopolist on source code; disclosure based on monopsony and market structure (Case 3)	Monopolist on source code; disclosure based on how open-standards help profits (Case 4)
Government Systems	Information sharing dilemma (help attackers & defenders); public choice model & under-disclosure (Case 5)	Turf maximization & under-disclosure, e.g., FBI vs. local police for the credit (Case 6)

Despite this greater-than-expected convergence of practice for open source and proprietary software, there are strong reasons to believe that less-than-optimal disclosure happens for government systems. The tradition of military secrecy and the concern about tipping off attackers leads to a culture of secrecy for government security. Market mechanisms to force disclosure are less likely to occur for government agencies than for private companies. Competition for turf, such as the FBI's reputation for not sharing with local law enforcement, further reduces agency incentives to share information about vulnerabilities.

Part B of this chapter briefly recaps the relevant portions of the "Security Disclosure Model" I proposed in "Security Model." Part C shows the incentive problems that exist when large databases are breached and the personal data of individuals is leaked. This sort of breach appears to be accompanied by significant externalities, so breach-notification statutes or similar measures are likely appropriate. Part D looks at the six parts of the matrix, analyzing the incentives for disclosure or secrecy for security reasons and competitive reasons, for open source software, proprietary software, and government systems.

This research provides a general approach for determining when disclosure is efficient for society and for describing the incentives actors face in disclosure or non-disclosure. The actual decision of whether to disclose in a given instance will depend on assessment of the empirical magnitude of the factors set forth in this chapter. The research provides, however, the first theoretical structure for assessing the issues. This theory is important to the design of systems and software in our information-rich age.

B. THE MODEL FOR WHEN DISCLOSURE HELPS SECURITY

"Security Model" presented the model for when disclosure of vulnerabilities helps security. This part briefly summarizes "Security Model," with emphasis on the aspects that are relevant to the current chapter. In brief, "Security Model" analyzed when disclosure would be socially optimal for security, taking into account the costs and benefits to all the parties involved.[2] This chapter continues the investigation of disclosure, looking at the incentives facing the key actors—those who design software or operate systems. In some settings, the incentives for key actors may lead to a large divergence between the socially optimal disclosure and the amount of disclosure actually made.

1) The Security Disclosure Model[3]

The Security Disclosure Model begins with a paradox. Most experts in computer and network security are familiar with the slogan, "there is no se-

---

2   More specifically, the Security Disclosure Model examined when disclosure would help "security," which is defined as "preventing the attacker from gaining control of a physical installation or computer system." "Security Model," *ibid.* at 205. The Security Disclosure Model does not explicitly address other important goals, such as disclosure to promote accountability (e.g., the *Freedom of Information Act*) or preventing disclosure in order to protect individual privacy. Important goals such as accountability and privacy should be considered in any overall decisions about the best levels of disclosure. *Ibid.* at 166–67 and 205.

3   "Security Model," *ibid.* at 167–75.

curity through obscurity."[4] For proponents of open source software, revealing the details of the system will actually tend to improve security, notably due to peer review. On this view, trying to hide the details of the system will tend to harm security because attackers will learn about vulnerabilities, but defenders will not know where to patch the vulnerabilities. In sharp contrast, a famous World War Two slogan warns "loose lips sink ships."[5] Most experts in the military and intelligence areas believe that secrecy is a critical tool for maintaining security. Both views — that disclosure helps security and hurts security — cannot be simultaneously correct, therefore we have a paradox. The task of "Security Model" was to explain the conditions for when each view, the open source view and the military view, is correct.

The first step toward resolving the paradox is to examine the effects of disclosure on attackers and defenders. Where disclosure on balance helps the attackers, then those defending the systems should rationally keep secrets. Where disclosure on balance helps the defenders, then disclosure should result.

By focusing on "effects on attackers"[6] and "effects on defenders,"[7] the Security Disclosure Model highlights the conditions under which the open source and "military" views are each correct. For open source, the usual assumption is that disclosure will not help attackers much or at all in a world of rapid communications among attackers, where exploits are rapidly learned by others. For open source, the next assumption is that disclosure of a flaw will prompt other programmers to improve the design of defences. In addition, disclosure will prompt many third parties — all of those using the software or the system — to install patches, or to otherwise protect themselves against the newly announced vulnerability. In sum, disclosure does not help attackers much but is highly valuable to the defenders who create new code and install it.

In contrast, the military assumptions highlight the ways that disclosure will assist the attackers. For a military base, for instance, the precise location of machine guns and other defences is closely guarded. A major goal is to hide the defences until it is too late for attackers, and they fall into traps.

---

4   *Ibid.* at 165 note 2.

5   *Ibid.* at 165 note 4.

6   See *ibid.* at 165–66. ("The first variable is the extent to which disclosure is likely to help the attackers, by tipping off a vulnerability the attackers would otherwise not have seen.")

7   See *ibid.* at 166. ("The second variable is the extent to which the disclosure is likely to improve the defence.")

In terms of disclosure helping defenders, the military traditionally uses its chain of command to tell fellow defenders what they need to know. There is no general broadcast of security flaws because such a broadcast would help the attackers but provide little or no information to fellow defenders.[8]

An important intermediate case for the present chapter is what I call the "information sharing paradigm," such as when the FBI or CIA is considering whether to share with officials in other agencies. To the extent the information is shared with the "good guys," then there can be strong assistance to the defenders because they might catch the terrorists before the attack occurs. To the extent the information is shared with the "bad guys," however, the information sharing can be the tip off that lets the attackers escape or change their plans. This dual effect of information sharing, to help defenders *and* attackers, is a helpful way to understand why it has been so important and yet so difficult a topic since the attacks of September 11, 2001.[9]

A fourth case concerns situations where additional disclosure about vulnerability will have small effects on attackers and defenders. An example is information in the public domain, such as detailed maps of Manhattan or Washington, DC. With maps so readily available in an online age, disclosure of one more map will make little difference to the risks of an attack against those cities.

---

8   In a workshop on this chapter, John Duffy made an excellent point: The "help-the-attacker" and "help-the-defender" effects can be described more generally as the prices that attackers and defenders face in gathering information about vulnerabilities. Widespread disclosure reduces information costs, such as when a software company publicly releases a patch to help defenders (i.e., users of software). Defenders still face the cost, however, of learning about the patch and deciding whether and how to implement it, with the result of substantially less than full implementation even of "free" patches.

9   One forum for extensive study of information sharing has been the Markle Foundation Task Force on National Security in the Information Age ("Task Force"). See Markle Foundation, "Task Force on National Security in the Information Age," online: www.markle.org/markle_programs/policy_for_a_networked_society/national_security/projects/taskforce_national_security.php. I was named an Associate to the Task Force in early 2005. My experiences there have confirmed my views that information sharing is often helpful but that poorly implemented information sharing also poses serious security and privacy risks. For my discussion of "The Bush Doctrine of Information Sharing," see Peter P. Swire, "America Faces the World on Privacy Four Years After 9/11" (Keynote Address at the Edinburgh Privacy Conference, 5 September 2005) [unpublished], online: www.peterswire.net/edinburgh_0905.ppt. I am currently writing a law review version of the topic for a symposium edition of the Villanova Law Review.

Table 2 pulls the four scenarios together. Notably, the open source scenario shows reasons for openness, with disclosure having a large "help-the-defenders" effect and a low "help-the-attackers" effect. The military scenario shows the opposite, with disclosure harming the defenders and helping the attackers. For information sharing, disclosure helps both the attackers and the defenders, making it unclear when to disclose. For the public domain, additional disclosure has minor effects.

Table 2

"Help-the-Attackers" Effect		
	Low	**High**
"Help-the-Defenders" Effect **High**	Open Source	Information Sharing
"Help-the-Defenders" Effect **Low**	Public Domain	Military/Intelligence
Greater Disclosure Up and to the Left		
Greater Secrecy Down and to the Right		

2) Why Computer and Network Security Often Varies from Other Security[10]

Table 2 simplifies reality by asserting that open source situations should lead to disclosure and military situations should lead to secrecy. A chief goal of Table 2 is to organize the reader's thinking into when there is "no security through obscurity" or when instead "loose lips sink ships." Whatever the reader's prior assumptions about the desirability of disclosure, the 2 × 2 matrix shows that disclosure in some situations will help security (the open source scenario) and in other situations will hurt security (the military/intelligence scenario).

The next task in "Security Model" was to explain the conditions under which each scenario is likely to exist. For instance, one might believe that disclosure will help in computer security situations (which may use open source software), but hurt in military and other physical security situations.

---

10   This section is based on Parts II and III of "Security Model." See, generally, "Security Model," above note 1 at 175–207.

"Security Model" explained why there is no *logical* or *necessary* difference between cyber security and physical security.[11] Nonetheless, there are important reasons why there are *commonly* differences between the two. The organizing concept for when hiddenness helps security is that a hidden feature is more likely to be effective against the first attack, but less likely to be effective against repeated attacks. For example, imagine a path up to a fort that has a pit covered with leaves, with a sharpened stick at the bottom. The first time an attacker comes up the path, he might fall into the pit. Even if it works the first time, though, later attackers will likely not "fall" for the same trick. In short, obscurity may work against the first attackers, but it will not work once the attackers learn to watch for the hidden pit.

"Security Model" explored in detail the factors that affect when an attack is very unique—much like a first-time attack—or instead has low uniqueness and is like a repeated attack in which learning occurs. The function for uniqueness (*U*), or the usefulness of hiddenness for the defence, is

$$U = f(E, N, L, C, A)$$

Under this terminology, "high uniqueness" refers to situations where hiddenness is effective, due to a combination of high values of initial effectiveness (*E*) and ability to alter the defence (*A*), and low values for the number of attacks (*N*), learning from previous attacks (*L*), and communication among attackers (*C*). "Low uniqueness" refers to situations where the values are reversed.

Using this approach, major categories of computer and network security turn out to have much lower uniqueness than typical physical attacks. For firewalls, mass-market software, and encryption, the analysis is similar. They are all subject to repeated attacks (high *N*), attackers learn from previous attacks whether they succeed or not (high *L*), and they can communicate the exploit to other attackers (high *C*). Even if a hidden defensive trick is effective against an initial attack (high *E*), the effects of repeated, low-cost attacks will generally overwhelm the usefulness of hidden defences. Defenders can issue patches and new versions of the software (high *A*), but repeated attacks will, once again, soon reveal any secrets. In short, the open source assumptions are often a good approximation of reality for these computer-security situations. Disclosure of vulnerabilities can enlist others to write improved code (increasing *A*) and encourage other users to patch their systems (increasing *A*). Along with this high help-the-defenders effect,

---

11   *Ibid.* at 175.

disclosure will often have a low help-the-attackers effect because communication among attackers is already effective.

The equation suggests a different outcome for physical attacks on a military installation. For many physical attacks, the first attack is crucial (very low N). People might die in the first attack, which is far different than the costs to an attacker of trying to hack a firewall or software package. Even if attackers get into the fort, they might not capture the entire thing (low L), and they might not be able to radio out to their comrades what they learn (low C). Under such circumstances, hidden defences can be quite useful against the first attack, and defenders can often alter the location and types of defences before a second or third attack (high A). In short, the military/intelligence assumptions seem to be a good approximation of reality. Disclosure about defences, perhaps by a spy, will help the attackers but provide little or no benefit to the defenders.

"Security Model," explained in greater detail using the variables just discussed, demonstrates some situations where secrecy will help, even for computer and network security.[12] Notable examples include encryption and other private keys and passwords; situations under which it is difficult to discover software flaws; and surveillance where attackers do not learn about the surveillance in the course of the attack.[13] Similarly, "Security Model" explained some situations in which disclosure will help even for military and other physical security.[14] Examples include disclosure for deterrence (which helps the defenders by reducing the likelihood of attack); material that is already in the public domain; and situations in which there are repeated attacks (high N) and disclosure will help defenders learn how to respond (increasing A).[15]

More complete explanations of these topics are available in "Security Model." For now, the hope is that the reader has a basic sense of the approach. "Security Model" sought to explain when disclosure would either aid or harm overall security. The current chapter focuses instead on the incentives of actors to make the best level of disclosure.

---

12   *Ibid.* at 186–87 and 190–93 (indicating instances in which disclosure will hurt the defender and help the attacker).

13   *Ibid.*

14   *Ibid.* at 206.

15   *Ibid.*

C. SECURITY BREACH NOTIFICATION TO INDIVIDUALS

The discussion of incentives to disclose security flaws begins with a topic that has recently been the subject of intense legislative activity: notification about security breaches to the individuals whose data has been compromised.[16]

1) Describing the Externality

The problem is straightforward to describe. The first party is the organization that holds personal information in a database. The second party is the attacker — the outside hacker or malicious insider who is trying to get the data. The third parties are those whose personal information is in the database. The personal information may include items that create risks of harm to the third parties if the data is leaked. For instance, disclosure of bank account numbers might allow theft from the accounts, and disclosure of social security numbers might let the second party or others perpetrate identity fraud.

What is the incentive of the first party (the organization holding the data) to disclose the information or prevent it from being disclosed? It is possible that the incentives of the first party are aligned with those of the third parties. This is true, for instance, when two conditions are met: (i) third parties become aware of leaks of their data from the database; and (ii) market or other mechanisms are effective in disciplining the first party for data leaks.[17]

If these conditions are not met, however, then the first party will likely have an incentive to under-invest in protecting the data of third parties. Consider the possibility that leaks of data are hard to trace back to the first

---

16   See, for example, US, Bill S. 751, *Notification of Risk to Personal Data Act*, 109th Cong., 2005, [*Notification Act*] (proposing a bill that would require disclosure of unauthorized acquisitions of such information).

17   Discipline on the first party might occur in the market if its reputation is harmed in the event of breaches. Discipline might also occur, for instance, through legal mechanisms. An example would be if the third parties could sue for losses caused by the data breach.

 The difficulty of tracing data leaks has also been a longstanding argument in favour of legislation or other measures to protect the privacy of individual information against sale or other intentional disclosure by the first party. See, for example, Peter Swire, "Markets, Self-Regulation, and Government Enforcement in the Protection of Personal Information by the U.S. Department of Commerce" (1997), online: www.ntia.doc.gov/reports/privacy/selfreg1.htm (examining the "uses and limitations of self-regulation" regarding the protection of personal information).

party where the leak occurred. This possibility happens often for personal data. It is usually very difficult for an individual, for instance, to figure out which of the databases containing her social security number was the source of a leak. Once a leak occurs, the individual may eventually discover that a criminal has used her bank account or social security number. The source of the leak, however, very often cannot be traced.

Untraced leaks from a database thus create a classic externality. In environmental protection, the factory (the first party) faces the cost of protecting against leaks, but the actual harms are on the third parties who are downstream from water pollution or downwind from air pollution.[18] In such circumstances, the factory has an incentive to pollute more than is desired by society. Much of environmental law consists of efforts to get the first party to face accurate incentives, so that the private decision by the factory owner matches the socially optimal decision, which includes effects on third parties.

Similarly, for protection of information in the database, the data holder (the first party) faces the cost of protecting against leaks, but the actual harms are on the third parties who suffer from the leaks. The incentives of the first party are thus to permit more leaks—more disclosure—than is desirable.

2)   What, if Anything, to Do About the Externality?

Given the likelihood of an externality, the next question is what measures, if any, to take in response. Description of the externality shows that the problem arises from lack of disclosure to third parties about data leaks by the first party. A tailored response to that problem would be to change incentives so that third parties learn of the leaks.

California was the first to take this approach when it enacted Senate Bill 1386 in 2002.[19] In the wake of large data leaks early in 2005, many other states moved to create breach notification statutes. As of December 2005, at least eighteen states have passed legislation,[20] and Congress is seriously considering a federal breach-notification standard.[21]

---

18   For one explanation of the basic theory of environmental externalities, see US, Congressional Budget Office, "Federalism and Environmental Protection: Case Studies for Drinking Water and Ground-Level Ozone" (November 1997) c. 1, online: www.cbo.gov/showdoc.cfm?index=250&sequence=2.

19   Cal. Civ. Code § 1798.82 (West Supp. 2005).

20   BNA Privacy Law Watch, online: www.bna.com/products/ip/pwdm.htm.

21   See US, Bill H.R. 3140, *Consumer Data Security and Notification Act of 2005*, 109th Cong., 2005 (a bill requiring "consumer reporting agencies, financial institutions,

The California statute essentially provides that individual notice shall be given to California residents "whose unencrypted personal information was, or is reasonably believed to have been, acquired by an unauthorized person."[22] The breach is to be disclosed in writing without unreasonable delay, with certain exceptions.[23] "Personal information" means a person's name in combination with any listed data element, such as social security number, driver's licence number, or "[a]ccount number, credit or debit card number, in combination with any required security code . . . that would permit access to an individual's financial account."[24]

In terms of the best approach for breach notification, I would like to make a few suggestions based on my experience with system owners, consumer groups, and regulators. The goal is to avoid both under-disclosure and over-disclosure. Under-disclosure quite likely exists in the absence of a statute (because of the incentives for under-disclosure described above). Over-disclosure could also be a problem. For first parties, there would be the expenses of first-class postage to very large classes, perhaps even for small and everyday levels of security flaws. For consumers, a blizzard of disclosures would swamp the signal in the noise. That is, consumers who received numerous notices would not know how to respond to the subset that posed a serious threat. Individual consumers would generally prefer to get notice when there are reasonable measures they should take in response.

To avoid both under- and over-disclosure, it makes sense to look at a security breach as a systemic issue over time. First, there should likely be a sunset on breach-notification statutes. We are at the early stages of knowing how to implement such statutes, and the sunset would likely spur better re-examination of the issue over time. Second, we should seriously consider a two-step regime. For more serious breaches, there would indeed be first-class mail notice to individuals, especially where there are concrete steps the individuals should take in response to the risks. For less serious breaches,

---

and other entities to notify consumers of data security breaches involving sensitive consumer information"); *Notification Act*, above note 16, (a bill requiring "Federal agencies, and persons engaged in interstate commerce, in possession of data containing personal information, to disclose any unauthorized acquisition of such information").

22 Above note 19, § 1798.82(a).

23 *Ibid.*, §§1798.82(a), (c), and (g). Email notices are only allowed if they comply with federal law regarding electronic signatures. § 1798.92(g)(2). In our current world of spam and phishing attacks, email notices might easily be filtered out or ignored by the recipient.

24 Above note 19, §1798.82(e).

which do not merit this individualized notice, there should be mandatory reporting to some agency such as the Federal Trade Commission. This sort of reporting would serve two major goals. It would mean that significant breaches, which do not merit notice to individuals, would be subject to action by the database holder. In this way, significant-but-not-major breaches would be addressed by data holders. In addition, it would allow the Federal Trade Commission to accumulate data about breaches, preparing the way for better re-examination of breach notification statutes over time.

More can be said about the best system for handling security-breach notification. For purposes of this chapter, the recent legislative activity shows the importance of addressing the incentives of organizations to provide the proper level of disclosure about security issues.

D. INCENTIVES FOR DISCLOSURE AND SECRECY FOR SECURITY AND COMPETITIVE REASONS

Part C of this chapter, on breach notification, concerned disclosure of information about third parties (customers) for data held by a first party (the system owner). The key point of this discussion was to show a potentially significant externality—that the system owner would not expend resources to protect third parties against harm from release of their data.

This part engages in a wider inquiry into incentives of system owners and software writers ("first parties") to disclose information or keep it secret. A new concept here is that system owners have a distinct calculus based on two different motives, the "security motive" and the "competitive motive." The security motive concerns the incentive of the first party to disclose or not, based on achievement of the security goals of the first party and other parties. Notably, what is the rational calculus for when disclosure will help ("there is no security through obscurity") or when instead secrecy will lead to better security ("loose lips sink ships")?[25] The competitive motive concerns the incentive of the first party to win in the marketplace against its competition. Notably, the first party will seek to determine when greater secrecy will help it competitively, such as with trade secrets, or when, instead, greater openness will enhance competitiveness, such as when use of an open standard attracts more business for a software writer.

---

25   As in "Security Model," security is defined as "preventing the attacker from gaining control of a physical installation or computer system." "Security Model," above note 1 at 205.

The two motives are generally analyzed separately in this chapter. In many instances, the security motive will not have a large effect on a company's bottom line—the question is whether enhanced security or secrecy is more effective at protecting security. In other instances, the security motive does significantly affect the bottom line, and analysis of the security motive proceeds here based on what helps the security of the affected parties. By contrast, the competitive motive includes all the incentives that a company faces that are not based on achieving security for itself or for other relevant parties. To the extent that disclosure for security purposes affects a company's bottom line, then analysis of the security motive will affect the rational degree of disclosure for competitive purposes.

The analysis here focuses on three categories of actors: (i) open-source-software writers, (ii) proprietary software writers, and (iii) government agencies. The three categories generate quite different and interesting results. In addition, the three categories map the terrain: private actors with a presumption of disclosure (open source); private actors with a presumption of secrecy (proprietary software where source code is not revealed); and public-sector actors.

Table 1 summarizes the more detailed discussion below. The table shows the key findings for open source, proprietary, and government actors, for both the security and competitive motives.

1) Case One: Security Incentives and Open Source Software

The first case examines, from a security standpoint, the incentives to disclose or not for designers and users of open source software.[26] Here is where the maxim that "there is no security through obscurity" has its greatest support. Proponents of open source, including the GNU General Public License, are proud that there is far greater disclosure than for proprietary software:

> The twist in the principal open-source model—including the General Public License ("GPL"), among the oldest and best-known public licence—is that if the software is distributed to third parties, it MUST be distributed using the open source licensing model, making the model "self-perpetuating." Thus, instead of guarding the "secret sauce," the

---

26 For a discussion of the legal, technical, and developmental differences between open source and proprietary software, see Jonathan Zittrain, "Normative Principles for Evaluating Free and Proprietary Software" (2004) 71 U. Chicago. L. Rev. 265 at 268–73.

GPL-Open Source approach not only makes it available but also mandates that all "secret sauce improvements" are made available in the same
manner.[27]

Even here, however, there turns out to be unsuspected areas where hiddenness—the use of "secret sauce"—is used for security purposes.

a)   When hiddenness can help open source security

As the previous quote indicated, any use of hiddenness for open source software seems inherently contradictory. After all, the GNU General Public License, Version 2.0, says to those who distribute software under that licence:
"[Y]ou must give the recipients all the rights that you have. You must make
sure that they, too, receive or can get the source code."[28] The heart of the
open source requirement, as the name implies, is that the source code will
be open. It may seem, thus, that there can be no secrecy.

Nonetheless, there are at least three respects in which secrecy can be
and is used to help security for open source software. The first, password
and encryption key secrecy, is entirely uncontroversial and was discussed
in detail in "Security Model." Even encryption experts, who argue most
vehemently against "security through obscurity," agree that passwords and
encryption keys should remain secret.[29] It is good common sense that revealing one's passwords will help the attackers but not provide any benefit
to defenders. Modern encryption systems are designed, in fact, to have the
clearest possible separation between the password or key (kept secret) and
the rest of the cryptosystem (kept open so that other experts can test for
flaws).[30] In short, a secret key or password is essential to use the system, but
there is no benefit to allowing outsiders to have the key.

---

27   Randall M. Whitmeyer, "Open Source Legal Issues and Controversies" (7 August
      2004), online: www.techjournalsouth.com/news/article.html?item_id=649.

28   "GNU General Public License," online: www.gnu.org/copyleft/gpl.html ["GNU
      General Public License"]. For an extensive set of links about the GNU Public
      Licence, see Groklaw, "GPL Resources," online: www.groklaw.net/staticpages/index.
      php?page=20050131065655645.

29   "Security Model," above note 1 at 190–91.

30   Interview with Whitfield Diffie, Vice President, Sun Fellow & Chief Security Of-
      ficer, Sun Microsystems (9 September 2005). Research for this project included an
      enlightening conversation with Whitfield Diffie, one of the authors of the founda-
      tional Diffie-Hellman algorithm for public key encryption. Diffie observed that the
      "security through obscurity" debate may have been led somewhat astray because
      techniques for separating the key from the cryptosystem were well developed for
      encryption but much less developed (and perhaps not applicable) for other security

The second area of potential secrecy involves surveillance by the defenders. As discussed in "Security Model,"[31] disclosure about surveillance, and especially its sources and methods, often helps the attackers more than the defenders. With surveillance, there is typically low learning by attackers (L), because the surveillance is designed specifically to make it difficult for attackers to detect. Because of this low L, it is often rational for defenders to keep surveillance techniques secret. (Also as described in "Security Model," secret surveillance may or may not be ultimately desirable, based on concerns including privacy, accountability, and long-run improvement of the security of systems.[32])

One common type of surveillance by defenders is an intrusion detection system, which seeks to detect the existence and nature of intrusions by attackers.[33] Intrusion detection software is available in both proprietary and open source forms.[34] Logically, there appear to be advantages to keeping some aspects of intrusion detection software secret, much as one would try to keep secret the placement of hidden cameras that watch for burglars.

Secrecy is even more important, though, for the aspect of intrusion detection software known as "honeypots," which "emulate real running operating systems to serve as a bait for potential attackers."[35] The idea of a honeypot is that the intruder is attracted to the honey — the apparently sweet target. The honeypot is under surveillance, however, and the defenders thereby learn about the type and number of attacks. Honeypots are available in open source code, and are used regularly by open-source programmers,[36] yet they rely on secrecy. Having a honeypot obviously will not work if the intruder knows that it is a fake. The use of honeypots illustrates how surveillance relies on secrecy, even for open source systems.

---

problems. For situations in which it is not feasible to separate the key from the rest of the security system, the clear distinction between hidden elements (the key) and public elements (the system) would not be sustainable.

31 "Security Model," above note 1 at 191–93.

32 *Ibid.* at 193.

33 For a detailed set of questions and answers about intrusion detection, see: SANS Institute, "Intrusion Detection FAQ," online: www.sans.org/resources/idfaq ["Intrusion Detection FAQ"]. SANS Institute defines "intrusion detection" as "the art of detecting inappropriate, incorrect, or anomalous activity."

34 Snort is one well-known intrusion detection system that is open source. See "About Snort," online: www.snort.org/about_snort.

35 Alexander Prohorenko, "Open Source Intrusion Detection: No-cost System Lockdown" (9 November 2004), online: www.devx.com/security/Article/22442.

36 *Ibid.*

Along with passwords and surveillance, the third area of potential secrecy is anything outside the scope of an open source licence, such as the GNU General Public License or others approved by the Open Source Initiative.[37] Even for the GNU Public License, the most widely used, there appear to be significant ways that programmers can use secrecy. One notable way is for programmers to use non-standard configurations and settings for the system. The term "configurations" is used in computer systems essentially to refer to the choice of software and other components in ways that affect system function.[38] The term "settings" has been defined as "[p]arameters of a system or operation that can be selected by the user."[39] The terms "configurations" and "settings" do not appear in the GNU General Public License, but the text of the licence seems to permit users to create or alter configurations and settings.[40]

The importance of non-standard configurations and settings was highlighted to me by an experienced open source programmer, Jon Callas, who said: "I'm not afraid to use a little secret sauce."[41] Callas gives the example of

---

37   It is not my intention here to enter the debate about what should be considered a true "open source licence." At the time of this writing, the Open Source Initiative has recognized over fifty licences as qualifying for its service mark. For a list of licences, helpful definitions, and links about the relevant terms, see "Open Source Licence," online: http://en.wikipedia.org/wiki/Open-source_license.

38   See National Communications System Technology & Standards Division, *Telecommunications: Glossary of Telecommunication Terms* (1996), online: www.tiaonline.org/market_intelligence/glossary/index.cfm?term=%26%23TOZRR%23M%0A (Configuration is, "[i]n a communications or computer system, an arrangement of functional units according to their nature, number, and chief characteristics . . . . Configuration pertains to hardware, software, firmware, and documentation.").

39   Glossary—Networking Terms Related to Remote Scope, online: www.micro2000.co.uk/products/remotescope/glossary.htm.

40   See "GNU General Public License," above note 28. For instance, paragraph o of the licence states: "Activities other than copying, distribution and modification are not covered by this License; they are outside its scope. The act of running the Program is not restricted . . . ."

41   Email from Jon Callas, Founder, Chief Technical Officer & Chief Security Officer, PGP Corp., to author (20 September 2005) (on file with author). The term "secret sauce" may trace back to the "special sauce" in a McDonald's ad that played often during the childhood of many current-day programmers: "Two all beef patties, special sauce, lettuce, cheese, pickles, onions on a sesame seed bun." Readers who can illuminate the history of the terms "secret sauce" or "special sauce" in programming are welcome to contact the author.

secret sauce he implemented for Secure Socket Layers (SSL), a cryptographic protocol that provides secure communications on the Internet. He says:

> In the generic case of SSL, we want secure interoperation of arbitrary web browsers and web servers. In the case I mentioned where I did some tweaks to SSL's security I didn't want interoperability, I only want *my* systems to interoperate, so there is usefulness in combining nonstandard configurations with a standard architecture.[42]

Using unknown and non-standard configurations and settings can have significant advantages to system owners. Notably, this use of obscurity can frustrate standardized attacks by "script kiddies" or other inexpert hackers.[43] Even for more skilled attackers, it may be rational to shift to an easier target when a target initially resists an attack.[44] It may thus be rational for a defender to use hidden and non-standard configurations and settings even where they would not withstand a determined attack. In terms of the model for when disclosure helps security, the non-standard configurations and settings increase the uniqueness—they reduce N (the number of attacks against a particular defence)—and make it more like a first-time attack. In such circumstances, hiddenness is more likely to be effective. In the words of Jon Callas: "Obscurity is camouflage, security is armor."[45] Either can be useful, depending on the circumstances. They can also be useful when working together, much like tanks that are often camouflaged.[46]

A second current example of secrecy in open source software, the so-called "stealth firewall,"[47] fits the idea of camouflage. A standard way to

---

42   *Ibid.*

43   For discussion of script kiddies, who are unskilled programmers who merely follow a script rather than understanding how to write code themselves, see Swire, "Security Model," above note 1 at 180 note 21.

44   See *ibid.* at 189 (discussing how relatively strong security may shift an attack to a different target).

45   Email from Jon Callas, above note 41.

46   See "Tank Research and Development," online: http://en.wikipedia.org/wiki/Tank_research_and_development. Indeed, some experts emphasize the need for stealth technologies, believing that "the future of tanks lies in invisibility rather than in invincibility." For an essay on tank camouflage when tanks were introduced in World War I, see Patrick Wright, "Cubist Slugs" (2005) 27(12) London Review of Books, online: www.lrb.co.uk/v27/n12/wrig01_.html.

47   The discussion here of stealth firewalls is based on (i) Interview with Chris Palmer (14 April 2005); and (ii) Michael Shinn & Scott R. Shinn, "Stealth Firewalling with Linux," *Linuxworld Magazine* (27 February 2005), online: http://linux.sys-con.com/read/48126.htm.

attack a firewall is to scan it, checking its existence and behaviour. A nice attribute of a stealth firewall is that it does not have to have an IP address that is scannable. The stealth firewall thus resists a common attack.

In this example, the source code for the stealth firewall may well be open source. The defence, however, depends on hiddenness from observation by the attacker. More generally, "Security Model" described the usefulness of hiddenness where the attacker has low learning (L) from attacks.[48] Similar to stealth firewalls, intrusion detection systems and other surveillance by the defender are more effective if attackers cannot tell how they operate.[49] Once again, the low level of L from prior attacks means that hiddenness is more likely to be effective, even against repeated attacks. Disclosure of the details of a stealth firewall or an intrusion detection system helps the attackers, but offers little likelihood of helping the defenders.

b) Implications of hiddenness in open source security

The discussion here highlights the incentives for open source programmers to use secrecy to produce a low N, such as through non-standard configurations and settings, or a low L, such as through stealth firewalls and hidden intrusion detection systems. These strategies will often be permitted under open source licences because the secrecy is not at the level of source code that must be disclosed under the licence.

These reasons to use secrecy have not been highlighted in the open source literature to date. Some open source proponents may be uncomfortable using the secrecy strategies discussed here, believing they smack too much of "security through obscurity." However, the examples used here came directly from interviews over time with open source programmers, who responded to the question: "Where, if anywhere, is there secrecy to promote the security of open source systems?" Within the overall paradigm of open source software, which so emphatically emphasizes the security advantages of disclosure, there are situations where secrecy appears to improve security. Those situations, as described here, fit well into the model of disclosure presented in "Security Model."

As a policy matter, the next question is whether there are externalities or other reasons to be concerned about harm from secrecy as used by open source programmers. The answer appears to be no. The uses of "secret sauce," such as stealth firewalls or non-standard configurations, affect the

---

48   See "Security Model," above note 1 at 176.
49   The role of secrecy for effective surveillance is discussed *ibid.* at 191–93. See also "Intrusion Detection FAQ," above note 33.

system owners themselves. There does not appear to be any significant externality where the failure to disclose leads to harm to others. In contrast to the large externality, discussed above, for disclosures of security breaches, the analysis here does not support any call for legislation or other measures with respect to disclosure for open source systems.

2) Case Two: Competitive Incentives and Open Source Software

For open source programming today, the use of secrecy is likely even more prevalent for competitive reasons than for the security reasons just discussed. My discussion in this section is deliberately somewhat provocative—the emergence of large firms in open source software and large corporate-users of open source software has changed practices considerably in the last decade. My prediction is that secrecy for competitive reasons will become an increasingly evident part of the open source world in the coming years.

a) The openness of open source software

As with the security discussion, it is important to begin with an understanding about the baseline of open source disclosure before examining ways that hiddenness also exists.

Open source software eschews key legal and technological measures that are used by proprietary software companies to protect their work. Most fundamentally, open source licences such as the GNU General Public License require disclosure of the source code.[50] For those who wish to reverse engineer a proprietary program, it is often expensive and difficult to do so and get usable source code. The closed or hidden nature of proprietary code often creates a large obstacle for those who wish to compete with the proprietary company. By contrast, the readability of open source code means that a competent coder may be able to quickly equal or surpass the insights of the person who wrote the original code.

Open source software not only lacks technical protection against competition and disclosure, but it lacks traditional legal protections. The "copyleft" nature of the GNU General Public License means that a later coder is forbidden from getting a copyright on material derived from licensed code.[51] If the open source movement is successful in ongoing patent disputes

---

50 "Open Source Initiative," online: www.opensource.org/docs/definition.php.
51 "GNU General Public License," above note 28.

such as the SCO litigation,[52] then patents will not be available to protect, at least, most open source code, nor, according to one expert in the field, will trade secret protection be available: "[T]rade secret protection is singularly inapplicable to open source software. The accessible and open source code would almost always defeat the trade secret status by disclosing the secret."[53]

The commitment to openness in the open source movement goes beyond these technological and legal commitments to openness. The ideology of free software, developed most prominently by Richard Stallman and the Free Software Foundation,[54] has had a powerful influence on a vast community of programmers. The view that free software is morally superior to proprietary software is accompanied, in turn, by influential academic commentary that provides theoretical explanations for how the open source movement initially developed and why it seems especially well-suited to creating software in a networked setting.

Yale Professor Yochai Benkler has offered a clearly defined theory for situations in which open source collaboration will have particular advantages over a proprietary approach: "[T]here will be conditions under which a project that can organize itself to offer social-psychological rewards removed from monetary rewards will attract certain people, or at least certain chunks of people's days, that monetary rewards would not."[55] Benkler emphasizes three conditions. First, the project must be modular, so that many people can contribute incrementally over time. Second, the project should have the right level of lumpiness, so that individuals can make contributions of a manageable size. Third, "a successful peer production enterprise must have low-cost integration, which includes both quality control over the modules and a mechanism for integrating the contributions into the finished product."[56] The peer-review aspect of open source production can

---

52   The SCO Group has sued IBM and other companies, with a principal allegation being infringement of patents that it says applies to code contributed to open source projects. See Amended Complaint, *SCO Group, Inc. v. IBM* (16 June 2003), Utah, No. 03-CV-0294 (Dist. Ct.), online: www.sco.com/scoip/lawsuits/ibm/ibm-25.pdf.

53   Greg R. Vetter, "The Collaborative Integrity of Open-Source Software" (2004) Utah L. Rev. 563 at 588.

54   Richard Stallman is the President and Founder of The Free Software Foundation. Free Software Foundation, GNU's Who-GNU Project, online: www.gnu.org/people/people.html. For more information about the Free Software Movement or Stallman, see Free Software Foundation, online: www.fsf.org.

55   Yochai Benkler, "Coase's Penguin, or, Linux and The Nature of the Firm" (2002) 112 Yale L.J. 369 at 378 [Benkler].

56   *Ibid.* at 378–79.

serve this integration function. Where all three conditions exist, a peer-production process, based on openness, can succeed, even in the absence of substantial monetary awards.

b) Hiddenness and the competitive incentives of open source users

Before looking at the incentives that face those who create open source code—the coders, developers, programmers, and so on—it is useful first to examine the users of that code. As open source code becomes more pervasive in modern organizations, decisions about openness versus hiddenness will increasingly turn on the needs of these open source users, such as manufacturers, services companies, government agencies, and so on. These users have their own imperatives about what should be disclosed.

Take the example of the widget manufacturer who uses open source code for standard tasks, such as supply-chain management, inventory control, or product testing. Using expertise about the widget sector, suppose that persons working for the manufacturer find a way to cut costs by 5 percent. They write new code, for use inside the company, that implements the cost-cutting measures.

Next, suppose you are the chief information officer (CIO) for the manufacturer, and you meet with the company president to decide whether to disclose the new code. As CIO, you might try to explain the beliefs of the open source community, including the importance of giving back code for use by the broader community.[57] The president is likely to be unimpressed, and perhaps even incredulous: "You mean we should tell our competitors how to get the 5 percent savings, after we invested all that time and money to learn how to do it!?"

This story of the widget manufacturer can be generalized. Corporations routinely make decisions about what to disclose or keep secret for competitive purposes. Confidential business information is a broad category, with common examples including business strategies, research that is not fully protected by patents, know-how relevant to ongoing operations, and trade secrets. To the extent that release of code will tip off competitors or other-

---

57   For one influential discussion of the philosophy of the free software movement, see Eric S. Raymond, *The Cathedral and the Bazaar: Musings on Linux and Open Source by an Accidental Revolutionary*, rev. ed. (Beijing: O'Reilly, 2001).

wise reduce profits, the rational corporate decision maker will decide to keep the code in-house.[58]

Open source proponents hope and expect that open source code will pervade business organizations in the future. If and as this occurs, public release of that code will increasingly provide clues to competitors about the activities of the company that used and modified the code. The incentives for open source users to keep their competitive secrets will then be in conflict with the norm of open source programmers to disclose the code.[59]

c) The puzzle of why corporations invest in producing open source software

Along with the incentives for secrecy for open source users, there is the well-recognized puzzle about why individuals and firms will rationally develop open source code. Benkler's theory coherently sets forth certain conditions under which social-psychological rewards can provide the motivation.[60] Later, he briefly examines what he calls "indirect appropriation mechanisms."[61] He writes, "These range from the amorphous category of reputation gains to much more mundane benefits, such as consulting contracts, customization services, and increases in human capital that are paid for by employers who can use the skills gained from participation in free software development in proprietary projects."[62]

The discussion here, by contrast, emphasizes that the appropriation mechanisms are often direct rather than indirect.[63] More surprisingly, *the*

---

58   Note that this discussion does not assume that the secrets would be protected against a determined adversary, such as one who resorted to industrial espionage. In business competition, it will often be rational not to disclose information if keeping the information secret simply raises costs to competitors or reduces the likelihood that they will learn the competitive secrets.

59   The extent to which the open source community can develop strategies to reduce such conflict with incentives for users to guard competitive secrets is a topic for further research. For instance, in some settings, source code might be released in ways that do not reveal corporate secrets. If readers are aware of such efforts to reconcile these conflicting norms of secrecy and disclosure, the author would be glad to learn of them.

60   See Benkler, above note 55 at 378–79.

61   *Ibid.* at 424.

62   *Ibid.* at 424–25 (footnote omitted).

63   As the draft of this chapter was being completed, Ronald Mann released an excellent working paper that addresses the puzzle of why corporations are investing large sums in open source software. Ronald J. Mann, "The Commercialization of Open Source Software: Do Property Rights Still Matter?" online: http://papers.ssrn.com/

economics of open source programming increasingly relies on (at least temporary) secrecy. The incentives facing those developing open source systems rely on secrecy in at least three distinct and substantial ways: staying ahead of the curve; systems integration and related services; and web services.

d) Hiddenness and the competitive incentives of open source developers

Significant incentives exist for secrecy on the part of open source developers in order to stay ahead of the curve, offer system integration and related services, and create open source code in ways that do not trigger disclosure obligations under the relevant licence.

i) Staying ahead of the curve

As I spoke to open source programmers about secrecy and openness, one who preferred not to be identified said, "I always try to stay six months ahead of the curve."[64] This programmer has regularly contributed code to various open source projects. He does not disclose, however, some aspects of his work that will give him a competitive advantage. A similar point has been made by Robert Lefkowitz, former director of Open Source Strategy at Merrill Lynch: "And then, there's the secret sauce for which you wish to

---

sol3/papers.cfm?abstract_id=802805. Professor Mann agrees with arguments made in this chapter that the financial incentives for investment are direct, as opposed to the indirect approach emphasized by Benkler, *ibid.* at 19–20. Professor Mann explains that much of open source investment follows the classic "value chain" model, which dictates that a company should "foster the commoditization of those portions of the stack in which the company does not have a core competency, so that it can earn high(er) returns for those portions of the stack in which it can defeat its competitors." *Ibid.* at 20. Essentially, the open source approach serves as a precommitment strategy, in which the major open source corporations cannot profit directly from sales of Linux or other open source software, but all of them become committed to an open source approach.

Professor Mann makes a number of points that are similar to those made here, including his description of how open source companies are able to profit from services. Nonetheless, it is not clear how well his precommitment strategy explains the large investments he documents. The company-specific returns emphasized in this chapter seem like a more straightforward way to explain the investments of hundreds of millions or billions of dollars by individual companies.

64 The programmer's reluctance to be named is a sign, perhaps, of the culture of openness that is prevalent in the open source community. Admitting that one is holding back information from the community can be a source of shame.

capture an innovation premium. You can take that open source stuff, add your secret sauce, and create some very nice commercial products."[65]

The idea of staying ahead of the curve is a powerful one. Although it is sometimes risky to be out front, there may be a substantial first-mover advantage in a particular market niche.[66] More generally, there are ongoing advantages to being somewhat ahead of the curve. As your competitors work to catch up to where you were at one point, you can seek to keep your lead through ongoing investment.

For writers of software, the payoff can come in various forms, such as through general reputation or positive reviews from satisfied clients. Applied to open source programmers, the idea of staying ahead of the curve suggests the business sense of what the anonymous programmer has done — release some code to the community to build reputation, while holding some valuable code back in order to provide premium service to clients.

The idea of staying ahead of the curve is essentially one of temporary secrecy. In a rapidly changing environment, getting the source code from a year or two ago will often not be very satisfying. Purchasers will be motivated to go to the suppliers of up-to-date solutions.

ii)   Systems integration and services

Why have corporate giants such as IBM and many others invested so heavily in open source in recent years? The elegant peer-production model of Yochai Benkler is designed to explain why individual programmers will seek social-psychological rewards rather than monetary profit.[67] That model, by its own terms, does not apply to profit-maximizing corporations. The proposal here is that the corporations will differentially invest in ways that the competitive advantage does not need to be disclosed under the open source licences. A major category of corporate effort is in the area of systems integration and related services.

IBM employee Michael Nelson said it succinctly: "We take very valuable open source software, and build it into a suite of services that's even

65   "Open Source Gets Down to Business" *Technology Review* (25 July 2003), online: www.technologyreview.com/Infotech/13258/?a=f (interview with Robert Lefkowitz, former Director of Open Source Strategy, Merrill Lynch).

66   See Jonathan M. Barnett, "Private Protection of Patentable Goods" (2004) 25 Cardozo L. Rev. 1251 at 1257–66 (discussing generally the economics of first-mover advantage).

67   Benkler, above note 55 at 378.

more valuable."[68] The logic behind this bland statement is important. The economic incentive is that the innovation and comparative advantage happen elsewhere (i.e., not in the source code). Under the licence terms, the source code must be revealed upon distribution. The techniques of services and system integration do not. The importance of integration is echoed by *Computerworld* columnist Frank Hayes:

> Once, IT would have looked for unique advantage by writing big custom applications. But today that takes too long and is too inflexible. Instead, open source-using companies like Google and Yahoo have figured out that their secret sauce is in the way they put together pieces of IT—software, hardware, networks and practices. Anyone can acquire the gear these companies use. How they put it together is the difference.[69]

A company's comparative advantage in systems integration also responds directly to Professor Benkler's model. He postulated that "a successful peer production enterprise must have low-cost integration, which includes both quality control over the modules and a mechanism for integrating the contributions into the finished product."[70] There is an empirical question about when a peer-production model will be superior to a corporate-production model for these aspects of quality control and integration. It seems plausible, however, that the reputation of a large company for providing quality control and integration will often give it an advantage in the marketplace.[71] To the extent that an advantage does occur, the lucrative market for quality control and integration may shift to corporate players, and away from the peer-production process.[72]

---

68 Email from Michael Nelson, IBM Employee, to author (21 October 2005) (on file with author).

69 Frank Hayes, "Deliver the Goods" *Computerworld* (8 August 2005) 54 at 54, online: www.computerworld.com/softwaretopics/software/appdev/story/0,10801,103728,00.html.

70 Benkler, above note 55 at 379.

71 For a thorough examination of the factors that can give comparative advantages to firms to internalize activities, including quality control and reputation effects, see, generally, Oliver E. Williamson, *Markets and Hierarchies: Analysis and Antitrust Implications* (New York: Free Press, 1975).

72 A web posting made by a frustrated open source programmer offers insight into how such marketplace advantages look to someone competing with the big companies:

> IBM often brags about billions in profits from Open Source because of consulting revenues. The problem with that is the guy who contributed most to the

iii)   Web services and other in-house use of open source

The current structure of the GNU General Public License creates another financial incentive for secrecy. As noted above, that licence requires publication of the source code upon distribution.[73] Before distribution occurs, however, there is no requirement to reveal the source code.

A famous example of a company adopting this approach is the online retailer Amazon.com (Amazon). Publishing impresario Tim O'Reilly has analyzed the subject: "Even though *amazon.com* is built on top of open source software, the licences compel no release of Amazon source because its software is never distributed. In the new world of the Internet, software is a service, not an artifact."[74]

The Amazon example illustrates the powerful business incentive that exists under the current GNU General Public License — open source code can be used, but need not be made public so long as the code is not "distributed" to others.[75] This "use-but-don't-disclose" aspect of the General Public License creates the possibility of supplying proprietary solutions over the Internet. Amazon uses its code, its "secret sauce," inside of Amazon. In this respect, Amazon acts in part as a developer of open source code — its employees and agents write code that may give Amazon a competitive advantage as an online retailer. Amazon also, in part, acts as a user of open source code. Like the widget manufacturer discussed above, Amazon may be reluctant to reveal proprietary information that is not about the code itself. In addition, companies that provide software as a service, but do not

---

original source code who did it for the love of coding probably didn't see too many of those dollars.

While it is possible for guy [*sic*] who did the coding to sell his consulting services, how does he compete with IBM global services? He doesn't have 1/100th the reputation, sales, and marketing force of IBM global services. IBM global services can just take your GPL code and implement it however they want. Once in a while, they might throw you a few crumbs for you [*sic*].

Posting of george_ou to TalkBack on ZDNet (14 June 2005), online: www.zdnet.com/5208-10535-0.html?forumID=1&threadID=11136&messageID=222450&start=-30.

73   See "GNU General Public License," above note 28 and accompanying text (providing that distributors of software under the General Public License must "give the recipients all the rights that [they] have").

74   O'Reilly Network, "Ask Tim: Amazon and Open Source" (February 2004), online: www.oreilly.com/pub/a/oreilly/ask_tim/2004/amazon_0204.html.

75   "GNU General Public License," above note 28.

trigger the General Public License by distribution through a CD or floppy disk are under no obligation to reveal their source code.[76]

iv) Implications of the analysis

The discussion here has highlighted important reasons why those involved with open source software will rationally rely on secrecy, at least to some extent. On the user side, the incentives to protect confidential business information will remain even for businesses that use open source software. For developers, there are incentives to use secrecy to stay ahead of the curve, to provide systems integration and related services, and to use open source software in ways that do not involve "distribution" and thus do not trigger obligations to disclose. One result has been an open source universe that is dominated by services, where profits can be captured by leading companies, rather than by the commodity software products that are so prominent in the proprietary software space.

In response to this possible shift toward secrecy, there has been discussion of a Version 3.0 of the GNU General Public License, which would address the disclosure issue. According to Sleepycat Software CEO Mike Olson, the next generation of the licence will address the distribution "loophole": "If you look at the market, Yahoo, eBay, IBM, Amazon, Google have all sunk millions into the GPL infrastructure."[77] When it comes to the distribution loophole, Olson added, "Not only are we changing the rules, we are changing them retroactively."[78]

The exact language for Version 3.0 is not known yet, and Eben Moglen, the head of the Software Freedom Law Center and a leader of the drafting process, has withheld comment until a discussion draft is released.[79] Nonetheless, it will be most interesting to see the extent to which major corporate players are willing to shift to Version 3.0 along the lines discussed by Mike Olson. The analysis in this chapter suggests that Version 3.0 will be a very tough sell. The business strategies of major corporations seem to have evolved to what is permitted under Version 2.0, with secrecy an important competitive advantage. If Version 3.0 looks the way Mike Olson has stated, then there may be a major moment of decision for open source developers: to what extent will the requirements for openness be extended, as Olson

---

76   Michael Singer, "Insider Hints at GPL Changes" (7 April 2005), online: www.internetnews.com/dev-news/article.php/3495981.

77   *Ibid.*

78   *Ibid.*

79   See *ibid.*

suggests, or to what extent instead will corporate business plans rely on the categories of secrecy described in this chapter?

3)   Case Three: Security Incentives and Proprietary Software

The third case examines, from a security standpoint, the incentives to disclose or not for designers of proprietary software. The analysis here shows a surprisingly diverse set of factors that create incentives to disclose security vulnerabilities.

a)   The hiddenness of proprietary software
Proprietary software traditionally uses both technological and legal methods to protect against unauthorized use by others. The technological method is to not reveal the source code. Outsiders who wish to reverse engineer the software thus need to engage in often elaborate efforts to figure out how to write code that will have the same function as the proprietary program.[80] The legal methods often include copyright on the program, and may also include patent and trade-secret protection. Both the technical and legal mechanisms make it more difficult for outsiders to see the source code. For security purposes, this implies that outsiders will, at least initially, not see the source code. For competitive purposes, as discussed below in Case Four, this implies that outsiders are limited in their ability, at least initially, to see the source code and use it for derivative or competing works. In these technical and legal ways, proprietary software is at the opposite pole from the open source software discussed in the previous sections.

b)   Proprietary software and a monopoly model for information about vulnerabilities
In order to understand the incentives to disclose for security purposes, this chapter begins with a simple monopoly model. When proprietary software is released, one can consider the company to have a monopoly of information about the source code. Employees of the company may not be the *only* persons to have experience with the software at the time of release. For instance, outside alpha and beta testers may have been used for the new software, and the new release may overlap with previous software releases.

---

80   The object code is accessible to authorized users of the software, but the source code is not. For one explanation of the meaning of object and source code, and the relative ease for humans of reading the latter, see *Universal City Studios, Inc. v. Corley*, 273 F.3d 429 at 438–39 (2d Cir. 2001).

Nonetheless, it is helpful to imagine at the moment of release that only employees of the software company have knowledge about the software, including its vulnerabilities.

Consider, next, the incentives that face the company when it learns about a vulnerability. Should the company disclose the vulnerability? Major disadvantages of disclosure would include an immediate reduction in sales of the program and an overall harm to the company's reputation for quality software. Advantages of disclosure would be more indirect—buyers might learn that they could trust the company to disclose vulnerabilities, thus increasing the company's long-term reputation for quality. Another advantage would be similar to the open source model—outside programmers might suggest how to fix the problem. Looking at these disadvantages and advantages of disclosure, a rational corporation might often conclude that it is better to keep the vulnerability secret. This reluctance to disclose vulnerabilities was indeed widespread not long ago in the proprietary software industry.

This simple model at first blush seems quite similar to the breach notification issues discussed in Part C above. The analysis there showed important reasons to support the breach-notification statutes that are now spreading in the US.[81] In both situations, there is a first party (the data holder or software company) and a second-party attacker. In both situations, there are potential harms to third parties (the individuals whose data is lost or the users of the software). For data breaches, the conclusion was that breach-notification statutes are likely appropriate because it is so difficult for individuals to trace harm back to the source of the breach. There are important differences, however, for proprietary software. One difference is that users of software will often (not always) be able to figure out what software program to blame if something goes wrong.[82] A second important difference is that third parties may have important assistance for software vulnerabilities that they did not have in the data-breach setting.

The Security Disclosure Model from "Security Model" helps to show how the monopoly problem tends to erode over time. Even if the software company has a monopoly of information about its product at the time of release, outsiders can and do learn about the software. For standardized

---

81   See Section C(2), above in this chapter.

82   Many computer users have had the experience of a software vendor blaming a problem on the hardware vendor or another software vendor. Even in such cases, the user generally knows that there is a problem and has a short list of suspects for who caused it. Both of these factors are often missing in the breach-of-data scenario.

software products, outsiders can probe and attack the software repeatedly (high N for number of attacks). When the software has a vulnerability or otherwise fails to perform appropriately, the outsiders learn about the flaws (high L). They can then communicate (high C) with other outsiders about the flaws.

To the extent that high N, L, and C thus exist, the monopoly of information may evolve quite rapidly to a competitive situation. Under fully competitive conditions, outsiders would have the same ability to discover and report on vulnerabilities as the software company itself. "Security Model," indeed, used mass-market software as an example of a situation where "security through obscurity" is unlikely to succeed.[83] For the new release of a video game, websites arise almost instantly advising how to "beat the game."[84] This is also the case for new proprietary software programs. Users can and do learn and communicate rapidly about programs after they are released.

To the extent that this analysis is convincing, the rational proprietary vendor is much more likely than it initially appeared to try to discover and fix vulnerabilities. When outsiders predictably discover and publicize flaws, the previous advantages of keeping a secret plummet. Keeping the vulnerability secret not only will likely soon fail, but the company will then have the additional reputation problem of explaining why it did not tell its customers that they were at risk. In such circumstances, it will often be rational for the company to disclose vulnerabilities.

c)   The importance of market structure

The discussion thus far has shown some interestingly strong reasons why the market is likely to work well to encourage disclosure of vulnerabilities, even for proprietary software. The next step is to notice that the analysis depends on an assumption that outsiders are effective at discovering and publicizing vulnerabilities. The validity of that assumption will depend on the empirical realities for any given software, and especially on the market structure. One risk is that the closed source in the software will be a strong barrier against outsiders learning about vulnerabilities. A related risk is that skilled and malicious hackers may learn about a vulnerability, but not reveal their knowledge until they use it in a major attack.

The nature of software buyers is important in determining whether a software company will rationally keep a vulnerability hidden. The exist-

83   See "Security Model," above note 1 at 181–82.

84   *Ibid.* at 182.

ence of large buyers who care about security increases the likelihood that disclosure will occur. At the extreme, imagine that a software vendor sells to a single buyer (a "monopsonist"), and that the buyer has a high taste for security. What will happen if the software has a serious vulnerability, known to the seller, and the buyer does not know about it? Quite simply, the vendor may lose all its sales.

To choose a vivid example, which, as far as I know, is not true, imagine a company that sells communications software to the US Air Force. Suppose that hackers learn about a vulnerability, and the software company also knows about it but does not disclose its knowledge to the Air Force. Then, on an important mission, the software tells the pilot to turn left when he is supposed to turn right. The mission therefore fails.[85] The Air Force, shall we say, is likely to go ballistic.

This Air Force example brings home the importance to a vendor of pleasing large buyers who care about security.[86] The vendor might then respond with a halfway disclosure, seeking to disclose to its "important" customers but not to its "unimportant" customers. But secrets once shared among many "important" customers are unlikely to stay secret for long.[87] Major proprietary software companies today now disclose vulnerabilities widely, to their own customers and through mechanisms such as the Computer Emergency Response Team (CERT).[88]

The Air Force example highlights the possibility that important customers will get contractual or other legal assurances that they will be notified about vulnerabilities. Although a purchaser of a single desktop does not bargain for such assurances, large customers can and do. The legal assurances might be in an individually negotiated licence to use the software throughout a large organization. For military and other government con-

---

85   If the plane therefore flies into a mountain, that would be a "system crash" of a different sort than usual.

86   In the language of Oliver Williamson, the buyer and seller would have a high level of transaction-specific capital in the use of the software by the organization. Oliver E. Williamson, *The Economic Institutions of Capitalism* (New York: Free Press, 1985) at 30 (discussing transaction-specific capital). The organization would therefore have important incentives to bargain to protect its investment in the software, such as insisting on requirements of disclosure of vulnerabilities.

87   For a discussion of the weaknesses of selective disclosure, see "Security Model," above note 1 at 203.

88   See CERT Coordination Center, online: www.cert.org (providing information about the CERT Coordination Center as a center of Internet security expertise).

tracts, the legal assurance might also come from a statute or other legal mandate from the government.

In addition to buyers with market power and government buyers, another check on under-disclosure is the existence of ethical bug hunters.[89] These individuals or firms seek to find vulnerabilities (bugs) in software. Upon finding a bug, in many instances, they notify the authors of the code in order to provide an opportunity to issue a patch before the vulnerability is publicly announced. To the extent that such bug hunters systematically discover flaws and provide an opportunity to fix them, disclosure will tend to occur even for proprietary software.

d) Historical experience and implications

In considering the likelihood of disclosure for security flaws in mass-produced software, it is helpful to remember the relative youth of the market. The IBM PC was introduced in the early 1980s. Attacks from a distance, including contagious phenomena such as viruses, only became significant with the growth of the Internet in the late 1990s. As late as 1998, the topic of cyber security was practically invisible to government agencies and law professors who were immersed in the law of cyberspace.[90] During the bubble of the late 1990s, many software companies emphasized adding new features and growing quickly instead of writing secure software.[91]

In the past several years, security has generally become a more prominent issue in computing and in mass-market proprietary software in particular. Purchasers, led by large corporations and government agencies, have pushed for and received greater access to the source code from Microsoft and other vendors.[92] An important literature exists within law and economics that shows how effective market discipline by a subset of sophisticated buyers (such as large purchasers of software) can provide a high

---

89   Jennifer Stisa Granick, "The Price of Restricting Vulnerability Publications" (2005) 9 Int'l. J. Comm. L. & Pol'y 1.

90   See Peter P. Swire, "Elephants and Mice Revisited: Law and Choice of Law on the Internet" (2005) 153 U. Pa. L. Rev. 1975 at 1977 note 4 (describing the low level of awareness of Internet security as of the late 1990s).

91   One sign of the shift in industry attitude came in a widely publicized email from Bill Gates to all Microsoft employees on 15 January 2002: "So now, when we face a choice between adding features and resolving security issues, we need to choose security." Email from Bill Gates, Microsoft Chairman & Chief Software Architect, to Microsoft Employees (15 January 2002), online: www.wired.com/news/business/0,1367,49826,00.html.

92   Interview with Dave Ladd, Microsoft Research (28 July 2005).

level of quality for many other buyers (such as mass-market purchasers of software).[93] The strong taste for security from prominent buyers, and the growth of CERT and other disclosure institutions over time thus suggests that the level of disclosure is and will be substantially better for proprietary software in the future than it was in the 1990s.

In conclusion, on the security motive for disclosure for proprietary software, the analysis here does not describe some idealized world where proprietary software vendors always disclose vulnerabilities promptly. Instead, the analysis identifies conditions under which the disclosure is likely to be done relatively effectively: high N, L, and C so that flaws are discovered; buyers with monopsony power who can force disclosure; governments that require disclosure; and effective bug hunters who make the disclosure market more efficient. Where those conditions do not exist, there remains a significant risk that the incentives for vendors to hide their flaws will result in harm to third-party users.

4) Case Four: Competitive Incentives and Proprietary Software

The incentive is clear for why proprietary software companies would keep source code secret. The technological protection of keeping source code hidden complements the legal protection from copyright or other intellectual property regimes. These technological and legal measures raise the costs for competitors to create equivalent software. The proprietary company expects to profit from greater sales of the software.

This incentive to keep source codes hidden is indeed powerful. There are major counter-incentives, however, that often lead proprietary software companies to disclose significant amounts of source code for competitive reasons.

a) Network effects and disclosure for standards

Software companies do not face a simple choice between keeping all source code hidden and revealing all of their code. Instead, there is a continuum. At the closed end of the spectrum, a company can rely entirely on its in-house programmers and not permit anyone else to see any source code. At the opened end of the spectrum, the company can adopt a strong open

---

93   This approach is developed in Alan Schwartz & Louis L. Wilde, "Intervening in
     Markets on the Basis of Imperfect Information: A Legal and Economic Analysis"
     (1979) 127 U. Pa. L. Rev. 630 at 662–66.

source licence, and perhaps even make disclosure about consulting and other activities that are outside the scope of that licence.

Choosing where to be on that spectrum requires a complex calculus that has strong elements of game theory. How will other actors react to various levels of openness? Being more open has the potential advantage of attracting other developers. If enough developers work with the software program, then a critical mass might result. There can thus be "network effects," where "the value that consumers place on a good increases as others use the good."[94] However, being more open has the potential disadvantage that the other participants may get sales from participation with your software. At the extreme, this sounds like the complaint quoted earlier from the open source programmer who gets, at most, "a few crumbs" from the code she has written.[95] In essence, the software company is trading-off the expanded size of the market that can come from openness versus the diminished share of that market that can come from the participation of the other competitors.

A recent announcement by VMware shows this dynamic at work. In August 2005, *The New York Times* reported: "VMware, the leader in the fast-growing market for virtual machine software, plans to announce today that it will share its code with partners like I.B.M., Intel and Hewlett-Packard in an effort to make the VMware technology an industry standard."[96] The article stated, "The move by VMware is an attempt to defend against Microsoft before that company accelerates its drive into virtual machine software."[97]

The VMware announcement nicely illustrates four points already made in this chapter. First, disclosure is on a continuum between an open and a closed source: "The partners will be able to modify the basic code for their own products, to be sold to customers. But the VMware program does not go so far as to allow the code to be freely distributed to anyone, as is the case with Open Source software projects."[98] Second, openness is a strategy to expand the overall market for a software project. In the words of

---

94   Mark A. Lemley & David McGowan, "Legal Implications of Network Economic Effects" (1998) 86 Cal. L. Rev. 479 at 481. Lemley & McGowan provide a comprehensive examination of the legal implications of such network effects, including a number of software-related issues.

95   See Posting on ZDNET, above note 72 and accompanying text.

96   Steve Lohr, "VMware to Share Its Code: Hoping to Be the Standard" *New York Times* (8 August 2005) C6 [Lohr].

97   *Ibid.*

98   *Ibid.*

an IBM executive: "This is a move toward open standards, and that is the path toward accelerating market growth and innovation."[99] Third, the shift to openness is accompanied by a strategy for the proprietary company to continue to reap financial rewards. VMware's chief executive Diane Greene said she "sees continued growth opportunities by adding features and services on top of its basic technology."[100] This quote matches the discussion above of open source competitive strategies: stay ahead of the curve; provide services where competitors do not learn easily about innovations; and, in general, seek a significant percentage of the growing market that uses VMware code. Fourth, complex game-theory calculations determine the optimal degree of openness for the software company. VMware is trying to stay closed enough to reap financial awards, but it is being pushed by other large players to become more open: "VMware's big industry partners have become increasingly concerned that it is becoming too powerful, and could potentially become a crucial, proprietary layer of software in data centers, much as Microsoft's Windows rules the market for personal computer operating systems."[101] In short, if VMware had not decided to become more open, the big industry partners may have abandoned it and gone elsewhere.

One way that this dynamic often plays out is through the standards process. The "effort to make the VMware technology an industry standard"[102] highlights the way that companies often face the question of how much to disclose; what should go into an open standard versus what should be kept in-house? My discussions with market participants reveal a high level of awareness about the importance of this standards issue. I have not found, however, any persuasive general account of how to decide how much to disclose in the standards process.[103]

For purposes of this chapter, I suggest two thoughts about the standards issue. First, because of the importance of the interactions among a few or several players, the optimal analysis is likely to depend on game theory.[104] Second, the rational level of disclosure for a vendor will often

---

99 *Ibid.* (quoting Susan Whitney, a general manager in IBM's server business).

100 *Ibid.*

101 *Ibid.*

102 *Ibid.*

103 For a thorough examination of legal issues arising from standard-setting organizations, see generally Mark A. Lemley, "Intellectual Property Rights and Standard-Setting Organizations" (2002) 90 Cal. L. Rev. 1889.

104 See Martin Shubik, *Game Theory in the Social Sciences: Concepts and Solutions* (Cambridge: MIT Press, 1982) at 300. Shubik explained that "[f]ew-player games are ones in which the players number anywhere from three to around twenty." *Ibid.*

be at an intermediate position between the extremes of open and closed source. This intermediate position is consistent with a theme of this chapter: movement along the continuum between an open and a closed source is a strategically and theoretically important topic.

b) Developer mindshare and "get them while they're young"

Proprietary software companies have an incentive to keep the source code in-house and only among software writers who have signed non-disclosure agreements. In this way, the company keeps maximum control over who gets to work with the code and can manage how all aspects of the code are developed over time. The number of software writers is then limited to the number of persons hired by the company.

Companies simultaneously face an incentive to get the maximum number of skilled software developers to work with the code. Greater developer "mindshare" leads to greater innovation on the company's code. Developer enthusiasm for this software, in turn, may reduce the amount of developer innovation that goes into competing software offerings.

Taking the conflicting incentives together, we see that a proprietary software company would rationally weigh the profits that come from increased control against the profits that result from innovation and other activity by those outside of the firm.

Two strategies illustrate how companies seek to resolve the conflicting incentives. First, companies can try to "get them while they're young." Apple Computer has famously placed its computers in elementary and other schools, hoping to train a new generation of loyal users.[105] Similarly, Microsoft has been licensing significant and increasing amounts of source code to universities since the early 1990s.[106] Computer science professors and their graduate students thus get to work directly on the source code. If programmers learn the intricacies of a software program during their student days, then it seems more likely that they will continue to work with that code after they leave school. Second, companies can release code to de-

---

He added, "Oligopoly theory, the formation of political coalitions, international negotiations, ecological struggles, and cartel problems all fall into this category." *Ibid.* His examples of oligopoly theory and cartel problems are closely related to the industry-structure issues implicated by the decision of companies about whether to cooperate (share source code) or compete (keep source code hidden).

105 Apple.com, "25 Years of Education Experience," online: www.apple.com/ca/education/whyapple/25years.html (charting Apple's investments in education from 1980 to the present).

106 Interview with Dave Ladd, above note 92.

velopers in the hopes of having the outside developers engage more deeply with the software. This strategy was used by Microsoft when it launched the Shared Source Initiative, under which it has released considerably more source code.[107]

c) Overcoming collective action problems

Proprietary software companies may use open approaches for another reason: to overcome collective action problems. Mancur Olson, a pioneer in researching such issues, memorably explained that for groups with common interests "there is a systematic tendency for 'exploitation' of the great by the small!"[108] Olson analyzed the incentives for large and small actors who would share in the benefit of a collective good.[109] His key point is that the large actor may have a rational basis for investing in the collective good because its own return from the investment may be large enough to justify the cost. A small actor, by contrast, would not get a large enough return from its own investment to justify the action. In such cases, the small actors would rationally be free riders, not investing even in a good that benefits all concerned. Thus, only the large actors will invest in the public good—the "exploitation" that Olson described.[110]

Turning to software, proprietary firms in some circumstances may find it rational to invest in open software in order to solve a collective-action problem. A notable current example would be an improved system for authentication on the Internet.[111] Put simply, it would be a great help to e-commerce and many other activities on the Internet for each of the two parties

---

107 For a discussion of the Shared Source Initiative, see Microsoft Shared Source Initiative, online: www.microsoft.com/resources/sharedsource/Initiative/Initiative.mspx.

108 Mancur Olson, *The Logic of Collective Action; Public Goods and the Theory of Groups* (Cambridge: Harvard University Press, 1965) at 29 [emphasis omitted] [footnote omitted].

109 Olson defines a public good or collective good "in terms of [the] infeasibility of excluding potential consumers of the good." *Ibid.* at 14 note 21. Modern definitions stress that a public good is not only non-excludable but also non-rival (i.e., use by one person does not reduce use by another). Robert P. Merges *et al., Intellectual Property in the New Technological Age*, 3d ed. (New York: Aspen Law and Business, 2003) at 11–12. A classic example of a public good is clean air. If a factory puts filters on its smokestacks, reducing pollution, it has no feasible way to exclude potential consumers of the good, those who breathe it. *Ibid.*

110 Olson, *ibid.* at 28–29.

111 Effective privacy protections do not necessarily preclude improved authentication. For an excellent National Academies of Science report on the topic, see National Research Council Committee on Authentication Technologies and their Privacy Im-

to be confident of the identity of the other party. Sellers and credit card companies have long faced the risk that buyers were using false identities or credit cards. More recently, the problem has grown more acute for buyers, who can no longer trust that the apparent seller's site is what it seems to be. Ordinary individuals today face the problem of phishing, defined as "the process of tricking or socially engineering an organisation[']s customers into imparting their confidential information for nefarious use."[112] A growing threat is pharming, defined as manipulation of the way that a customer "locates and connects to an organisation's named hosts or services through modification of the name lookup process."[113]

The lack of good authentication poses risks not only to websites and Internet users, but also to the overall growth of computing and the Internet. Large companies who benefit from this overall growth thus may have an incentive to take actions that will improve authentication.

The actions of Microsoft in the Internet-authentication area illustrate the way that this collective-action problem might be addressed either by a proprietary or open approach. Microsoft's first big authentication effort was heavily proprietary. Its Passport program, as proposed in 2000, contemplated that users would have a unique username that Microsoft would issue.[114] To make the system even more proprietary, data about sites the user visited would go through the Microsoft system.

The reaction to Passport was negative and overwhelming — on security, privacy, and competitive grounds.[115] A main security problem was that

plications, *Who Goes There? Authentication through the Lens of Privacy* ed. by Stephen T. Kent & Lynette I. Millett (Washington, DC: National Academies Press, 2003).

112   Gunter Ollman, *Next Generation Security Software Ltd., The Phishing Guide: Understanding and Preventing Phishing Attacks* (2004) at 3, online: www.ngsconsulting. com/papers/NISR-WP-Phishing.pdf. I am currently serving as reporter for a process convened by the National Consumers League on strategies for addressing phishing.

113   Gunter Ollman, *Next Generation Security Software Ltd., The Pharming Guide: Understanding and Preventing DNS-Related Attacks by Phishers* (2005) at 3, online: www.ngsconsulting.com/papers/ThePharmingGuide.pdf.

114   See Electronic Privacy Information Center, online: www.epic.org/privacy/consumer/ microsoft. Passport was initially proposed as part of broader Microsoft initiatives called "Hailstorm" and ".NET." See *ibid.*

115   See, for example, SOA World Magazine News Desk, "WSJ Exclusive Interview: Single Sign-On is a Single Point of Failure, Says EPIC Counsel" (1 January 2000), online: http://webservices.sys-con.com/read/39389.htm [SOA World Magazine News Desk] (discussing the privacy risk of central authentication). The Federal Trade Commission also initiated a complaint on security grounds, stating that Microsoft's disclosures about security were deceptive under section 5 of the *Federal Trade Com-*

Microsoft's role at the centre of the system created a single possible point of failure—if the Microsoft system was hacked, then all of the identifying information could be compromised. On privacy, advocacy groups sharply criticized the amount of identifiable data that would be gathered,[116] and the EU brought a major privacy complaint.[117] On competitive grounds, online retailers and other key players did not want Microsoft to have the "crown jewels" of electronic retailing (e-tailing), namely information about identified persons, including where they surfed and shopped.[118] The original Passport plans were halted, and a scaled-down Passport system has been used principally to sign into Hotmail, MSN, and other Microsoft-specific activities.[119]

In late 2005, Microsoft announced an entirely different approach to Internet authentication based on openness.[120] The new InfoCard approach

---

mission Act, 15 U.S.C. § 34 (2000). See Federal Trade Commission, Press Release, "Microsoft Settles FTC Charges Alleging False Security and Privacy Promises" (8 August 2002), online: www.ftc.gov/opa/2002/08/microsoft.htm (discussing Microsoft's agreement to settle the FTC's "charges regarding the privacy and security of personal information collected from consumers" through Passport); see also Complaint para. 21, *In re Microsoft Corp.*, No. 012-3240 (8 August 2002), online: www. ftc.gov/os/caselist/0123240/microsoftcmp.pdf ("The acts and practices of respondent as alleged in this complaint constituted unfair or deceptive acts or practices in or affecting commerce in violation of Section 5(a) of the *Federal Trade Commission Act*.").

116   See, for example, SOA World Magazine News Desk, above note 115 ("'It's bad practice to create personally identifiable records unless it's necessary. Microsoft, through Passport, is creating personally identifiable records.'" (interviewing Chris Hoofnagle, legislative counsel for Electronic Privacy Information Center (EPIC)).

117   See Paul Meller, "Microsoft to Alter Online System to Satisfy Europe" *The New York Times* (31 January 2003), online: http://query.nytimes.com/gst/fullpage.html?res=95 03EFDE1638F932A05752C0A9659C8B63 (reporting that Microsoft agreed to make "radical" changes to .Net Passport to "avert a clash with European regulators over data privacy").

118   Byron Acohido, "Microsoft, Banks Battle to Control Your E-Info" *USA TODAY* (13 August 2001), online: www.usatoday.com/tech/news/2001-08-13-microsoft-banks-e-info.htm.

119   For the current privacy policies for Passport, see "Microsoft.com Privacy Statement," online: www.microsoft.com/info/privacy.mspx#E6D.

120   For a good overview of this approach, called InfoCard, see Robert McMillan, "InfoCard Not Son of Passport, Says Microsoft Executive" *INFOWORLD* (21 September 2005), online: www.infoworld.com/article/05/09/21/HNinfocard_1.html [McMillan], who notes that, unlike Passport, "InfoCard is being designed to work on client and server software that was not developed by Microsoft." As in "Security Model," I note that I am a member of Microsoft's Trustworthy Computing Academic Advisory

is designed to make it easy for users to keep track of their passwords and other credentials,[121] while also making it far harder to impersonate a buyer or seller. InfoCard is a standard (or a set of standards) rather than a solution provided by one company. The approach is designed to be open on the client side—working with browsers such as Firefox and Opera—and on hardware running Apache, Linux, and other systems.[122] Unlike the original Passport, Microsoft would not see the data that moves between surfers and websites. In addition, Microsoft has announced it will not charge for its work on InfoCard.[123]

The suggestion I make here is that the InfoCard project is an illustration of what Mancur Olson described as the "'exploitation' of the great by the small."[124] It would benefit a very wide range of players to have effective authentication on the Internet, so that a wide variety of surfers and websites can interact with less risk of spoofing and fraud. It will likely take large investment by one or more major players, however, to make a dent in the collective-action problem of how to authenticate such a range of surfers and websites. Microsoft showed with Passport that it would prefer to have a proprietary approach to solving the authentication problem. That effort did not succeed. As a next-best solution, Microsoft is now investing resources in the open InfoCard process.

It is useful to compare the ways in which InfoCard is similar to or different from the VMware account discussed above. The similarity is based on the role of standards and the way that critical mass may develop where there is openness in development. The difference essentially boils down to the extent that there is a private good versus a public good. For VMware, the goal was to create a private good so that its software would succeed

---

Committee, which is a group of nineteen academics that has been asked to provide advice on security and privacy issues to Microsoft "Security Model," above note 1 at 198 note 51. I have heard presentations on InfoCard both in public, and in connection with that committee's work. The views expressed in this chapter are entirely my own, and I have not been compensated by Microsoft in connection with this research. I have also spoken about the issues in this chapter at great length with many open source supporters.

121   McMillan, *ibid.*

122   *Ibid.*

123   See Mary Branscombe, "Credit Where It's Due" *The Guardian* (9 June 2005), online: www.guardian.co.uk/microsoft/Story/0,,1501893,00.html.

124   Olson, above note 108 at 29 [emphasis omitted]. A similar argument would support the investment in another authentication project, the Liberty Alliance, by a coalition of large companies engaged in e-commerce, online: www.projectliberty.org.

competitively against Microsoft. VMware strategically chose the degree of openness in order to gain allies such as IBM and HP, and to get direct profits based on "adding features and services on top of its basic technology."[125] By contrast, InfoCard seems designed to create a public good, which is non-excludable (anyone can use the standard) and non-rival (use by one person does not limit use by another). Speakers for Microsoft have stressed instead the goal of growing the entire space of e-commerce and computing, rather than forcing users to buy Microsoft for authentication.[126] The incentive for Microsoft is that it will gain enough new sales from overall growth to justify its investment in creating InfoCard.[127]

d) Convergence of open source and proprietary approaches

In summary of Case Four, there are complicated interactions that affect when a proprietary software company will reveal source code for competitive reasons. Significant incentives exist for such disclosure, including: the possibility of network effects; the strategic use of open standards; the enticement of students and other developers; and the possibility of overcoming collective-action problems. Taken together, there are major incentives for proprietary software to shift toward disclosure, just as there are major incentives for open source software to use secrecy in substantial ways. The overall trend appears to be toward substantial convergence of the two previously separate approaches.

5) Case Five: Security Incentives and Government Agencies

From the discussion of open source and proprietary software, we now shift to examination of the incentives for government agencies to disclose or not. Case Five examines the incentives to disclose in connection with promoting security. Case Six looks at the competitive incentives of government agencies and focuses on agency incentives to protect and expand their own turf.

---

125 Lohr, above note 96.

126 Microsoft Corporation, "Microsoft's Vision for an Identity Metasystem" (May 2005), online: http://msdn.microsoft.com/en-us/library/ms996422.aspx.

127 Note that the Mancur Olson argument shows why the large company may invest substantial funds in the creation of a public good. The investment in the public good may still be less than is societally optimal.

a)   Government agencies and national security

To begin, the government agency can be modeled similarly to the proprietary software company. The agency has information about its own systems and activities. The agency has various incentives to keep information secret, including the hope that attackers will not learn about any vulnerabilities. The agency also has various incentives to disclose information, including the gain the agency may realize if more defenders know and respond to the information.

As discussed in "Security Model," there are often good reasons for categories of military and intelligence information to be kept secret. First, the high cost of each military attack, including the risk of casualties, means the number of attacks (N) is often low. In such instances, secrecy is often a rational strategy.[128] Second, many government secrets concern sources and methods, and other aspects of surveillance where secrecy is, again, rational.[129] Third, the chain of command and hierarchical nature of the military often make it more feasible to disclose to allies selectively, without disclosing to all parties.[130]

Related to the low N is the fact that significant portions of government activities are different from activities in the private sector. For example, nuclear launch codes and stealth aircraft are not (presumably) used in the private sector. To the extent that government activities are different, attackers gain less experience from attacking private-sector systems. In such situations, there is low N and L, and secrecy is more likely to be rational. Even if an agency knows about a vulnerability, the benefits of non-disclosure to the attackers quite possibly outweigh the benefits of disclosure to the defenders.

b)   Information sharing and third-party effects

There are other government activities where the calculus is more complex. Consider the incentives for an agency, such as the FBI, to disclose information about suspected terrorists to state and local agencies and private-sector actors. The various third parties might help the FBI by spotting and arresting the suspects, but disclosure to the third parties might also help the terrorists by tipping them off that their identities are known. In this infor-

---

128   See "Security Model," above note 1 at 177 (commenting that hiddenness will benefit military defenders because the cost of each attack will lower the total number of attacks and prevent the attackers from taking advantage of increased knowledge about the defences).

129   *Ibid.* at 191–93.

130   *Ibid.* at 203–4.

mation-sharing instance, disclosure quite possibly will help both attackers and defenders, and it is difficult to generalize about when to disclose.

In other instances, the third parties may receive clear benefits from disclosure, but the first party may not share in those benefits. Consider the possibility that the FBI learns that a certain type of attack is likely to occur, such as a nighttime attack on a power plant in an American or foreign city. The FBI may decide not to disclose because it places a higher priority on continuing its investigation of the entire terrorist group. The area that is attacked, however, is likely to place a much greater value on damage to its city.[131] In this example, the benefits of disclosure to the city may be external to the FBI's calculus. The FBI may err on the side of less disclosure than would have occurred if the localities and the FBI had made the decision jointly.

This possibility of external, negative effects on third parties can occur much more generally as a result of government action. One sad and dramatic example is the way that environmental decisions were made in the Soviet Union before its dissolution. Essentially, government agencies made decisions based on their incentives to meet production quotas and other government goals. Meanwhile, very serious environmental spillover effects often occurred. Due to one especially large disaster, the entire Aral Sea now appears to be on course to dry up, with numerous secondary consequences.[132]

c) Public choice and the weak constraints on government secrecy

The potentially large effect of government secrecy on third parties is analogous to the potentially large effect of proprietary software secrecy on third-party users. For proprietary software, the discussion above identified a number of mechanisms that push toward disclosure of vulnerabilities, even for companies that initially prefer to keep the vulnerabilities secret. These mechanisms included: (i) high N, L, and C so that flaws were discovered; (ii) buyers with monopsony power who could force disclosure; (iii) governments that required disclosure; and (iv) effective bug hunters who made the disclosure market more efficient.

---

131   The locality, in this example, is analogous to the users of proprietary software who would benefit from the disclosure of vulnerabilities by the software creator. Both the locality and the software users can suffer negative effects due to the incentives facing the first party.

132   For discussion of the environmental effects of Soviet-era decision making on the Aral Sea, see Nicola Jones, "South Aral 'Gone in 15 Years'" *New Scientist* (19 July 2003) at 9; Joshua Calder & Jim Lee, "Inventory of Conflict and Environment, Case Study Number 69: Aral Sea and Defense Issues" (1995), online: www.american.edu/ted/ice/aralsea.htm.

The question is the extent to which those market mechanisms have an analogy for government agencies. Public choice theory is the branch of political economy that analyzes political institutions by use of economic theory.[133] In some instances, agencies and other institutional actors may get to good outcomes because the organizational incentives are well-designed. When it comes to the optimal level of disclosure for vulnerabilities, however, the mechanisms to force disclosure seem much less likely to be successful than for proprietary software. The number of attacks and learning by attackers will often be less due to the backdrop of national security and secrecy. Rarely will there be any equivalents of monopsony purchasers who can force disclosure.[134] Laws such as the *Freedom of Information Act*[135] are indeed a crucial mechanism for creating openness and accountability, but discovery of any specific vulnerability depends at best on the serendipity of whether someone makes the right *Freedom of Information Act* request. Finally, bug hunters are discouraged in various ways in the public sector: stealing classified information is a crime; there are legal and personnel sanctions against those who "leak"; and whistleblowing is typically risky to do.

In short, it is difficult to be optimistic about the mechanisms in place to ensure the optimal level of disclosure from government agencies. As the next section shows, the magnitude of the problem is likely even greater when one considers an agency's competitive incentives.

6)   Case Six: Competitive Incentives and Government Agencies

When examining incentives to disclose, Case Five shows that government agencies would consider the effects on their own security goals but would not internalize the effects on third parties. Those risks are magnified when one considers the overall competitive position of a government agency.

---

133   See Daniel A. Farber & Philip P. Frickey, *Law and Public Choice: A Critical Intro-duction* (Chicago: University of Chicago Press, 1991) at 1 and 6–7 (defining public choice theory).

134   For instance, it seems unlikely that foreign or American localities will be effective at forcing the FBI or other federal agencies to disclose information when the FBI does not believe it is in the Bureau's best interest to do so. One partial exception, where the incentive effects lead to fuller disclosure, is when the Presidency and Congress are held by different parties. My experience in the Clinton Administration was that the Republican Congress vigorously investigated even small alleged problems. The level of oversight fell sharply when the same Republican majority was in office with a Republican, President George W. Bush, in the White House,.

135   5 U.S.C. § 552 (2002).

A prominent strand of public choice theory posits that agencies will seek to maximize "turf."[136] That is, agencies will have goals such as expanding their budget, maximizing their flexibility vis-à-vis other institutions, avoiding embarrassment, and so on. One example is when different law-enforcement agencies compete to get credit on a high-profile case. There have long been laments in law enforcement that information sharing (i.e., disclosure) is lacking because agents do not want to lose control of a case.[137]

Under this model, consider the incentives of a government agency when there is a known problem, such as a vulnerability, in a project where the agency is supposed to be in charge. The disadvantages of disclosure are evident—disclosure will expose problems in the agency's area of responsibility. There could well be hostile public hearings, as well as possible reductions in budget and agency discretion. The advantages of disclosure may be only indirect. If the embarrassing details will come out later, it may make sense to disclose the problem earlier, spun in a way that favours the agency. In many instances, these indirect benefits of disclosure are small. The incentive of government agencies in many situations, when they know about a vulnerability or mistake, is to deny, deny, deny.

To what extent are there market or similar mechanisms to correct for this tendency to err on the side of secrecy? Some such mechanisms can exist. An opposing political party has the incentive to expose corruption or wrongdoing in the current administration. Depending on the degree to which it is beholden to the current administration, the media may have incentives to "break a story" that shows mistakes or wrongdoing in government. The analysis here is consistent with the grand tradition of checks and balances because opposition political parties and a free press set limits on secrecy and wrongdoing by incumbents.

On a more day-to-day level, however, the political opposition or reporters may not be able to learn about many agency secrets. In that instance, it is good policy to have additional accountability institutions. In the US federal government, such institutions include the following: inspector generals in each agency; reports from the General Accountability Office;

---

136   See, for example, William A. Niskanen, Jr., *Bureaucracy and Representative Government* (Chicago: Aldine-Atherton, 1971) at 111–12 (arguing that bureaus seek to provide the broadest possible range of services in order to garner the most power possible).

137   For one article that gives a vivid flavour of ongoing turf wars at the federal and state level, see Mike Kelly, "State Counter-Terror Organization in Disarray" *The (Bergen County, NJ) Record* (9 October 2005) O1.

congressional hearings; the *Freedom of Information Act*;[138] and other open-government requirements. Creation of these institutions and these laws is crucial. Without them, there will undoubtedly be too much secrecy and self-protection by agencies. Even with them, I believe that agencies err on the side of secrecy and excessive use of classified documents far too often.[139]

In response, I believe there should be ongoing and significant efforts to detect and correct areas of excessive government secrecy. For instance, I have proposed modifying the "gag rules" under the foreign intelligence surveillance laws.[140] More generally, this entire project on security and obscurity has developed systematic approaches to describing and assessing the limited circumstances under which obscurity actually helps security.

E. CONCLUSION

An organizing theme of this chapter has been that the incentives to disclose are based on two distinct calculations. How does disclosure help or hurt security? How does disclosure help or hurt the organization competitively? Discussions about disclosure of vulnerabilities have typically failed to address the competitive issues. Discussions about the economics of open source versus proprietary software have typically failed to address the security disclosure issues. Understanding of the incentives to disclose or hide requires attention to both questions.

For the open source movement, one theme of this chapter has been to identify and highlight ways that secrecy is used for security and competitive reasons, despite the ideology of openness. The repeated use of the term "secret sauce" is suggestive here — even cute. The image of the sauce is a small layer of secrecy on top of the main course, which is not secret. The secret sauce is tasty, adding zest and individuality to each dish. The term suggests that the use of secrecy is, after all, a minor ingredient.

---

138 Above note 135.
139 For one excellent source on overclassification, including quotations about the extent of the problem, see US, *Emerging Threats: Overclassification & Pseudoclassification: Hearing Before the Subcommittee on National Security, Emerging Threats, and International Relations of the House Committee on Government Reform*, 109th Cong. (2005) (statement of Thomas Blanton, Executive Director, National Security Archive, George Washington University) at 121–24, online: www.fas.org/sgp/congress/2005/030205overclass.html.
140 Peter P. Swire, "The System of Foreign Intelligence Surveillance Law" (2004) 72 Geo. Wash. L. Rev. 1306 at 1356–60.

I speculate that use of the term "secret sauce" is a linguistic effort to downplay the use of secrecy, in recognition that any lapse from openness risks being viewed as a shameful act among the open source community. To the extent that the analysis here shows multiple, significant ways that secrecy-for-security and secrecy-for-competitiveness coexist with open source projects, the linguistic effort may be a sign of guilty consciences among true believers who nonetheless employ secrecy. The ideology of openness is not necessarily a good match for how the rational open source programmer acts.

Do I write this out of some admiration or preference for secrecy over openness? Not at all. I am a great supporter, for instance, of the *Freedom of Information Act*, openness in government, and robust rights of a free press. For breach notification, I support measures to ensure that third parties are not harmed by the externality described in this chapter. For software vulnerabilities, I applaud the many measures taken in recent years that have accelerated discovery, notice, and patch-creation for vulnerabilities. Where there is evidence that the incentives to disclose and fix vulnerabilities are not working, further measures should be explored.

This chapter, instead, has been primarily descriptive. It began with an attempt to explain when it is correct to say "there is no security through obscurity" and when instead it makes sense to say that "loose lips sink ships." "Security Model" examined when disclosure would help or hurt security, considering the effects on all the relevant actors. This work took on the next task, identifying the incentives for key actors to disclose or not, for both security and competitiveness reasons. Together, the hope is to create systematic ways to decide when it makes sense to disclose or keep a secret. In a world of pervasive new information flows and systems, that is no small thing.

CHAPTER 4

FLOW Licensing and Contracting: Applied Intellectual Resource Economics in the Canadian Public Sector

*Joseph R. Potvin**

A. INTRODUCTION

The paper explains and illustrates a generic approach to licensing and contracting for free-libre-open works (FLOW). Concepts in economics, accounting, and copyright law are summarized to provide a view of the business purposes of free-libre-open resource availability. An original way is presented to summarize the differences amongst various major free-libre-open licence types, emphasizing their rules for the distribution of derivative works. The paper also offers a generic naming convention for comprehensive models that combine sets of licensing and contracting choices for communities working on free-libre-open resources. A particular model described in the paper is named FLOW.through.1, and the example used to illustrate its application is the first free-libre-open project to be initiated by the Treasury Board Secretariat of the Canadian Government.

---

* This article was prepared and submitted by Joseph Potvin as a private citizen. Nothing he expresses in this article, or in discussions related to it, can be taken to represent the views, directions, or policies of his employer, the Treasury Board Secretariat of the Canadian Government. This article is licensed under the Creative Commons Attribution License (http://creativecommons.org/licenses/by/2.5/ca/ in Canada, and http://creativecommons.org/licenses/by/3.0 elsewhere). It is a detailed elaboration and extension of the presentation given by the author at the F/LOSS as Democratic Principle conference (April 2007), which was licensed Creative Commons Attribution, under Crown Copyright (Treasury Board Secretariat, Government of Canada).

B. FLOW

FLOW refers to any data, information, or knowledge resource created and distributed under free or open source software licensing, under similar licensing for content, or under "public domain" status. The "flow" metaphor emphasizes that intellectual works constitute dynamic "streams" of meaning. This idea is opposed to treating intellectual works as fixed property[1]. In the book *I Seem to Be a Verb*, R. Buckminster Fuller wrote: "I live on Earth at present, and I don't know what I am. I know that I am not a category. I am not a thing—a noun. I seem to be a verb, an evolutionary process."[2] Accordingly, in this paper, FLOW is used in place of FLOSS (Free/Libre Open Source Software).[3]

C. CONSIDERATIONS IN ECONOMICS, ACCOUNTING, AND COPYRIGHT LAW

In his *Principles of Economics*,[4] Alfred Marshall described "land," "labour," "capital," and "organization/knowledge" as the four primary factors of production. The boundaries cannot depend solely upon their biophysical

---

1 Richard Stallman, "Did You Say 'Intellectual Property'? It's a Seductive Mirage" (2008), online: www.gnu.org/philosophy/not-ipr.html

2 R. Buckminster Fuller, Jerome Agel, & Quentin Fiore, *I Seem to Be a Verb* (New York: Bantam Books, 1970) at 1.

3 It was in the trivial act of creating a filename for this article that typing "Free-Libre-Open" led me to think that all I needed was a good "W" word to complete what could be a deeply metaphorical acronym. "Works" is the generic term used in law and economics for all sorts of creative output. "Flow" is usually perceived first as a verb, and even when it is a noun, such as in "the flow of water," it refers to movement. The result is that the subject of discussion is less likely to be mistaken for a commodity, as in: "Yes, please, I'll have another flow." (Though, if you did say that at the pub, the second one would probably be delivered!) I've never liked FLOSS (Free/Libre Open Source Software), because it is meaningless within the licensing context, and brings to mind the dental hygiene context to anyone outside the jargon circle. Furthermore, FLOSS refers just to software, whereas I find that most of the issues we concern ourselves with in this community are relevant to a wide spectrum of intellectual resources. I had already reinterpreted FLOSS in the original title of my presentation at the April 2007 workshop, to refer to services instead of software: "Licensing in a Free/Libre Open Source Services (FLOSS) Oriented Architecture: An Experiment in Applied Intellectual Resource Economics in the Canadian Public Sector." As an economist, I have always held the view that a software programmer is a service provider, not a manufacturer.

4 Alfred Marshall, *Principles of Economics*, 8th ed. (London: Macmillan, 1920).

characteristics. Whether landscaped features should be treated as capital or land, and whether management strategy is to be considered labour or knowledge, will always be debatable, due to different legitimate objectives underlying various accounting or analytical efforts. Marshall also did not clearly distinguish organization/knowledge from capital. But he did observe:

> The distinction between public and private property in knowledge and organization is of greater importance than that between public and private property in material things; and partly for that reason it seems best sometimes to reckon Organization apart as a distinct agent of production.[5]

A hundred years earlier, on 13 August 1813, Thomas Jefferson wrote a letter to Isaac McPherson to articulate the practical distinction between public/private property considerations in relation to intellectual versus material things:

> If nature has made any one thing less susceptible than all others of exclusive property, it is the action of the thinking power called an idea, which an individual may exclusively possess as long as he keeps it to himself; but the moment it is divulged, it forces itself into the possession of every one, and the receiver cannot dispossess himself of it. Its peculiar character, too, is that no one possesses the less, because every other possesses the whole of it. He who receives an idea from me, receives instruction himself without lessening mine; as he who lights his taper at mine, receives light without darkening me.[6]

Jefferson's emphasis that the possession of intellectual things can be infinitely concurrent, while the possession of material things is ultimately exclusive, even when held "in common," is obviously critical to any consideration of licensing and contracting. In general, it is useful to maintain a distinction between intellectual "organization/knowledge" and physical "capital."

The significance of distinguishing between organization/knowledge and physical capital is most evident today in relation to software. In legislation, software is considered to constitute a type of literary work. Under the Canadian *Copyright Act*,[7] the term "literary work" explicitly "includes

---

5   *Ibid.* at 114.
6   Letter from Thomas Jefferson to Isaac McPherson (13 August 1813) in Philip Kurland & Ralph Lerner, eds., *The Founders' Constitution*, vol. 1 (Chicago: University of Chicago Press, 1987) c. 16, Document 25.
7   R.S.C. 1985, c. C-42.

tables, computer programs, and compilations of literary works."[8] It further specifies that "computer program" means "a set of instructions or statements, expressed, fixed, embodied or stored in any manner, that is to be used directly or indirectly in a computer in order to bring about a specific result."[9] The *Agreement on Trade-Related Aspects of Intellectual Property Rights (TRIPS)*,[10] similarly states: "Computer programs, whether in source or object code, shall be protected as literary works under the Berne Convention (1971)."[11] Accordingly, an expression in the C programming language, such as:

```
#include
int main()
{
    std::cout << "Hello, world!\n";
}
```

. . . or in the Ruby programming language, such as

```
for i in 1..1
    puts "Hello World!"
end
```

has the same essential characteristics in law as the English statement in pre-formatted text, such as:

```
Print: ?Hello World!?
```

The text you are reading presently is machine-readable via optical character recognition technology; the C++ source code of the word processor used by the author to write this text is readable by someone fluent in that programming language.

In 1928–29, the Belgian surrealist painter René Magritte depicted a pipe on canvas, below which he also painted the words: "Ceci n'est pas

---

8   *Ibid.*, s. 2.

9   *Ibid.*

10 *Agreement on Trade-Related Aspects of Intellectual Property Rights*, 15 April 1994, Marrakesh Agreement Establishing the World Trade Organization, Annex 1C, 1869 U.N.T.S. 299 [*TRIPS*]. On terminology, see Richard Stallman, "Did You Say 'Intellectual Property'? It's a Seductive Mirage" (2008), online: www.gnu.org/philosophy/not-ipr.html.

11 *Ibid.*, art. 10(1).

une pipe," (this is not a pipe).[12] His intent was to play with the human propensity to confuse the mere depiction of something, with the thing itself. His paradox is solved with the realization that one is not looking at a pipe, but at a painting of a pipe. As obvious as it may seem here, this type of misunderstanding frequently characterizes current perceptions of digital works, as many feel the software and the hardware are similar. But each, in their own ways, of Jefferson, Marshall, Magritte, and Canadian federal legislators have all emphasized the essential difference between a folder and an image of a folder, used as a metaphor.

Nevertheless, many public sector organizations institutionalize the confusion between the computer and the algorithmic instructions for the computer in their management of licensing and contracting. We can see the problem right in the name of the "Software Commodities Division" of the Acquisitions Branch of the Department of Public Works and Government Service Canada. The name suggests that federal acquisition of computer programming code is like acquiring hard drives, as one might consider stories to be similar to books. The methods of commerce applied to trade in licences for "seats" of restricted-access software since the early 1990s have made it seem common sense for procurement professionals to treat software programs in terms of commodity units. But spending for programming code that is prepared under contract is accounted for under "professional services"; and when the code is written in-house, the money shows up as "salaries." There are no financial transactions to be accounted for at all when code is downloaded under free-libre-open licence terms, or when personnel from other organizations volunteer improvements or extensions to software that one's in-house developers created and published under free-libre-open licence terms. Yet all of these are genuine "software acquisitions." A higher-level of common sense suggests we can probably find common ground by treating computer programs as literary works; that is to say, as they are already considered as such in federal and international law.

Unfortunately, we cannot turn to the Canadian Institute of Chartered Accountants (CICA) for clarity. From 2001 forward the CICA has also allowed the treatment of spending on software as tangible capital expenditure for accounting purposes, whether in the form of licence purchases, contracted development, or own-account development. Recently, Professor

---

12   René Magritte, *La trahison des images*, 1928–29. Oil on canvas. Los Angeles County Museum of Art.

Charles Mulford and Jack Roberts[13] at the Georgia Institute of Technology analyzed how the capitalization of software expenditure by firms causes financial reports to significantly overstate earnings for the fiscal year in which the money is spent, and then through amortization, to cause earnings to be understated in subsequent years. Finding that the majority of software development companies, in fact, do not capitalize software spending, and that amongst firms where it is done, the methods are arbitrary, they recommend that accounting standards bodies should revoke the provisions that permit this practice. Their study is in reference to the US market, however the issue they discuss is not significantly different in Canada.

Payments to vendors for unit licences are really "rental fees" (usage royalties), bundled with fees for financial services and support services. A typical end-user licence agreement, such as for the Microsoft XP operating system, states: "The Product is protected by copyright and other . . . laws and treaties. Microsoft or its suppliers own the title, copyright, and other . . . rights in the Product. The Product is licensed, not sold." Clearly, the vendor is emphasizing that no asset ownership is acquired by the customer. The organization purchasing a licence cannot logically capitalize this expenditure. In March 2008 the quasi-judicial Commissioner of Income Tax (Appeals) in New Delhi ruled on the very point:

> A copy of software supplied by the appellant admittedly did not amount to a sale but it is a licence to use the software as stipulated in software licence agreement.[14]

Accounting and acquisitions policies and practices that perceive royalties and service agreements as commodity unit sales are at best inadequate, and at worst misleading. From a pragmatic point of view, they tend to restrict an organization's consideration of licensing and contracting options to the confines of a single business model.

Mulford and Roberts propose that software development costs should be returned to the pre-2001 treatment as research and development (e.g., new capabilities), which is expensed, or as operations and maintenance expenditures (e.g., bug fixes), which will depend upon the type of work

---

13   Charles Mulford & Jack Roberts, "Capitalization of Software Development Costs: A Survey of Accounting Practices in the Software Industry" (2006), online: http:// smartech.gatech.edu/handle/1853/15598.

14   Tax India Online Legal Bureau, "Microsoft Softwares: The Product is Licensed, Not Sold" (2008), online:www.taxindiaonline.com/RC2/inside2.php3?filename=bnews_ detail.php3&newsid=7095.

actually undertaken. Such a step "would be more closely aligned with the realities of the software industry today."[15]

D. SOMETHING GAINED IN TRANSLATION: COPYRIGHT AND *DROITS D'AUTEUR*

In this global digital age of data warehouses, mash-ups, wikis, and free-libre-open licensing, it is useful, albeit frustrating, to realize that the key concepts and definitions in each country's copyright legal tradition started off and remain a little different, which inevitably leaves much room for confusion. Even within our own Canadian legal context, it is challenging for software and database professionals to steer clear of misunderstanding due to the conceptual differences between the English copyright tradition that emphasizes artistic and literary works as articles of commerce, and the *droits d'auteur* continental *civiliste* tradition that emphasizes personal reputation. There's value in briefly reviewing the historical origins of Canadian copyright, and their implications for licensing and contracting.

After Johann Gutenberg invented the printing press in 1440, it became easier for people to disseminate heretical and seditious works, challenging both church and state. In order to control what was being said, Henry VIII of England invoked a royal prerogative in 1538, on dubious constitutional grounds, to establish printing patents as a form of censorship. By a royal charter in 1557, the Stationers' Company was created by the British Crown to oversee a guild system in which the right to print a book was limited to members of the guild, who were the printers and sellers of books, not the authors. Much has changed in 450 years, but Canada's own current *Copyright Act*[16] should still be viewed in its historical context, with attention to the evolution of the legislation, caselaw, and international conventions.

When the UK ratified the *Berne Convention for the Protection of Literary and Artistic Works* in 1887,[17] they also ratified it on behalf of Canada. Under section 91(23) of the *Constitution Act, 1867*,[18] the federal government was granted exclusive power to enact laws within Canada related to copyright. But Canada remained under British copyright until 1921, when the Canadian Parliament passed its own *Copyright Act*. This came into force in

---

15   Above note 13 at 18.
16   *Copyright Act*, R.S.C. 1985, c. C-42.
17   9 September 1886, as revised at Paris on 24 July 1971 and amended in 1979, S. Treaty Doc. No. 99-27 (1986).
18   (U.K.), 30 & 31 Vict., c. 3, reprinted in R.S.C. 1985, App. II, No. 5.

1924,[19] although it was still closely modelled on the English *Copyright Act of 1911*.[20] As a separate country Canada only ratified the *Berne Convention* in 1928.

It is a common experience in bilingual and multilingual settings to encounter problems of confusion when semantic meaning gets lost in translation. In Canada's case, we find something has been gained in translation with the French phrase *droits d'auteur*, which is evidently not "*droit de copier*." The English word "copyright" refers to a straightforward economic right to make copies of a work. The meaning is extended in the French *droits d'auteur* in a way that draws upon the European continental civil law (*civiliste*) tradition. It holds that the right of reproduction goes beyond the simple right to make new copies of a work to the more complex notion of protecting the integrity and paternity of the work, because it is linked to the author's reputation in society.

In Canadian legislation, Parliament has sought to draw upon both English and French traditions in an attempt to balance a right that is centred on the reputation of the person of the author with a right centred on the economic role of the work as an object of commerce. (In the English language, the reputation element is the denoted "moral right," although this would have been better communicated with the word "morale.") *Droits d'auteur*, or "author's rights," does not refer strictly to the dollars-and-cents linkage between an author and the creative work. Instead, the work is considered to represent something about the author, whose dignity deserves protection, and thus the right to defend the integrity of a work and, where reasonable in the circumstances, to be associated with the work as its author by name or under a pseudonym, or to remain anonymous. Under international agreements and national legislation, authors of creative works hold moral rights of integrity, association, and attribution, although how these rights are understood varies from country to country. Section 28.2(1) of Canada's *Copyright Act* specifies that "the author's right to the integrity of a work is infringed only if the work is, to the prejudice of the honour or reputation of the author" as a result of the work being "distorted, mutilated or otherwise modified" or "used in association with a product, service, cause or institution."[21] In Canada, the reputation (moral) rights of an author can be waived but not transferred through assignment or sale, whereas copyright can be sold or assigned to a person or entity other than the original author.

---

19   *An Act to amend and consolidate the Law relating to Copyright*, S.C. 1921, c. 24.

20   *Copyright Act 1911* (U.K.), 1 & 2 Geo. V, c. 46.

21   Above note 7, s. 28.2(1)(b).

The *Theberge v. Galerie d'Art du Petit Champlain Inc.*[22] case provides an excellent description of these concepts.

E. RELEVANCE AND LIMITATIONS OF COPYRIGHT FOR DATA AND DATABASE PROFESSIONALS

The application of copyright should be considered by parties to contracts involving the use of or creation of databases, which are implemented in software. The boundary line regarding the applicability of copyright law to data was clarified in a 1997 case at the Canadian Federal Court of Appeal (*Tele-Direct (Publications) Inc. v. American Business Information, Inc.*).[23] In his decision, Judge J.A. Denault explained:

> Under subsection 5(1) of the (Copyright) Act, copyright subsists not in a compilation of data per se, but in an original work . . . the selection or arrangement of data only results in a protected compilation if the end result qualifies as an original intellectual creation.[24]

He reiterated a US Supreme Court decision,[25] which found that listings of routine factual data, such as names, towns, and telephone numbers in a telephone directory, are "uncopyrightable" facts, because they are not selected, coordinated, or arranged in an original way.

The *TRIPS* agreement also states:

> Compilations of data or other material, whether in machine readable or other form, which by reason of the selection or arrangement of their contents constitute intellectual creations shall be protected as such. Such protection, which shall not extend to the data or material itself, shall be without prejudice to any copyright subsisting in the data or material itself.[26]

Further, subsection 2.1(2) of the *Copyright Act* states that the "mere fact that a work is included in a compilation does not increase, decrease or otherwise affect the protection conferred by this Act in respect of the copyright in the work." The courts have consistently found that the amount of effort required to collect and manage the information is not a criterion for copyrightability.

---

22   *Théberge v. Galerie d'Art du Petit Champlain inc.*, 2002 SCC 34.

23   [1997] F.C.J. No. 1430, 1997 CanLII 6378 (C.A.).

24   *Ibid.* at para. 16.

25   *Feist Publications, Inc. v. Rural Tel. Serv. Co.*, 499 U.S. 340 (1991).

26   *TRIPS*, above note 10, art. 10(2).

Rights in the other constituent parts of a database warrant separate consideration. Copyright title to generic documentation of the source data model and metadata schema may be held by an international standards body, such as the International Public Sector Accounting Standards Board. However, technical documentation, implemented database tables, indices and functions, data entry forms, queries, and output views are typically covered by copyright. Title to these discrete parts of the database would be determined according to what organizations the database analysts/architects worked for, their terms of employment with those organizations, and the terms of the federal contracts under which the work was performed.

F. TERMS AND CONDITIONS OF AVAILABILITY DISTINGUISH INTELLECTUAL ASSETS FROM INTELLECTUAL RESOURCES

A *resource* is any available supply of wealth that may be drawn upon when needed. Only that part of an asset, such as an in-ground mineral deposit or oil *reservoir*, that is technologically and financially available for extraction is correctly referred to as a *reserve*, or natural *resource*. *Intellectual resources* refer to the available supply of data, information, or knowledge assets that may be drawn upon when needed. Therefore the terms and conditions of availability associated with an intellectual asset, especially provisions related to the creation and distribution of derivative and associated works throughout a community of creators and users, establish whether that asset can be considered a resource.

Figure 1: An Intellectual Resource Community

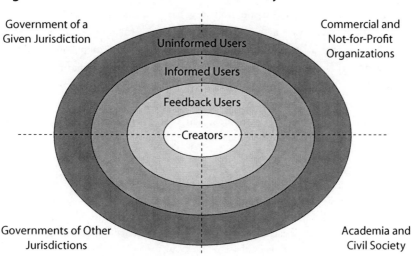

Government of a Given Jurisdiction

Commercial and Not-for-Profit Organizations

Uninformed Users

Informed Users

Feedback Users

Creators

Governments of Other Jurisdictions

Academia and Civil Society

Figure 1, developed in conversation with Mike Lachapelle of Public Works and Government Services Canada, illustrates creators of intellectual resources at the centre of a given community. The resource may be used by people who are unaware that they are using it, such as visitors to www.canada. gc.ca,[27] who do not realize that the site is delivered from a system running a compilation of more than 200 software community resources distributed as the "Apache Webserver."[28] The name is derived from an early reference to this compilation of complementary resources, by one of its original creators, as "a patchy webserver." Being told this fact, users of the site are introduced into the group of informed users, which includes some who locate and download a copy of this set of resources for use in other contexts. A small part of this group may have reason, on occasion, to offer feedback to the creators of a given intellectual resource like Apache. By communicating with the creators, these "feedback users" can influence its further evolution. They can also have the source code to Apache and modify it themselves. To the extent that some contribute substantively to the Apache resources themselves, they participate as co-creators.

Formal access rules, such as nondisclosure agreements, licences, and role-based access protocols, as well as informal "us/them" social dichotomies, may restrict participation in an intellectual resource community to a defined group within one of the sector quadrants indicated, such as a single branch of a given organization, or to identified participants within or across sectors.[29] To anyone outside that boundary, those exclusive assets are not resources. Business interests in restrictive licensing and contracting of intellectual assets depend upon the ability of rights owners to maintain some degree of exclusive possession of these assets, as if they were physical.

There are numerous business reasons for creators in various contexts to declare their asset to be a free-libre-open resource for any participant from any sector, under an explicit or implicit governance agreement and management process. Their reasons can be grouped as augmenting benefits, reducing costs, and managing risk, summarized in Table 1. Some of the terminology in this list reflects its origins relating to software. But most of the elements can be easily interpreted in connection with other intellectual resource types.

---

27 Government of Canada, "Canada: The True North Strong and Free," online: www. canada.gc.ca.

28 The Apache Software Foundation, online: www.apache.org.

29 An example across sectors would be a public-sector study, or software project team, the design of which is exclusive to staff and selected external commercial contractors, even if it invites public feedback on the results.

Table 1: Business interests in FLOW Licensing and Contracting

Augment Benefits	Reduce Costs

• Knowledge-sharing and innovation through agile private-public-academic collaboration
  » International
  » Cross-sector/Cross-departmental
  » Cross-industry
• Leverage of intellectual assets that have already been paid for
• Leverage of the most competitive approaches
• Better in-house and independent security, management, and financial control
• Diversify and decentralize
  » Customization for niche requirements
  » Opportunities for participation of small and medium enterprise outside major cities
• Engage internal and external expertise
  » Designers/architects/ planners
  » Quality assurance community
  » Implementation community
	• Cost management
	  » Configuration flexibility
	  » Migration flexibility (no forced obsolescence)
	  » Reuse components (own and others')
	  » Externalize certain costs
	  » Simplify licence management
	• Reduce start-up and delivery times
	• Engage international standards by default
	• More elegant modular architecture
	• More agile systems development
	Manage Risk
	• Provide/obtain independent security assurance
	• Distribute risk amongst multiple investors
	• Protect the "knowledge commons"
	• Sustainability (outlast team/organization)
	• Learn from peer review feedback
	  » Praise and/or criticism
	  » Confirmation/rejection of assumptions
	• Employee retention and succession management

One of the primary business interests/reasons for creators in an intellectual community to choose FLOW arrangements is that the scope of feedback influences the depth of learning. Almost half a century ago, Jay Forrester observed that the basic structural element of an organization (or a community) is the "information-feedback loop."[30] He believed that it is really the set of interacting feedback loops that comprise the underlying structure of a system. More recently, Chris Argyris described learning that takes for granted certain goals, values, and frameworks as "single-loop

---

30 Jay W. Forrester, *Industrial Dynamics* (Cambridge: MIT Press, 1961) and Jay W. Forrester, "Industrial Dynamics: A Major Breakthrough for Decision Makers" (1958) 36 Harvard Business Review 37.

learning."[31] Since participants in open communities are more often challenged to reconsider their goals, strategies, and assumptions, these influences lead to what Argyris called "double-loop learning," by which he means they learn how to learn more effectively.

FLOW terms and conditions of supply around data, information, or knowledge, and the associated provisions for derivative and associated works, are expressly designed to foster the most diverse set of interacting feedback loops possible. If Forrester and Argyris are correct, participants in FLOW communities can be expected to experience more opportunities to learn, and to learn more deeply, than those operating under restrictive arrangements.

G. A SPECTRUM OF FLOW LICENCE TYPES

The key to understanding the differences amongst alternative FLOW licences is to consider how they accommodate derivative and associated works. Figure 2 is an original way to illustrate the three basic types of software licences used by FLOW communities. The large squares at the top represent software "programs," and their smaller internal squares represent component "files" that constitute the functional elements of those programs. (As before, the terminology here is related to software because that is the most advanced area of FLOW licensing, offering the clearest examples. The essential concepts can be leveraged for many other types of works also, such as for "stories" that contain chapters.")

For software, the most popular "unified licence" is the GNU General Public License (GPL).[32] Under its terms, anyone is free: to change elements of the work, represented here as a square that is modified to be a circle; to add new elements into it, seen as the addition of the diamond and the triangle; and, to "wrap" other software around it, on the condition that the entire resulting program is distributed under the same GPL, the shading of the illustration with diagonal lines. The business intent of such a licence is to ensure that terms and conditions for users, contributors, and distributors remain simple and consistent for the whole resource, hence the term "unified." It also establishes a prohibition against distribution of elements or derivatives under any other licence. This protects the interests of the original software creators where competitors would make derivatives of their

---

31   Chris Argyris, *On Organizational Learning*, 2d ed. (Oxford: Blackwell, 1999).
32   GNU Operating System, "GNU General Public License," online: www.gnu.org/copyleft/gpl.html.

Figure 2: How Different FLOW Licences Accommodate Derivative and Associated Works

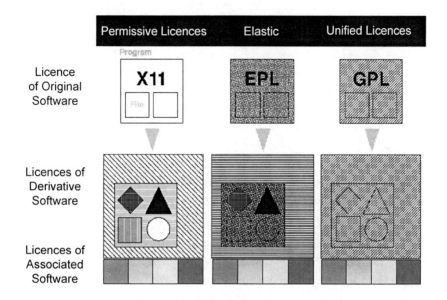

creative work. This licence does accommodate the distribution of other intellectual resources under different licences in association with the program that is under the unified licence, and this is represented by the multi-shaded squares along the bottom. Only derivatives and extensions of the original work must remain under the unified licence.

At the other end of this FLOW licensing spectrum are options such as the "X11" licence and revised BSD License.[33] This "permissive" class of licences leaves anyone the right to maintain or change elements of the original work, to add new elements, and to "wrap" other software around it, under any licences at all. The main business intent of permissive licences is to propagate a given solution. For this reason it is particularly suited to reference implementations of international standards because the business goals of these resource creators are met even when others re-license the solution under restrictive royalty-based terms and conditions.

A hybrid approach is referred to here as "elastic" licensing of intellectual resources, best represented by the Eclipse Public License (EPL).[34] The GPL-styled share-alike requirements of unified licensing apply to component

---

33   XII License, online: www.xfree86.org/3.3.6/COPYRIGHT1.html#1
34   Revised BSD, online: www.xfree86.org/3.3.6/COPYRIGHT2.html#5

files and their derivatives and extensions, but the X11 style of laissez-faire permissive licensing applies to the whole functional program. Under this scenario, anyone may change discrete elements of the work, shown here as a square that is modified to be a circle, on the condition that the derivative element is redistributed under the original EPL licence, the inner box inside the box shaded with horizontal lines. Anyone may also add new elements, and "wrap" other software around the entire set, under any licences at all. The business intent of this type of licence is to ensure that terms and conditions for users, contributors, and distributors of individual components and their derivatives remains consistent, but that anyone can create derivative programs by adding different features and functions under any licence at all, including restrictive royalty-based terms and conditions. The elastic licence fosters more complex, composite licensing scenarios for complete programs than either the unified or permissive scenarios:

- The unified GPL requires application of the original single licence to the whole program
- The permissive X11 permits the option of applying any other single licence to all adopted components licensed under it
- The elastic EPL restricts licensing to some parts, but not all.

H. THE FLOW.through.1 MODEL FOR LICENSING AND CONTRACTING BY AN INTELLECTUAL RESOURCE COMMUNITY

1) A Naming Convention for Licensing and Contracting Models

FLOW licences provide rules governing the wide availability and distribution of intact, derivative, and associated works from an intellectual resource community. But none of these licences are designed to address, nor do they imply, any assumptions about the original intellectual rights of creators, whether they are individuals or organizations, as autonomous original contributors of data, information, and knowledge to the community.

Walter Pitkin of Columbia University observed that "there are a few right ways of doing anything (some say there is only one, but that is not true); and there are a million easy ways of doing each thing wrongly."[35] There are several potential "right" ways for an intellectual resource community as a whole, and its contributors individually, to complement FLOW

---

35   Walter B. Pitkin, *A Short Introduction to the History of Human Stupidity* (London: George Allen & Unwin Ltd., 1935) at 16.

licensing with contractual foundations for intellectual rights in original contributions, as well as for ongoing rights and licence management. But at present there is no easy way to name alternative approaches to contracting and licensing.

A three-part generic-naming convention is suggested here for comprehensive models that combine sets of licensing and contracting choices. The first part is the FLOW acronym, which refers to any stream of data, information, or knowledge that is created and distributed under free or open source software licensing, under similar licensing for content, or under "public domain" status. The second part is any word in lowercase to distinguish each model, the preference being to select words that extend or qualify the metaphor. The third part appends conventional version numbering to the model's name, so that incremental improvements can be easily signalled. A particular model described below is named "FLOW.through.1." A similar naming convention can be used to distinguish FLOW from exclusive models. For example, the label RENT ("Restrictive/Exclusive/Negotiated Title") emphasizes particular terms of compensation, and can be used in the following form: "RENT.thought.1."

2) FLOW.through.1 Intellectual Rights Contract Provisions Among Contributors

The FLOW.through.1 model outlined in this section borrows ideas from four sources. Its treatment of primary copyright ownership is derived from the Canadian Government's "Policy on Title to Intellectual Property Arising Under Crown Procurement Contracts," specifically Appendix A, Part 1: "Contractor Owns."[36] Provisions for community copyright management are adapted from the "Joint Copyright Assignment" of OpenOffice.org.[37] Risk management relating to potential and perceived liability builds upon the rationale presented by the CICA regarding the application of joint and several liability to professional defendants, and incorporated into subsequent recommendations by the Canadian Senate Standing Senate Com-

---

36 Treasury Board of Canada Secretariat, "Policy on Title to Intellectual Property Arising under Crown Procurement Contracts (Appendix A, Part 1: Contractor Owns)" (2006), online: www.tbs-sct.gc.ca/Pubs_pol/dcgpubs/Contracting/tipaucpca_e.asp.

37 Sun Microsystems, "OpenOffice.org Open Source Project Joint Copyright Assignment by Contributor to Sun Microsystems, Inc.," online: www.openoffice.org/licenses/jca.pdf.

mittee on Banking, Trade and Commerce.[38] The synthesis of all of these elements into an approach for FLOW licensing and contracting that maintains an attractive incentive structure for voluntary knowledge sharing and inter-organizational learning, is the outcome of many conversations with private, public, and academic participants in the GOSLING Community.[39]

The FLOW.through.1 model vests authors' rights to original work with the contributor most directly associated with authorship, whether the author's legal status is as a contractor, subcontractor, organization, employee, or individual. When an author is subcontracted through another firm, such as a professional services broker that holds a standing offer with a paying client, the brokering firm and the paying client will need to waive all intellectual rights claims to the creative work contributed in favour of the author.[40] When the author is an employee, an employer gaining original title would assign independent joint copyright to the individual(s).

The FLOW.through.1 model for licensing and contracting has each author participating in the intellectual resource community sign an attestation upon first seeking to join the ranks of contributor. It states that any work to be contributed shall be either:

- Directly authored by or herself, such that she holds moral rights of integrity, association, and attribution for the contributions, and also holds author's rights to issue licences and to assert controls on copying and distribution of these contributions (copyright). The FLOW. through.1 model then has each author commit to a waiver of her moral rights to the integrity of the work, thereby authorizing anyone else to make derivative works, and a waiver of her moral rights of as-

---

38   Canada, Parliament, Standing Committee on Banking, Trade and Commerce, "Corporate Governance" in *Journals of the Senate* (August 1996), online: www.parl. gc.ca/35/2/parlbus/commbus/senate/com-e/bank-e/rep-e/cgo-tc-e.htm ["Corporate Governance"].

39   GOSLING (Getting Open Source Logic INto Governments) is a voluntary, informal learning and knowledge-sharing community of practice, involving civil servants and other citizens who actively assist the engagement of free/libre/open methods and software solutions in government operations. Participation in GOSLING involves individuals in their personal capacities, such that activities are driven by the research, interests, and views of the members, which may or may not reflect the official stances of the organizations in which they may work. See online: www. goslingcommunity.org.

40   All brokering firms I have approached with this FLOW.through.1 model have agreed to sign such a waiver, or were able to demonstrate that they were making no intellectual rights claims in the work of their contractors.

sociation, which authorizes anyone else to combine or distribute the contributed work in relation to any product, service, cause, or institution. However each author retains the moral right of attribution to the original contributed form of the work (right to claim authorship; to remain anonymous; to use a pseudonym).

- Third-party data, information, or knowledge, accompanied by identification of sources, and documentation of permissions from those who hold moral rights and authors' rights, which may be in the form of licences. The FLOW.through.1 model has each contributor commit to a statement that any such work will only be contributed if it is known to be under permissions and licences that are compatible with the licensing regime use by this community. The statement also commits the contributor to respect all requirements of third-party permissions and licences, and to provide the community clear rights or authorizations to modify and distribute under its chosen community licensing regime. The contributor is obliged to identify in writing any issues or uncertainties regarding appropriate use or distribution. The statement also requires that the terms and conditions of externally acquired supporting resources needed to work with or implement the community resource shall be read and respected by the contributor.

It is essential that an intellectual resource community be able to exercise management authority over licensing and distribution of its resources, under whatever governance structure it happens to engage. This requires that the governing entity of the community obtain unrestricted, independent, joint authors' rights over all contributions taken together, without limiting the intellectual rights of individual contributors. Otherwise, at some future date, the community could find it entirely impractical to implement even the most minor and obvious adjustments to the licensing of the combined works. If authors' rights vest only with each individual contributor, then any change in any licence clause covering the whole would have to be approved by each and every contributor. Some of the contributors may be impossible to reach and, indeed, some may only be represented by their estates. Companies that held rights might have been absorbed by other firms, or they may no longer exist. This is the bind that the Linux kernel community got itself into during the past fifteen years. Since most kernel contributors have always retained exclusive individual rights in their contributions, negotiation related to changing from version 2 to version 3 of the GNU General Public License was significantly complicated beyond any substantive differences of opinion. Some kernel contributors who did not agree with elements of the version 3 licence viewed this limitation as beneficial. They argue that consent was required from all the authors who had ever contributed to the Linux kernel, which would have remained entirely impractical to obtain. Not everyone agrees that complete expressed consensus was required. However, lingering differences on this point demand that both views be considered.

The present FLOW.through.1 model is suitable for any intellectual resource community whose participants would vest authority with their governing authority to manage licensing of the whole, yet want to leave intact the intellectual rights of individual contributors. Therefore, before any original contribution can be accepted as part of the combined resource, the owner of the authors' rights is required to assign "unrestricted, independent, joint" authors' rights (copyright) to the governing entity. That means both the author and the governing entity will hold full, autonomous rights to distribute, license, and sublicense the contribution, and while the original author will always be attributed (within the limited provisions of the licence), both may independently register a copyright in the contribution in any jurisdiction. But by these means, the governing entity is granted by all contributors, unrestricted and independent derivative and distribution rights in the synthesized whole, or any part, including the right to make these available under any licence, for a fee or otherwise, to re-license, sublicense, and/or multiple-license, without seeking any additional authorizations from any contributors.

3)   The FLOW.through.1 Community Risk Management Strategy

The FLOW.through.1 model explicitly does not encompass the supply of financial services, such as warranties, insurance, and indemnifications, to any part of the community, directly, indirectly, or by implication. However, some observers of free-libre-open activities have raised the question of whether an intellectual resource community could be considered a legal partnership, in which case it would be subject to rules about joint and several liability, such that all contributors and distributors could be considered liable for the actions of each contributor and distributor individually. Although the contributors, distributors, and other participants in such a community typically do not intend to establish a legal partnership, some argue that a legal partnership could potentially be deemed to be created, particularly in cases where a community may be managing a fund, maintaining a well-defined Internet presence, sharing management responsibilities for copyrighted works, and perhaps even referring to itself as a "partnership" in the colloquial sense. These analysts point to numerous cases related to physical property in which courts have found the existence of partnerships, contrary to the intent of the participants, even in cases where signed agreements expressly declared that no partnership was created. The administrative requirement to register partnerships for reporting and taxation purposes gives people the impression that such a declaration is required for a partnership to come into existence. But legally, a partnership exists commercially or does not exist, regardless of what the parties might have declared or believed. In the Australian case *Weiner v. Harris*, Cozens-Hardy M.R. explained:

> Two parties enter into a transaction and say "It is hereby declared there is no partnership between us". The Court pays no regard to that. The Court looks at the transaction and says "Is this, in point of law, really a partnership?" [41]

Conversely, in *Commissioners of Inland Revenue v. Williamson*, the Lord President of the Scottish Court of Session, Lord Clyde, said:

> My Lords, you do not create . . . a partnership by saying there is one. The only proof that a partnership exists is proof of the relations of agency and of community in losses and profits. . . .[42]

Therefore, participants in an intellectual resource community should consider whether a court examining the facts of their relationship under their chosen licences and contracts might declare it to be a legal partnership, notwithstanding what their licences or contracts say, in which case joint and several liability would apply.

In 1996, representatives of the CICA appeared before the Standing Senate Committee on Banking, Trade and Commerce[43] to explain that auditors were facing just this sort of liability crisis, which they blamed on the application of joint and several liability to professional organizations. The Senate Committee went further and "expressed the view that the issue of joint and several liability . . . affects all professional defendants, not just auditors,"[44] and agreed to hold hearings on the subject later the same year. Its interim

---

41   *Weiner v. Harris*, [1910] 1 K.B. 285 at 290 (C.A.).
42   *Commissioners of Inland Revenue v. Williamson* (1928), 14 T.C. 335 at 340.
43   "Corporate Governance," above note 39.
44   *Ibid.* at 6.

report "Joint and Several Liability and Professional Defendants"[45] identified Limited Liability Partnerships (LLPs) as a practical solution, because they would:

> allow firms to retain their partnership structure while protecting the personal assets of partners who have no involvement in a negligence action. The firm is liable for the acts committed by its members in the ordinary course of the firm's business, but individual members will not be liable for each other's acts. Individual partners, however, continue to maintain responsibility for their own acts and for those over which they have a direct supervisory role or knowledge.[46]

With further input from the Canadian Bar Association (CBA) and the CICA, the Committee issued the fourteenth report on "Modified Proportionate Liability"[47] in September 1998, recommending a limited liability regime for all types of professionals, to replace joint and several liability. Specifically it recommended that

- a form of modified proportionate liability should replace joint and several liability for claims for financial loss arising by reason of an error, omission, statement or misstatement;
- joint and several liability should continue to apply to claims made against a defendant who knowingly or intentionally engaged in fraudulent or dishonest conduct;
- the modified proportionate liability regime should distinguish between sophisticated and unsophisticated plaintiffs.[48]

Subsequently, Canadian provinces updated their legislation to recognize LLPs, but some jurisdictions (such as Ontario) declined to accommodate the Senate Committee's expressed concern that joint and several liability was inappropriate to professional membership organizations of all types of disciplines. Instead they restricted LLP protections only to chartered accountants, certified general accountants, and lawyers, presumably because

---

45   Canada, Parliament, Standing Committee on Banking, Trade and Commerce, "Joint and Several Liability and Professional Defendants: Options Discussion Paper" in *Journals of the Senate* (October 1997), online: www.parl.gc.ca/36/1/parlbus/ commbus/senate/com-e/bank-e/report-e/report-02-e.htm.

46   *Ibid.*

47   Canada, Parliament, Standing Committee on Banking, Trade and Commerce "Modified Proportionate Liability" in *Journals of the Senate* (September 1998), online: www. parl.gc.ca/36/1/parlbus/commbus/senate/com-e/bank-e/rep-e/rep14sep98-e.htm.

48   *Ibid.*

of the leading roles that the CICA and the CBA played in the Senate Committee's consultations.

To address potential scenarios in which a court examining the facts of an intellectual resource community may deem a legal partnership to exist, the FLOW.through.1 model includes an explicit conditional declaration of intent by each contributor and distributor to the effect that if the relationship would be considered a partnership of some form, then the participants intend that it would exist as an LLP within the jurisdiction of the governing entity of the community, and in every other jurisdiction, as an extra-territorial LLP. Granted, such an interpretation might not be supported in current provincial legislation; however, the declaration stands as a statement of intent by the community to challenge, if necessary, the unwarranted restriction of LLP protections according to field of endeavour in light of the Senate Committee's expressed view that joint and several liability presented a problem relevant to all types of professional defendants, not just auditors. Obviously, further analysis on this question is required.

While some lawyers have expressed concern that there is very little caselaw to review in relation to disputes over work covered by free-libre-open licences, this is because almost all such disputes are settled through negotiation, not litigation. In general, the conflict management environment around FLOW licensing and contracting tends to differ qualitatively from scenarios driven by exclusive rights and restrictive licensing. Most available caselaw stems from incidents at that dangerous intersection on the corner of "Exclusive-Restrictive Road" and "Free-Libre-Open Street," rather than just along Free-Libre-Open Street *per se*.

4) FLOW.through.1 Community-Level Licence Management

The intellectual rights contracts described above are intended to enable effective community-level licence management under a diversity of FLOW licensing scenarios. Since moral rights of integrity and association are waived, and the governing entity is granted unrestricted and independent authors' rights to the community resources, the intellectual resource community is at liberty, by whatever governance process it has adopted, to make the synthesized resources available in whole or in part, for any purpose and under any licence, without seeking additional authorizations from any or all of the contributors. This provides a basis for genuine community-level licence management that is not fettered by the inevitable plurality of views on any future issue.

Under the FLOW.through.1 model, both the individual contributor and the community's governing entity have their own licensing decisions to make, since both autonomously hold authors' rights.

The FLOW concept in general is not congruent with any licences that place conditions on the field-of-endeavour, such as the Creative Commons Attribution Non-Commercial License. A no-royalties licence would be within the scope of FLOW models, because it would address terms of compensation, and remain useable by any type of organization. However, the Creative Commons family of standardized licences does not include a no-royalties option at this time.

Under the FLOW.through.1 model, the governing entity of an intellectual resource community uses licences for resources under management by the community that are optimized to attract back, under unified business terms and conditions, the improved, derivative and/or combined works that anyone may create for distribution. That is to say, a governing entity using this model would select from amongst the major unified licences:

FLOW.through.1 Community Licenses

Software
- GNU General Public License (GPL) Version 3
- GNU Affero License (New adaptation of the GNU GPL, for software run on a network. This licence is not yet "widely used.")

Content[49]
- GNU Free Documentation License Version 1.2
- Creative Commons Attribution Share-Alike License Version 3.0.

Having said this, however, the governing entity of an intellectual resource community under the FLOW.through.1 model does not impose any preconceived licence choices on contributors. Each contributor, having retained full authors' rights in their own creative work, can use, modify, and distribute their work, in whole or in part, through any channel, for any purpose, under any licence at all. They are not required to attach their own licence to these contributions since the governing entity of the intellectual resource community will, under its own authority, apply the appropriate unified licence(s). That contributors, including those internal to the

---

49 Work that is both programming code and descriptive text or architecture graphics, such as descriptive comments in the source code that are not executable, as well as source-code samples that are used in textual documentation, can be distributed dual-licensed, for example, under the FDL and the GPL.

governing entity, can apply licences distinct from the community licence might appear contradictory or redundant. But there are often good reasons for using different licences for different contexts, and the FLOW.through.1 model maintains each contributor's right to do so. In the interest of licence standardization and compatibility, however, the FLOW.through.1 model suggests, but does not require, that contributors choose from amongst any of the licences that are widely used,[50] and that they are also compatible with the most widely used unified licences:[51]

FLOW.through.1 Contribution Licences (Recommended Only)

Software
- Apache License, 2.0
- Revised ("Modified"; "3-Clause") BSD License
- GNU General Public License (GPL)
- GNU Library or "Lesser" General Public License (LGPL)
- GNU Affero License
- XII (MIT) License
- Public Domain (if not licensed)

Content
- Creative Commons Attribution Share Alike License (CC-by-sa)
- Creative Commons Attribution License (CC-by)
- GNU Free Documentation License (FDL)
- Public Domain (if not licensed)

The right of each contributor to license their own creative work does not extend to the combined or derivative works involving contributions of other rightsholders in the community. Nevertheless, any subset of contributors under FLOW.through.1 are at liberty to establish separate written agreements amongst themselves to distribute their synthesized or collective works in any way they please.

---

50   Open Source Initiative, "Report of License Proliferation Committee and Draft FAQ" (31 July 2006), online: www.opensource.org/proliferation-report.

51   See GNU Operating System, "Various Licenses and Comments about Them," online: www.gnu.org/philosophy/license-list.html; David A. Wheeler, "The Free-Libre/ Open Source Software (FLOSS) License Slide" (27 September 2007), online: www. dwheeler.com/essays/floss-license-slide.html; and Wikipedia, "Life of FSF Approved Software Licences," online: http://en.wikipedia.org/wiki/List_of_FSF_approved_software_licenses.

I.   THE ITERation PROJECT: IMPLEMENTING THE FLOW. through.1 MODEL

Elements of the FLOW.through.1 model were researched and arranged through 2006 and 2007 as the basis for community development of the ITERation project (IT for Expenditure Reporting Automation). This project is an experimental "proof-of-concept" initiative led by the Canadian Government (Treasury Board of Canada Secretariat 2006)[52] to automate and simplify expenditure data assembly, mapping, and issue management from across multiple, non-confidential, authoritative sources, and to support repeatable trend analysis and reporting according to user-defined profiles. The government's 2007 "Federal Accountability Action Plan"[53] refers to Part III of the International Monetary Fund's "Manual on Fiscal Transparency,"[54] entitled "Public Availability of Information," which states that

> Making fiscal information available to the public is a defining characteristic of fiscal transparency. Principles and practices in this regard concern the provision of comprehensive information on fiscal activity and government objectives and the presentation of such information in a way that facilitates policy analysis and promotes accountability. A cornerstone for ensuring the timely and uniform availability of fiscal information is that it can be readily accessed free of charge on the internet.[55]

ITERation is therefore an experiment in applied information management according to the principles of "Open Services Oriented Architecture,"[56] which requires a process for "integrating structured and unstructured information sources so that they can be dealt with as if they were a single source."[57]

---

52   The Treasury Board of Canada Secretariat (TBS) provides advice and support to treasury board ministers in their role of ensuring value for money, and provides oversight of the financial management functions in departments and agencies. The Secretariat makes recommendations and provides advice to the Treasury Board on policies, directives, regulations, and program expenditure proposals with respect to the management of the government's resources.

53   Government of Canada, *Canada's New Government Federal Accountability Action Plan: Turning a New Leaf* (Ottawa: Government of Canada, 2006).

54   International Monetary Fund, "Manual on Fiscal Transparency," online: www.imf.org/external/np/pp/2007/eng/051507m.pdf.

55   *Ibid.* at Part III, Public Availability of Information, paras. 177–78.

56   Jeff Kaplan, "Roadmap for Open ICT Ecosystems," online: http://cyber.law.harvard.edu/epolicy.

57   Mei Selvage, Dan Wolfson, & John Handy-Bosma, "Information Management in Service-Oriented Architecture, Part 1: Discover the Role of Information Manage-

The ITERation project involves

1) *The ITERation Reference Implementation.*[58] This is a generic, structured data warehouse that includes data documentation control, business rules management, multi-source data mapping, data issue management, data cleansing, and formal revision control workflow, together with a web application that includes automated statistical analysis and visualization functions, and portfolio, issue management, and revision control systems for user-generated content and system software.

2) *The ITERation Web Service.* This is a functioning instance of the Reference Implementation at its ongoing state of development, populated with data that is formally cleared for unencumbered public use.[59]

The project is intended to help multiple organizations share a common approach to

- simplifying and accelerating data assembly, management, statistical analysis, and reporting;
- automating quarterly and annual trend reporting to precise requirements, based on reusable analytical elements;
- ensuring 100 percent auditability of all elements, functions, files, and data sources;

---

ment in SOA" (22 March 2005), online: www.ibm.com/developerworks/webservices/library/ws-soa-ims; and Mei Selvage, Dan Wolfson, & John Handy-Bosma, "Information Management in Service-Oriented Architecture, Part 2: Explore the Different Approaches to Information Management in SOA" (10 June 2005), online: www.ibm.com/developerworks/webservices/library/ws-soa-ims2.

58 The modules that comprise the Reference Implementation are architected to be substitutable with solutions from alternative suppliers. The forthcoming ITERation Version 1.0 operates on the following externally acquired software:
- PostgreSQL database, distributed by the PostgreSQL Global Development Group under the BSD License;
- R and R-project statistics and graphing environment, distributed by the R Foundation under the GNU General Public License;
- A web application environment. The alpha implementation was created using the PHP environment distributed by the PHP Group under the PHP License. This may be ported in 2008 to the Ruby Language on the Rails environment, distributed by the Rails Core Team under the MIT License.

59 Robert Howell asks: "Should some data, such as non-confidential information held by governments or public authorities, be declared public domain data or information?" See Robert G. Howell, *Database Protection and Canadian Laws (State of Law as of March 31, 2002)*, 2d ed. (Ottawa: Canadian Heritage, 2002).

- supporting user-customizable queries, data sources, adjustments, charts, etc.;
- providing analysts with a simple, secure web interface for analysis and reporting, with role-based access;
- ensuring flexibility, adaptability to change, and extensibility to other purposes; and
- assisting in conformance with policy, legislation, and standards.

The ITERation project is not the first FLOW project to be initiated by the Canadian Government; however, it is the first FLOW project led from within the Treasury Board of Canada Secretariat. It therefore has a demonstrative role as an experimental or "proof-of-concept" implementation of free-libre-open contracting and licensing by the Canadian federal public sector.

In the present author's role as a public servant, it appeared attractive that the X11 and CC-by licences provided a basis for offering unrestricted access to non-confidential intellectual resources that have been paid for by individual and business taxpayers across Canada.

From the present author's complementary perspective as the initial proponent and manager of the ITERation project, however, the GNU GPL, GNU FDL, Affero GPL, and CC-by-sa licences together afforded a well-understood incentive structure for attracting back to the project improved, derivative, and combined works.

Therefore, FLOW.through.1 licensing was arranged to accommodate both the "project manager's" and the "public servant's" priorities. This hybrid model evolved through discussions with numerous people inside and outside the public sector. In the particular case of contributions to the ITERation project authored by employees of the governance entity, the Treasury Board Secretariat, this creative work is licensed "prior to" contribution to the project under the X11 or CC-by licences, which enable unencumbered public access to these resources on terms as close to "public domain" as Canadian law provides. Once any contributions are "in" the ITERation project, they are at that point sublicensed by the project manager, on behalf of the Crown under the GNU GPL Version 3, Affero GPL Version 3, GNU FDL Version 1.2, or CC-by-sa Version 3.0 licences (or later versions). Putting these unified licences at the centre of the resource community leaves contributors the widest spectrum of options for their own work. The recent

GPL Version 3 licences also provide protections from software-patent litigation risk.[60]

At the time of writing, the ITERation project has not yet released a version 1.0 of the ITERation Reference Implementation, and the proof-of-concept web service is running only on an internal development server. However the ITERation project community from 2006 through 2008 has included public servants, paid consultants, and volunteers. Throughout this time, all FLOW.through.1 arrangements described in this paper have been implemented in the project's licensing, in the statements of work attached to consulting contracts, and in attached agreements.

---

60   Free Software Foundation, "FSF Releases the GNU General Public License, Version 3" (29 June 2007), online: www.fsf.org/news/gplv3_launched.

CHAPTER 5

Free Software and Software-defined Radio: An Overview of New FCC Rules

Matt Norwood

A. ABSTRACT

The US Federal Communication Commission (FCC) recently promulgated rules governing the use of free and open source software (FOSS) in software-defined radio devices. While the rules encourage the use of FOSS for some applications, they also express reservations about its employment in certain security-critical systems, taking the position that secrecy results in better security system design. This paper examines the immediate implications of this mixed ruling for hardware manufacturers and independent software developers, as well as its likely meaning for the long-term relationship between the FCC and developers of new technologies. The paper also makes a normative argument that regulators should re-examine their reliance on secrecy as a method for ensuring the design of secure systems.

B. INTRODUCTION

The free software movement has brought about a paradigm shift in software production. The retail software model — where initial production, incremental development, and ongoing support of software was centralized with a single vendor — has given way to decentralization of all these activities, carried out by entities motivated by market and non-market forces. This shift presents new challenges for regulators, who are forced to rethink old incentive models to account for this decentralization. Regulators must also examine the decoupling of activities once considered unitary because production, distribution, modification, end-user support, and deployment of software may each be performed separately by hardware manufacturers, software vendors, independent software developers, and users.

One domain of government regulation implicated in this shift from proprietary software to FOSS is the regulation of radio-spectrum use. As the wireless industry steps up production of radio devices whose operating parameters are controlled by computer software, regulators find themselves re-examining their assumptions about the most efficient points of account-ability in the wireless device industry, and about how the industry distrib-utes the labor of software production and support. In adjusting or rewriting rules to account for the new industrial landscape, there is a real danger of leaving certain assumptions unexamined even after they have lost their usefulness.

In the US, the FCC has recently made a positive step toward coming to terms with the new realities of the wireless industry, but it has failed to re-think some of its old assumptions that no longer hold, potentially inhibiting the rate of innovation among developers of new devices. This paper exam-ines the positive changes effected by the FCC in lifting some of the regula-tory barriers to wireless innovation, but also examines the ways in which the new regulations fall short of their stated purpose by hindering development of new technologies without any reciprocal gain in public welfare.

C. BACKGROUND

1) FCC Software-defined Radio Rules

The FCC regulates radio and wire communications in the US. Among its regulatory duties is the protection of radio broadcasts from harmful inter-ference caused by consumer products. To this end, it requires manufactur-ers of electronic devices to certify their products at FCC-approved testing labs to ensure that they comply with rules limiting the power and patterns of radio transmissions at various frequencies. This certification process has traditionally examined only the behaviour of the hardware itself, as the broadcast characteristics of most radio devices on the market were limited only by the device's antenna and other hardware components. In the late 1980s and 1990s, however, a new class of devices emerged whose radio char-acteristics were limited in part by computer software. These devices showed promise in a number of respects: they were much simpler and cheaper to manufacture than devices with complex hard-wired logic, and they could be reconfigured for different behaviours through a simple alteration of the operating software. This also meant that one device could be marketed in several regions under different regulatory regimes, and software could be used to bring the device into compliance with local regulations; this strategy presented significant efficiencies over the manufacture of different chipsets for sale in different countries.

The rise of these software-configurable radio devices presented the FCC with a regulatory challenge. Reconfiguration of software was one of the devices' main advantages, but under the existing certification rules any change to a device—including changes to its software—would require lengthy, expensive recertification with FCC labs. The FCC made efforts to accommodate the new devices under their existing certification rules, but it also put out a notice of proposed rule-making to streamline and standardize the treatment of software-configurable devices during certification.[1]

On 11 March 2005, the FCC released a set of rules outlining an alternative method for certification of devices whose radio frequency and power characteristics can be modified by software, designating such devices software defined radio (SDR) devices.[2] These rules allow manufacturers who have certified under the new process to update the software on the devices without recertifying the devices with the FCC.

The rules require any manufacturer certifying a device under the new process to take steps to prevent "unauthorized" changes to the software on the device that might alter its radio frequency and power parameters in a way that takes it out of compliance with the regulations known as FCC Part 15 regulations.[3] The specific technology implemented to accomplish this task is left to the manufacturers seeking certification, although the FCC suggests several possible mechanisms that can serve as such "security measures."[4]

In response to a petition from Cisco Systems, Inc., the FCC issued a *Memorandum Opinion and Order* on 25 April 2007, making two clarifications to the rules.[5] First, the FCC clarified the scope of the rules to require

---

1   US, Federal Communications Commission, *Notice of Proposed Rule Making and Order* (Doc. No. 03-322) (2003), online: http://hraunfoss.fcc.gov/edocs_public/attachmatch/FCC-03-322A1.pdf.

2   US, Federal Communications Commission, *Report and Order* (Doc. No. 05-57, 20 FCC Rcd 5486) (2005), online: http://hraunfoss.fcc.gov/edocs_public/attachmatch/FCC-05-57A1.pdf [*Report and Order*].

3   *Ibid.* at 5488.

4   *Ibid.* at 5509.

5   US, Federal Communications Commission, *Memorandum Opinion and Order* (Doc. No. 07-66) (2007), online: http://fjallfoss.fcc.gov/edocs_public/attachmatch/FCC-07-66A1.pdf [*Memorandum Opinion and Order*].

certification under the new process of any device that uses software to comply with the Part 15 regulations, if such software is "designed or expected to be modified by a party other than the manufacturer."[6] Second, the FCC stated a position regarding the use of FOSS on SDR devices. The FCC acknowledged the use of FOSS by device manufacturers and noted some of the advantages of FOSS for the industry. However, citing concerns regarding publishing information relating to security measures, the FCC stated that an SDR device that uses FOSS to build the "security measures" protecting the software against modification would face a "high burden" during the certification process "to demonstrate that it is sufficiently secure."[7]

2) Linux-based Wireless Devices

The FCC notes in its *Memorandum Opinion and Order* that the industry now commonly uses both the kernel named Linux and complete FOSS operating systems in wireless radio devices under its regulatory control. For example, many 802.11 wireless network routers use FOSS to provide a fully functional system, including network address translation (NAT), network firewalling, intranet web servers, and other network management features. Such functionality, which if licensed as individual proprietary components can be prohibitively expensive, is readily available with any FOSS operating system. Many manufacturers have therefore chosen to configure their devices with these FOSS systems rather than proprietary alternatives. In such a configuration, almost none of the FOSS on the device interacts directly with the FCC-regulated radio hardware. Typically, only small pieces of code, either running as a Linux kernel module and/or as a wholly independent firmware on the chip itself, actually constitute an SDR component whose modification would need to be limited by the "security measures" described in the FCC's rules. This paper focuses primarily on the impact of the rules on these small components, but the reader should not lose sight of how much software on the standard FOSS-based, FCC-regulated consumer devices remains far from the regulatory control of the FCC.

3) Industrial Adoption of FOSS

Free and open source software has been widely adopted by industries where its advantages of stability, standardization, and community support and de-

---

6   *Ibid.* at 3; *Report and Order*, above note 2 at 5504; 47 C.F.R. § 2.1.
7   *Memorandum Opinion and Order*, above note 5 at 4.

velopment outweigh the advantages gained by exclusive control and owner-ship of a proprietary software product. Although many FOSS projects are primarily developed by volunteer programmers, the support and develop-ment of FOSS is increasingly carried out by private industry, with com-panies and consultants sharing the development and support work among themselves and with the volunteer community. This decentralization of contribution to the success of FOSS projects distinguishes it from propri-etary software, which is usually developed and supported by a single entity. FOSS is also distinguished by the common availability of its source code, where proprietary software vendors tend to closely guard the secrecy of their code. This last distinction is the salient characteristic of FOSS seized on by the FCC's *Memorandum Opinion and Order* as presenting a problem for the design of secure systems: in its rules, the FCC discourages manufacturers from making their security software public if doing so would increase the likelihood of it being circumvented.

D. LEGAL CONSEQUENCES FOR DEVELOPERS AND MANUFACTURERS

After an extended period of uncertainty among software developers and wireless hardware manufacturers alike as to the FCC's stance on FOSS in wireless devices, the new rules provide substantial clarity and leeway to both hardware and software developers using FOSS. The rules eliminate the uncertainty in the industry as to FCC's stance on FOSS by explicitly addressing the subject. They unequivocally permit the use of FOSS for most applications used in wireless devices. And the only prohibition they create for FOSS is qualified in two respects: it applies only when FOSS can be shown to make a system less secure, and even then it is not an absolute bar on FOSS but only a "high burden" to prove the device's security.

The clarity and permissiveness of the rules allow wireless software and hardware developers to operate in a much more certain legal environment than has been available for several years. The boundaries of the activities permitted and barred by the rules can now be demarcated with a reason-able degree of confidence, as can the boundaries between the parties sub-ject to the rules and those unaffected by them. Specifically, FCC's lack of jurisdiction over independent software developers and the rules' explicit applicability only to device manufacturers seeking certification mean that independent software developers with no ties to radio hardware manufac-turers are not the subject of these regulations, and their activities are not affected by the SDR device certification rules. Hardware manufacturers, meanwhile, are still afforded significant leeway in the use of FOSS in their devices, with most applications being expressly cleared for implementation through FOSS. Only a completely FOSS-driven device would be implicated by the FCC's cautionary statement, and even then the FCC has presented guidance on how their resistance to FOSS can be overcome by a manufacturer seeking certification.

1)   FCC Jurisdictional Limits

It is unlikely that the FCC could promulgate rules regulating the activities of software developers unless those developers were engaged in the manufacture or distribution of devices capable of causing radio interference. The FCC is a statutory body with a grant of jurisdiction strictly defined by Congress.[8] First, it has the power to regulate "interstate and foreign communication by wire or radio."[9] This primary jurisdictional grant gives it wide latitude to make and enforce rules for broadcasters and telecommunication carriers. Second, it has ancillary jurisdiction to make rules and regulations necessary for carrying out its primary responsibilities.[10] This ancillary jurisdiction includes the power to make "reasonable regulations . . . governing the interference potential of devices which in their operation are capable of emitting radio frequency energy."[11] It is much more narrowly constrained than the FCC's primary jurisdiction over broadcasters and carriers because courts, fearful that the FCC's powers would become "unbounded" if it were allowed to make rules governing any activity or party that might have an effect on radio or wire transmissions, have precluded such a reading of the FCC's jurisdictional grant.[12] Thus, while the FCC's ancillary jurisdiction reasonably extends to regulating the marketing and sale of devices that create active radio interference, it does not extend to such activities as the construction of buildings that might interfere with radio signals.[13]

Similarly, the FCC's ancillary jurisdiction cannot reasonably extend to the development of software by parties uninvolved in the marketing or sale of radio devices. Congress did not contemplate the FCC as a gen-

---

8   *Michigan v. EPA*, 268 F.3d 1075 (D.C. Cir. 2001); *Louisiana Public Service Commission v. FCC*, 476 U.S. 355 (1986).

9   47 U.S.C. § 152(a).

10   47 U.S.C. § 154(i).

11   47 U.S.C. § 302(a).

12   *FCC v. Midwest Video Corp.*, 440 U.S. 689 (1979).

13   *Illinois Citizens Committee for Broadcasting v. FCC*, 467 F.2d 1397 (7th Cir. 1972) [*Illinois*].

eric technology-regulatory agency, and courts have repeatedly limited the FCC's reach when it attempted to make rules outside of the realm of the distribution or marketing of equipment capable of wire or radio signal transmission.[14] Attempts by the FCC to regulate the activities of software developers not engaged in the importation or marketing of radio devices and not employed by telecommunication carriers are likely to be met with similar judicial restriction.

2)   Scope of the Certification Rules

Even if the FCC did have the power to regulate independent software development, it has promulgated no rules governing such activity. Its new rules related to SDR are addressed to "manufacturers" of radio "equipment," modifying the rules for certification of such "hardware-based device[s]" prior to their "marketing or importation."[15] No other parties or activities are affected by the regulations. Thus, unless a given entity engages in the marketing or importation of hardware-based radio equipment, it is unaffected by these regulations.

3)   "Equipment" vs. Software

The FCC has promulgated the SDR rules as a modification to its existing regulations governing the certification for marketing and sale of devices that may interfere with radio transmissions.[16] These rules limit the ability to "manufacture, import, sell, offer for sale, or ship devices or home electronic equipment and systems, or use devices, which fail to comply with regulations promulgated pursuant to this section."[17]

Since software is a representation of a mathematical algorithm, it is not a "device," "home electronic equipment," or a "home electronic . . . system."[18]

---

14   *American Library Association v. FCC*, 406 F.3d 689 (D.C. Cir. 2005) (the FCC has no power to regulate television components unrelated to signal reception); *Illinois*, above note 13 (the FCC lacks jurisdiction over objects that interfere with television transmissions).

15   *Report and Order*, above note 2 at 5505.

16   *Ibid.* at 5487. Codified at 47 C.F.R. § 0.457, § 2.1, § 2.932, § 2.944, § 2.1033, § 2.1043, and §15.202.

17   47 U.S.C. § 302.

18   The only place where the FCC's rules or its enabling statute include software within the definition of any of these terms is in the context of regulating telecommunications carriers: the definition of "Telecommunications Equipment" in 47 U.S.C.

Further, there is no precedent for applying the device certification rules to software except as installed as a component of a specific hardware device. Indeed, the FCC has explicitly limited the certification requirements to "hardware-based device[s]."[19] Both of these facts make it clear that the FCC rules do not apply to software by itself, but only to hardware-based devices.

4) FCC Recognition of FOSS

The FCC's *Memorandum Opinion and Order*, clarifying its SDR certification rules, acknowledges the use of "open source software" by SDR device manufacturers and notes the advantages FOSS provides to the industry. It declines to forbid or restrict the use of FOSS on SDR devices. However, it discourages the use of FOSS in the "hardware and software security elements" of SDR devices by stating that systems "*wholly* dependent on open source elements" would have a "high burden" to demonstrate their security during the certification process.[20]

Nowhere do the rules restrict any party other than a manufacturer seeking certification for a device. Even in that case, they do not restrict the manufacturer's activities directly, but simply warn that the certification will be less likely to be granted if the manufacturer relies "*wholly*" on FOSS in building the device. The rules acknowledge the activities of the FOSS community in developing radio device software and, in keeping with the FCC's jurisdictional limitations, decline to formulate rules governing any participant in this activity except manufacturers seeking certification for their devices.

This reluctance on the part of the FCC to create regulations for technological development—beyond regulating the actual marketing of de-

---

§ 153(45) states that the term "includes software integral to such equipment." This definition explicitly excludes "customer premises equipment." Thus, it applies only to equipment used by carriers, on the premises of the carriers, to provide telecommunications services. The careful limitation of this definition to carrier equipment is consistent with the FCC's broad jurisdiction over carriers' business practices, allowing the FCC to regulate software in this specific domain where Congress is unwilling to grant jurisdiction over software developed or used by other parties not under the FCC's direct jurisdiction. In addition, the explicit inclusion of "software integral to such equipment" in this definition implicitly excludes software from other uses of the term "equipment" in the statute. If Congress had intended the general term "equipment" to include software, it would have defined it accordingly, as it did in the limited case of "Telecommunications Equipment."

19   *Report and Order*, above note 2 at 5505.
20   *Memorandum Opinion and Order*, above note 5 at 4 [emphasis added].

vices — is consistent with the FCC's position on experimental or specialized equipment. Such equipment is exempt from the certification requirements if it is not marketed to the public and is only used under controlled conditions.[21] It is allowed to be developed and distributed as long as it is used for such limited purposes. Thus, even entities that install and run software (FOSS or otherwise) on radio hardware devices for the purposes of testing, research, or development are exempt from the new SDR certification rules as long as they abide by the other applicable FCC rules.

E. POLICY ANALYSIS

The FCC's rules on SDR device certification present two positive developments for FOSS deployment in the wireless technology space. First, the FCC permits the use of FOSS in all but a very narrowly constrained subsystem on a specific type of device. Second, the FCC has provided much greater regulatory clarity than has existed on this issue since the commencement of the SDR rule-making process in 2003. This freedom to deploy FOSS and the clarity of the FCC's position allows hardware manufacturers and FOSS developers to openly collaborate on most parts of SDR device design, and it frees software developers from concerns that they might have to deal with legal issues related to the FCC.

Unfortunately, the FCC has not gone as far as it could in embracing and encouraging the use of FOSS by SDR device manufacturers. Its rules express reservations about the security of FOSS-based systems based on the notion that "making information on security measures publicly available could assist parties in determining ways to defeat them."[22] However, there is broad consensus among software security experts that public disclosure of security design actually results in more secure systems, especially when the system is subject to repeated, low-cost attacks by attackers who can share information freely among themselves.[23] Disclosure of security designs for such devices tends to benefit designers more than attackers, as the designers can learn from each other and improve their designs accordingly, offset-

---

21   47 C.F.R. § 2.803.

22   *Memorandum Opinion and Order*, above note 5 at 4.

23   Peter P. Swire, "A Model for When Disclosure Helps Security: What is Different about Computer and Network Security?" (2004) 2 J. on Telecomm. & High Tech. L. 163. Swire makes a technical, economic, and regulatory argument for different disclosure models maximizing security based on the nature of the system being designed. He finds that disclosure tends to result in higher security for systems like SDR consumer products that are exposed to multiple attackers who can share information with each other.

ting the advantages the attackers already have in information-gathering and sharing.[24] SDR devices used by consumers fit this description: the software on a cell phone or 802.11 card is exposed to virtually unlimited attack by anyone who purchases the device, and anything learned from such an attack can be communicated at low cost to fellow attackers. Design details disclosed by manufacturers, on the other hand, have tremendous benefits for other manufacturers' ability to spot security flaws, but they provide little benefit to attackers. These arguments are articulated in greater depth in a Petition for Reconsideration submitted to the FCC in June 2007 by the SDR Forum, a wireless industry consortium with a vested interest in the SDR rule-making process.[25] The SDR Forum's petition argues for the right of manufacturers to collaborate openly on the design of security systems. It notes the advantages for security design gained by open standards and public collaboration, condemning "security through obscurity" as an unworkable and self-defeating strategy for designing robust, secure systems.[26] It also points out the ambiguity of the FCC's language regulating disclosure of security design details: while the rules prohibit disclosure "if doing so would increase the risk" of circumvention, they do not make clear who determines whether this risk is increased, decreased, or unaffected by disclosure.[27]

On a positive note, the FCC does signal in its *Memorandum Opinion and Order* that it is open to persuasion on the subject of FOSS-based security systems. It states:

> manufacturers should not intentionally make the distinctive elements that implement that manufacturer's particular security measures in a software defined radio public, if doing so would increase the risk that these security measures could be defeated or otherwise circumvented to allow operation of the radio in a manner that violates the FCC's rules.[28]

This qualification suggests that the FCC is not committed to this proposition, as does the doubly qualified message that only devices "wholly" (not

---

24   Bruce Schneier, *Beyond Fear: Thinking Sensibly About Security in an Uncertain World* (New York: Copernicus Books, 2003) at 119–28. Schneier deconstructs the myth that "security through obscurity" is an effective strategy, noting the brittleness of systems designed under that approach.

25   SDR Forum, *Petition for Reconsideration* (Doc. No. SDRF-07-A-0012-V0.0.0) (2007), online: www.sdrforum.org/pages/documentLibrary/documents/SDRF-07-A-0012-V0_0_0_Response_to_MOO.pdf .

26   *Ibid.* at 3.

27   *Ibid.*, quoting *Memorandum Opinion and Order*, above note 5 at 4.

28   *Memorandum Opinion and Order*, above note 5 at 4 [emphasis added].

mostly, or partly) based on FOSS would face a "high" (not insurmountable) burden during certification. The FCC's refusal to categorically prohibit FOSS in any part of an SDR system reads as an invitation to the wireless device industry and the FOSS community to demonstrate the suitability of FOSS for the design of all software subsystems of SDR devices.

F. CONCLUSION

The SDR rules promulgated by the FCC represent a positive development for FOSS developers working in the wireless space. The rules allow FOSS developers not affiliated with device manufacturers to continue work on their software without restriction. They allow SDR manufacturers to employ FOSS for most of the functionality of their devices, and leave open the possibility that a device using a purely FOSS-based software platform could also pass FCC certification if it managed to demonstrate the soundness of its security strategy. The rules should spur FOSS developers and hardware manufacturers to collaborate on design strategies that maximize the efficiency, robustness, and freedom inherent in the FOSS development process, while ensuring that manufacturers satisfy the FCC's security mandate.

On the other hand, the SDR rules' overly conservative position on secrecy suggests that the FCC's regulatory decisions are being unduly influenced by the proprietary software production model that is currently losing market share to newer, more open and collaborative models. It also suggests that the FCC is willing to mandate specific technology choices for the industries it regulates, potentially hampering innovation as new technologies are not allowed to develop. Neither of these trends is positive, but each represents an opportunity for dialogue between the FCC, the wireless device industry, and the FOSS community, on how best to foster innovation while meeting the FCC's regulatory goals.

CHAPTER 6

The Legality of Free and Open Source Software Licences:
The Case of *Jacobsen v. Katzer*

Brian Fitzgerald & Rami Olwan

A. INTRODUCTION

In the last ten years "open source" has become a paradigm for thinking about innovation. While its origin can be found in the everyday activity of sharing knowledge in order to learn how to accomplish things, the application of these ideas in the area of technology and innovation have in recent times been most clearly associated with Richard Stallman and the Free Software Foundation. Stallman, after a frustrating experience trying to fix a printer in his lab, launched what is known as the free and open source software movement. The idea is that if we share and distribute the human readable software code (source code) and not just the machine readable code (binary code), then we will be able to understand how the software works more quickly and thereby take the necessary action. To achieve this goal Stallman employed the long-established legal notion of copyright (and its more recent application to computer software code) along with a copyright licence or permission that promoted sharing and openness of source code, but on the condition that improvements be shared on further distribution. As the default rule in copyright law is that you need permission to use material in a way that comes within the exclusive rights of the copyright owner (e.g., reproduction and communication to the public), the permission to use (i.e., the licence) was combined with conditions on use that required a commitment to further develop openness. "If you use my source code and improve upon it and then distribute it, you should share your source code with the person you are distributing the software to; in essence the community." This licence, known as the GNU General Public Licence (GPL), is said to be a "copyleft" licence because it licenses copyright not to restrict use, but to promote and further expand openness and reuse. To some, this amounts to turning copyright on its head in the name of community action, and thus the name copyleft.[1]

Many other licences emerged along with the GNU GPL. The Berkeley Software Distribution (BSD) licence allows the source code distributed under it to be reused in any way so long as there is a notice attributing copyright ownership, the BSD disclaimer is included, and there is no attempt to suggest endorsement of the derivative work by the organization or individual who developed the original code without their written permission.[2] This is a more permissive and less restrictive licence than the GNU GPL.

From the examples found in software development, organizations like Creative Commons developed licences to promote the notion of free culture or open content. They once again used the legal institution of copyright combined with copyright licences to condition reuse that would promote openness and access. Creative Commons licences allow content to be licensed to the world on the provision that attribution (BY) is given, and with the additional yet optional conditions of non-commercial use (NC), share alike (SA), and no derivatives (ND).[3]

Today there are numerous software and content products that are licensed through free and open copyright licences — much of it underpinning and implemented in the open and distributed world of the Internet.

---

1   On the notion of free and open source software (FOSS), see R. Dixon, *Open Source Software Law* (Boston: Artech House, 2004); R. Van Wendel, ed., *Protecting the Virtual Commons* (The Hague: T.M.C. Asser Pres, 2003); R.M. Stallman & J. Gay, *Free Software, Free Society: Selected Essays of Richard M. Stallman* (Boston: Free Software Foundation, 2002), online: www.gnu.org/philosophy/fsfs/rms-essays.pdf; L. Rosen, *Software Freedom and Intellectual Property Law* (Upper Saddle River, NJ: Prentice Hall PTR, 2004), online: www.rosenlaw.com/oslbook.htm; Brian Fitzgerald & Graham Bassett, eds., *Legal Issues Relating to Free and Open Source Software* (Brisbane, Qld.: Queensland University of Technology, School of Law, 2003), online: www. law.qut.edu.au/files/open_source_book.pdf; Brian Fitzgerald & Nic Suzor, "Legal Issues for the Use of Free and Open Source Software in Government" (2005) 29(2) Melbourne U.L. Rev. 412, online: www.law.qut.edu.au/staff/lsstaff/fitzgerald2.jsp.

2   Nelson, "Open Source Initiative OSI – The BSD License – Licensing" *Open Source* (31 October 2006), online: www.opensource.org/licenses/bsd-license.php.

3   "Creative Commons (CC) is a non-profit organization devoted to expanding the range of creative works available for others to build upon legally and to share." See online: http://wiki.creativecommons.org/FAQ.

The word "free" in this context means not "free as in beer," but "free as in speech" or "freedom to access and reuse."[4]

In August 2008 one of, if not the most, influential IP courts in the US, known as the Court of Appeals for Federal Circuit, upheld the validity of a free and open source software licence known as the Artistic License.[5] The case is significant because up until this point there has been little judicial discussion[6] of the legal operation of this new type of copyright licensing that is sweeping across the world fuelled by the ubiquity of the Internet. The decision in *Robert Jacobsen v. Matthew Katzer and Kamind Associates, Inc.*[7] issued on 13 August 2008 has changed all of that and will be necessary reading for anyone in the law, technology, and innovation sectors.

B. BACKGROUND TO DISPUTE

In March 2006, Jacobsen, a physics professor at the University of California, Berkeley, filed a lawsuit against Katzer and his company, Kamind Associates Inc.[8] (trading as "Kam" Industries), claiming that Kam was distributing a commercial software program that incorporated software code,[9] which Jacobsen had developed and licensed through a free and open source software licence.[10] Jacobsen accused Kam, which "developed commercial

---

4   See "The Free Software Definition," online: www.gnu.org/philosophy/free-sw.html; Sam Williams, *Free as in Freedom, Richard Stallman's Crusade for Free Software* (Sebastopol, CA: O'Reilly Media, 2002), online: http://oreilly.com/openbook/freedom/.

5   Version 1.0 and Version 2.0 of the Artistic License are certified as "open source" by the Open Source Initiative. See online: www.opensource.org/licenses/alphabetical. According to the Free Software Foundation, Version 1.0 of the Artistic License is not regarded as a free software licence as it "is too vague." See online: www.fsf.org/licensing/licenses/index_html#ArtisticLicense. JMRI, below note 10, appears to be licensed under the Artistic License Version 1.0.

6   See the German decision in *Harald Welte vs. Sitecom Deutschland GmbH*, online: www.groklaw.net/article.php?story=20040725150736471.

7   *Jacobsen v. Katzer*, 535 F.3d 1373 (Fed. Cir. 2008) [*Jacobsen*].

8   Katzer was CEO and Chairman of the Board of Directors of Kamind Associates Inc. See *Jacobsen v. Katzer*, 2007-1 Trade Cas. (CCH) P 75,589 (N.D. Cal. Oct. 20, 2006) at 1 [*Jacobsen* No. 1].

9   John Markoff, "Ruling is a Victory for Supporters of Free Software" *New York Times* (13 August 2008) C7, online: www.nytimes.com/2008/08/14/technology/14commons.html.

10 *Jacobsen*, above note 7 at 1376.

    Jacobsen manages an open source software group called Java Model Railroad Interface (JMRI) that had developed an application called DecoderPro, which

software products for the model train industry and hobbyists . . . [of] copying certain materials from Jacobsen's website and incorporating them into one of Kam's software packages without following the terms of the Artistic License."[11] To this end, he brought an action for copyright infringement and sought a preliminary injunction. At first instance the District Court, in denying the preliminary injunction, explained:

---

allowed model railroad enthusiasts to use their computers to program the decoder chips that control model trains. DecoderPro files were available for download and use by the public free of charge from an open source incubator website called SourceForge; Jacobsen maintained the JMRI site on SourceForge. The downloadable files contained copyright notices and refer the user to a COPYING file, which clearly sets forth the terms of the Artistic License. Katzer/Kamind offered a competing software product, Decoder Commander, which was also used to program decoder chips. During development of Decoder Commander, one of Katzer/Kams predecessors or employees is alleged to have downloaded the decoder definition files from DecoderPro and used portions of these files as part of the Decoder Commander software. The Decoder Commander software files that used DecoderPro definition files did not comply with the terms of the Artistic License. Specifically, the Decoder Commander software did not include (1) the authors' names, (2) JMRI copyright notices, (3) references to the COPYING file, (4) an identification of SourceForge or JMRI as the original source of the definition files, and (5) a description of how the files or computer code had been changed from the original source code. The Decoder Commander software also changed various computer file names of DecoderPro files without providing a reference to the original JMRI files or information on where to get the Standard Version.

11   *Ibid.* at 1375.

The Artistic License grants users the right to copy, modify, and distribute the software: provided that [the user] insert a prominent notice in each changed file stating how and when [the user] changed that file, and provided that [the user] do at least ONE of the following:

a)   place [the user's] modifications in the Public Domain or otherwise make them Freely Available, such as by posting said modifications to Usenet or an equivalent medium, or placing the modifications on a major archive site such as ftp.uu.net, or by allowing the Copyright Holder to include [the user's] modifications in the Standard Version of the Package.

b)   use the modified Package only within [the user's] corporation or organization.

c)   rename any non-standard executables so the names do not conflict with the standard executables, which must also be provided, and provide a separate manual page for each nonstandard executable that clearly documents how it differs from the Standard Version, or

d)   make other distribution arrangements with the Copyright Holder.

Ibid. at 1380.

The plaintiff claimed that by modifying the software the defendant had exceeded the scope of the license and therefore infringed the copyright. Here, however, the JMRI Project license provides that a user may copy the files verbatim or may otherwise modify the material in any way, including as part of a larger, possibly commercial software distribution. The license explicitly gives the users of the material, any member of the public, the right to use and distribute the [material] in a more-or-less customary fashion, plus the right to make reasonable accommodations. The scope of the nonexclusive license is, therefore, intentionally broad. The condition that the user insert a prominent notice of attribution does not limit the scope of the license. Rather, Defendants' alleged violation of the conditions of the license may have constituted a breach of the nonexclusive license, but does not create liability for copyright infringement where it would not otherwise exist.[12]

The District Court held that while Jacobsen might have an action for breach of contract (the non-exclusive licence), there was no action for copyright infringement based on a breach of the terms of the Artistic License. Further, they explained that while establishing a likelihood of success on the merits of a copyright infringement claim would create a presumption of irreparable harm and thereby support a preliminary injunction, there was no similar presumption that was created by the law for a breach of contract.

C. THE APPEALS COURT

Jacobsen appealed this decision, arguing that he did have an action for copyright infringement.

1) Nature of the Licensing Model

The Appeals Court commenced its analysis by examining the nature and scope of this new form of "public" licensing:

Public licenses, often referred to as open source licenses, are used by artists, authors, educators, software developers, and scientists who wish to create collaborative projects and to dedicate certain works to the public. Several types of public licenses have been designed to provide creators of copyrighted materials a means to protect and control their copyrights.

---

12 *Jacobsen v. Katzer*, 2007 U.S. Dist. LEXIS 63568 (N.D. Cal. Aug. 17, 2007) at 19 [*Jacobsen* No. 2].

Creative Commons, one of the *amici curiae*, provides free copyright licenses to allow parties to dedicate their works to the public or to license certain uses of their works while keeping some rights reserved.[13]

The Appeals Court also acknowledged the important role these licences are playing in a wide range of endeavours:

Open source licensing has become a widely used method of creative collaboration that serves to advance the arts and sciences in a manner and at a pace that few could have imagined just a few decades ago. For example, the Massachusetts Institute of Technology (MIT) uses a Creative Commons public license for an OpenCourseWare project that licenses all 1800 MIT courses. Other public licenses support the GNU/Linux operating system, the Perl programming language, the Apache web server programs, the Firefox web browser, and a collaborative web-based encyclopedia called Wikipedia. Creative Commons notes that, by some estimates, there are close to 100,000,000 works licensed under various Creative Commons licenses. The Wikimedia Foundation, another of the *amici curiae*, estimates that the Wikipedia website has more than 75,000 active contributors working on some 9,000,000 articles in more than 250 languages.[14]

Further the Appeals Court explained the rationale and operation of open source software projects:

Open Source software projects invite computer programmers from around the world to view software code and make changes and improvements to it. Through such collaboration, software programs can often be written and debugged faster and at lower cost than if the copyright holder were required to do all of the work independently. In exchange and in consideration for this collaborative work, the copyright holder permits users to copy, modify and distribute the software code subject to conditions that serve to protect downstream users and to keep the code accessible. By requiring that users copy and restate the license and attribution information, a copyright holder can ensure that recipients of the redistributed computer code know the identity of the owner as well as the scope of the license granted by the original owner. The Artistic License in this case also requires that changes to the computer code be tracked so that downstream users know what part of the computer code is the ori-

---

13   *Jacobsen*, above note 7 at 1378.
14   *Ibid.*

ginal code created by the copyright holder and what part has been newly
added or altered by another collaborator.[15]

Importantly the Appeals Court also highlighted the benefits of the open
source methodology:

> Traditionally, copyright owners sold their copyrighted material in ex-
> change for money. The lack of money changing hands in open source
> licensing should not be presumed to mean that there is no economic
> consideration, however. There are substantial benefits, including eco-
> nomic benefits, to the creation and distribution of copyrighted works
> under public licenses that range far beyond traditional license royal-
> ties. For example, program creators may generate market share for their
> programs by providing certain components free of charge. Similarly, a
> programmer or company may increase its national or international repu-
> tation by incubating open source projects. Improvement to a product
> can come rapidly and free of charge from an expert not even known to
> the copyright holder. The Eleventh Circuit has recognized the economic
> motives inherent in public licenses, even where profit is not immediate.
> *See Planetary Motion, Inc. v. Techsplosion, Inc.*, 261 F.3d 1188, 1200 (11th
> Cir. 2001) (Program creator derived value from the distribution [under a
> public license] because he was able to improve his Software based on sug-
> gestions sent by end-users . . . . It is logical that as the Software improved,
> more end-users used his Software, thereby increasing [the programmers]
> recognition in his profession and the likelihood that the Software would
> be improved even further).[16]

2) The Arguments

Jacobsen's claim to be the copyright owner was not challenged, nor was the
fact that software code was copied. Rather, Kam argued that there was no
infringement because they had a licence. The Appeals Court explained that

> [t]he heart of the argument on appeal concerns whether the terms of the
> Artistic License are conditions of, or merely covenants to, the copyright
> license. A series of US cases has held that where "a copyright owner who
> grants a nonexclusive license to use his copyrighted material waives his
> right to sue the licensee for copyright infringement and can sue only for

---

15   *Ibid.* at 1378–79.
16   *Ibid.* at 1379.

breach of contract[17] . . . [i]f, however, a license is limited in scope and the licensee acts outside the scope, the licensor can bring an action for copyright infringement."[18] Therefore if the terms of the Artistic License were "both covenants and conditions, they . . . [could] . . . serve to limit the scope of the license and . . . [be] . . . governed by copyright law [whereas] . . . [i]f they are merely covenants, by contrast, they are governed by contract law."[19] The District Court had not expressly resolved this issue, simply acting as though the limitations in the Artistic License were "contractual covenants rather than conditions of the copyright license."[20]

The Appeals Court summarized argument on this issue as follows:

> Jacobsen argues that the terms of the Artistic License define the scope of the license and that any use outside of these restrictions is copyright infringement. Katzer/Kamind argues that these terms do not limit the scope of the license and are merely covenants providing contractual terms for the use of the materials, and that his violation of them is neither compensable in damages nor subject to injunctive relief. Katzer/Kamind's argument is premised upon the assumption that Jacobsen's copyright gave him no economic rights because he made his computer code available to the public at no charge. From this assumption, Katzer/Kamind argues that copyright law does not recognize a cause of action for non-economic rights, relying on *Gilliam v. ABC*, 538 F.2d 14, 20-21 (2d Cir. 1976) (American copyright law, as presently written, does not recognize moral rights or provide a cause of action for their violation, since the law seeks to vindicate the economic, rather than the personal rights of authors.)[21]

3) The Artistic License

To resolve the issue the Appeals Court said it was necessary to consider the actual terms of the Artistic License. It noted that the "Artistic License states on its face that the document creates conditions" whereby it says: "The intent of this document is to state the *conditions* under which a Pack-

---

17   *Sun Microsystems, Inc. v. Microsoft Corp.*, 188 F.3d 1115 at 1121 (9th Cir. 1999) [*Sun Microsystems*]; *Graham v. James*, 144 F.3d 229 at 236 (2d Cir. 1998) [*Graham*].

18   See *S.O.S., Inc. v. Payday, Inc.* 886 F.2d 1081 at 1087 (9th Cir.1989).

19   See *Graham*, above note 14 at 236–37; *Sun Microsystems*, above note 14 at 1121.

20   *Jacobsen*, above note 7 at 1380.

21   *Ibid.* at 1380–81.

age may be copied." The Court went on to say that "[t]he Artistic License also uses the traditional language of conditions by noting that the rights to copy, modify, and distribute are granted 'provided that' the conditions are met. Under California contract law, 'provided that' typically denotes a condition."[22]

The Appeals Court further explained that "[t]he conditions set forth in the Artistic License are vital to enable the copyright holder to retain the ability to benefit from the work of downstream users."[23] It added that by requiring downstream developers who modify and distribute the code to provide notice of the original source files the copyright owner puts in place a mechanism for letting downstream users know about the collaborative project based at SourceForge and allows them to join in.

In disposing of the case the Appeals Court reasoned:

> The District Court interpreted the Artistic License to permit a user to "modify the material in any way" and did not find that any of the "provided that" limitations in the Artistic License served to limit this grant. The District Court's interpretation of the conditions of the Artistic License does not credit the explicit restrictions in the license that govern a downloader's right to modify and distribute the copyrighted work. The copyright holder here expressly stated the terms upon which the right to modify and distribute the material depended and invited direct contact if a downloader wished to negotiate other terms. These restrictions were both clear and necessary to accomplish the objectives of the open source licensing collaboration, including economic benefit. Moreover, the District Court did not address the other restrictions of the license, such as the requirement that all modification from the original be clearly shown with a new name and a separate page for any such modification that shows how it differs from the original. Copyright holders who engage in open source licensing have the right to control the modification and

---

22   *Ibid.* at 1381.

> See, e.g., *Diepenbrock v. Luiz*, 159 Cal. 716 (1911) (interpreting a real property lease reciting that when the property was sold, this lease shall cease and be at an end, *provided that* the party of the first part shall then pay [certain compensation] to the party of the second part; considering the appellant's interesting and ingenious argument for interpreting this language as creating a mere covenant rather than a condition; and holding that this argument cannot change the fact that, attributing the usual and ordinary signification to the language of the parties, a *condition* is found in the provision in question) [emphasis added].

23   *Ibid.*

distribution of copyrighted material. As the Second Circuit explained in
Gilliam v. ABC, 538 F.2d 14, 21 (2d Cir. 1976), the unauthorized editing of
the underlying work, if proven, would constitute an infringement of the
copyright in that work similar to any other use of a work that exceeded
the license granted by the proprietor of the copyright. Copyright licenses
are designed to support the right to exclude; money damages alone do
not support or enforce that right. The choice to exact consideration in
the form of compliance with the open source requirements of disclosure
and explanation of changes, rather than as a dollar denominated fee is
entitled to no less legal recognition . . . .

The Appeals Court went on to explain:

In this case, a user who downloads the JMRI copyrighted materials is authorized to make modifications and to distribute the materials provided
that the user follows the restrictive terms of the Artistic License. A copyright holder can grant the right to make certain modifications, yet retain
his right to prevent other modifications. Indeed, such a goal is exactly the
purpose of adding conditions to a license grant. The Artistic License, like
many other common copyright licenses, requires that any copies that are
distributed contain the copyright notices and the COPYING file . . . .

Finally, it noted:

It is outside the scope of the Artistic License to modify and distribute
the copyrighted materials without copyright notices and a tracking of
modifications from the original computer files. If a downloader does not
assent to these conditions stated in the COPYING file, he is instructed
to make other arrangements with the copyright holder. Katzer/Kamind
did not make any such other arrangements. The clear language of the
Artistic License creates conditions to protect the economic rights at issue
in the granting of a public license. These conditions govern the rights to
modify and distribute the computer programs and files included in the
downloadable software package. The attribution and modification transparency requirements directly serve to drive traffic to the open source
incubation page and to inform downstream users of the project, which
is a significant economic goal of the copyright holder that the law will
enforce. Through this controlled spread of information, the copyright
holder gains creative collaborators to the open source project; by requiring that changes made by downstream users be visible to the copyright
holder and others, the copyright holder learns about the uses for his soft-

ware and gains others knowledge that can be used to advance future software releases.[24]

In summary, the Appeals Court held that the form and the purpose of the terms of the Artistic License established that they were conditions and not merely contractual covenants. The consequence of this was that if those licence conditions were not satisfied, there would be a likelihood of copyright infringement and a preliminary injunction would lie.

However, in this case, the evidence presented at the trial level was not sufficient for the Appeals Court to finally determine the issue. While it moved to overturn the decision of the District Court, it sent the matter back to the District Court to determine on a factual basis whether Jacobsen could produce evidence to support the grant of a preliminary injunction.

4) Commentary

This is a landmark decision because it confirms that free and open source software copyright licences and, by analogy, open content licences that are similar in style to the Artistic License are

1)   copyright licences,
2)   which impose licence conditions which if not satisfied can found an action in and the grant of remedies for copyright infringement, and
3)   legally enforceable.[25]

This, in turn, provides individuals, businesses, universities, and governments that use these types of licences to distribute and acquire code and content with a greater degree of confidence in their legality.

However, the decision does not clearly settle the debate as to whether these licences are also contracts, although there is much in the judgment

---

24   *Ibid.*

25   See also *Curry v. Audax*, Rechtbank Amsterdam, Docket No. 334492 / KG 06-176 SR, 3/9/06, online: http://mirrors.creativecommons.org/judgements/Curry-Audax-English.pdf; Mia Garlick, "Creative Commons Licenses Enforced in Dutch Courts" *Creative Commons* (16 March 2006), online: http://creativecommons.org/weblog/entry/5823; Veni Markovski, "Creative Commons License Recognized in Bulgarian Court" *The Blog* (28 May 2008), online: http://blog.veni.com/?p=494; Thomas Margnoi, "English Translation of Spanish Provincial Court Decision" (29 November 2005), online: http://mirrors.creativecommons.org/wp-content/uploads/2007/02/luis-cc-spanish-decision-final.pdf.

to suggest this is the case.[26] It has been argued in the past that the GPL is not capable of being a contract in common law countries as there is no consideration.[27]

Some have argued that the decision should be treated with caution because the holding that a copyright licence with conditions is lawful could be used in negative way to restrict liberty and freedom.[28] One is driven to ask whether this is a dispute with the legal effect of this legal tool or more the legal or legislative environment in which it sits. Others might argue that a copyright licence should be limited as to the conditions that can attach to it. Furthermore, others have suggested that while the decision will have impact in common law jurisdictions it may not be received in the same way in civil law jurisdictions where it is argued the licence will be treated as though were it a contract.[29]

On the other hand the decision is significant in that it acknowledges the economic and social value of the "open source" paradigm of innovation and cultural exchange, commenting that "[o]pen source licensing has become a widely used method of creative collaboration that serves to advance the arts and sciences in a manner and at a pace that few could have imagined just a few decades ago"[30] and that "[t]here are substantial benefits, including economic benefits, to the creation and distribution of copyrighted works under public licences that range far beyond traditional licence royalties."[31]

---

26   Consider the following statements: "In exchange and in consideration for this collaborative work, the copyright holder permits users to copy, modify and distribute the software code subject to conditions that serve to protect downstream users and to keep the code accessible": *Jacobsen*, above note 7 at 1379. "The lack of money changing hands in open source licensing should not be presumed to mean that there is no economic consideration, however": *Jacobsen, ibid.* "The choice to exact consideration in the form of compliance with the open source requirements of disclosure and explanation of changes, rather than as a dollar denominated fee is entitled to no less legal recognition. Indeed, because a calculation of damages is inherently speculative, these types of license restrictions might well be rendered meaningless absent the ability to enforce through injunctive relief": *Jacobsen, ibid.* at 1382.

27   Fitzgerald & Suzor, above note 1 at 436–38.

28   Lawrence Lessig, "Huge and Important News — Free Licenses Upheld" *Lessig 2.0* (13 August 2008), online: www.lessig.org/blog/2008/08/huge_and_important_news_free_l.html.

29   *Ibid.*

30   *Jacobsen*, above note 7 at 1378.

31   *Ibid.* at 1379.

D. CONCLUSION

For people who are dealing with open content licences on a daily basis, the decision in *Jacobsen* provides a judicial confirmation and assurance of the legality of such public licences, which can be used to further educate the broader community and act as a catalyst for changing entrenched attitudes towards copyright management practices. In terms of legal practitioners, the judgment provides guidance on the way in which public licences can be drafted and how they work in practice. Ultimately, the decision gives a legal imprimatur to the notion of open innovation and how law might play a role in such a process.

The decision is a good antidote to the normal Fear Uncertainty and Doubt (FUD) that is thrown at open licensing models and their adopters to obfuscate their usefulness. Here we have one of the most well recognized IP courts in the world providing a very positive approach to the legal operation and effectiveness of public licences. While each jurisdiction will no doubt interpret this decision according to its own local legal environment, there is little doubt that it will be very useful in helping more people understand the benefit of open code and open content.

CHAPTER 7

Facilitating Meaningful Public Access to Primary Legal Information: Designing an Integrated Legal Environment

*Marcus Bornfreund & Phil Surette**

A. INTRODUCTION

In this chapter we, the authors, describe our experience building a tool for browsing statutes and other primary legal information in a rich, integrated electronic environment. This work builds upon an earlier project: a system for automatically extracting the structure inherent in the unstructured corpus of Canadian federal legislation, which is published in HTML format.

B. ENABLING FASTER, FREER ACCESS TO LEGAL INFORMATION

1) Introduction

In this chapter we briefly describe existing obstacles to the accessibility and usability of primary legal information currently available online. The main focus of the chapter is a description both of our progress thus far, and future plans to help address these problems, with a facilitative tool called the LawShare Browser.

2) What Is the Problem with How Legal Information Is Stored?

The structure of online legal information today reflects the limitations of the legal world's paper-based legacy. The foundational problem with the way legal information is currently stored is that the industry has simply carried forward the structures of a paper-based world to the digital environment. The following problems have been inherited:

---

* You can download the LawShare (ILE) Browser at http://lawshare.ca/resources.htm.

1) links between pieces of information are cumbersome and difficult to update;
2) information that could be organized in many different ways is stored in a single linear or hierarchical fashion; and
3) sharing of secondary information is time-consuming and slow.

Of course, paper is no longer the principal medium for storing legal information. We have large, private, searchable databases of caselaw, legislation, and secondary materials. However, these databases are little more than repositories of scanned print material combined with a search engine. This is an important first step but leaves much to be desired, as meaningful interaction is largely absent. Moreover, the existing structure in government-published legislation and caselaw is barely exploited; for example, links within a statute—and to revising acts—are rarely available, making it unnecessarily slow to navigate links between pieces of information.

a) Structured and unstructured legal repositories

An unstructured legal repository is a searchable database of largely non-formatted primary legal material. This definition is broad enough to capture normal legal web applications such as laws.justice.ca, CanLII, and commercial legal databases. At their most basic level, these applications marry a collection of primary legal materials with a search engine to allow searches for particular terms within statutes or caselaw. Statutes (or sometimes top-level sections) and cases are treated as basic or unstructured documents within the repository. Although they may also allow searches within statute or section titles, and may provide navigation to particular sections, very little of the structure of the underlying content is directly represented in the database. A defining characteristic of an unstructured legal repository is that it is stored in a presentation format (such as HTML or PDF) that presupposes that legal data will always be presented in the same way.

A structured legal repository is a legal repository of structured legal content. Structured legal content is represented using a data format such as XML, which exposes the relationships between parts, topics, sections, subsections, paragraphs, and metadata such as headings and marginal notes, but does not include presentation markup. The structured data supports the following key features:

- more precise linking (pinpoints);
- more precise searches; and
- different ways of organizing and representing the same data.

The capability to precisely link to pinpoints within a piece of legislation is a key enabler for effective annotation, topic construction, and concordance between sections and paragraphs of a statute across amendments. A structured legal repository will support a better, more accessible legal system.

b)   Lack of sharing or reuse of legal information

Because there is no free, public, high-quality legal repository (structured or not) that is linked to a legal collaboration system, the research results and insights of lawyers and students are not shared or reused outside the confines of a law firm. Instead, the wheel is constantly reinvented — resulting in more time spent researching, with poorer results than if each successive researcher could build upon the previous researcher's work.

Absent a shared repository of legal metadata, there will never be an authoritative, up-to-date source of information on a particular legal topic because legal information changes too rapidly for print-based secondary sources to be current. Every decision has the potential to change the law in unpredictable ways. Secondary legal materials provide the best resource here but always lag significantly behind the law and, due to the unfavourable ratio of the number of legal authors in a jurisdiction to the volume of law, generally address only the most common legal problems.

3)   Why Should We Fix It?

The current system for interacting with primary legal information is inefficient. If you are lucky, you may already know of some secondary sources that can point you in the right direction. Or you can perform unstructured searches of existing caselaw, hoping to find references to the section. This is error-prone: you will need to search for terms that are used in the section, the exact text of the section (hoping the judges have quoted it), or the appropriate section number somewhere near the name of the act (keeping in mind that sections are regularly renumbered). The odds are good that you will miss a lot or be swamped by too many results.

The following subsections describe in detail reasons why we should not be satisfied with current, unstructured legal repositories. Some of the reasons are related to building in support for the kind of legal collaboration system that is needed to enable sharing and building legal knowledge, and some relate to more direct benefits.

a) Islands of information and inefficient linking

To understand the meaning of a section of a statute, it is necessary to know what other legislation it relates to, what pronouncements the judiciary has made on the section, and what secondary materials may apply. Legal information is highly interrelated. But legal information is not stored in a way that facilitates finding this related information; today, the user is generally given nothing better than *ad hoc* search strategies to get to this information. Reliable and pervasive linking is required to convert legal information from a series of islands into a highly interconnected cloud of information.

In some ways, the legal world already has an advanced linking mechanism in the form of citations. However, citations are complex and (except for the neutral citation format) publisher-specific. Much of the time, online versions of legislation and cases are not marked up to allow pinpoint referencing to work effectively. But the biggest problem in this area is that citations are generally not live; that is, they are not linked to an online version of the case or statute. Over time this has been improving, but richer linking structures are required. We need full-fledged meta-information, arranged by topic through a collaboration system, with bi-directional links between a topic and related primary and secondary legal material.

b) The granularity problem

The "granularity problem" is a term used within the artificial intelligence discipline to describe the question of knowing at what level of detail to represent knowledge. Legal publishers have not explicitly addressed this problem. Primary legal materials are packaged as statutes, sections, and judgments. The amount of information in each of these units is too large, or too *coarse*, to allow optimal access to the information.

For instance, while judgments provide the appropriate level of granularity for resolving a dispute, as legal instruments they are far too rough. Lengthy judicial decisions are routinely reduced by practitioners to the legal principles they represent. Once the decision is rendered it is these simple principles that inform the law. The rest of the decision is largely irrelevant outside the scope of the decision itself. Because decisions are stored in unstructured legal repositories without any metadata to filter them, the irrelevant information in caselaw creates a substantial and often overwhelming amount of noise in the search result.

c) Hierarchical representation of data

Legislation is designed in a top-down, hierarchical fashion. This reflects the structure of paper documents and means that statutes can only be efficiently organized along one dimension. Current legal repositories exhibit the same limitations as the statutes themselves. These limitations can really only be overcome by superimposing an overlay of topic-centred meta-information on top of the legislation. This is what secondary legal materials have traditionally tried to do, though in a static way and in documents that are themselves often largely linear. What is needed today is something more powerful: a collaborative annotation system providing new ways of organizing and viewing legal data.

d)   Unacceptable response time

Response times of over 300 milliseconds are enough to interrupt a user's train of thought. Because existing legal repositories lack sophisticated linking facilities, finding legal information suffers from time lags caused by inaccurate searching, analysis of search results, and refining of criteria. Minutes, hours, or even days can elapse when trying to determine the legislation or caselaw that informs a particular law. The process is inordinately slow compared to other information-rich domains. For instance, software developers have access to integrated development environments that allow them to navigate through programming information instantaneously, even though the amount of information they have to navigate is similar in size and scope to what legal practitioners navigate.[1]

Because of these inefficiencies, legal research is slow. This results in poor access to law for legal professionals and laypeople alike, less well-informed legal decisions, and a legal process that is inefficient—with commensurate costs to society as a whole.

4)   Who Cares?

There will be no improvement to legal information without a demand for it. Legal practitioners are both the primary beneficiaries and the serfs of the current system. If the system was more efficient, it might result in higher-quality legal decision-making and less drudgery for legal professionals. But it might also mean less legal work. "Cheaper legal services" is not a rallying cry that many lawyers will instinctively support. Similarly, the legal pub-

---

1   For comparison, consider that the complete set of federal statutes and regulations, in XML format after conversion on laws.justice.gc.ca at the end of 2005, was 289 megabytes of data. The core API documentation for the popular programming language, Java, was about the same size—185 megabytes for JDK1.5.

lishers and database managers cannot be expected to independently facilitate significant liberalization of access to their "proprietary" information.

But there are some groups who should care, for example:

- Government: governments are presumed to take their duty to communicate their laws to citizens seriously.
- Citizens: citizens are governed by laws, many of which are complex and contextual, making it virtually impossible to understand, interpret, and apply them without both legal training and specialization. The public would benefit from more accessible primary legal information both directly, by being able to understand it themselves, and indirectly by improving the quality and efficiency of legal advice.
- Students: law students are struggling daily with the problems that stem from poorly structured legal information, and they should be more motivated than most to find a better way.
- Sole practitioners: a freely-accessible repository of legal information would help to level the playing field between sole practitioners and firms with access to (expensive) proprietary repositories and databases of in-house legal materials.
- Judiciary: more than anyone, the judiciary has an interest in ensuring that judicial decisions can be made quickly and accurately, with reference to current precedent.

5) The Solution: An Integrated Legal Environment

The solution to the limitations of the current legal repositories is to create a public, living repository of legal information that is easy to navigate and contribute to. This can be achieved through the development of an Integrated Legal Environment (ILE). The idea of an ILE is to try to build a tool that will provide legal practitioners with the level of tool support that is available for software development through Integrated Development Environments (IDEs) today. This means that you should be able to move between statutes, sections of statutes, relevant cases, and annotations almost instantaneously.

The following are key technical components of an ILE:

- a highly available, public, *structured legal repository*;
- a powerful *legislation browser* for navigating the repository; and
- a shared *legal annotation system* to support the creation of the legal metadata — topics, links, and notes that superimpose order on the mass of legal information.

C. DEVELOPMENT OF AN INTEGRATED LEGAL ENVIRONMENT

This section describes the current status and a longer-range plan for developing an ILE. The following issues are addressed:

- who will contribute to the ILE;
- the copyright regime under which the ILE will operate; and
- progress, plans, and a technical description of the ILE.

1) Who Will Contribute to an Integrated Legal Environment

An Integrated Legal Environment will be of limited value without a community of *contributors* or *annotators* willing to enhance the raw data in the structured legal repository. It is expected that people will contribute for the same types of reasons that motivate Wikipedia contributors, open source software developers, and even bloggers. Some possible reasons are

- to create a permanent record of one's research that is externally maintained and updated;
- to build an online reputation;
- to use a public forum to encourage (legal) reform;
- to share one's knowledge; and
- a philanthropic impulse to improve access to law.[2]

It is expected that the early adopters of the ILE will be law students, who can use an ILE as a way of making and sharing notes with one another.

2) Copyright Issues in an Integrated Legal Environment

An ILE will contain the following types of copyrighted information:

- federal legislation and caselaw; and
- contributed metadata in the form of annotations, categorization, link creation, and the like.

Federal legislation and case law can be freely reproduced if due diligence is taken under the statute appropriately named *Reproduction of Federal Law Order.*[3] Because the ILE will convert federal law from one format (HTML)

---

2   See WorldLII, "Declaration on Free Access to Law," online: www.worldlii.org/worldlii/declaration.

3   Department of Justice Canada, "Reproduction of Federal Law Order (S.I./97-5)," online: http://laws.justice.gc.ca/en/ShowDoc/cr/SI-97-5///en?page=1.

to another (XML), care must be taken to ensure that the due diligence requirement is met. For instance, it may be that special permission will be required from the registrar of the applicable court to include headnotes.

Contributions made to the ILE in the form of annotations or other metadata will use a Creative Commons Attributions-Share Alike licence[4] to ensure both free access to the content and to allow the content to be updated. A fully featured annotation engine will need to keep track of who contributed a particular piece of metadata so that both a chain of authority and (if the contributor desires it) attribution can be made for a particular contribution.

3) Development Plan for the ILE

The first component of the ILE that has been developed is the LawShare Browser, a legislation browser intended as a rich tool for exploring statutes. The intent is to provide smarter and faster statute navigation than is currently in use in web-based tools available both from governments and commercial sources.

The LawShare Browser is one piece of a long-range project aimed at providing an open source, free, shared legal development environment — similar to the collaborative, rich development environments that software developers currently enjoy with IDEs. This environment will couple rapid and intelligent navigation of legal materials with a rich knowledge-sharing mechanism. The following sections describe the various phases of the planned development process.

4) Phase 1: Adding Structure to Statutes (Completed)

The project must reach a certain level of usefulness before it will attract users and contributors. We have decided to target law students as a usergroup for whom we can provide a useful product quickly. For this group, simply providing access to a comprehensive set of federal statutes that are properly linked and easily navigated will provide significant value to their studies.

The federal statutes at laws.justice.gc.ca are published in HTML format. They are not very searchable, have links only to the section levels, and have no internal links. The first goal of the ILE project was to create

---

4   See the licence terms at Creative Commons, "Attribution-Share Alike 2.5 Canada," online: http://creativecommons.org/licenses/by-sa/2.5/ca/.

XML versions of these statutes. This phase was completed in 2006, with the complete collection of Canadian federal statutes and associated regulations being converted to an XML format that could be used by the LawShare Browser. The completed conversion consists of 9142 files containing 309 MB of data.

Since the time of conversion, the federal government has made slight modifications to the HTML format of its statutes, which may necessitate further changes to the conversion tool. Ultimately, governments should be convinced to publish structured versions of their laws, but this is a very long-range goal. In the meantime, subsequent converters will be simplified by using the following two-step process:

1)   convert the published representation of the statute to text-only; and
2)   use pattern-matching to identify the underlying structure.

This approach, which results in an intermediate text format, has the danger of potentially dropping some information when converting to text, but has the benefit that the same pattern-matching code can be used to parse legislations from all jurisdictions. The current converter uses a one-step process and tries to use cues from the HTML classes of the generated data to identify structure, but this process is too brittle in the face of changes to the presentation format in which the federal government chooses to publish.

The current conversion utility captures the following structures within a piece of legislation:

- containment relationships between parts, topics, sections, subsections, paragraphs, and clauses;
- the history of amendments to a particular section; and
- metadata such as keywords, titles, definitions, and marginal notes.

The work of creating links within statutes on this body of data remains to be completed and will never be fully automatable. For instance, when section 5 of the *Broadcasting Act*[5] refers to "subsection 3(1)," it should be possible to follow that link easily. Many of these links can be created automatically based on imprecise, language-dependent, and regular expression-matching. Imprecision arises from the many different possible ways of describing a reference, language difference, and the context-sensitivity of the reference.

However, it is expected that the vast majority of intra-statute references will be able to be identified with good reliability. A fully integrated LawShare Browser will identify which links were created automatically, and

---

5   S.C. 1991, c. 11.

will allow online contributors to correct and expand on the automatically created links, as well as presenting a list of possible endpoints for links that are suggested by the browser.

The creation of the containment relationships mentioned above creates many benefits. Users can link or navigate to components of the statute at a very fine-grain (clauses) or coarse-grain (parts) level. This is important to allow annotations to be properly scoped. It also allows LawShare Browser to dynamically display or hide useful contextual information, such as the list of amendments that apply to a section, marginal notes, or ultimately comments on the selected piece of legislation that have been provided by members of the community.

Other benefits of making the containment relations explicit include:

- allowing the calculation of intelligent differences between versions of a statute;
- allowing a web service to deliver only the amount of data required by the client (for better responsiveness in an AJAX or similar application); and
- allowing the generation of tables of sections, forms, schedules, parts, or other logical groupings of the statute.

5) Phase 2: LawShare Browser (completed)

The objective of this phase was to develop a prototype legislation browser, called the LawShare Browser, which would be able to demonstrate some of the benefits of structured statutes. In this section we describe the nuts and bolts of how the LawShare Browser prototype was built and the rationale behind the choices that went into building it.

A number of technologies were considered for developing the statute browser. The following factors guided the choice of technology:

1) The statute browser needs to be cross-platform to reach the broadest possible audience. In particular, it should be supported on open source operating systems (Linux and other open source unices). Java-based (Swing or Eclipse-based) or web-based (HTML and XUL) applications meet this criterion.

2) The technology upon which the statute browser is based needs to provide a rich and responsive user experience. This rules out traditional (pre-AJAX) web-based applications that require a round trip to the server for every user interaction, which introduce overly long latencies between performing an action (such as expanding a tree node) and get-

ting a response. The statute browser must follow "good human-factors engineering principles," which dictate that responses must occur within 300ms to avoid interrupting the user's thought process.

3) The underlying technology needs to be easily deployed over the web. The model for the LawShare Browser is to download entire statutes and store them entirely locally, but in a full deployment the original statutes will be pulled from a central repository of "XMLized" statutes that will be made available over HTTP and continually updated.

4) The underlying technology must allow the statute browser to keep a large cache of information locally, including both cached statutes and local annotations of the statutes. This rules out unsigned Java applets or normal HTML applications.

5) It must be possible to develop the statute browser in a timely fashion.

6) The statute browser must be built on open, preferably open source, software.

XUL was chosen as the underlying technology of the LawShare Browser. It is the open source user-interface definition language that is used both to build the Firefox web browser and to deploy applications within Firefox. Because XUL applications run *within* a browser, they can take full advantage of the very rich document manipulation capabilities of a full-fledged web browser. XUL applications can be installed *within* a browser and can take full advantage of the very rich document manipulation capabilities and, as trusted applications, they can also get access to the file system.

An annotated screenshot of the LawShare Browser is shown in Figure 1. Features of the current version of the LawShare Browser include:

- A side-by-side *hierarchical* view of a piece of legislation and an HTML/CSS *content* view of the associated text—both views are always synchronized.
- An optional display of amending legislation for particular sections.
- A direct pinpoint search: enter a pinpoint and the browser will take you directly to the relevant part/topic/paragraph/section.
- A structured search within text, titles, marginal notes, or definitions.

Some features that are yet to be added include:

- integration with an annotation engine;
- integration with a back-end repository of legislation (the current implementation is file-based); and
- the ability to generate a correctly formatted citation for the selected section or paragraph (a relatively simple feature to add).

Figure 1: The LawShare Browser

The hierarchy view provides an outline view for exploring the legislation and also provides context for what is displayed in the content view.

The content view uses faint dotted lines and indentation to clearly demarcate the scope of a part, topic, section, or paragraph.

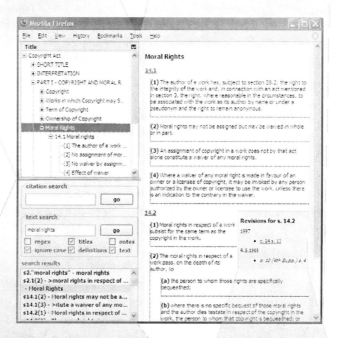

Citation searches provide direct access to known sections by simply typing in the pinpoint, e.g. S14.2(2)(b).

Text searches are structured searches through the statute. In this case, the Copyright Act was searched for all occurrences of "moral rights" that appear in titles, definitions, or paragraph text. Occurrences of "moral rights" that appear in marginal notes have not been returned.

Sections that have been amended over time have clickable headings. In this example, the user has clicked the s. 14.2 heading to reveals that the section was last amended in 1997. There is a direct link to the amending act.

6) Phase 3: Deployment of Structured Legislation into a Shared Legal Repository

This phase has yet to be completed. The goal of this phase is to design a highly available, remotely accessible legal repository.

A legal repository needs to support the following features:

- Full indexing of legal text, headings, and metadata such as marginal notes;
- Multi-language support;
- Efficient search capability;
- The ability to store multiple versions of the same statute to support point-in-time searches;
- The ability to maintain and navigate the structure of legislation and caselaw;
- Storage of the following types of legal material:
  » Legislations
  » Caselaw
  » Metadata about jurisdictions, courts, judges, *et cetera*; and
- Integration with an annotation system.

Content repositories are an emerging technology that is well-suited to support the above features. For example, JSR-170[6] content repositories have built-in text indexing capabilities and native XML support, including a query engine that is based upon XPath. The content repository sits on top of a file system or a database and adds in the kind of support for text indexing, searching, and navigating hierarchical data that would need to be built in any event if a flat file system or database was used directly. XML databases are a similar maturing technology that are also a good match and could possibly be used in conjunction with a content repository.

A high-level design of the repository has been proposed based on the capabilities of a content repository, which is a kind of hierarchical database. The core legal information in the repository will be organized at the following levels:

1) Jurisdiction;
2) Lawmaking body (a court or a legislature);
3) Legal document (decision or legislation);
4) Document version (in the case of legislation, each amendment results in a new version of the legislation);
5) Language; and
6) The internal organization of the legal document itself (e.g., opinions, sections, and/or paragraphs).

---

6   See further at Java Community Process, "Community Development of Java Technology Specifications," online: http://jcp.org/en/jsr/detail?id=170.

The following sections examine some aspects of the proposed structured legal repository in detail.

a) How to handle different languages in the content repository

The problem of how to represent multiple languages must be carefully addressed when designing the content repository. Multiple languages mean that you will have multiple versions of various units of legislative information (legislation and decisions). This does not sit easily with a hierarchical layout. There are two approaches that are generally used to address the issue of multiple languages in a hierarchical repository:

- Early splitting: Parallel hierarchies are created, beginning at the root of the repository. This is the approach that the Government of Canada uses for its legal repository.[7]
- Late splitting: A single hierarchy is used, with branching between languages occurring only at the leaf nodes.

Figure 3 (page 144) exemplifies the differences between these two approaches. The clouds indicate the point in the hierarchy at which duplication begins.

For the structured legal-content repository we have decided to follow a late-splitting strategy. It has the following advantages:

- The hierarchical relationship between nodes is preserved as far as possible.[8]
- There is less duplication of information.
- There is less need to keep separate branches in sync.
- It is a more flexible model for allowing the addition of new languages.[9]

---

7   See French: Ministère de la Justice Canada, "Site Web des Lois du Canada," online: http://laws.justice.gc.ca/fr, and English: Department of Justice Canada, "Justice Laws Web Site," online: http://laws.justice.gc.ca/en. For these websites there is a common homepage which directs you to either the English or the French website, both of which are for all intents and purposes entirely independent.

8   This avoids difficulties that can arise where only one translation is available for a particular node. In the early splitting strategy, for example, if the *Patent Act* was not available in English, and the *Copyright Act* was not available in French, then the only way to discover that full set of facts in the federal jurisdiction would be to perform a merge of the various translations of the Acts.

9   For instance, with early splitting, if you wished to add Inuit as a third language for federal Canada, you would need to create a new hierarchy containing all Inuit translations at once. With late splitting, you can just add Inuit translations as they become available.

The Government of Canada can achieve its goals with an early-splitting strategy because federal legislation is required by law to be published simultaneously in English and in French. However, the structured legal-content repository is intended to be applicable to all jurisdictions, and some jurisdictions may provide different levels of support for different languages, which means that translations into some languages will not always be available. Late splitting is more tolerant of translation gaps.

The final question that remains is: Given that we intend to use late splitting of languages, precisely how late should the splitting occur? The obvious place to split is at the level of individual pieces of legislation or decisions. This is the policy that we intend to pursue. However, another strategy would be to push the splitting even later. For instance, a given statute will have precisely the same number of parts, sections, and subsections in both languages (to allow interoperability between languages), so the split could be deferred all the way down to leaf nodes within the statutes. Because this is even later splitting, this is an attractive strategy for all the reasons listed above.

Nevertheless, we have chosen not to utilize late splitting because it is extremely intolerant of mismatches between different language versions of the same statute, which are likely to occur due to typographical errors in the source statute, or from errors in the parsing process used to convert source statutes into structured (XML) statutes.

b) How to design jurisdictions within the repository

One of the most obvious constraints on searches within the structured legal-content repository will be to limit a search to relevant jurisdictions. This division is so familiar that some commercial repositories store material from different jurisdictions in separate databases.

Although it is obvious at first glance that jurisdictions are hierarchically organized within nations, there are some subtle aspects to jurisdictions that need to be handled carefully:

- Jurisdictions come and go over time—for example, the Canadian territorial jurisdiction of Nunavut is relatively new and the jurisdictions of upper and lower Canada have evolved into the provinces;
- Jurisdictions can merge or split—how do we represent the relationship between Nunavut and the Northwest Territories (from which Nunavut emerged)?; and
- Jurisdictions can move between national units—for example, Newfoundland joined the Canadian federation in 1949, and Czechoslovakia split into two jurisdictions in 1993.

Figure 2: Hierarchical Position of the *Patent Act* within the Content Repository

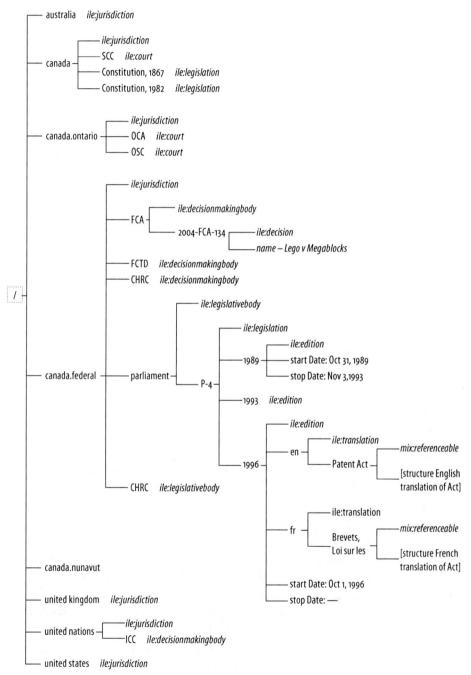

We think the correct approach to these questions is to not answer them at all. While jurisdictions appear to be stable, hierarchical structures at any point in time, over time they merge, split, and disappear. In order for the content repository to remain accurate, it should store jurisdictions as a flat structure. In other words, the repository should not explicitly represent the relationship between Nunavut and the Northwest Territories; this will be left to the realm of annotations.

Figure 3: Early vs. Late Hierarchy Splitting to Support Multiple Hierarchies

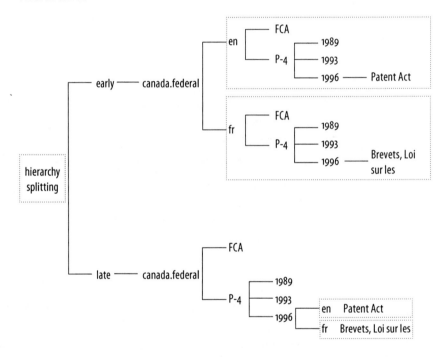

Jurisdictions will be represented within the structured legal-content repository as a completely flat list at the root of the repository, using a dotted naming convention (similar to that used for domain names) to group jurisdictions. Figure 4 shows the difference between the hierarchical approach and the flat approach to jurisdictions that we intend to pursue.

Note that although there is an explicit representation of a nation in the flat model, it will contain very little. For instance, in Canada the only objects that truly belong to the jurisdiction called "Canada" would be constitutional documents and the Supreme Court of Canada; these are in their own jurisdiction that supersedes all other jurisdictions in Canada, but this is not represented in the repository other than through the hint that the dotted naming convention provides. The Parliament of Canada, its legislation, and federal courts all reside within the Canadian federal jurisdiction.

c) Representing courts and decisions

In a complete, structured legal-content repository, decisions should be linked to the decision-making bodies that make them. A special node type, "ile:decisionmakingbody," will represent courts, tribunals, and the like. Decisions will be represented by the "ile:decision" node type and will be children of ile:decisionmakingbody nodes.

Another important component of decisions is the group of judges, tribunal members, or arbitrators who made the decision. These will be represented within the repository as children of an ile:decisionmakingbody with the type "ile:decisionmaker," and these nodes will contain meta-information about the decision maker, indicating the periods in which they were active in the decision-making body, as well as links to their participation in other decision-making bodies.

Individual decisions will contain references to the list of ile:decisionmakers that participated in the decision. Decisions will also have links to earlier and later decisions in the case history, where available.

d) Representing legislation and legislation-making bodies

The relation between legislation and legislation-making bodies is similar to that between decisions and decision-making bodies. This relationship is visible in Figure 2 (page 143).

e) Interfaces to the shared legal content repository

The repository will be accessible as a web application and as a web service. The web application will be used by end-users from a standard web browser. The web service will be available to rich clients such as a statute browser, and will be designed to be easily integrated with AJAX applications. The web service will also be available for other custom applications such as data-mining applications.

Figure 4: Hierarchical Representation of Jurisdictions vs. the Proposed Flat Model

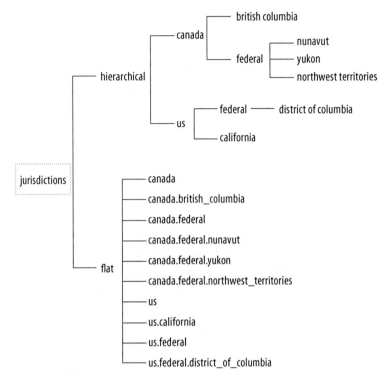

7) Phase 4: Annotations

Annotations and topics or articles (similar to Wikipedia articles) will provide the key means of providing both links between laws and non-obvious perspectives on how different laws interrelate.

It is currently envisioned that annotations will not be stored directly in the legal repository. Every node in the legal repository will be uniquely identifiable with a structured URL that will contain the same type of information currently available in the neutral citation format, with implementation-dependent extensions. The annotation engine will be a separate database that links to the legal repository using these identifiers. The design of the annotation repository must make it possible to quickly identify which annotations apply to a piece of law.

Annotations should be supported anywhere in the repository. The annotation system has to support the following:

- links to the annotator;

- date of annotation;
- links to external resources;
- an annotation history; and
- codified rules for who can contribute annotations (the initial model will be informed by the social rules of Wikipedia).

8) Phase 5: Structured Caselaw

This phase will structure caselaw in much the same way as Phase 1 added structure to statutory materials. The targeted caselaw is that of the Supreme Court of Canada, since it is both the most widely applicable jurisprudence in Canada, and the most complicated jurisprudence. Because of the complexity of having multiple opinions and references interwoven in a single judgment, the Supreme Court judgments will benefit the most from being structured.

9) Future Developments

Other functionality that may be added includes:

- The ability to navigate amendments to a statute through time, preferably through a diff-based mechanism;
- Providing quick navigation between equivalent English and French versions of legislation; and
- Advocating the integrated legal environment approach for adoption by third parties (such as the Government of Canada itself).

D. SUMMARY

In this chapter we have briefly described our plans to build an integrated legal environment. A working version of the first application, the LawShare Browser, is already a useful tool and, with a little more work, will be a compelling application in its own right. However, it is not until it is integrated with a web service that provides easy access to structured versions of all federal statutes, together with a common annotation engine, that the full power of an integrated legal environment will be measurable.

The prototype LawShare Browser demonstrates some of the benefits of XML-structured statutes by providing access to a select set of federal statutes that are properly linked and easily navigated. It is available for download from www.lawshare.ca/resources.htm.

CHAPTER 8

Blogs and the Law: Key Legal Issues for the Blogosphere

Damien O'Brien*

A. INTRODUCTION

Over the past few years the blogosphere (the community or social network of blogs) has experienced an unprecedented level of growth, in terms of both the popularity of blogs and the number of blogs in existence. The very nature of a blog—a short, instantaneous, highly personalized form of on-line communication that is accessible throughout the world—fundamentally challenges the application and operation of traditional legal doctrines. However, this relationship between the blogosphere and the law is yet to be fully conceptualized from a legal perspective. Therefore, the purpose of this chapter is to consider from an Internet-law perspective some of the most critical legal issues that are currently facing blogs, their authors, bloggers, and the intermediaries that host blogs. The chapter will first provide a broad overview of blogs by examining the nature of a blog, how the courts have interpreted blogs, the rise of the blogosphere, and the emergence of so-called "new generation blogs." The chapter will then consider some of the key legal issues affecting blogs, including copyright law, defamation law, Internet jurisdiction, employment law, and intermediary liability of blog providers. Finally, the chapter will conclude with some thoughts on how blogs and the blogosphere will survive the many challenging legal issues that they are likely to encounter.

---

* The author owes special thanks to Professor Brian Fitzgerald for his guidance and assistance with this article, and to Professor Mark Perry. The law as it appears in this chapter is based on Australian Law.

B. AN OVERVIEW OF BLOGS

1) The Definition of a Blog

A blog is a public online journal that features individually authored entries or posts in reverse chronological order, along with hypertext links, and, in some cases, the opportunity for readers to post comments and responses to an author's entry.[1] In their simplest form, a blog is nothing more than a webpage that consists of a number of different entries on a particular topic, which are arranged in reverse chronological order, from the most recent entry to the oldest entry.[2] Beyond this generic definition, there are also a number of other variations that blogs may use, for example: some blogs feature each entry on a new page, while others organize entries by topic or the date the entry was created.[3] However, the key distinguishing feature of a blog is the time-stamping, reverse chronological format that arranges entries from most recent to oldest, according to their date of creation.[4] New entries are then simply added through a simplified interface that operates in a similar way to a word-processing application.

Commonly, blogs also contain links to other blogs and websites within the individual blog.[5] Indeed, many of the first blogs relied heavily upon material from other websites to create their entries. However, many of today's blogs now feature a greater amount of original and creative material, which is very much akin to a personal journal or diary of the author.[6] Most blogs take the form of a personal journal or diary and as such are non-commercial in nature. However, blogs are also increasingly being used by corporations and organizations as a communications and public relations tool.

---

1   Axel Bruns & Joanne Jacobs, "Introduction" in Axel Bruns & Joanne Jacobs, eds., *Uses of Blogs (Digital Formations)* (New York: Peter Lang, 2006) 1 at 2 [Bruns & Jacobs].

2   Bausch *et al.*, *We Blog: Publishing Online with Weblogs* (Indianapolis, IN: Wiley, 2002) at 7.

3   *Ibid.*

4   Axel Bruns, *Gatewatching: Collaborative Online News Production (Digital Formations)* (New York: Peter Lang, 2005) at 173 [Bruns].

5   For an overview of the legal issues relating to collaborative blogging activities, see Eric Goldman, "Co-Blogging Law" (Paper presented to the Berkman Center for Internet & Society, Bloggership: How Blogs are Transforming Legal Scholarship Conference, 28 April 2006), online: http://papers.ssrn.com/sol3/papers.cfm?abstract_id=898048.

6   Bruns, above note 4 at 173.

There has so far been very limited judicial consideration of the legal nature of a blog. In the few cases that have examined blogs, it would appear that the definitions provided by the courts have been somewhat misguided, often mistakenly likening a blog to a traditional website or bulletin board. In the US, one of the major decisions to have considered the legal nature of a blog was *Cahill v. Doe*,[7] where the Superior Court of Delaware described a blog as

> [a]n Internet website where users interested in a particular topic can post messages for other users interested in the same topic to read and answer if they wish. When users post information on a blog, they often do so using a pseudonym referred to as a "user name."

In the Australian decision of *Y & H*,[8] Federal Magistrate Baumann described a blog as "a sort of Internet accessible private diary," which in this case had been used as a forum for debate and comment about the respondent's life and experiences. Similarly, in a decision of the Supreme Court of New South Wales in *Kaplan v. Go Daddy Group Inc.*,[9] White J. described a blog as a "website . . . which enables anyone with Internet access to post comments." Again, in a recent decision of the Supreme Court of Victoria in *Melbourne University Student Union Inc. (in liq) v. Ray*,[10] Hollingworth J. defined a blog as "essentially an online diary."

2) The Rise of the Blogosphere

The blogosphere has evolved over the past few years to create an entirely new form of media and content production. Blogs have played a significant role in major events throughout the world, and are now regarded by many as a personalized alternative to the mainstream media.[11] As Bruns and Jacobs argue, the main reasons for the rise of the blogosphere have been the social networking aspect of blogs, and the potential large-scale collaboration that provides the human and personal dimension to the publishing and publicizing of information online.[12] It is this personalization of content production that enables blogs to go beyond a purely passive and informative role to generate a new platform for social, political, and cultural expres-

---

7   879 A.2d 943 at 945 (Del. Super. Ct. 2005).

8   [2005] FMCAfam 229 at para. 25.

9   [2005] NSWSC 636 at para. 3 [*Kaplan*].

10   [2006] VSC 205 at para. 3 [*Ray*].

11   Bruns, above note 4 at 175.

12   Bruns & Jacobs, above note 1 at 5.

sion.[13] Indeed, blogs are in many ways replacing traditional websites as a forum for ideas and information because they give authors the opportunity to interact with their audience, unlike any other form of media.[14] The rise of the blogosphere can also be attributed to the highly democratic nature of blogs and the decentralized nature of the blogosphere.[15]

Over the past year, the blogosphere has experienced an unprecedented level of growth. In the October 2006 "State of the Blogosphere" report released by the blog-tracking website Technorati, it was found that the blogosphere doubled in size every six months and is now a hundred times bigger than it was three years ago.[16] Similarly, according to Technorati's report "State of the Live Web," April 2007, there are now over 75.2 million blogs, with over 120,000 new blogs created every day and 1.5 million new entries made daily.[17] Interestingly, Technorati's figures show that blogs and the blogosphere act as a barometer for the digitally connected world, with current news and events triggering a rapid increase in blog entries. For example, the July 2006 Israel-Lebanon conflict caused an increase in daily blog entries of over 2.5 million.[18] The "State of the Live Web" report also demonstrates the global nature of the blogosphere, with English accounting for only 36 percent of blogs, Japanese at 37 percent, Mandarin at 8 percent, and a number of other languages making up the remaining 19 percent.[19]

3) The New Generation Blogs: MP3 Blogs, Vlogs, and Photoblogs

Recently there have also been a number of variations to the traditional blog, including MP3 blogs, vlogs or videoblogs, and photoblogs. An MP3 blog is

---

13 *Ibid.*

14 *Ibid.*

15 *Ibid.*; see also Urs Gasser & Silke Ernst, "From Shakespeare to DJ Danger Mouse: A Quick Look at Copyright and User Creativity in the Digital Age" (2006), online: http://papers.ssrn.com/sol3/papers.cfm?abstract_id=909223 at 4–8 [Gasser & Ernst].

16 David Sifry, "State of the Blogosphere, October, 2006" (6 November 2006), online: http://technorati.com/weblog/2006/11/161.html [Sifry]; see also Candace Lombardi, "There's a Blog Born Every Half Second" (7 August 2006), online: http://news.com. com/Theres+a+blog+born+every+half+second/2100-1025_3-6102935.html.

17 David Sifry, "The State of the Live Web, April 2007" (5 April 2007), online: www. sifry.com/alerts/archives/000493.html [Sifry, "State of the Live Web"]; See also Technorati, "About Us," online: http://technorati.com/about/.

18 *Ibid.*; see also Sifry, above note 16.

19 Sifry, "State of the Live Web," above note 17.

a type of blog in which the author makes music files—generally in MP3 format—available for download.²⁰ Most MP3 blogs only make available a very small number of songs, sometimes only one or two tracks from an album, which are freely available to download for a short period of time. These MP3 files are then usually annotated with biographical and contextual notes about the artist and music available for download. In an attempt to distance themselves from peer-to-peer file-sharing services, readers are encouraged to download the music for sampling purposes only, and then to purchase the artist's music if they like it. Generally, the music available on MP3 blogs is restricted to a particular musical genre or theme, usually that which is not termed as contemporary or mainstream, and is often difficult to locate.

A vlog or videoblog is simply a blog which uses video as its primary source of content, as opposed to the traditional text format that is featured on most blogs. Typically, a vlog will combine videos, which are directly uploaded to the vlog, along with embedded and linked videos, which are supported by text, images, and metadata.²¹ The growth and popularity of vlogs on the Internet can largely be attributed to two factors: the introduction of video iPods capable of playing videos, along with the introduction of videos to the Apple iTunes Store, and the emergence of the online "clip culture," in particular video-sharing websites such as YouTube, which enable uploaded videos to be embedded directly to vlogs. ²²

A photoblog is a form of blog that primarily uses photographs or images as its main source of content. Generally, a photoblog can be distinguished from a blog, as its main emphasis is on photography, with the associated photos and images not simply being used to illustrate the text entries. Similar to traditional blogs, photoblogs contain photos that are posted to the blog, time stamped, and then listed in chronological order, along with the provision for readers to post comments related to the particular entry.

---

20   For an overview of MP3 blogs see Brian Fitzgerald & Damien O'Brien, "Digital Sampling and Culture Jamming in a Remix World: What Does the Law Allow?" (2005) 10 Media and Arts Law Review 279 at 288 [Fitzgerald & O'Brien].

21   Katie Dean, "Blogging + Video = Vlogging" (13 July 2005), online: www.wired.com/news/digiwood/0,1412,68171,00.html?tw=rss.TOP.

22   For an overview of YouTube, see Damien O'Brien & Brian Fitzgerald, "Digital Copyright Law in a YouTube World" (2006) 9(6 & 7) Internet Law Bulletin 71 [O'Brien & Fitzgerald, "Digital Copyright Law"].

C. COPYRIGHT LAW

1) Key Copyright Issues

One of the major legal issues facing blogs and the blogosphere in general is copyright law—in particular to what extent bloggers will be legally permitted to reproduce and communicate existing material as a source of content for their blogs.[23] In this regard, it is necessary to consider whether the unauthorized reproduction and communication of text, images, videos, and MP3s on blogs will constitute an infringement of copyright. As a general principle, the *Copyright Act*[24] provides protection for either subject matter that falls within the category of Part III "works" or Part IV "subject matter other than works." The following discussion will consider the copyright implications of some of the most common content featured on blogs, including copyright infringement, the application of the defence of fair dealing, and the infringement of moral rights.

2) Text

The term "literary work" is not defined exhaustively within section 10 of the *Copyright Act*,[25] although it is taken to incorporate a broad category protecting any work that is expressed in either print or written form.[26] As such, the term "literary work" has been held by the courts to include works as diverse as computer programs,[27] telephone directories,[28] examination papers,[29] and even betting forms[30]. Furthermore, the term "literary" does not prescribe that the work must reach any particular standard of literary style or merit; thus there is no quality requisite, it must simply be original.[31] Therefore, in the context of blogs, all original text posted to a blog by either the blogger themselves, or blog contributors, will be protected under the *Copyright Act* as a literary work.

---

23 See, generally, Gasser & Ernst, above note 15.
24 *Copyright Act 1968* (Cth.) [*Copyright Act*].
25 *Ibid.*, s. 10.
26 Anne Fitzgerald & Brian Fitzgerald, *Intellectual Property: In Principle* (Sydney: Law Book Co., 2004) at 97 [Fitzgerald & Fitzgerald].
27 *Computer Edge Pty. Ltd. v. Apple Computer Inc.*, [1986] HCA 19, 161 C.L.R. 171.
28 *Desktop Marketing System Pty. Ltd. v. Telstra Corp.* (2002), 55 I.P.R. 1.
29 *University of London Press Ltd. v. University Tutorial Press Ltd.*, [1916] 2 Ch. 601.
30 *Ladbroke (Football) Ltd. v. William Hill (Football) Ltd.*, [1964] 1 W.L.R. 273 (H.L.) [*Ladbroke*].
31 Fitzgerald & Fitzgerald, above note 26 at 97.

3) Images

The term "artistic work" is defined extensively (although not exhaustively) under section 10 of the *Copyright Act* to include, from the perspective of a blog, photographs, irrespective of the artistic quality.[32] Therefore, a wide range of artistic works will be afforded copyright protection, including drawings, diagrams, maps, charts, plans, prints, photographs, paintings, photocopies, and designs.[33] Thus, in relation to blogs, generally most of the images featured on a blog, in particular on photoblogs, will be protected as an artistic work under the *Copyright Act*.

4) MP3s

The *Copyright Act* provides protection for sound recordings, which are defined in section 10(1) of the *Copyright Act* as meaning the aggregate of sounds embodied in a record,[34] therefore extending to the recording of sounds on some of the most common mediums, including a CD and an MP3 file.[35] Therefore, blogs, in particular MP3 blogs, which contain MP3 files, will be protected under the *Copyright Act* as a sound recording.[36]

5) Videos

The *Copyright Act* protects videos in the form of cinematograph films and sound and television broadcasts.[37] A cinematograph film is defined in section 10(1) of the *Copyright Act* as being the aggregate of the visual images embodied in an article or thing capable of being shown as a moving picture.[38] Notably, this also includes the aggregate of the sounds embodied in

---

32   Above note 24, s. 10(1); Fitzgerald & Fitzgerald, *ibid.* at 99.

33   For example, see *Australian Chinese Newspapers Pty. Ltd. v. Melbourne Chinese Press Pty. Ltd.* (2003), 58 I.P.R. 1; *Melbourne Chinese Press Pty. Ltd. v. Australian Chinese Newspapers Pty. Ltd.*, [2004] FCAFC 201, 63 I.P.R. 38..

34   Above note 24, s. 10(1).

35   Also note that copyright may subsist in other underlying works, including lyrics — literary work and the musical score or composition — and musical work; see Fitzgerald & O'Brien, above note 20 at 282.

36   *Universal Music Australia Pty. Ltd. v. Cooper*, [2005] FCA 972 at paras. 49–53 [*Universal v. Cooper*]; *Universal Music Australia Pty. Ltd. v. Sharman License Holdings Ltd.*, [2005] FCA 1242 at para.412 [*Universal v. Sharman*].

37   Above note 24, s. 87.

38   *Ibid.*

a soundtrack that is associated with the visual images.[39] Thus, films, videos, television programs, and multimedia works will all be protected as a cinematograph film.[40] Similarly, section 87 of the *Copyright Act* provides protection for sound and television broadcasts that are based on underlying copyrighted works or subject matter, as well as on live broadcasts of news, sports events, and unscripted interviews that have no underlying copyright content.[41] The term "television broadcast" is defined to mean the visual images that are broadcast by way of television, along with any associated sounds broadcast with those images.[42] Therefore, videos featured on blogs, in particular vlogs, will be protected as either a cinematograph film or sound and television broadcast under the *Copyright Act*.

6) Copyright Infringement

Copyright infringement will occur where a person who is not the copyright owner does or authorizes someone else to do, without the licence of the copyright owner, any of the acts within the copyright owner's exclusive rights.[43] Assuming that it has been established that the person has infringed the exclusive rights of the copyright owner — as will be likely where there has been an unauthorized reproduction or communication of one of the above works or subject matter other than works on a blog — it is then necessary to determine whether this act has been done in relation to a substantial part of the work or subject matter other than work.[44]

---

39   *Ibid.*, ss. 10(1) and 23(1); *Phonographic Performance Company of Australia Ltd. v. Federation of Australian Commercial Television Stations* (1998), 40 I.P.R. 225.

40   *Galaxy Electronics Pty. Ltd. v. Sega Enterprises Ltd.* (1997), 37 I.P.R. 462; *Kabushiki Kaisha Sony Computer Entertainment v. Stevens*, [2003] FCAFC 157, 57 I.P.R. 161; *Stevens v. Kabushiki Kaisha Sony Computer Entertainment* (2005), 65 I.P.R. 513.

41   Fitzgerald & Fitzgerald, above note 26 at 103; *TCN Channel Nine Pty. Ltd. v. Network Ten Pty. Ltd. (No. 2)*, [2005] FCAFC 53; *Network Ten Pty. Ltd. v. TCN Channel Nine Pty. Ltd.* (2004), 59 I.P.R. 1; *TCN Channel Nine Pty. Ltd. v. Network Ten Pty. Ltd.* (2002), 55 I.P.R. 112.

42   Above note 24, s. 10(1). Also see Melissa de Zwart, "Copyright in Television Broadcasts: *Network Ten v. TCN Channel Nine* — 'A Case Which Can Excite Emotions'" (2004) 9(4) Media Arts and Law Review 277.

43   *Copyright Act, ibid.*, ss. 36(1) and 101(1). For literary works, see ss. 31(1)(a), (c), & (d); for artistic works, see s. 31(1)(b); for sound recordings, see s. 85; for cinematograph films, see s. 86; and for television and sound broadcasts, see s. 87.

44   *Ibid.*, s. 14(1).

The general test for a substantial part was stated by Lord Pearce in *Ladbroke*[45] as "whether a part is substantial must be decided by its quality rather than its quantity." This test was affirmed by Mason C.J. in *Autodesk Inc. v. Dyason (No 2)*[46] who held that "in determining whether the quality of what is taken makes it a 'substantial part' of the copyrighted work, it is important to inquire into the importance which the taken portion bears in relation to the work as whole: is it an 'essential' or 'material' part of the work?" The High Court approved Mason's C.J. statement in *Data Access Corporation v. Powerflex Services Pty. Ltd.*[47] where it was held that "in determining whether something is a reproduction of a substantial part of a [copyright work], the essential features of the [work] should be ascertained by considering the originality of the part allegedly taken."

The High Court referred to the definition of a substantial part again in *Network Ten Pty. Ltd. v. TCN Channel Nine Pty. Ltd.*[48] In this case, Kirby J. explained that a small portion in quantitative terms may constitute a substantial part, having regard to its materiality in relation to the work as a whole.[49] More recently, in *TCN Channel Nine Pty. Ltd. v. Network Ten Pty. Ltd. (No 2)* it was held that whether a part taken is a substantial part or not, involves an assessment of the importance of the part taken to the work as a whole.[50]

An analysis of whether a substantial part of the work or other subject matter is involved will be particularly important given the nature of blogs as short pieces of commentary that very often contain material which is protected by copyright. Where the material posted by a blogger or a contributor is a complete reproduction or communication of the original material, generally a substantial part of the work or subject matter other than work will almost always be involved. However, it becomes more difficult to determine substantiality in relation to very small reproductions or communications, which contain only very small parts of the original material. Such assessments of substantiality will need to be made on a case-by-case basis, and, even then, it may be that the court interprets the substantial part doctrine narrowly, so that even highly transformative derivatives are held

45   Above note 30 at 293.
46   [1993] HCA 6, 176 C.L.R. 300 at 305.
47   (1999), 45 I.P.R. 353 at para. 84.
48   (2004), 78 A.L.J.R. 585.
49   *Ibid.* at 605; see also McHugh A.C.J., Gummow, and Hayne JJ. at 589.
50   Above note 41 at paras. 12 and 50–52; see also *Network Ten Pty. Ltd. v. TCN Channel Nine Pty. Ltd.*, [2005] HCA Trans 842.

to be a substantial part of the work or subject matter other than work.[51] In this regard, it should be noted that thus far, there is yet to be a major reported decision involving issues of copyright infringement on a blog, although there have been a number of cases filed against bloggers that have failed to proceed to trial.[52]

7) Fair Dealing

After determining that an infringement of copyright has occurred in relation to material posted to a blog, it is then necessary to consider whether any of the fair dealing defences will apply. Under the *Copyright Act*, copyright in a work or subject matter other than a work will not be taken to have been infringed where it falls within one of the five fair dealing exceptions,

---

51 For example, see *Bridgeport Music Inc. v. Dimension Films Inc.*, 401 F.3d 647 (6th Cir. 2004) where it was held in relation to a sound recording, that a very small amount of music sampling is substantial for the purposes of copyright infringement. For a discussion of the uncertainty in relation to the substantial part doctrine, see Michael Spence & Timothy Endicott, "Vagueness in the Scope of Copyright" (2005) 121 Law Q. Rev. 657. Also note a person may be criminally liable for copyright infringement under the *Copyright Act*, above note 24, ss. 132AA–132AO; Brian Fitzgerald, "Copyright Vision: Copyright Jails" (26 October 2006), online: www.onlineopinion. com.au/view.asp?article=5068; Kimberlee Weatherall, "Copyright Amendment Bill: The Criminal Provisions" (25 October 2006), online: http://weatherall.blogspot. com/2006_10_01_weatherall_archive.html.

52 For example, a Maine advertising agency in May 2006 filed a copyright infringement suit against a local blogger who had posted a number of draft advertisements from the Maine Department of Economic and Community Development website to his blog. The case was eventually withdrawn by the advertising agency. See *Warren Kremer Paino Advertising v. Duston*, Civil No. 06-047 (5 May 2006); Harry Wessel, "Orlando Lawyer Is Web Hero after Defending Blogger" *Orlando Sentinel* (12 May 2006) C.1; Robert Weisman, "Blogger who Criticized Maine Tourism Office Faces Lawsuit" (28 April 2006), online: www.boston.com/business/articles/2006/04/28/ blogger_who_criticized_maine_tourism_office_faces_lawsuit. Also see *NXIVM Corporation and First Principles Inc. v. Ross Institute*, WL 22298756 (N.D.N.Y. 2003) [*NXIVM N.D.N.Y.*]; *NXIVM Corporation and First Principles Inc. v. Ross Institute*, 364 F.3d 471 (2nd Cir. 2004) [*NXIVM 2nd Cir.*]; *NXIVM Corporation and First Principles Inc. v. Ross Institute*, 543 U.S. 1000 (2004) [*NXIVM U.S.S.C.*]. Also note that the recent decisions involving Google may have copyright implications for bloggers; see *Field v. Google Inc.*, *412 F. Supp. 2d 1106 (Nev. Dist. Ct. 2006); Parker v. Google Inc., 422 F. Supp. 2d 492 (E.D. Pa. 2006); Perfect 10 v. Google Inc., 416 F. Supp. 2d 828 (C.D. Cal. 2006); Copiepresse v. Google Inc. 2006/9099/4* (Court of First Instance of Brussels, 29 August 2006).

and its use is deemed to be fair. These fair dealing exceptions are for the purposes of

- research or study;[53]
- criticism or review;[54]
- parody or satire;[55]
- reporting news;[56] or
- judicial proceedings or professional advice.[57]

In the context of blogs with a focus of criticism or review, such as academic or scholarly blogs, or even MP3 blogs, it may be argued that they fall within the fair dealing defence of criticism or review. Under this provision, a work or audiovisual item will not infringe copyright provided it is used for the purposes of criticism or review, its use is fair, and sufficient acknowledgement has been made.[58] There is no definition of criticism or review within the *Copyright Act*, however, it has been held that the words "criticism" and "review" are of "wide and indefinite scope which should be interpreted literally."[59] In *Warner Entertainment Co. Ltd. v. Channel 4 Television Corp. PLC*,[60] Henry L.J. stated that the question to be answered in assessing whether a dealing is fair or not is, "is the [work] incorporating the infringing material a genuine piece of criticism or review, or is it something else, such as an attempt to dress up the infringement of another's copyright in the guise of criticism." The question that will arise for blogs will be whether the comments posted to a blog will be sufficient to constitute criticism or review. Given the varying nature of blogs, it is likely that such an assessment will need to be made on a blog-by-blog basis.[61]

---

53   Above note 24, ss. 40 and 103C.

54   *Ibid.*, ss. 41 and 103A.

55   *Ibid.*, ss. 41A and 103A.

56   *Ibid.*, ss. 42 and 103B.

57   *Ibid.*, ss. 43 and 104.

58   *Ibid.*, ss. 41 and 103A; Fitzgerald & Fitzgerald, above note 27 at 170.

59   *TCN Channel Nine Pty. Ltd. v. Network Ten Pty. Ltd.* (2001), 50 I.P.R. 335 at paras. 16–17 and 66; *TCN Channel Nine Pty. Ltd. v. Network Ten Pty. Ltd.*, [2002] FCAFC 146 at paras. 2–6, 15–25, and 94–131. Also see Melissa de Zwart, "Seriously Entertaining: The Panel and the Future of Fair Dealing" (2003) 8 Media and Arts Law Review 1.

60   (1993), 28 I.P.R. 459 at 468.

61   For a discussion of the application of the criticism or review defence to MP3 blogs, see Fitzgerald & O'Brien, above note 20 at 288; Brian Fitzgerald & Damien O'Brien, "Bloggers and the Law" in Bruns & Jacobs, above note 1, 223 at 227–28. Also see Evan Brown, "Big Time Blogger Faces Big Time Copyright Suit" (17 December

Similarly, blogs that provide news or current affairs perspective may be entitled to the fair dealing defence for the reporting of news. Under this provision, copyright in a work or audiovisual item will not be infringed where it is dealt with for the purposes of, or is associated with, the reporting of news, by means of a communication, and its use is fair.[62] Again, in determining whether a blog will be entitled to the fair dealing exception for the reporting of news, it will be necessary to assess the nature of the blog in question and its content on an individual basis.

In regard to the operation of the fair use doctrine in the US, it is arguable that this doctrine provides a broader (although not unlimited) scope for bloggers and blog contributors to rely upon the defence of fair use.[63] In determining whether a use by a blogger or blog contributor of copyrighted material will be classified as fair or not, and thus exempted from copyright infringement, the courts will have to regard the following four factors:

- the purpose and character of the use, including whether such use is of a commercial nature;
- the nature of the copyrighted work;
- the amount and substantiality of the portion used in relation to the copyrighted work as a whole; and
- the effect of the use upon the market or potential market for or value of the copyrighted work.[64]

8) Moral Rights

The potential for the infringement of moral rights will also need to be considered in relation to blogs. Moral rights are personal rights belonging to the author or creator of the copyrighted work, which exist independently from the economic rights mentioned above.[65] Under the *Copyright Act* there are three types of moral rights that are protected:

2006), online: http://blog.internetcases.com/2006/12/17/big-time-blogger-faces-big-time-copyright-suit/.

62   Above note 24, ss. 42 and 103B; Fitzgerald & Fitzgerald, above note 26 at 171.

63   *Copyright Act*, 17 U.S.C. § 107 [US *Copyright Act*]; Attiya Malik, "Are You Content with the Content? Intellectual Property Implications of Weblog Publishing" (2003) 21 J. Marshall J. Computer & Info. L. 439 at 498–503 [Malik].

64   US *Copyright Act*, *ibid.*; Electronic Frontier Foundation, "Bloggers' FAQ - Intellectual Property," online: www.eff.org/bloggers/lg/faq-ip.php.

65   Fitzgerald & Fitzgerald, above note 26 at 118; note that for the purposes of Part IX a "work" is defined to include "a literary work, a dramatic work, a musical work,

- the right of attribution of authorship;[66]
- the right not to have authorship falsely attributed;[67] and
- the right of integrity of authorship.[68]

The right of attribution of authorship involves the right to be identified as the author/creator of the work if any "attributable acts" are done in respect of the work. The second moral right provides the author/creator of the work the right not to have authorship of the work falsely attributed. The third moral right of integrity involves the right not to have the work subjected to derogatory treatment that would demean the author/creator's reputation.[69] It should also be noted that moral rights in respect of a work will only apply in relation to a substantial part of the work and, therefore, in instances where a substantial part has not been reproduced or communicated, infringement will not be an issue.[70]

In the case of blogs, the possibility for the infringement of moral rights will arise where bloggers reproduce or communicate an author/creator's copyrighted work on their blog. In particular, issues of infringement will arise where a blogger fails to attribute the author/creator of the work in question, where a blogger claims attribution in the work as if it were their own, and where a blogger subjects the work to derogatory treatment that could be interpreted to demean the author/creator's reputation, particularly where acts of remix are involved.[71]

D. DEFAMATION LAW

1) Uniform Defamation Acts

Given the nature of a blog—a highly personalized online journal—it is inevitable that they will encounter many challenging issues in regard to defamation law. It should be noted that significant changes have been made to all defamation laws across Australian states, largely in an attempt by the

---

an artistic work or a cinematograph film," but not sound recordings (*Copyright Act*, above note 24, s. 189).

66 *Copyright Act, ibid.*, s. 193.
67 *Ibid.*, s. 195AC.
68 *Ibid.*, s. 195AQ.
69 *Ibid.*, s. 195AQ.
70 *Ibid.*, s. 195AZH.
71 Damien O'Brien & Brian Fitzgerald, "Mashups, Remixes and Copyright Law" (2006) 9 Internet Law Bulletin 17.

Commonwealth attorney-general to establish a uniform defamation law.[72] This has resulted in largely standardized defamation laws being established throughout all Australian jurisdictions, instead of the single, proposed Commonwealth law.[73] However, the new defamation laws are accompanied by an intergovernmental agreement, which provides that all laws are to remain uniform and retain the common-law elements.[74]

The uniform state *Defamation Acts 2005* came into effect on 1 January 2006 in Queensland, New South Wales, Victoria, Tasmania, South Australia, and Western Australia.[75] These uniform Acts continue to make no distinction between libel and slander, and, interestingly, in some states and territories the Acts abolish the previous definition of the term "defamation."[76] Instead, a plaintiff will have an action for defamation where they can establish under the common law that the defendant published a defamatory matter about them.[77] Generally, under the common law a plaintiff will be able to establish a defamatory matter where it can be proved that the imputation satisfies one of the following three tests:

1) the imputation is likely to injure the reputation of the plaintiff by exposing them to ridicule, contempt, or hatred;[78]

---

72 Kevin Lynch, "Uniform Defamation Law: An Overview" (2006) 2 Privacy Law Bulletin 137 [Lynch].

73 See Australia, Commonwealth, Attorney-General's Department, *Revised Outline of a Possible National Defamation Law* (July 2004), online: www.ag.gov.au/www/agd/ rwpattach.nsf/VAP/(03995EABC73F94816C2AF4AA2645824B)-revised+defamation %5B1%5D.pdf/$file/revised+defamation%5B1%5D.pdf.

74 Lynch, above note 72 at 137.

75 Note the *Defamation Act 2006*, No. 8 of 2006 (N.T.) commenced on 26 April 2006, and the amendments to the *Civil Law (Wrongs) Act 2002*, No. 40 of 2002 (A.C.T.) commenced on 23 February 2006.

76 *Defamation Act 2005*, No. 55 of 2005 (Qld.), s. 7; *Defamation Act 2005*, No. 77 of 2005 (N.S.W.), s. 7; *Defamation Act 2005*, No. 75 of 2005 (Vic.), s. 7; *Defamation Act 2005*, No. 73 of 2005 (Tas.), s. 7; *Defamation Act 2005*, No. 50 of 2005 (S.A.), s. 7; *Defamation Act 2005*, No. 44 of 2005 (W.A.), s. 7; *Defamation Act 2006*, No. 8 of 2006 (N.T.), s. 6; *Civil Law (Wrongs) Act 2002*, No. 40 of 2002 (A.C.T.), s. 119; Amanda Stickley, "*Defamation Act 2005* (Qld): A Step Towards National Uniformity?" (2006) 26 Queensland Lawyer 192 [Stickley].

77 *Defamation Act 2005* (Qld.), s. 6; *Defamation Act 2005* (N.S.W.), s. 6; *Defamation Act 2005* (Vic.), s. 6; *Defamation Act 2005* (Tas.), s. 6; *Defamation Act 2005* (S.A.), s. 6; *Defamation Act 2005* (W.A.), s. 6; *Defamation Act 2006* (N.T.), s. 5; *Civil Law (Wrongs) Act 2002* (A.C.T.), s. 118; Frances McGlone & Amanda Stickley, *Australian Torts Law* (Chatswood, NSW: LexisNexis Butterworths, 2005) at 379 [McGlone & Stickley].

78 *Ettingshausen v. Australian Consolidated Press Ltd.* (1991), 23 N.S.W.L.R. 443 (S.C.).

2) the imputation is likely to make people shun or avoid them;[79] or

3) the imputation has the tendency to lower the plaintiff's reputation in the estimation of others.[80]

Finally, for an action of defamation to be established under the *Defamation Act 2005*, the plaintiff is required to show that the defamatory matter that refers to them was published in some way.[81] The previous definition of "publication" in some states and territories has been removed; however, it is suggested that it will retain the same meaning—the imputation must be published to someone other than the person who is defamed.[82] The uniform Acts do, however, define the term "matter" for the purposes of reference to a "defamatory matter," as including, from the perspective of blogs, a report or other thing communicated by means of the Internet.[83] Therefore, a defamatory matter will extend to comments or entries posted to a blog by virtue of the operation of this definition.

It is clear from the preceding discussion that defamatory comments or entries posted to a blog, which satisfy one of the three tests of imputation and are published to a third party, will give rise to an action for defamation in all states and territories throughout Australia. It should also be noted that there are a number of defences under both the uniform Acts and the common law that may provide a defence to defamatory comments posted to a blog. Some of the applicable defences that may be available to blog-

---

79   *Henry v. TVW Enterprises*, [1990] W.A.R. 475.

80   McGlone & Stickley, above note 77 at 380.

81   *Defamation Act 2005* (Qld.), s. 8; *Defamation Act 2005* (N.S.W.), s. 8; *Defamation Act 2005* (Vic.), s. 8; *Defamation Act 2005* (Tas.), s. 8; *Defamation Act 2005* (S.A.), s. 8; *Defamation Act 2005* (W.A.), s. 8; *Defamation Act 2006* (N.T.), s. 7; *Civil Law (Wrongs) Act 2002* (A.C.T.), s. 120; note that under these sections a person has only a single cause of action for the publication of a defamatory matter about the person, even though more than one defamatory imputation may exist.

82   McGlone & Stickley, above note 77 at 26; *Pullman v. Walter Hill & Co. Ltd.* [1891] 1 Q.B. 524.

83   *Defamation Act 2005* (Qld.), s. 4; *Defamation Act 2005* (N.S.W.), s. 4; *Defamation Act 2005* (Vic.), s. 4; *Defamation Act 2005* (Tas.), s. 4; *Defamation Act 2005* (S.A.), s. 4; *Defamation Act 2005* (W.A.), s. 4; *Defamation Act 2006* (N.T.), s. 3; *Civil Law (Wrongs) Act 2002* (A.C.T.), s. 116.

gers include justification,[84] contextual truth,[85] absolute privilege,[86] qualified privilege,[87] honest opinion,[88] innocent dissemination,[89] and triviality.[90]

2) Defamation Cases Involving Blogs

Despite the significant risks that defamation laws pose to blogs, so far there have been relatively few cases for defamation brought against blogs and bloggers.[91] In Australia there is very little judicial authority outlining how the courts will apply defamation law to blogs. However, there have been two related decisions (although not actions for defamation) in Australia

---

84 *Defamation Act 2005* (Qld.), s. 25; *Defamation Act 2005* (N.S.W.), s. 25; *Defamation Act 2005* (Vic.), s. 25; *Defamation Act 2005* (Tas.), s. 25; *Defamation Act 2005* (S.A.), s. 23; *Defamation Act 2005* (W.A.), s. 25; *Defamation Act 2006* (N.T.), s. 22; *Civil Law (Wrongs) Act 2002* (A.C.T.), s. 135.

85 *Defamation Act 2005* (Qld.), s. 26; *Defamation Act 2005* (N.S.W.), s. 26; *Defamation Act 2005* (Vic.), s. 26; *Defamation Act 2005* (Tas.), s. 26; *Defamation Act 2005* (S.A.), s. 24; *Defamation Act 2005* (W.A.), s. 26; *Defamation Act 2006* (N.T.), s. 23; *Civil Law (Wrongs) Act 2002* (A.C.T.), s. 136.

86 *Defamation Act 2005* (Qld.), s. 27; *Defamation Act 2005* (N.S.W.), s. 27; *Defamation Act 2005* (Vic.), s. 27; *Defamation Act 2005* (Tas.), s. 27; *Defamation Act 2005* (S.A.), s. 25; *Defamation Act 2005* (W.A.), s. 27; *Defamation Act 2006* (N.T.), s. 24; *Civil Law (Wrongs) Act 2002* (A.C.T.), s. 137.

87 *Defamation Act 2005* (Qld.), s. 30; *Defamation Act 2005* (N.S.W.), s. 30; *Defamation Act 2005* (Vic.), s. 30; *Defamation Act 2005* (Tas.), s. 30; *Defamation Act 2005* (S.A.), s. 28; *Defamation Act 2005* (W.A.), s. 30; *Defamation Act 2006* (N.T.), s. 27; *Civil Law (Wrongs) Act 2002* (A.C.T.), s. 139A.

88 *Defamation Act 2005* (Qld.), s. 31; *Defamation Act 2005* (N.S.W.), s. 31; *Defamation Act 2005* (Vic.), s. 31; *Defamation Act 2005* (Tas.), s. 31; *Defamation Act 2005* (S.A.), s. 29; *Defamation Act 2005* (W.A.), s. 31; *Defamation Act 2006* (N.T.), s. 28; *Civil Law (Wrongs) Act 2002* (A.C.T.), s. 139B.

89 *Defamation Act 2005* (Qld.), s. 32; *Defamation Act 2005* (N.S.W.), s. 32; *Defamation Act 2005* (Vic.), s. 32; *Defamation Act 2005* (Tas.), s. 32; *Defamation Act 2005* (S.A.), s. 30; *Defamation Act 2005* (W.A.), s. 32; *Defamation Act 2006* (N.T.), s. 29; *Civil Law (Wrongs) Act 2002* (A.C.T.), s. 139C.

90 *Defamation Act 2005* (Qld.), s. 33; *Defamation Act 2005* (N.S.W.), s. 33; *Defamation Act 2005* (Vic.), s. 33; *Defamation Act 2005* (Tas.), s. 33; *Defamation Act 2005* (S.A.), s. 31; *Defamation Act 2005* (W.A.), s. 33; *Defamation Act 2006* (N.T.), s. 30; *Civil Law (Wrongs) Act 2002* (A.C.T.), s. 139D.

91 Glenn Harlan Reynolds, "Libel in the Blogosphere: Some Preliminary Thoughts" (Paper presented to the Berkman Center for Internet and Society, Bloggership: How Blogs are Transforming Legal Scholarship Conference, 28 April 2006) [unpublished] [Reynolds].

that have examined the nature of defamatory comments posted to a blog. These two decisions confirm the principle that the courts will treat blogs in exactly the same manner as if the defamatory comments had been communicated in the non-digital, paper-based world.

The first case, *Kaplan v. Go Daddy Group & 2 Ors,*[92] involved an action for the tort of injurious falsehood. The second defendant in the case created a disparaging blog about the plaintiff, which encouraged other users to post derogatory comments about the plaintiff's business. The result was that six comments were posted to the blog, all of which contained defamatory comments about the plaintiff's business. The plaintiff subsequently brought an application to the court for an injunction to prevent the second defendant from maintaining the defamatory blog. In granting the injunction, White J. held that there was a serious question to be tried in that the second defendant had committed and threatened to commit the tort of injurious falsehood through the posting of defamatory comments about the plaintiff to his blog.[93]

In *Y & H,*[94] the Federal Magistrates Court considered the question of whether the respondent, a prominent blogger, should be restrained from publishing information about pending court proceedings in a family law matter. In granting the injunction to restrain the respondent from posting comments to her blog, Baumann F.M. held that it was in the child's best interests that the respondent-blogger be restrained from posting defamatory comments to her blog.[95]

In the US there have also been a number of cases that have considered the nature of defamatory comments posted to a blog. In one of the most notable, *John Doe No. 1 v. Cahill,*[96] a case considering whether an Internet service provider was required to disclose the identity of an anonymous blogger, the Supreme Court of Delaware considered the question of whether anonymous comments posted to a blog could amount to defamation.[97] In

---

92   Above note 9.

93   *Ibid.* at paras. 36–42.

94   Above note 8.

95   *Ibid.* at paras. 29–30; also see *Ray*, above note 10, concerning an action for contempt of court against the defendants for posting defamatory comments about the conduct of a liquidator to a blog.

96   884 A.2d 451 (Del. 2005), rev'g *Cahill v. Doe*, above note 7.

97   See "Court Outlines Standard for Unmasking Blogger of Criticism of Public Figure" (2005) 22(12) The Computer and Internet Lawyer 25; Sylvia Mercado-Kierkegaard, "Blogs, Lies and the Doocing: The Next Hotbed of Litigation?" (2006) 22 Computer L. and Sec. R. 127 at 130 [Mercado-Kierkegaard].

this case, the appellant had anonymously posted defamatory comments on a Delaware community blog, claiming that the appellant, a councilman, was unfit for office. At first instance, the Superior Court of Delaware, applying a "good-faith standard," held that Cahill had made out on a claim for defamation a good-faith basis.[98] However, on appeal the Supreme Court rejected the application of the good-faith standard, instead finding that the stricter "summary-judgment standard" applied, which requires a plaintiff to demonstrate sufficient evidence to establish a *prima facie* case for defamation.[99] Applying this summary-judgment standard, the Supreme Court held that in the context of a blog, no reasonable person could have interpreted the allegedly defamatory comments as being anything other than mere opinion.[100]

While the Supreme Court of Delaware expressly stated that it did not hold as a matter of law that comments posted to a blog could never be defamatory, interestingly, the Court did make some observations about the nature of defamation law and blogs.[101] First, the Supreme Court noted that a potential plaintiff in an action for defamation involving a blog has a powerful form of extra-judicial relief, in that they can respond instantly to the allegedly defamatory comments on the blog, thereby mitigating any harm the plaintiff might suffer.[102] However, this may not always be possible given that some blogs do not enable readers to leave comments and thereby respond to the allegedly defamatory comments. Furthermore, the fact that there are over 57 million blogs in multiple languages means that it is unlikely that a potential plaintiff would be aware of the allegedly defamatory comments at the time that they were made; thereby somewhat eroding the argument that a plaintiff, by responding to comments made on a blog, can mitigate the damage they might otherwise suffer.

Second, the Supreme Court stated that it is important to consider certain factual and contextual issues relevant to blogs when considering a defamation claim regarding comments posted to a blog.[103] Expanding on this, the court

---

98 *Cahill v. Doe*, above note 7 at 954–56.

99 *John Doe No. 1 v. Cahill*, above note 96 at 457–61; *McMann v. Doe* (18 January 2007), Maricopa County, Case No. CV 2006-092226 (Ariz. Super. Ct.).

100 *John Doe No. 1 v. Cahill*, *ibid.* at 466–68.

101 *Ibid.* at 467.

102 *Ibid.* at 464; Larry Ribstein, "From Bricks to Pajamas: The Law and Economics of Amateur Journalism" (2006) University of Illinois Law and Economics Research Paper No. LE06-008 at 40, online: http://papers.ssrn.com/sol3/papers.cfm?abstract_id=700961 [Ribstein].

103 *John Doe No. 1 v. Cahill*, *ibid.* at 465.

noted that, in terms of reliability, there is a spectrum of sources on the Internet, and blogs tend to be vehicles for the expression of opinion and not a source of facts or data upon which a reasonable person would rely.[104] The court stated:

> A reasonable person reading a newspaper in print or online can assume that the statements are factually based and researched. However, this is not the case when statements are posted on a blog. When viewing the allegedly defamatory statements on a blog in context—both the immediate context and the broader social context—it becomes apparent that many of the allegedly defamatory statements cannot be interpreted as stating actual facts, but instead are either subjective speculation or merely rhetorical hyperbole.[105]

While in many cases blogs act as nothing more than vehicles for the expression of personal opinions, there are, however, many blogs that could be classed as scholarly, authored by prominent academics and commentators, which might be just as reliable as *The New York Times*, for example. Furthermore, many organizations and media outlets now use blogs as a source to disseminate reliable information, facts, and news. It is therefore difficult to label blogs as simply vehicles for the expression of personal opinions that cannot constitute defamation.[106] It should also be noted, that it would seem

---

104 *Ibid.*; for the application of this argument in relation to Internet chat rooms and bulletin boards, see *Rocker Management LLC v. John Does 1 through 20, 2003 US Dist LEXIS 16277; Global Telemedia International Inc. v. Doe 1*, 132 F. Supp.2d 1261 (C.D. Cal. 2001); *SPX Corporation v. Doe*, 253 F. Supp.2d 974 (N.D. Ohio 2003).

105 *John Doe No. 1 v. Cahill*, above note 96 at 466.

106 Other related United States cases which have been filed involving defamatory comments posted to a blog include: California—*Holmes v. Ford*, No. BC221609 (2000), *Lake v. Ford*, No. SC059805 (2001), *Wald v. Ford*, No. SC086263 (2005); District of Columbia—*Steinbach v. Cutler*, Civil No. 05-00970 (2005); Florida—*Bell v. Shah*, Civil No. 06-21063 (2006), *Hunt v. Patten*, CA002857 (2006), *Johnson v. Tucker Max*, CA004867 (2003), *Lexington Homes Inc v. Siskind*, No. CA01018 (2006); Georgia—*Banks v. Milum* (2006), *Goodens v. Milum* (2005), *Fisher and Phillips LLP v. Doe*, Civil No. 05-01719 (2005); Illinois—*Emmanuel Welch v. Nyberg*, No. 2005L009751 (2005), *Bill Welch v. Nyberg*, No. 2005L009752 (2005); Maine—*The Gentle Wind Project v. Garvey*, Civil No. 04-103 (2006), *Warren Kremer Paino Advertising v. Duston*, Civil No. 06-047 (2006); Minnesota—*Olson v. Brodkorb* (2005); Mississippi—*Moore v. O'Bannon* (2006); Nevada—*Software Development and Investment of Nevada d/b/a Traffic-Power.com v. Wall*, Civil No. 05-1109 (Nevada 2006) [*Software Development*]; New Jersey—*Landmark Education LLC v. The Rick A. Ross Institute of New Jersey*, Civil No. 04-3022 (2005); New York—*Choy v. Boyne*, No. 115577/2005 (2006), *Citywide Sewer and Drain Service Corporation v. Carusone*, No.

somewhat unlikely that the reasoning in this decision would be applied and followed under Australian defamation law. However, it is worthwhile noting that, in this regard, the uniform *Defamation Acts* do provide for the non-litigious resolution of a defamation claim through the provision of an offer to make amends, although this does not entirely absolve liability.[107]

Although not strictly involving a blog, it is worth noting the recent UK decision in *Keith-Smith v. Williams*,[108] which dealt with defamatory comments posted to a Yahoo! bulletin board.[109] In this case, the English High Court awarded the plaintiff Keith-Smith £10,000 in damages against Williams, who had anonymously posted a number of defamatory comments to a Yahoo! bulletin board about Keith-Smith.[110] It would seem likely that courts in the UK would take a similar approach when considering defamatory comments posted to a blog.

E. INTERNET JURISDICTION

The decentralized, global nature of blogs and the blogosphere means that comments that are posted or uploaded to a blog in one jurisdiction will be

---

05-018160 (2005), *Penn Warranty Corporation v. DiGiovanni*, Index No. 600659/04 (2005), *Sollami v. Sheppard*, 21 A.D.3d 408 (N.Y. Sup. Ct. 2005); Ohio — *Ohio v. Baumgartner*, No. CR-05-470184-A (2005), *Ohio v. DuBois*, No. CR-05-470184-B (2005); Pennsylvania — *Deon v. McMonagle*, No. 2005-08774 (2005), *D'Alonzo v. Truscello*, WL1768091 (2006); Texas — *Cisneros v. Sanchez*, No. 2005-CCL-01024-A (2005), *R.L. Lackner Inc. v. Sanchez*, No. 2005-CCl-1032-C (2005); Utah — *Thalin v. Misbach* (2004); Virginia — *Council on American-Islamic Relations Inc. v. Whitehead*, No. CL04000926-00 (Va. Cir. Ct. 2006), *Hargrave Military Academy v. Guyles*, Civil No. 06-00283 (2006); Wisconsin — *Miranda v. Sykes* (2005). Also see Laura Parker, "Jury awards $11.3M over Defamatory Internet Posts" (10 October 2006), online: www.usatoday.com/news/nation/2006-10-10-internet-defamation-case_x.htm; Laura Parker, "Courts Are Asked to Crack Down on Bloggers, Websites" (2 October 2006), online: www.usatoday.com/tech/news/2006-10-02-bloggers-courts_x.htm.

107 *Defamation Act 2005* (Qld.), ss. 12–19; *Defamation Act 2005* (N.S.W.), ss. 12–19; *Defamation Act 2005* (Vic.), ss. 12–19; *Defamation Act 2005* (Tas.), ss. 12–19; *Defamation Act 2005* (S.A.), ss. 12–19; *Defamation Act 2005* (W.A.), ss. 12–19; *Defamation Act 2005* (N.T.), ss. 11–18; *Civil Law (Wrongs) Act 2002* (A.C.T.), ss. 124–31.

108 [2006] EWHC 860 (Q.B.).

109 See also *Lewis v. King*, [2004] EWCA Civ 1329 [*Lewis*]; *Bunt v. Tilley*, [2006] EWHC 407 (Q.B.).

110 See Catherine Bond, "Can I Sue Google If It Says I'm Gay? The Tales of Internet Defamation in the UK" (2006) 64 Computer and Law 1 at 5 [*Bond*]; Jennifer McDermott, "UK Defamation Law Update" (2006) 11 Media and Arts Law Review 212 at 218.

accessible instantaneously in not only that jurisdiction, but in every other jurisdiction where the blog is capable of being comprehended. In particular, bloggers need to be mindful of the law pertaining to Internet jurisdiction in relation to defamation because a potentially defamatory comment that is posted or uploaded to a blog will be capable of being viewed across jurisdictions. This transnational nature of the blogosphere fundamentally challenges the traditional concept that a nation state is able to exercise sovereignty over citizens within a defined territory.[111] One view is that jurisdiction in the blogosphere will be established in every state where the blog is accessible. Another view is that jurisdiction will only be established where there is some proximate connection or relationship between a state and the blog.

However, the decision of the High Court in *Dow Jones & Co. Inc. v. Gutnick*[112] suggests that under Australian law, Internet jurisdiction—at least in relation to defamation—will be established on the basis of where the content is downloaded or comprehended. In this case, content that was produced in New York, uploaded to a server in New Jersey, and then made available on the Internet for access in Victoria, was held to be actionable in the courts of Victoria.[113] In considering the three key issues of whether jurisdiction could be established, whether Victorian law applied, and whether Victoria was a clearly inappropriate forum, the High Court essentially dispensed with all three issues by holding that "publication" for the purposes of defamation occurred where the defamatory material was comprehended.[114]

Although *Gutnick*[115] suggests that Internet jurisdiction may be established on a broad basis of where the content is downloaded or comprehended, this approach is not universal. Indeed, only days later a US court came to the opposite conclusion on similar facts, holding that unless the website containing the defamatory statement was targeted towards the forum state, jurisdiction could not be established.[116] However, generally,

111   Brian Fitzgerald *et al.*, *Jurisdiction and the Internet* (Pyrmont, NSW: Law Book Co., 2004) at 101 [Fitzgerald *et al.*]; Brian Fitzgerald, "*Dow Jones & Co. Inc. v. Gutnick*: Negotiating 'American Legal Hegemony' in the Transnational World of Cyberspace" (2003) 27 Melbourne U.L. Rev. 590 at 596.

112   [2002] HCA 56, 210 C.L.R. 575 [*Gutnick*].

113   Fitzgerald *et al.*, above note 111 at 120–21.

114   *Ibid.* at 121; *Gutnick*, above note 112 at 582.

115   *Gutnick*, *ibid.*

116   *Young v. New Haven Advocate*, 315 F.3d 256 (4th Cir. 2002) [*Young*]. See also *Griffis v. Luban*, 646 N.W.2d 527 (Minn. 2002); *Yahoo! Inc. v. La Ligue Contre le Racisme et l'Antisémitisme*, 379 F.3d 1120 (9th Cir. 2004).

from the decided cases in the US, there have been two approaches to Internet jurisdiction that have emerged:

- the *Zippo Manufacturing v. Zippo.com*[117] sliding scale approach; and
- the *Calder v. Jones*[118] "effects" and "targeting" approach.

In *Zippo*,[119] the court held that a finding of jurisdiction was contingent upon the nature of the website and sought to employ a sliding scale test.[120] A fully interactive website would establish jurisdiction, while a passive website used for mere advertising would not. In principle, in order to establish jurisdiction, the website would have to reach out and touch the forum in question. The *Calder*[121] "effects" and "targeting" test has also been applied in relation to Internet jurisdiction.[122] Under this approach, in essence where an act is done intentionally that has an effect within the forum state and is directed or targeted at the forum state, jurisdiction will be established.[123]

The issue of Internet jurisdiction was also recently considered in the Canadian decision of *Bangoura v. Washington Post*,[124] where allegedly defamatory articles were published about the plaintiff and subsequently made available on *The Washington Post*'s website. In considering whether the courts of Ontario should assume jurisdiction, the Court of Appeal for Ontario held that there was no real or substantial connection between the action and Ontario, as the plaintiff was not a resident of Ontario when the articles were originally published, thus jurisdiction could not be established.[125]

In the UK there have also been a number of recent cases involving the issue of Internet jurisdiction. In *Harrods Ltd. v. Dow Jones & Company Inc.*,[126] the English High Court held that England was the appropriate

---

117   952 F. Supp. 1119 (W.D. Pa. 1997) [*Zippo*].
118   465 U.S. 783 (1984) [*Calder*].
119   Above note 117.
120   Fitzgerald *et al.*, above note 111 at 107–10.
121   *Calder*, above note 118.
122   Fitzgerald *et al.*, above note 111 at 107–16.
123   *Metro-Goldwyn-Mayer Studios Inc. v. Grokster Limited*, 243 F. Supp.2d 1073 (C.D. Cal. 2003); *Metro-Goldwyn-Mayer Studios Inc. v. Grokster Limited*, 545 U.S. 913 (2005) [*Grokster*, 2005]; *Young*, above note 116; compare *Pavlovich v. DVD Copy Control Association*, 29 Cal.4th 262 (Sup. Ct. Cal. 2002).
124   2005 CanLII 32906 (Ont. C.A.).
125   *Ibid.* at paras. 21–23 and 46; for an analysis of the approaches relating to publication on the Internet in Canada, see paras. 47–49. See also *Bangoura v. Washington Post*, 2006 CanLII 4742 (S.C.C.).
126   [2003] EWHC 1162 (Q.B.) [*Harrods*].

forum for a defamation action against Dow Jones concerning an allegedly defamatory article published on the online edition of *The Wall Street Journal*.[127] In deciding this, the court held that English law does not recognize a single-publication doctrine, thus under English law there may be separate publications in other jurisdictions that are sufficient to found a separate cause of action.[128]

However, more recently, in *Dow Jones & Company Inc. v. Yousef Jameel*,[129] the English Court of Appeal refused to allow a Saudi businessman's defamation action in the UK against Dow Jones. In this case, an article published on the online edition of *The Wall Street Journal* incorrectly alleged that the respondent had been involved with Al Qaeda and Osama bin Laden.[130] The respondent subsequently commenced proceedings for libel in the English High Court. However, on appeal, the Court of Appeal dismissed the respondent's action on the basis that the article had only been viewed by five individuals within the English jurisdiction and thus the respondent had suffered only minimal damage to his reputation.[131]

The landmark Australian High Court decision in *Gutnick*[132] is of particular significance for blogs and the blogosphere, as it is the authority for the principle that defamatory comments published on the Internet will be actionable in not only the jurisdiction where they are uploaded, but in every other jurisdiction where they are able to be downloaded and comprehended. It is likely that in Australia a similar approach would be taken by a court in regard to issues of Internet jurisdiction concerning defamatory comments posted to a blog.[133]

---

127 Bond, above note 110 at 1; *Fitzgerald et al.*, above note 111 at 133.

128 Above note 126 at paras. 36–38; also see *Lewis*, above note 109.

129 [2005] EWCA Civ 75 [*Yousef Jameel*].

130 Jennifer McDermott, "UK Defamation Law Update" (2005) 10 Media and Arts Law Review 161 at 167; *Bond*, above note 110 at 1; Kylie Howard & Yee Fen Lim, "Defamation and the Internet One More Time: *Dow Jones & Co. v. Yousef Abdul Latif Jameel*" (2005) 8 Internet Law Bulletin 21.

131 *Yousef Jameel*, above note 129 at paras.69–71 and 74–77.

132 *Gutnick*, above note 112.

133 For example, in regard to Internet jurisdiction in relation to authorization of copyright infringement, see Jane Ginsburg & Sam Ricketson, "Inducers and Authorisers: A Comparison of the US Supreme Court's *Grokster* Decision and the Australian Federal Court's *KaZaa* Ruling" (2006) 11 Media and Arts Law Review 1 at 23–24 [Ginsburg & Ricketson]; *Cooper v. Universal Music Australia Pty. Ltd.*, [2006] FCAFC 187 at paras. 10–12 [*Cooper v. Universal*].

F. EMPLOYEE BLOGS

1) Employment Contracts

One of the most contentious legal issues in the blogosphere at the moment is employee blogs. Employee blogs are those blogs in which the author either predominantly or implicitly makes reference to their employment or employer in some way.[134] In this regard, it becomes particularly important to ascertain whether an employee's contract of employment will permit them to post comments about their employment and other work-related matters to their personal blog. As such, bloggers need to be aware of any blogging-specific polices in the terms and conditions of their contract of employment, which may enable an employer to terminate their employment.[135] Most commonly, a company's information technology policy will prohibit employees from using computer equipment for personal use.[136] However, it becomes less clear where an employee posts comments to a blog away from the workplace.[137] In this regard, there have been a number of high profile cases where employees have been dismissed for blogging.[138] A well-known example of this was Ellen Simonetti, a Delta Airlines stewardess whose employment was terminated for posting images of herself in uniform onto her blog, despite never mentioning her employer, Delta Airlines.[139]

As a result of this case and many other similar cases, many employers now incorporate a blogging-specific policy into the existing terms and conditions of employment. In this regard, it is common for such policies to prohibit employees from blogging about work-related matters or refer-

---

134 Ken Ebanks "Into the Blogosphere: Managing the Risks and Rewards of Employee Blogging" (2005) 22 The Computer and Internet Lawyer 1 [Ebanks].

135 Judy Skatssoon, "Blogging May Get You the Sack" (3 May 2006), online: www.abc. net.au/science/news/stories/s1627903.htm.

136 Ebanks, above note 134 at 2.

137 *Ibid.* at 2–3.

138 Laura Smith-Spark, "How To Blog—And Keep Your Job" (20 July 2006), online: http://news.bbc.co.uk/2/hi/europe/5195714.stm; Mercado-Kierkegaard, above note 97 at 132–33; A US soldier was demoted and fined for posting comments to his blog criticizing the war in Iraq in *United States v. Clark* (U.S. Army Ct. Martial 2005).

139 See the stewardess' blog, online: http://blogs.myspace.com/index. cfm?fuseaction=blog.ListAll&friendID=77318790. A British-based French blogger has also filed a workers tribunal claim after she was dismissed from international accounting firm Dixon Wilson for comments posted to her blog. See Angela Donald, "Blogger in France Sues after Being Fired" (20 July 2006), online: www.usatoday. com/tech/news/2006-07-20-france-blogger_x.htm.

ring to a company's name. However, it becomes more contentious where a blogging policy contains an outright prohibition on all blogging, including personal blogging in an employee's own time. These responses, which may be perceived as harsh, are a result of growing fears among employers about what an employee may disclose on their blog, either intentionally or inadvertently, as even the most inconspicuous of comments may be potentially damaging for an employer.

Employers also need to be mindful of the fact that they could be found vicariously liable for employee blogs where the employer provides the means to blog or where an employee's blog is perceived as being endorsed by their employer.[140] In the context of employee blogs, employers need to clearly establish whether or not the employee is authorized to blog on behalf of the employer. The effect of such authorization will be that the employer will be held vicariously liable for any damage caused by the employee's blog. Generally, in cases where an employee is permitted to blog, the employer will ensure that the employee's blog contains a disclaimer that makes clear that the blog is a personal blog and does not represent the views of the employer.

It should also be noted that some states in the US have legislation that prevents employers from terminating employees for engaging in lawful activities outside of the workplace. For example sections 96(k) and 98.6 of the *California Labor Code*[141] prohibit employers from terminating employees for "lawful conduct during non-working hours away from the employer's premises."[142] In this regard, it has been suggested that these sections may be invoked by an employee who is dismissed for blogging during their own time outside of the workplace.[143]

2) Confidential Information and Trade Secrets

In relation to employee blogs, bloggers will also need to ensure that they do not breach any duty of confidentiality by disclosing confidential infor-

---

140 Ebanks, above note 134 at 2; see, generally, *Broom v. Morgan* (1953), 1 Q.B. 597 (C.A.); *Darling Island Stevedoring & Lighterage Co. Ltd. v. Long* (1957), 97 C.L.R. 36.

141 Cal. Lab. §§ 96(k) and 98.6 (West Supp. 2006), online: www.leginfo.ca.gov/cgi-bin/calawquery?codesection=lab&codebody=.

142 Stacey Leyton, "Bloggers' FAQ: Labor Law" (2006), online: www.eff.org/bloggers/lg/faq-labor.php [Leyton]; *Grinzi v. San Diego Hospice Corporation*, 120 Cal. App.4th 72 at 86–88 (2004); *Barbee v. Household Automotive Finance Corporation*, 113 Cal. App.4th 525 at 534–36 (2003). Also see *Konop v. Hawaiian Airlines Inc.*, 302 F.3d 868 (9th Cir. 2002).

143 Leyton, *ibid.*

mation or trade secrets. Generally, a duty of confidentiality will be formed whenever one party imparts to another party either private or secret matters with the express or implied intention that the communication is for a restricted purpose.[144] In such circumstances, the person to whom the information has been communicated to (the confidant) will be restrained in equity from making any unauthorized use of the information.[145]

Therefore, bloggers need to ensure that where confidential information has been imparted to them in circumstances where an obligation of confidence exists, or they are under a contractual obligation, the information remains confidential and is therefore not posted to a blog. Bloggers also need to be cautious about either deliberately or inadvertently posting comments to their blog that have the effect of exposing trade secrets.[146] In this regard, there have been a number of cases brought against bloggers in the US for disclosing confidential information and trade secrets on their blogs.[147]

G. INTERMEDIARY LIABILITY OF BLOGS

Issues involving Intermediary liability of blogs, particularly in regard to copyright infringement and defamation, will also need to be considered from the perspective of blog-providers or online service providers who host blogs.

1) Copyright Infringement

The most common issue which will arise in relation to intermediary liability of blogs will be in regard to copyright infringement—in particular, whether blog providers can be held liable for authorizing copyright infringement. The premise behind intermediary liability for copyright infringement was

---

144 Gino Dal Pont & Tina Cockburn, *Equity and Trusts in Principle* (Pyrmont, NSW: Law BookCo., 2005) at 74.

145 *Ibid.*

146 Mercado-Kierkegaard, above note 97 at 133.

147 *Apple Computer Inc. v. DePlume*, No. 05-CV-33341 (Cal. Super. Santa Clara County filed Jan. 4, 2005); *Apple Computer Inc. v. Doe*, No. 1-04-CV-032178 (Cal. Super. Santa Clara County Mar. 11, 2005); *The Permanente Medical Group Inc. v. Cooper*, No. RG05-203029 (Cal. Super. Alameda County 2005); *Software Development*, above note 106; *NXIVM N.D.N.Y.*, above note 52; *NXIVM 2nd Cir.*, above note 52; *NXIVM U.S.S.C.*, above note 52. For a recent example, see the action brought by Target against a blogger for posting Target's anti-theft procedures to a blog, *Target Corp. v. Doe* (6 February 2007), Atlanta, Complaint No. 1:06-CV-2116 (Dist. Ct.).

identified by the US Supreme Court in *Grokster* 2005[148] where it held that where a widely distributed service is used to commit copyright infringement, it may be impossible to enforce rights against all direct infringers, so the only practical alternative is to pursue the distributors or hosts for intermediary liability.

Under the *Copyright Act*, a person or organization that authorizes another person to do an infringing act, without the licence of the owner, will themselves infringe copyright.[149] In determining whether a person or organization has authorized the doing of an act that infringes copyright, it is necessary to consider:

(a) the extent (if any) of the person's power to prevent the doing of the act concerned;

(b) the nature of any relationship existing between the person and the person who did the act concerned; and

(c) whether the person took any other reasonable steps to prevent or avoid the doing of the act, including whether the person complied with any relevant industry codes of practice.[150]

It should be noted that, in this regard, the reference to "(if any)" in subparagraph (a) tends to suggest that liability for the authorization of copyright infringement may be established, even if the blog provider has no power to prevent the infringement, or where they deliberately put themselves in a position where they are powerless to prevent the infringement.[151] Furthermore, the reference in subparagraph (b) to the "nature of the relationship" between the authorizer (blog provider) and the user (blogger) has important implications in the online environment. In the traditional relationship of vendor-purchaser, the relationship has a distinct end. However, from the perspective of blog providers and bloggers, the relationship is most likely to be one of a continuing nature.[152]

---

148   *Grokster, 2005,* above note 123 at 930; also see *In re Aimster Copyright Litigation,* 334 F.3d 643 at 645-646 (7th Cir. 2003) [*Aimster*]; Mark Radcliffe, "Grokster: The New Law of Third Party Liability for Copyright Infringement under United States Law" (2006) 22 Computer L. & Sec. R. 137 at 144.

149   Above note 24, s. 101(1).

150   *Ibid.,* ss. 36(1A) and 101(1A); *University of New South Wales v. Moorhouse,* [1975] HCA 26, 133 C.L.R. 1.

151   Ginsburg & Ricketson, above note 133 at 13–14.

152   *Ibid.* For example, blog providers provide their customers, bloggers, with ongoing technical, administrative, and other support and services which do not cease until the blogger ends his relationship with the blog provider.

However, in order to protect the position of intermediaries, such as carriage service providers (CSPs), a defence to authorization liability was introduced under sections 39B and 112E of the *Copyright Act*. This defence provides that a person, including CSPs, will not be held to have authorized copyright infringement merely because the facilities provided by them for making a communication are used by someone else to infringe copyright.[153] The effect of this defence was first considered in *Universal Music Australia Pty. Ltd. v. Cooper*[154]. The Federal Court held that section 112E did not apply, as Cooper had done more than simply provide the facilities for the making of communications by encouraging users to download infringing music files.[155] Similarly, in *Universal Music Pty. Ltd. v. Sharman Licence Holdings*,[156] the Federal Court held that the defence under section 112E did not apply to the defendants, as they had committed positive acts designed to encourage copyright infringement.[157]

There remains little judicial guidance on the interpretation of sections 39B and 112E of the *Copyright Act*. However, from the decided cases it would appear that where the person or organization is intimately involved with the infringing content, then the defence to authorization liability will not apply. For example, in *Universal Music Pty. Ltd. v. Sharman Licence Holdings*, Wilcox J. held that something more is required to be held liable for authorization than simply providing the facilities for someone else to infringe copyright.[158] Notably, Wilcox J. held that the legislative intention of section 112E was to "protect the messenger," that is, CSPs and Internet service providers (ISPs).[159]

The critical question for blog providers will be, first, whether they will be held liable for authorizing copyright infringement for the infringing acts of bloggers, and second, whether they will be entitled to the defence to authorization of copyright infringement. In this regard, it should be noted that this is a very uncertain area of copyright law, with there being no clear precedent. However, it is suggested that blog providers would be more likely than other online service providers, such as YouTube and peer-to-peer file-sharing services, in, first, avoiding liability for authorization of copyright

---

153   Above note 24, ss. 39B and 112E; note this also applies to moral rights under s. 195AVB.

154   *Universal v. Cooper*, above note 36.

155   *Ibid.* at paras. 97–99; aff'd *Cooper v. Universal*, above note 133.

156   *Universal v. Sharman*, above note 36.

157   *Ibid.* at para. 405.

158   *Ibid.* at para. 401.

159   *Ibid.* at para. 418.

infringement, and, second, successfully invoking the defence to authorization liability.

However, if blog providers were to be held liable for authorizing copyright infringement and the defence to authorization liability were to be denied, it is then necessary to consider the safe harbour provisions under the *Copyright Act*. As a result of the *US Free Trade Agreement Implementation Act 2004*,[160] a number of changes have been made to the *Copyright Act* concerning the liability of CSPs for the infringement of copyright.[161] These new provisions are an attempt to bring Australian copyright law in line with the "safe harbour provisions" in the US under the *Digital Millennium Copyright Act 1998*.[162] Notably, these provisions do not provide a complete defence for CSPs for copyright infringement; instead, they act to mitigate liability by limiting the remedies available against CSPs for copyright infringement in certain circumstances.

There are four categories of online activities outlined in sections 116AC to 116AF that will qualify for a limitation of remedies for the authorization of copyright infringement under the *Copyright Act*. In the case of blog providers, they will most likely fall within the category C activity under section 116AE, which refers to the storing of copyrighted material at the discretion of the user on a system or network operated by or for the CSP. Under this category, in order for a CSP to qualify for the limitation of remedies they must comply with each of the conditions outlined in section 116AH of the *Copyright Act*, including: adopting and implementing a policy to terminate the accounts of repeat infringers; complying with relevant industry codes; avoiding receipt of a financial benefit that is directly attributable to the infringing activity where they have the right and ability to control the activity; and expeditiously removing or disabling access to infringing material they are hosting when they become aware of it, or facts that make it apparent that the material is infringing.

Again, the key question to be determined in considering whether blog providers will be entitled to the limitation of remedies under the safe harbour provisions will be whether blog providers fall within the definition of a CSP. Under section 87 of the *Telecommunications Act 1997*,[163] a CSP is defined narrowly as a person supplying a carriage service to the public using a network. It would seem unlikely that blog providers would fall within this

---

160   *US Free Trade Agreement Implementation Act 2004* (Cth).
161   Above note 24, s. 116AA.
162   *Digital Millennium Copyright Act of 1998*, Pub. L. No. 105-34 [*DMCA*].
163   *Telecommunications Act 1997* (Cth.).

definition, as they do not *per se* supply a carriage service to the public, unlike ISPs or CSPs. Blog providers do not provide Internet access or any other carriage services, but simply provide the facilities and services to host blogs. Therefore, blog providers are unlikely to be classified as a CSP and, thus, will not be entitled to the benefit of the safe harbour provisions under the *Copyright Act*. However, it is hoped that as a result of the attorney-general's review of the application of the safe harbour provisions, that the definition of a CSP will be extended to cover new user-generated intermediaries that extend beyond the traditional definition of a CSP.[164]

It should be noted that under the equivalent safe harbour provision in section 512(c) of the *DMCA*[165] in the US, blog providers will most probably be entitled to the protection of the safe harbour provisions, provided that they comply with the necessary pre-conditions.[166] This provision in the US has a somewhat broader operation, due to the fact that it applies to not only service providers, but also to online service providers. An online service provider is defined broadly under section 512(k)(1)(b) of the *DMCA* as a provider of online services or network access, or the operator of facilities therefore. This broad definition will therefore include virtually every online service, including blog providers.[167] The courts have also endorsed the expansive nature of the definition of an online service provider, holding that peer-to-peer file-sharing services, Amazon, and eBay all fall within the definition of an online service provider.[168] Indeed, in *Re Aimster Copyright Litigation,*[169] the US District Court for the Northern District of Illinois held that the term "online service provider" "is defined so broadly that we have trouble imagining the existence of an online service that would not fall under the definitions . . . ."

---

164   See, for example, O'Brien & Fitzgerald, "Digital Copyright Law," above note 22 at 72–73.

165   Above note 162.

166   Malik, above note 63 at 439, 486–92, and 503–8.

167   Fred von Lohmann, "*DMCA* 'Safe Harbors' for Online Service Providers" (2006) 237 InfoSys 1 at 3.

168   *Corbis v. Amazon.com,* 351 F. Supp.2d 1090 (W.D. Wash. 2004) [*Corbis*]; *Hendrickson v. Amazon.com,* 298 F. Supp.2d 914 at 915 (C.D. Cal. 2003) [*Hendrickson*]; *Re Aimster Copyright Litigation,* 252 F. Supp.2d 634 (N.D. Ill. 2002); *Aimster,* above note 148; *Hendrickson v. eBay Inc.,* 165 F. Supp.2d 1082 at 1087 (C.D. Cal. 2001) [*eBay*].

169   *Re Aimster Copyright Litigation, ibid.* at 658.

2) Defamation

In regard to defamation, blog providers and individual bloggers who enable comments to be posted to their blogs need to be aware that they may be held liable for authorizing defamatory comments which are posted to the blogs that they host.[170] However, under both the common law, and state and territory uniform Defamation Acts, blog providers may be able to rely upon the defence of innocent dissemination.

The defence of innocent dissemination applies where an intermediary publishes a defamatory statement made by a person who uses that intermediary's facilities or services to publish the statement.[171] In particular, the defence of innocent dissemination provides that a person will not be the primary distributor merely because they were involved in the publication of the matter in the capacity of a service provider. The question again will be whether blog providers fall within the ambit of a "provider of services." It is suggested, however, that this provision is intended to have a broader operation, and thus will include not only ISPs and CSPs, but also providers of other Internet and online services, such as blog providers.[172] Therefore, blog providers will most likely be entitled to the statutory defence of innocent dissemination under the relevant state and territory uniform *Defamation Acts*, provided that they can establish the necessary statutory elements.

In Australia there is yet to be a major decided case involving the liability of Internet intermediaries for authorizing the publication of defamatory comments.[173] It should also be noted that the common law defence of innocent dissemination may have some application for blog providers and

---

170 See, generally, Michael Geist, "Free Speech, Libel and the Internet Age" (31 July 2006), online: http://news.bbc.co.uk/go/pr/fr/-/2/hi/technology/5230776.stm.

171 For the statutory elements of innocent dissemination, see *Defamation Act 2005* (Qld.), s. 32; *Defamation Act 2005* (N.S.W.), s. 32; *Defamation Act 2005* (Vic.), s. 32; *Defamation Act 2005* (Tas.), s. 32; *Defamation Act 2005* (S.A.), s. 30; *Defamation Act 2005* (W.A.), s. 32; *Defamation Act 2006* (N.T.), s. 29; *Civil Law (Wrongs) Act 2002* (A.C.T.), s. 139C.

172 *Defamation Act 2005* (Qld.), s. 32; *Defamation Act 2005* (N.S.W.), s. 32; *Defamation Act 2005* (Vic.), s. 32; *Defamation Act 2005* (Tas.), s. 32; *Defamation Act 2005* (S.A.), s. 30; *Defamation Act 2005* (W.A.), s. 32; *Defamation Act 2006* (N.T.), s. 29; *Civil Law (Wrongs) Act 2002* (A.C.T.), s. 139C.; Stickley, above note 76 at 194; also see the Explanatory Notes to the *Defamation Bill 2005* (Qld.), cl. 32 at 20, which gives the example that a provider of an internet email service will generally not be a primary distributor.

173 For a discussion of this issue, see *Bristile Ltd. v. The Buddhist Society of Western Australia Inc. & Anor*, [1999] WASC 259; *Kaplan*, above note 9.

bloggers. However, the operation of this defence remains uncertain and is arguably somewhat narrower than the statutory provisions.[174]

In the US, section 230(c)(1) of the *Communications Decency Act 1996*[175] states that "no provider or user of an interactive computer service shall be treated as the publisher or speaker of any information provided by another information content provider."[176] The term "interactive computer service" is defined broadly under section 230(f)(2) as including "any information service, system, or access software provider that provides or enables computer access ... to a computer server, including specifically a service or system that provides access to the Internet . . . ."[177] The crucial question in this regard will be whether blog providers and bloggers will fall within the definition of an "interactive computer service" and will thus be entitled to the protection under the so-called "good Samaritan provisions." It has been suggested that these provisions will apply to blogs. Thus, blog providers and bloggers will be immunized from liability for defamation in the US under the *Communications Decency Act 1996*, where defamatory comments are uploaded by either bloggers, in the case of blog providers, or contributors, in the case of bloggers.[178]

---

174 Richard Potter, "Flamers, Trolls and Bloggers—Are ISPs and Webhosts at Risk from Online Anarchy?" (2004) 57 Computers and the Law 6 at 7–8; *Thompson v. Australian Capital Television Pty. Ltd.*, [1996] HCA 38, 186 C.L.R. 574; also see *Broadcasting Services Act 1992* (Cth.), s. 91(1). For the position in the UK, see *Defamation Act 1996* (U.K.), s. 1; *Electronic Commerce (EC Directive) Regulations 2002*, S.I. 2002/2013, rr. 17–19; *Godfrey v. Demon Internet Limited*, [1999] 4 All E.R. 342 (Q.B.); *Bunt v. Tilley & Ors*, [2006] EWHC 407 (Q.B.); Law Commission, "Defamation and the Internet: A Preliminary Investigation" Scoping Study No. 2 (2002), online: www.lawcom.gov.uk/docs/defamation2.pdf; Bond, above note 110 at 3–5.

175 *The Telecommunications Act of 1996*, Pub. L. No. 104-104 §§ 501–561, 110 Stat. 56 [*CDA*].

176 *Ibid.*, § 230(c)(1); *Zeran v. America Online Inc.*, 129 F.3d 327 (4th Cir. 1997).

177 *CDA*, above note 175; see also the definition of an "information content provider" under § 230(f)(3.)

178 Reynolds, above note 91 at 3–4; Electronic Frontier Foundation, "Bloggers' FAQ: Section 230 Protections" (2006), online: www.eff.org/bloggers/lg/faq-230.php; Ribstein, above note 102 at 43–44; Mercado-Kierkegaard, above note 97 at 134–35; *Barrett v. Rosenthal*, 40 Cal.4th 33 (Sup. Ct. 2006); *CLC v. Craigslist* (1 November 2006), Illinois 1:06-CV-00657 (N.D. Ill. Dist. Ct.); *Carafano v. Metrosplash.com*, 339 F.3d 1119 (9th Cir. 2003); *Batzel v. Smith*, 333 F.3d 1018 (9th Cir. 2003); *Ben Ezra, Weinstein & Co. v. American Online*, 206 F.3d 980 (10th Cir. 2000); *Optinrealbig. com LLC v. Ironport Systems Inc.*, 323 F. Supp. 2d 1037 (N.D. Cal. 2004); *Gentry v. eBay Inc.*, 99 Cal. App.4th 816 (App. Ct. 2002); *Schneider v. Amazon.com Inc.*, 31 P.3d 37 (Wash. App. Ct.); *Perfect 10 Inc. v. CCBill LLC*, 340 F. Supp.2d 1077 (C.D.

H. CONCLUSION

Blogs, bloggers, blog providers, and the blogosphere in general, will be fundamentally challenged by the application of traditional legal doctrines, which remain firmly embedded in the non-digital world. In particular, copyright law, defamation law, Internet jurisdiction, employment law, and the law of authorization for intermediaries will all prove to be a significant impediment to the functioning of the blogosphere. The many challenges that these areas of the law will have on the blogosphere have, to a small degree, already been experienced, with an increase in actions filed against bloggers, specifically for defamation. It is expected that the amount of litigation in the courts involving blogs will increase dramatically, as blogs become a mainstream form of online communication. While it will be interesting to witness the application of these legal doctrines to the blogosphere over the next few years, the law, and in particular the judiciary, should embrace the potential of blogs in a proactive manner and not apply these laws counterproductively so as to stifle the very great potential of the blogosphere. The evolution of this new chapter in online communication has placed content production firmly in the hands of billions of people throughout the world. Blogs and the blogosphere have in many ways democratized the mainstream media, by providing the impetus for an extremely powerful form of social and political expression, which the law should not unduly restrict.

Cal. 2004); *Donato v. Moldow*, 865 A.2d 711 (N.J. Super. Ct. App. Div. 2005); *Grace v. eBay Inc.*, 16 Cal. Rptr.3d 192 (App. Ct. 2004); *Barrett v. Fonorow*, 343 Ill. App.3d 1184 (App. Ct. 2003). For the application of the *Communications Decency Act 1996* to Wikipedia see Ken Myers, "Wikimmunity: Fitting the *Communications Decency Act* to Wikipedia" (2006) 20 Harv. J.L. & Tech. 163. Also note there are a number of other legal issues which may arise in relation to blogs and the law. These include privacy issues. For example, see Electronic Frontier Foundation, mentioned previously in this note; Bruce Johnson, "*Steinbuch v. Cutler*: When is a Personal Blog Considered Publicity?" (29 March 2006), online: www.privsecblog.com/archives/blogging-steinbuch-v-cutler-when-is-a-personal-blog-considered-publicity.html. There are also sedition issues. For example, see Samtani Anil, "Singapore Media Law Update" (2006) 11(1) Media and Arts Law Review 75 at 81–82; Edmund Tadros, "Australian Bloggers Muzzled" (7 December 2005), online: http://blogs.smh.com.au/entertainment/archives//002970.html.

CHAPTER 9

The School Girl, the Billboard, and Virgin: The Virgin Mobile Case and the Use of Creative Commons Licensed Photographs by Commercial Entities

Emma Carroll & Jessica Coates

A. INTRODUCTION

It's Friday afternoon. That one drink at lunch turned into more than a couple, resulting in an emergency nap under your desk back at the office. The boss need never know. But unfortunately it's 2007: the digital age. Someone in the office that day had a camera, and unbeknownst to you that photograph of you snoring under the computer was posted on the Internet. All in good fun, right? But what if the photographer who decided to post the embarrassing photograph online did so under a Creative Commons licence that allows commercial reuse and the image is subsequently plucked off the Internet for use in a nationwide advertising campaign?

This is exactly what happened in June 2007 when billboards were put up across Australia displaying Creative Commons licensed photographs from the Yahoo! Flickr[1] website as part of an advertising campaign for the Australian-based corporation Virgin Mobile.[2] The result saw a lawsuit brought against the international corporation, by both the photographer

---

1   Online: www.flickr.com.
2   See Jude Townend, "Virgin Backs Down on Ads" *The Australian* (25 July 2007), online: www.theaustralian.news.com.au/story/0,25197,22130223-7582,00.html [Townend]; Asher Moses, "Virgin Sued for Using Teen's Photo" *The Sydney Morning Herald* (21 September 2007), online: www.smh.com.au/news/technology/virgin-sued-for-using-teens-photo/2007/09/21/1189881735928.html [Moses]; David Koenig, "Family Sues Phone Company over Ad" *San Francisco Chronicle* (20 September 2007), online: www.sfgate.com/cgi-bin/article.cgi?file=/n/a/2007/09/20/national/a170859D28.DTL&type=printable; Noam Cohen, "Use My Photo? Not without My Permission" *The New York Times* (1 October 2007), online: www.nytimes.

of one of the images used in the campaign and the Texan schoolgirl it featured.[3]

Drawing on other examples of the use of Creative Commons licensed Flickr photos by corporate entities, this paper looks at the wider ramifications of Virgin Mobile's conduct. It will consider not only the issue of whether Virgin Mobile has complied with the Creative Commons copyright licence, but also what the incident can tell us about additional legal issues not contemplated by the Creative Commons licences, such as privacy rights, model clearances, and defamation. Finally, it will consider the ethical issues that arise from corporate use of Creative Commons licensed content, and the ramifications of this case for the Creative Commons community in general.

B.   FLICKR, CREATIVE COMMONS, AND BIG BUSINESS

The Yahoo!-owned Flickr website has proven itself to be a popular choice for online photo management.[4] Its user-friendly application enables images to be catalogued and shared either selectively or to the public at the photographer's discretion. To increase the flexibility of its copyright management tools, the service provides the option for users to license their photographs under the Creative Commons licensing scheme, which lets creators give permission in advance for uses such as commercial dealings and remixing that would not ordinarily be permitted under standard copyright law.[5]

The inclusion of Creative Commons as an option on Flickr has led to a vast increase in Creative Commons licensed photos. As of April 2008, there were over 65 million Creative Commons licensed photos listed on Flickr,[6] making Flickr the biggest repository of photographs available for reuse

---

com/2007/10/01/technology/01link.html?_r=1&ex=1348977600&en=8b50f28a0b8334 ob&ei=5088&partner=rssnyt&emc=rss&oref=slogin [Cohen].

3   The case of *Chang v. Virgin Mobile USA LLC* was filed 19 October 2007 in the Texas District Court in Dallas. On 16 January 2009, the court dismissed the case due to lack of personal jurisdiction. The court held that the circumstances did not have the minimum contacts to satisfy the constitution due process requirements for the case to be heard in the state of Texas. See *Chang v. Virgin Mobile USA, LLC*, 2009 WL 111570 (N.D. Tex January 16, 2009) [*Chang*].

4   Yahoo! purchased the Canadian company Flickr in 2005.

5   See "Creative Commons," online: www.flickr.com/creativecommons.

6   As of 19 April 2008, there were 65,670,475 Creative Commons licensed photos on Flickr. Flickr reached 2 billion images in November 2007. See Michael Arrington, "2 Billion Photos on Flickr" (13 November 2007), online: www.techcrunch.com/2007/11/13/2-billion-photos-on-flickr/.

under open content licences. To assist navigation of this vast collection, the Flickr site includes a page dedicated to its Creative Commons licensed photographs,[7] grouped according to licence type. This makes it simple for those searching for an image to use, in a publication, website, or advertising campaign for example, to find a photograph suited to their purpose.

However, the increased profile and usage that Flickr's incorporation of Creative Commons has engendered has not come without controversy. Debates about the use of Creative Commons licences and material are common within the Flickr discussion boards.[8] Because of the nature of photography and the manner in which third parties use images, the growth of Creative Commons licensed content on Flickr has had (or at least it is feared it will have) a strong effect on the pro-am photographer community, and particularly the market for stock-photographs, which has traditionally been the main and often only source of income for many photographers. Where previously stock-photograph companies such as Getty Images were the primary source of generic photographs, companies motivated by cost and convenience are increasingly using Creative Commons licensed photographs available for free from Flickr. This has led many photographers to be highly vocal in their opposition to Creative Commons licensing and the use of Creative Commons licensed photographs by third parties. To quote Scott Baradell from the prominent Black Star Rising photography blogzine:

> Before Creative Commons, a corporation or ad agency that wanted to use your photo would have to contact you or your photo agency for permission to use it. You could negotiate a price based on the particular use, making sure you got a fair deal. Through Creative Commons, hundreds of thousands—if not millions—of photographers have thrown away this right forever . . . . the end result is that you are building a system enabling commercial buyers to use your images without paying for them.[9]

With all this controversy, combined with the complexity of copyright law and the casual attitude many people have to using material available online, it is hardly surprising that the Virgin Mobile case is not the only time over the past few years that the use of Creative Commons licensed images

---

7   Above note 5.
8   See, for example, Flickr discussion board, "Dump Your Pen Friend" (27 May 2007), online: www.flickr.com/photos/sesh00/515961023/.
9   Scott Baradell, "Why Photographers Hate Creative Commons"(20 December 2007), online: http://rising.blackstar.com/why-photographers-hate-creative-commons-2.html.

sourced from Flickr by commercial entities has led to public debate and even legal action. Before turning to analysis of the circumstances of the Virgin Mobile case, we will first consider two of the more prominent incidents of commercial usage of Creative Commons licensed Flickr photographs below.

1)   *Curry v. Audax*[10]

The first court decision involving Creative Commons, *Curry,* concerned the commercial publication of Creative Commons licensed photographs downloaded from Flickr. In a typical celebrity-versus-the-tabloids dispute, the claimant, former MTV music video jockey and reality television star Adam Curry, brought proceedings in the District Court of Amsterdam in 2006 against Audax, publishers of the weekly tabloid magazine *Weekend.* Curry had uploaded photographs of his family onto Flickr under a Creative Commons Attribution-Noncommercial-Sharealike (BY-NC-SA) Licence, which allows use of the photographs for non-commercial purposes where the author is attributed and where any derivative works (i.e., new works that make use of or draw from the original photograph) are also licensed under the BY-NC-SA licence. Curry alleged that Audax had infringed both the terms of the "some rights reserved" licence and his right to privacy when they published four of the photographs in a magazine feature about his children.[11]

The case focused on the issue of the validity and clarity of the Creative Commons licensing. Instead of trying to argue that the publication of the photographs in *Weekend* (clearly a commercial use) was permitted by the licence, Audax instead claimed that the Creative Commons licence link was not obvious and they were misled by the notice on Flickr stating that "these photos are public" (a standard feature on all Flickr photographs that are marked for public viewing). They argued that they had published the photographs in good faith and had not committed any copyright breach. With regards to the right to privacy, Audax claimed that Curry had courted publicity for years, broadcasting details of his family's private life through his weekly reality TV show, frequent podcasts, and weblogs, and that because the photographs were freely available for public viewing via his

---

10   *Curry v. Audax* (9 March 2006), Amsterdam 334492 / KG 06-176 SR (District Court of Amsterdam); English translation, online: http://mirrors.creativecommons.org/ judgements/Curry-Audax-English.pdf [*Curry*]; published under Creative Commons-BY-2.5 licence by Lennert Steijger and Nynke Hendriks of the Institute for Information Law of the University of Amsterdam.

11   *Ibid.*

Flickr account, the celebrity had not suffered any damage or privacy breach through their publication.

Rejecting Audax's defence, the court held that the Creative Commons licence under which the photographs had been made available was valid and that the prominent link to the licence included on the Flickr page provided sufficient notice as to its terms. Once this decision had been made, Audax's publication of the photographs in a commercial magazine was clearly in breach of the licence. Audax were also chastised for not taking the care that a professional media organization in their position should have when publishing Internet-sourced material. If they had done so, the court argued, they would have investigated the link to the "some rights reserved" licence and been made aware of the licence terms. While accepting that Audax were misled by Flickr's "public" notice, the court advised Audax that, in case of any doubt, they should have sought permission from Curry to use the photographs. They awarded Curry damages of €1000 (noting the limited commercial value of the images because of their presence on Flickr) and issued an injunction against Audax prohibiting them from using content placed on Flickr by Curry without prior permission, unless done so in accordance with the Creative Commons licence conditions.

This case was important in addressing the practical implications of publishing under a Creative Commons licence and confirming that the licences have full legal standing, at least in the Netherlands. It clarified the misconception held by Audax and many others that content published on the Internet falls automatically into the public domain and provided legal authority that the limitations on Creative Commons licensed content must be adhered to.

2) *El País*

More recently, a similar incident occurred in Colombia. In December 2007, photographer Maria Claudia Montano discovered that an image she had uploaded onto her Flickr page under a Creative Commons Attribution-Non-commercial-No Derivatives Licence (which allows non-commercial use as long as the photograph is not altered in any way and the photographer is attributed) had been used by regional newspaper *El País* to advertise a photographic exhibition in their weekly magazine.[12] As with the Curry case, the

---

12   Juliana Rincón Parra, "Colombia: Bloggers Fight for Creative Commons Rights" (10 December 2007), online: www.globalvoicesonline.org/2007/12/10/colombia-bloggers-fight-for-creative-commons-rights/ [*El País*].

magazine's use was clearly in breach of the terms of the Creative Commons licence—not only had the photograph been used in a commercial publication, it had also been modified in breach of the "No Derivatives" term and the publication had failed to attribute Montano as owner of the image.

Upon making this discovery Montano promptly announced via her online weblog that *El País* had done this without her knowledge or permission. *El País* replied publicly that the photograph had been used to advertise an exhibition of which Montano was a participant; a fact which Montano flatly denied.[13] Even if this were the case, Montano argued, it did not have any effect on the licence terms and did not excuse the infringement. As with the *Curry* case, *El País* did not argue that its use was permitted by the licence, but rather challenged the notification of the licensing terms and the validity of copyright in "online" material. According to online sources, Montano's complaints to *El País* were responded to by newspaper spokespeople with the following: "Why did you upload the picture to a place where it can be easily downloadable [sic]? One cannot tell from the site that the picture is not available for others to use."[14] This is a remarkable reaction coming from a professional media organization that could be expected to have a solid understanding of the boundaries of copyright.

After Montano's case came to light a number of similar occasions were uncovered by the online community in which *El País* had used Creative Commons Non-commercial licensed Flickr photographs without authority.[15] Although at the time of writing no legal action had commenced against *El País*, the incident is receiving online media[16] and attention in the web 2.0 community,[17] and a number of photographers, including Montano, who have had their rights infringed are contemplating bringing suit. Considering the case is factually similar to *Curry*,[18] in the event of the matter going to court, it appears likely that a similar outcome would result.

---

13   María Elvira Domínguez Lloreda, "Carta de El País a María Claudia Montaño" *El Pais* (7 December 2007), online: www.elpais.com.co/paisonline/notas/Diciembre072007/mariaclaudiamontano.html.

14   Caro Botero, "Using Flickr Photos in the Traditional Media" (16 December 2007), online: http://icommons.org/articles/using-flickr-photos-in-the-traditional-media.

15   Above note 12.

16   *Ibid.*

17   See, for example, Flickr Discussion Board: "Scrambled Eggs with Smoked Salmon — Babka" (11 September 2006), online: www.flickr.com/photos/avlxyz/240472820.

18   *Curry*, above note 10.

C. THE VIRGIN MOBILE CASE

What unites the cases discussed above is that, setting aside spurious arguments as to the existence of copyright in publicly available photographs, the facts and legal ramifications are fairly straightforward. The images in question were licensed under Creative Commons licences that prohibited commercial use. Thus their use in profit-based media without attribution was a clear violation of the licence terms and of the copyright in the images.

The Virgin Mobile case is interesting precisely because it is not nearly so clear-cut. In contrast to *Audax* and *El País*, not only does Virgin Mobile appear to have been aware of the Creative Commons licences that applied to the photographs they chose to use, they also appear to have made at least a good-faith attempt to respect their terms. The case therefore raises far more complex questions about the precise legal and ethical issues surrounding use of Creative Commons material by corporate entities.

1) The Facts

In May 2007[19] Virgin Mobile launched its "Are you with us or what?" advertising campaign.[20] The campaign saw billboards[21] across Australia displaying amateur photographs, which had been branded with comical captions in what Virgin Mobile stated was "part of an approach designed to reject clichéd advertising in favour of more genuine and spontaneous shots."[22] On each of the billboards was the address of a website on which more, similar advertisements were available, and which linked through to Virgin Mobile's

---

19   Although the exact date the campaign was first launched is unknown, it is mentioned in online news postings from early June 2007. See Duncan, "Virgin Mobile Cheap Text Ads From Flickr" (2 June 2007), online: www.print.duncans. tv/2007/virgin-mobile-cheap-texts. The campaign is first referenced on Flickr on 28 June 2007. See "Virgin Mobile Advertising Campaign Using Flickr Photos" (28 June 2007) online: www.flickr.com/groups/central/discuss/72157600541608353. A photograph of a campaign billboard was labelled as being taken on 27 May 2007. See "Dump Your Pen Friend" (27 May 2007), online: www.flickr.com/photos/seshoo/515961023/.

20   Online: www.areyouwithusorwhat.com (accessed 28 June 2007). Note that the website has since been disabled.

21   For images of the billboards, see "Virgin Mobile — Are You with Us or What?" Online: www.flickr.com/groups/379879@N24/pool/.

22   See "Virgin Mobile — Are You with Us or What?" (16 July 2007), online: www. flickr.com/groups/379879@N24/discuss/72157600858275458.

main website. With the possible exception of one photograph,[23] all of the photographs used in the campaign had been sourced from Flickr and were available under the Creative Commons Attribution Licence, which not only allows commercial use, but also allows modification of the photographs through cropping and the addition of captions. The only significant restriction imposed by this licence is that the original author must be attributed. Virgin Mobile included a link to the Flickr profile of the photographer in fine print at the bottom of each advertisement, presumably to comply with this term.

At least some of the Flickr photographers featured were "excited"[24] to see their photos used as the face of Virgin Mobile. In response to being told of a billboard featuring his photograph of his hand pushing an unmarked button captioned with "pressing buttons for the hell of it is a basic human right,"[25] Blake Emrys made the following comments:

> Woohoo, that's my thumb! :) I can't really speak for everyone, but most of my photos are licensed as CC attribution, noncommercial, share alike. This was one of the few where I thought "Eh, what the heck—let 'em do whatever they want and let's see what happens!" so all I asked for was attribution. I'm glad I did.[26]

Meanwhile, "Qole Pejorian"[27] (Alan Bruce) responded to negative comments by other users about his photograph being used: "I got a picture of mine used on billboards and magazines in Australia! Doesn't sound wrong to me."[28] In a similar vein, "Merfam" (Jason Meredith) had this to say about the use of a photograph of his daughter in the campaign:

---

23   See babasu, "Scary Andrew" (5 November 2006), online: www.flickr.com/photos/babasu/289444685/, which is currently listed as being under a BY-NC-SA licence. See online: http://creativecommons.org/licenses/by-nc-sa/2.0/deed.en. Considering the fact that all other photographs used in the campaign were under an attribution-only licence, it seems likely to have been re-licensed under a more restrictive licence following Virgin's usage.

24   See Qole Pejorian [Alan Bruce]'s comment, "Virgin Mobile Advertising Campaign Using Flickr Photos" (28 June 2007), online: www.flickr.com/groups/central/discuss/72157600541608353/#comment72157600694703907.

25   See josiejose, "CIMG0158.JPG" (27 May 2007), online: http://flickr.com/photos/awaketodream/517157852/.

26   Blakeemrys [Blake Emrys]' comment, "Dump Your Pen Friend" (27 May 2007), online: www.flickr.com/photos/seshoo/515961023/#comment72157600541633523/.

27   See "Qole Pejorian's photostream," online: www.flickr.com/photos/qole/.

28   Qole Pejorian [Alan Bruce]'s comment, "Ruined Irish Church Graveyard" (24 July 2006), online: www.flickr.com/photos/qole/197513122/#comment72157600560006468.

I can say that my photography has been used in a national ad campaign (magazine and billboard) by a Major Corporation. How many armature [*sic*] photographers can say that? I'm going to add this experience to my resume and consider it a feather in my cap . . .

I feel it was innovative of Virgin Mobile to use a Web 2.0 site like Flickr for their ad campaign. This is a company that understands the power of technology.[29]

Congratulatory statements and positive comments were also made by Flickr users whose photographs had not been used in the campaign.[30]

However some photographers and subjects of the photographs did not find the ads quite so humorous.[31] The campaign led to intensive online discussion, both on Flickr[32] and individual blogs,[33] about the legal and ethical implications of corporate use of Creative Commons licensed photographs, with the prevailing attitude being that Virgin Mobile had not acted entirely "by the book." It also gained considerable media attention, making the front page of www.news.com[34] and several prominent national and international newspapers,[35] and was reported on the Australian Broadcasting

---

29   Merfam [Jason Meredith]'s comment, "Crazy" (26 November 2006), online: www. flickr.com/photos/merfam/307113221/comment72157601338373225/. Merfam now lists the use of his photograph by Virgin Mobile as one his "photo accomplishments" on his Flickr profile: Jason Meredith, "About merfam" (2007), online: www.flickr.com/people/merfam.

30   See "Ruined Irish Church Graveyard" (24 July 2006), online: www.flickr.com/photos/qole/197513122/#comment72157602107221466; See also "Virgin Mobile Advertising Campaign Using Flickr Photos" (28 June 2007), online: www.flickr.com/groups/central/discuss/72157600541608353/72157602105180125.

31   See, for example, the following comment by gillicious: "I am, however, annoyed (as some of you are) that I wasn't informed that my photo was being used, and only know because a stranger wrote down my flickr address from the poster and contacted me . . . How much trouble would it have been for a Virgin representative to create a user on flickr to comment on each photo being used, just to inform us that it was? Just to be polite! They're a huge company, they could afford to hire a lackey to do it." Online: www.flickr.com/groups/central/discuss/72157600541608353/#comment72157600669104564.

32   Above note 8.

33   Rogers Cadenhead, "Virgin Mobile Botches Creative Commons-driven Ad Campaign" (11 July 2007), online: www.cadenhead.org/workbench/news/3232/virgin-mobile-botches-creative.

34   See Townend, above note 2.

35   Above note 2.

Corporation's popular youth radio network, Triple J.[36] Most criticized the fact that Virgin Mobile had made no attempt to inform the photographers that they were using their images in such a way, or to obtain clearance from the people featured in the photographs.

2)   Dump Your Pen Friend

American high-school student Alison Chang was surprised to find herself the focus of one of the advertisements.[37] The advertisement, featuring Alison flashing the universal two-fingered peace sign under the caption "Dump your Pen Friend," was brought to her attention when a Flickr user saw it on a billboard in Adelaide, South Australia. They photographed the billboard and posted it to Flickr, congratulating the Flickr user "Chewywong" for having his photograph used in the campaign.[38] "Chewywong" was the username for Justin Wong, Alison's youth counsellor who had taken the picture at a fundraising carwash and uploaded it to Flickr under a Creative Commons Attribution Licence.

Alison's brother spoke out publicly both on the Flickr community boards and to a number of newspapers about the discomfort the family felt at Alison's image being used in the campaign.[39] They felt that the tagline was derogatory[40] and that Alison's permission should have been asked before the photograph was used to promote Virgin Mobile's product.[41] It was not long before a suit was filed in the District Court of Dallas County, Texas, by the Changs and the photographer, Wong.[42] Named as defendants in the initial suit were Virgin Mobile Pty Ltd. (the Australian company), their American constituents Virgin Mobile USA, LLC, and the Creative Commons Corporation.

---

36   See online: www.abc.net.au/triplej/hack/notes/mp3s/hack_flikr.mp3.
37   Aleeviation [Alison Chang]'s comment, "Dump Your Pen Friend" (27 May 2007), online: www.flickr.com/photos/seshoo/515961023/#comment72157600541633523.
38   Above note 8.
39   Teacherjamesdotcom [Damon Chang]'s comment, "Virgin Mobile Advertising Campaign Using Flickr Photos" (28 June 2007) online: www.flickr.com/groups/central/discuss/72157600541608353/#comment72157600614863168; See also Moses, above note 2.
40   Moses, *ibid.*
41   Teacherjamesdotcom [Damon Chang]'s comment "Virgin Mobile Advertising Campaign Using Flickr Photos" (28 June 2007) online: Flickr www.flickr.com/groups/central/discuss/72157600541608353/72157602096415462.
42   *Chang,* above note 3.

The papers filed seek to bring suit on a number of bases. Alison's parents allege that Virgin Mobile's use of the photograph of their daughter constituted a violation of her privacy and that the insulting caption amounted to libel. Wong further claims that the company's inclusion of a link to his Flickr profile was not sufficient to satisfy the attribution requirements of the Creative Commons licence under which the photograph had been made available. With regards to Creative Commons, Wong claimed that the organization owed him a duty as a user and beneficiary of a Creative Commons licence, and that they breached this duty by failing to "adequately educate and warn him . . . of the meaning of commercial use and the ramifications and effects of entering into a license allowing such use."[43]

Not long after the furor erupted, Virgin Mobile removed most of the photographs in which particular people could be identified from their website and replaced them with related but less controversial images. For example, one ad using the line "People who talk in lifts have bad breath," which originally pictured a group of people talking in a elevator,[44] was replaced with a picture of an overflowing ashtray. This seems an appropriate response, especially considering the following disgruntled blog post by the subject of the "talking in the lift" photograph, computer-book author Molly Holzschlag:

> There's a level of irony in this particular picture . . . . The person I'm talking with is the head of Web Development for Yahoo! Europe—and Yahoo! is of course Flickr's big daddy. Virgin really stepped in it but [*sic*] good.[45]

Virgin Mobile also appears to have since taken down both the website and the billboard advertisements, although this may merely have been due to the campaign coming to an end.

As a final note, since the initial filing of the legal papers, Virgin Mobile USA has been removed as a respondent to the case on the basis that they are an entirely separate company to Virgin Mobile Australia and were in no way involved in the campaign.[46] In late November 2007, Creative Commons was also dropped as a defendant.[47] Although no reason was provided,

---

43   *Ibid.*

44   See Daniel Morrison, "Molly Holds Court in the Elevator" (12 March 2007), online: www.flickr.com/photos/danielmorrison/419368629/.

45   Above note 33.

46   Andrew D. Smith, "Bedford Mom Sues Virgin Mobile over Teen's Photo in Ad" *The Dallas Morning News* (21 September 2007), online: www.dallasnews.com/sharedcontent/dws/bus/stories/DN-suevirgin_21bus.ART.State.Edition1.35bdb09.html.

47   Lawrence Lessig, "From the Why-a-GC-from-Cravath-is-great Department: The Lawsuit is Over" (28 November 2007), online: http://lessig.org/blog/2007/11/from_

the general consensus seems to be that Creative Commons was removed due to the lack of a legal cause against them.[48]

D. LEGAL ANALYSIS

1) Compliance with the Creative Commons Licence

Unlike the *Curry*[49] and *El Pais* cases discussed above, Virgin Mobile's use does not immediately appear to be a breach of the Creative Commons licences used for the photographs included in the campaign. With the possible exception of one photograph, the licence of which may have been altered after the campaign, all the images were made available under the Creative Commons Attribution Licence, which clearly allows the kind of commercial use and alterations undertaken by Virgin.[50] Indeed, Virgin Mobile appears to have chosen the photographs on this basis; as one Flickr member has indicated, he was contacted by an advertising agency to obtain his permission to use an "all rights reserved" image in the campaign, only to later receive an apology that "[t]he client went for a different shot."[51]

Nevertheless, there is still some question as to whether Virgin Mobile did in fact comply with all the Creative Commons licence conditions. As the legal claim filed by Wong and the Changs points out, it is arguable that Virgin Mobile's attribution does not satisfy the Creative Commons licence requirements. The licence deed (i.e., plain English summary) of the Creative Commons licences specifically states that the licence requires attribution "in the manner specified by the author or licensor." By reading the full licence (accessible from the deed), Virgin Mobile would have been made aware that the required attribution should include:

(i)   the name of the author (or pseudonym, if applicable), and/or the name of any other party designated by the licensor;

(ii) the title of the work; and

---

the_whyagcfromcravathisgr.html [Lessig, "The Lawsuit is Over"].

48   *Ibid.*

49   *Curry,* above note 10.

50   Above note 23.

51   Steve Rhodes' comment, "Virgin Mobile Advertising Campaign Using Flickr Photos" (28 June 2007), online: www.flickr.com/groups/central/discuss/72157600541608353/72157601393029582/.

(iii) to the extent reasonably practicable, any uniform resource identifier (e.g., link) associated with the Work that refers to the copyright notice or licensing information for the Work.[52]

The licensee is also required to provide a link to the appropriate Creative Commons licence with every copy of the work they distribute.[53] Yet both the billboard and web versions of the advertisements merely included a link to the home page of the photographer's Flickr account in the bottom corner. Virgin did not directly name the photographers, reference or link to the Creative Commons licence the photo was under, or link to the image itself. Even a link to the Flickr page of the photograph itself would have come closer to complying with the licence requirements, as it would at least have provided the means for the viewer to seek the attribution information available on the page for themselves. As it is, with many Flickr photographers having hundreds or even thousands of photographs posted to their profile, it would be virtually impossible for any person seeking to use the particular photograph to identify it, its title, or the licence it was under.

Although the licence allows users to vary most of the attribution requirements when it is "reasonable" to do so, it is questionable whether Virgin Mobile had reason not to give greater attribution in this case. Following the logic in the *Curry* case, as a large corporation there is a strong onus on Virgin Mobile to fully read the licence of any material they use and to follow its provisions exactly. If only from a risk management point of view, it would be shrewd for the company to implement best practices for a national advertising campaign. The Creative Commons attribution requirements, as they currently exist, act not only to recognize the moral rights of the author, but also to ensure others are notified of the existence of the licence and are given the opportunity to locate and use the photograph themselves, should they so wish. By merely linking to the photographer's profile, Virgin Mobile has in effect undermined the "openness" of the photographs.

It should be noted that, were the case being heard in an Australian court, the question of the validity of Virgin Mobile's attribution could also give rise to a cause of action for breach of the moral rights of the photographers. Accurate attribution is one of three moral rights recognized by Australian copyright law.[54] These rights are personal to the author and cannot be waived or assigned by contract. Furthermore, by adding insulting captions, there is

---

52   Creative Commons Attribution licence cl. 4(b), online: http://creativecommons.org/licenses/by/3.0/legalcode.

53   Creative Commons Attribution licence cl. 4(a), *ibid*.

54   *Copyright Act 1968* (Cth.), ss. 189–195AZR.

also a possibility that Virgin Mobile has breached the photographers' moral right of integrity, which prohibits distortions of, or a material alteration to, artistic works that are "prejudicial to the author's honour or reputation."[55] Moral rights law is still in its fledgling stages in Australia, with the first case to award moral rights infringement only decided in December 2006.[56] As such, the elements of the rights are yet to be defined, and it is difficult to determine the chances of success of any suit on such grounds. Nevertheless, the fact that the insulting captions applied by Virgin Mobile are aimed at the subjects of the photo, rather than the photographer or photograph, makes a cause of action based on the right of integrity unlikely.

2) Personal Rights

As the libel and privacy causes of action raised in the legal filings fall outside the scope of the Creative Commons licences on which this paper focuses, we do not intend to provide substantive legal analysis of the likelihood of their success. Nevertheless, it is interesting to note that, were Australian law to be applied, it is questionable whether the causes would succeed. Although Australia has steadily developed its privacy law, there currently exists no distinct right of publicity to the same extent as in the US.[57] Rather, defamation, passing-off law, trademark law, or the *Trade Practices Act 1974* (Cth.)[58] have been used to address similar situations to those in publicity rights cases in the US.[59] While defamation could potentially be raised as a remedy if publication of the photograph impaired the reputation of the subject, proof would be required that Alison had a public reputation that had been lowered, exposing her to hatred, contempt, or ridicule, or causing her to be shunned or avoided.[60] It seems unlikely that such an argument would succeed. While

---

55   *Ibid.*, s. 195AK(a).

56   *Meskenas v. ACP Publishing Pty. Ltd.*, [2006] FMCA 1136.

57   An Australian Law Reform Commission review was initiated in 2006 to bring Australian privacy laws further in line with modern developments; however, its recommendations are yet to be handed down. Austl., Commonwealth, Australian Law Reform Commission, *Review of Australian Privacy Law* (Discussion Paper No. 72) (Sydney: Australian Law Reform Commission, 2007).

58   *Trade Practices Act 1974* (Cth.) [*Trade Practices Act*].

59   See, for example, *Henderson v. Radio Corp. Pty. Ltd.* (1960), S.R. (N.S.W.) 576 (S.C.) [*Henderson*]; *Ettinghausen v. Australian Consolidated Press Ltd.* (1991), 23 N.S.W.L.R. 443 (S.C.) [*Ettinghausen*].

60   Publication alone without permission does not prove defamation. See, for example, *Ettinghausen, ibid.*

Alison and her family were clearly offended at the "dump your pen friend" caption over her image,[61] public discussion shows that interpretation of the caption's meaning is subjective, with many of those who viewed the ad publicly stating that they did not believe it had ridiculed or insulted Alison.[62]

More relevant to the paper at hand, and closely related to the issues of libel and privacy, is the question of model clearances. Much of the public discussion of the case has focused on the question of whether Virgin Mobile should have obtained permission from the people who are identifiable in the photographs. The Flickr forums in particular contain numerous posts debating the issue, with statements both in favour of [63] and against[64] the use of model clearances. Even a person claiming to be Flickr's general manager wades into the debate, stating "in the US, Canada, the EU (and presumably Australia and most of the rest of the world) use of a recognizable person in a commercial context (here 'commercial' generally means in advertising or promotions) definitely requires a model release."[65]

However, there is a real question as to whether this is true. Although it seems to be industry practice to obtain a model clearance where a photograph is being used for commercial purposes,[66] it is questionable as to whether, in the circumstances of this case, this is a legal requirement under Australian law. Section 53 of the *Trade Practices Act*[67] does prohibit commercial conduct that misleads or deceives consumers into thinking a particular person has purchased or is affiliated with a product. However, existing cases in this area tend to involve a person who is a celebrity (or is at least well-known to the public) and are limited to circumstances where it is clear that consumers were falsely led to believe that person was endorsing the

---

61 Moses, above note 2.

62 Above note 8.

63 See, for example, "Virgin Mobile Advertising Campaign Using Flickr photos" (28 June 2007), online: www.flickr.com/groups/central/discuss/72157600541608353/ 72157600542126986.

64 See, for example, "Virgin Mobile Advertising Campaign Using Flickr Photos" (28 June 2007), online: www.flickr.com/groups/central/discuss/72157600541608353/ 72157600960543755.

65 Stewart's comment, "Virgin Mobile Advertising Campaign Using Flickr Photos" (28 June 2007), online: www.flickr.com/groups/central/discuss/72157600541608353/ #comment72157600545426189.

66 See, for example, "Model Release Primer," online: www.danheller.com/model-release-primer.html; and Andrew Nemeth, "Australian Street Photography Legal Issues" (10 May 2008), online: www.4020.net/words/photorights.php.

67 Above note 58, s. 53.

product.[68] The Virgin Mobile ads, with their deliberate "amateur" style and sarcastic bylines, can hardly be said to clearly imply endorsement — if anything, they suggest that the person is an unwitting participant in the joke.

The failure to obtain model clearances may hold more clout in the US, where the right to control how one's persona is commercialized by third parties is more readily recognized. Yet, while Alison's counsel asserts that Texan law requires that "if a company uses your face in its ads without your consent, then you're entitled to whatever money those ads generate for the company,"[69] it is not clear that this is the case. As with Australian law, judicial consideration of the right of publicity in US courts has focused more on celebrities than members of the general public.[70]

Regardless of the legal situation, from a best practice standpoint it would have been advisable for Virgin Mobile to seek clearances from the individuals involved in such a widespread advertising campaign, whether they were a celebrity or otherwise. Public sentiment certainly appears to condemn Virgin's failure to obtain a model clearance, and doing so would have reduced the likelihood of legal action. It certainly seems unlikely that any lawyer would advise a company like Virgin Mobile to launch such a campaign without first contacting the photographers — if only to avoid the kind of public backlash that has occurred.

E. AFTERMATH OF THE VIRGIN MOBILE CASE

Although the outcome of the legal action commenced by Wong and the Changs is yet to be seen, it has already had a substantial effect on the Creative Commons and Flickr communities. The public debate surrounding the Virgin Mobile case has raised a number of issues about Creative Commons ethics and practices that are likely to have an effect on the development of the licences and their take-up in the wider community. These are discussed further below.

---

68   See also *Talmax Pty. Ltd. v. Telstra Corp. Ltd.*, [1996] QSC 34; *Pacific Dunlop Ltd. v. Hogan* (1989), 23 F.C.R. 553 (F.C.A.); *Honey v. Australian Airlines Ltd.* (1990), 18 I.P.R. 185 (F.C.A.).

69   Above note 47.

70   See, for example, *Henderson*, above note 59.

1) Free Culture or Free Ride?

One of the common themes running through the Virgin Mobile, *Curry*, and *El País* cases is a lack of understanding as to exactly what uses the Creative Commons non-commercial licences permit. Despite the fact that in each of the cases there seems to be little doubt as to the commercial nature of the use of the photographs, all three circumstances raise the question as to whether the commercial-use element has been properly explained and delineated to the creators and users. It is clear from a legal perspective that the claim in the Virgin Mobile filings of negligence against Creative Commons for failing to adequately explain its licences was weak at best. The Creative Commons website provides substantial explanatory materials regarding the details of its licences, which are linked to the Flickr licensing page. If anything, Creative Commons provides more publicly accessible information about the details of their licences than your average attorney, not to mention the vast majority of licences used by online entities. Nevertheless, the case provides evidence that there is still room for additional steps by Creative Commons to inform users about the implications of their licensing decisions.

The "non-commercial" term is the most popular of the Creative Commons licence elements, and is applied to 67.5 percent of all Creative Commons works.[71] However, it is also the most controversial of the licence elements. It has been described as "vague,"[72] "dangerously ill-defined,"[73] and "confusing,"[74] and its value has been debated by many of Creative Commons' most well-known advocates and critics.[75] The Creative Commons or-

---

71   "Distribution of License Properties across Licenses Deployed" (2006), online: http://wiki.creativecommons.org/License_statistics..

72   Nick Sweeney, "Introducing Creative Commons" (March 2006), online: www.artslaw.com.au/LegalInformation/IntroducingCreativeCommons.asp; Gordon Haff, "Why and How to Fix Creative Commons" (15 January 2008), online: www.cnet.com/8301-13556_1-9849881-61.html; Erik Möller, "The Case for Free Use: Reasons Not to Use a Creative Commons-NC License" (2005–2007), online: http://freedomdefined.org/Licenses/NC.

73   Gordon Haff, "Does the Noncommercial Creative Commons License Make Sense?" (27 November 2007), online: www.cnet.com/8301-13556_1-9823336-61.html.

74   Joan McGivern, "10 Things Every Music Creator Should Know About Creative Commons Licensing" (2007), online: http://ascap.com/playback/2007/fall/features/creative_commons_licensing.aspx.

75   Mako [Benjamin Mako-Hill], "Towards a Standard of Freedom: Creative Commons and the Free Software Movement" (29 July 2005), online: www.advogato.org/article/851.html; Lawrence Lessig, "CC in Review: Lawrence Lessig on Important Freedoms" (7 December 2005), online: http://creativecommons.org/weblog/entry/5719;

ganization recognizes this, and has launched a number of public initiatives aimed at clarifying and educating users about the meaning of non-commercial in the Creative Commons licences. In late 2006, it launched a set of proposed non-commercial guidelines for comment by the Creative Commons community. Although still in draft form, these guidelines aim to assist with determining whether a particular use is non-commercial based on a series of standardized questions about the use.[76] Creative Commons has also announced that during 2009 they will be undertaking a study of the non-commercial term, which could result in changes to the licences and/or additional explanatory material on the website.[77]

Nevertheless, the cases discussed can hardly be attributed to confusion over the meaning of non-commercial. In each of their circumstances, the nature of the use was clearly commercial, as has been noted on the Flickr discussion boards,[78] and neither the artists involved nor the corporations using the photographs can truly claim to have thought otherwise. Instead, Audax's, El Pais's, and even Virgin Mobile's (potential) infringements seem to be based either on failure to read the licences or misunderstanding of standard copyright law. The response from the newspaper spokesperson in the *El País* case in particular demonstrates how many users are still of the opinion that, at least ethically if not legally, material on the Internet is a free-for-all. Creative Commons' ability to address the issue may therefore be limited.

2)   Creative Commons Licence and Model Clearance Compatibility

As is indicated above, some commentators have suggested that the failure to deal with the issue of model clearances represents a flaw in the Creative Commons licences.[79] The argument goes that, as the licences purport to provide

---

See Klauss Graff comment on Lawrence Lessig, "On the Texas Suit against Virgin and Creative Commons" (22 September 2007), online: http://lessig.org/blog/2007/09/on_the_texas_suit_against_virg.html [Lessig, "On the Texas Suit"].

76   Mia Garlick, "Discussion Draft — NonCommercial Guidelines" (10 January 2006), online: http://creativecommons.org/weblog/entry/5752.

77   Eric Steuer, "Creative Commons Launches Study of 'Noncommercial Use'" (18 September 2008), online: http://creativecommons.org/weblog/entry/9557.

78   See "Virgin Mobile Advertising Campaign Using Flickr Photos" (28 June 2007), online: www.flickr.com/groups/central/discuss/72157600541608353/72157600972448807/.

79   Shelley Powers, "Virgin Bites Creative Commons on the Butt" (10 July 2007), online: http://burningbird.net/connecting/virgin-bites-creative-commons-on-the-butt.

permission to use the photographs commercially, they should cover all rights required to do so, including model clearances. Other commentators have suggested that the responsibility is on the photographers, and that licences that allow commercial use should not be applied to photographs in which individuals are identifiable unless such clearances have been obtained.[80]

However, the Creative Commons licences make it clear that the licensors are merely providing copyright permissions, and that this permission does not purport to extend to any other area of law. Indeed, they have an extensive disclaimer clause that specifically states that they provide no warranty, express or implied, as to merchantability, marketability, or fitness of purpose.[81] Due to the vast number of uses that can be made of Creative Commons licensed material and the multitude of legal jurisdictions in which such uses can occur, the laws that can come into play (e.g., defamation, privacy, and competition, to name but a few) is significant. It would be impossible for the licences, or the person issuing the licence, to definitively cover all potential legal issues that may arise in releasing the work for general use. There is therefore a strong argument that, if only for practical reasons, the onus must be on the person or company making use of the work to identify any laws their particular actions might breach, and to make an effort to obtain any additional permissions that are needed. By using a Creative Commons licence they are obtaining a copyright clearance; however, they must seek any additional permissions or clearances that might arise from other relevant areas of law. Such precautionary steps would seem particularly important if their use is large-scale and commercial, and even more so if the image is that of a minor, as in Alison's case.

Although the principle legal onus is on the user of the photograph, any creator using Creative Commons licences on their work without obtaining model clearances does potentially expose themselves to some risk if their content is reused or published commercially in jurisdictions with broad personality rights. Creative Commons Chairman Joichi Ito acknowledged this when he relayed to an audience at the 2007 iSummit the importance of understanding the legal aspects of publishing an individual's photograph. While he admitted to not obtaining model clearances for any of his photos published under a Creative Commons Attribution Licence, he also stated

---

80 See, for example, "Virgin Mobile Advertising Campaign Using Flickr Photos" (28 June 2007), online: www.flickr.com/groups/central/discuss/72157600541608353/72157600610121981/.

81 Creative Commons Attribution 3.0 United States License, cl. 5, online: http://creativecommons.org/licenses/by/3.0/us/legalcode.

that he makes a point of not publishing any unflattering images of people. He further emphasised the importance of ensuring licence-users understand the risks they are taking by not obtaining clearances.[82]

Although the Creative Commons founder, Stanford Law Professor Lawrence Lessig, has been careful to note that Creative Commons should not provide "what looks like legal advice,"[83] several recent actions by Creative Commons suggest it may prove itself receptive to addressing the obstacle that the lack of availability of model release forms potentially presents to the uptake of the Creative Commons licences.[84] Even prior to the Virgin Mobile case, Creative Commons had added additional information to its "Frequently Asked Questions" page dealing with the issue of publicity rights, with links to a detailed section in its podcasting guide.[85] Other suggestions put forward include Creative Commons offering a model clearance rights tutorial such as that found on www.istockphoto.com,[86] or even altering the licence deed to acknowledge additional rights that may not have been cleared.[87] A project devised by Joichi Ito called "Freesouls," which aims to provide high-quality Creative Commons Attribution Licensed images of interesting people and offer them for reuse as simplistically as possible, seems likely to go even further towards addressing the issue of privacy rights and Creative Commons.[88] Such steps would seem to be particularly important if Creative Commons wish to extend their user-base to those in the professional and institutional arena or to encourage the use of Creative Commons content in commercial settings without the legal complications brought about by the Virgin Mobile advertising campaign.

The Virgin Mobile case has certainly raised public awareness of model clearances. Wikimedia, an online community that licenses their material

---

82   See, David Harris, "CC Not in a Theater Near You w/o Model Releases" (25 June 2007), online: www.icommons.org/articles/cc-not-in-a-theater-near-you-wo-model-releases [Harris].

83   Cohen, above note 2.

84   Harris, above note 82.

85   See "Frequently Asked Questions" (14 February 2008), online: http://wiki.creative-commons.org/FAQ#When_are_publicity_rights_relevant.3F; and David Gerard's comment on Lessig, "On the Texas Suit," above note 75.

86   See Henri Laupmaa's comment on Lessig, "On the Texas Suit," *ibid.*; and Harris, above note 82.

87   Gavin Baker, "Let's All Sue Creative Commons: A Defense, and Suggestions for Publicity *et al.*" (22 September 2007), online: www.gavinbaker.com/2007/09/22/lets-all-sue-creative-commons.

88   Lessig, "On the Texas Suit," above note 75.

in a similar manner to Creative Commons, has added the following notice to their Wikimedia Commons webpage, which provides information on reusing content outside of Wikimedia:

> **Warning on images of people:** Even if a given image is pre-cleared with regard to copyright, this does not mean the image is pre-cleared with regards to possible personality rights, moral rights or model releases, depending on jurisdiction. Take care with context when reusing images of people.[89]

Flickr also has responded to the incident, and now reportedly provides the following message to photographers who have made high resolution images available under Creative Commons licences that allow commercial use:

> Any user can download this photo because you've applied a Creative Commons license to it. Change license?[90]

3) Ethics and the Creative Commons

What the public reaction to the Virgin Mobile incident has perhaps most emphasized is the ongoing difference of opinion as to the ethics of, and motivations for, Creative Commons usage. From a technical-legal standpoint, if the photographs that Virgin Mobile used were licensed to allow commercial use and the company had complied with all other licence restrictions (i.e., attribution), then this use appears to be permitted under the Creative Commons model. But even if they had no legal duty to do so, should Virgin Mobile have used photographs that had been provided online as part of a sharing culture in such a widespread commercial campaign, rather than seeking out similar photographs through professional avenues? More notably, should they at least have notified the photographers that they were planning on using their photographs before doing so?

Public opinion in the Flickr forums certainly seems to be that they should have. To quote "gillicious," one of the photographers whose image was used in the campaign:

---

89   "Commons: Reusing Content outside Wikimedia", online: http://commons.wikimedia.org/wiki/Commons:Reusing_content_outside_Wikimedia. Wikimedia uses GFDL rather than Creative Commons licensing—however the principles are not dissimilar.

90   Qole Pejorian [Alan Bruce]'s comment, "Virgin Mobile Advertising Campaign Using Flickr Photos" (28 June 2007), online: www.flickr.com/groups/central/discuss/72157600541608353/72157601662536021/.

How much trouble would it have been for a Virgin representative to create a user [profile] on flickr [*sic*] to comment on each photo being used, just to inform us that it was? Just to be polite! They're a huge company, they could afford to hire a lackey to do it.[91]

But, there is also an argument that this is exactly why Creative Commons includes the non-commercial term as an optional element of their licences: people can choose to share their material even with large corporations if they wish to. As Flickr-user Alan Bruce puts it:

> The thing about the Creative Commons Attribution-Only license is that you are telling other people, "go ahead, use this picture as you wish, just credit me," without any requirement to tell the photographer or even be "nice" with the photo. So I guess this license isn't for the faint of heart . . . On the other hand, if you sell your photo to a stock photo bank, the same things apply . . . people who buy your photo can use it however they like. But I would prefer fame instead of money, and this license certainly has gotten me a bit of fame![92]

4) The Importance of Education

One thing noted by several Flickr users is that the Virgin Mobile case clearly demonstrates the importance of both creators and users understanding the Creative Commons licences before they use them.[93] Wong's anger at Virgin Mobile's use of his material would appear to indicate that he did not fully comprehend the implications of the licence when he chose to apply it to his work. Despite the weakness of the legal claim of negligence against them, Creative Commons has taken the matter seriously, with Professor Lawrence Lessig publicly apologizing for any trouble that confusion about the Creative Commons licences might have created in this case, and undertaking to work harder to make the licences as clear as possible.[94]

---

91   Gillicious' comment, "Virgin Mobile Advertising Campaign Using Flickr Photos" (28 June 2007), online: www.flickr.com/groups/central/discuss/72157600541608353/72157600669104564/.

92   Above note 28.

93   See, for example, the following comment by Flickr member ellipse: "yeah i mean seriously people there was a license, they used it why are they the bad party? to me the issue is people not understanding licenses when they apply them," online: www.flickr.com/groups/central/discuss/72157600541608353/72157600961016540/.

94   Lessig, "The Lawsuit is Over," above note 47; See similarly Lessig, "On the Texas Suit," above note 75.

These cases also clearly demonstrate the need for a better understanding of copyright in general. It can be hoped that the existence of the Creative Commons licences may assist to educate both creators and users about their rights and responsibilities with respect to copyright law, and even to help combat copyright piracy online. With "all rights reserved" copyright restrictions so often ignored, even by large scale commercial entities, a licence on content, such as is offered by Creative Commons, works to draw attention to the existence of legal rights over the material that must be considered in any use. In the event that their rights are infringed, it also gives the copyright owner a written document to point towards, which sets out the exact terms of use permitted, without needing to resort to the more obtuse provisions of copyright law. It can be hoped that third-party users of Internet content, acting innocently or in good faith, will be more likely to adhere to copyright restrictions if they have clear instructions from the owner as to how the work can (or cannot) be reused. As Alan Bruce puts it,

> Ironically, I find the [attribution only] license to be more of a deterrent to theft than marking the photo "All rights reserved." For some reason, people think it's "cheap" to attribute the photo. It's actually stealing attention away from your ad and focusing some of it on the photographer. Which is great for the photographer![95]

F. CONCLUSION

The Virgin Mobile case is currently in the discovery stage and a suspenseful stay awaits, to see if the case makes it to an outcome.[96] As the case requires a far more subtle analysis than either the *Curry* or *El País* cases, it has the potential to clarify a number of hitherto untouched legal issues relating to the use of Creative Commons licences. However, even without a legal decision, the public debate prompted by the case has already served a valuable purpose in the continuing evolution of the Creative Commons movement in that it has highlighted the ongoing disparity in views of what constitutes an ethical use of open-content material, and the potential for public backlash if these ethics are not obeyed. It is likely that Virgin Mobile will have learnt its lesson from the experience, and that the case will herald a new awareness of best-practice standards, particularly in circumstances involving the use of Creative Commons licensed material by commercial entities. But as long

---

95   Above note 24.
96   *Chang*, above note 3.

as the *El País* newspapers of the world continue to flout copyright law, the potential for contention remains. Perhaps what this case most highlights is the controversy that is always likely to surround any project that aims to provide standardized legal tools to a large number of users, each with their own motivations, interpretations, and understandings, and the importance of continuous clarification and education to movements such as Creative Commons in their ongoing quest to develop and promote free culture.

CHAPTER 10

Abandoning Eden: The Google Print Library Project

Dilan Thampapillai

A. INTRODUCTION

No one who has travelled to Oxford, Cambridge, or Harvard would deny the quaint pleasure of visiting the small bookstores that nestle in the streets around these universities. Certainly, John Updike, writing in the *New York Times Book Review* acknowledged this fact whilst bemoaning the spectre of a digital library.[1] Barnes & Noble, Borders, and Kinokuniya may well have established themselves as large commercial bookstores, but they cannot replicate the atmosphere of their smaller counterparts. Similarly, Amazon and other online booksellers have little chance of coming close to the shops of the dreaming spires. But the experience of the Harvard Bookstore, which is by no means small, is not something that everybody has the chance to enjoy. As such, it was certainly fair that Siva Vaidhyanathan, writing in the *University of California Davis Law Review*, would criticize Updike's remarks as elitist.[2]

When it first appeared, the Google Print Library Project (GPLP) seemed a way to bring the elite experience to the masses. The notion of an online digital library hosting all the knowledge of mankind, accessible to all persons, seemed too good to be true—and it was. From the start, the

---

1   John Updike, "The End of Authorship" *New York Times (Sunday Book Review)* (25 June 2006), online: www.nytimes.com/2006/06/25/books/review/25updike.html.

2   Siva Vaidhyanathan, "Copyright, Creativity, Catalogs: The Googlization of Everything and the Future of Copyright" (2007) 40 U.C. Davis L. Rev. 1207. Vaidhyanathan ultimately concludes that there may be dangers in the GPLP for "public rights" under copyright.

project suffered from the interminable obstacles of copyright law. Google's attitude did not help. At the outset Google seemed to want to steamroll over authors and publishers by relying on a vague and poorly defined notion of fair use. Google soon changed its tack and became somewhat more consultative.[3] Then the writs were issued by some publishers and authors. The GPLP quickly narrowed itself to become Google Book Search. Even then the legal problems remain.

But the lure of the GPLP still persists. Like an Eden of knowledge, it is an idea that is too powerful and attractive not to be considered. In some respects Google came to the idea first, abandoning it only when the legal realities became too obvious. Yet for policy-makers there is something in the whole GPLP that should be revisited. The democratic and egalitarian ideals of freedom of access to information demand that some policy be put in place to provide an online library for the citizenry. Every developed nation has public libraries that provide physical hard copies of books to their patrons. These libraries are limited only by geography and physical scope. Similarly, the National Library of Australia keeps a copy of every work published in Australia. In this context, the GPLP offered only a digital extension of the physical reality.

Regrettably, where the entry of copyright works onto the Internet has been accompanied and propelled by piracy, the GPLP was always going to be controversial. The spectre of Napster and Grokster created fears in the minds of most copyright owners. The possibility that e-books might be pirated due to the GPLP would have irked publishers. There have been endless debates and studies on whether peer-to-peer piracy actually costs money for the content industries. But it is impossible to go past the logical proposition that once a consumer has obtained a good for free they are hardly likely to go and pay for it. Accordingly, the content industries have adopted an ultra-conservative approach to Google and other digitization efforts. The piracy issue, along with the success of the copyright owners in seeking stronger copyright laws, has provided Google with a difficult environment in which to operate.[4]

3   In August 2005, Google announced that it would stop copying and offer an opt-out process.
4   For a discussion of the strengthening of copyright laws, see Neil Netanel, "Why Has Copyright Expanded? Analysis and Critique" in Fiona MacMillan, ed., *New Directions in Copyright Law*, vol. 6 (Cheltenham: Edward Elgar, 2007).

To succeed, Google needs strong copyright exceptions. In the US it has the possibility of the fair use doctrine.[5] At best, this equitable doctrine is a last resort defence. Though many American commentators have viewed it as an affirmative right, it is in fact merely a defence under the US *Copyright Act*.[6] In Australia, the UK, Canada, and other common law jurisdictions, Google would need to rely on the fair dealing provisions of the respective statutes. Put simply, the legal task facing the GPLP appeared, and still does appear, to be somewhat insurmountable.

There are still two questions that need to be answered. Firstly, can the Google Book Search Project (GBSP), in its current form, be deemed to be permissible under the fair use doctrine in the US and under the fair dealing laws of other common law nations, such as Australia? Secondly, could a government ever undertake a project like the original GPLP and remain compliant with its international obligations? In answering these two questions I have focused on the laws of the US and Australia.

B.   THE GOOGLE PRINT LIBRARY PROJECT

Google is an amazing commercial success. The company was created by two Stanford graduate students, Larry Page and Sergey Brin, in the mid-1990s and rapidly became a Silicon Valley success story. From the outset, Google's rise was marked by an unorthodox and daring approach to commercialization. The founders were reluctant to agree to an orthodox commercial figure as CEO, but eventually agreed to Eric Schmidt (former CEO

---

5   Academic opinion on the fair use defence and the GPLP is divided. Those who argue in favour of Google and fair use tend to consider only the online book search itself. See, for example, Melanie Constantino, "Fairly Used: Why Google's Book Project Should Prevail under the Fair Use Defense" (2006) 17 Fordham I. P. Media & Ent. L.J. 235; Thomas Wilhelm, "Google Book Search: Fair Use or Fairly Useful Infringement" (2006) 33 Rutgers Computer & Tech. L.J. 107; Emily Proskine, "Google's Technicolor Dreamcoat: A Copyright Analysis of the Google Book Search Library Project" (2006) 21 Berkeley Tech. L.J. 213. In contrast, those who argue against GPLP being defensible under fair use consider many of the steps in the overall process. See, for example, Steven Hetcher, "The Half-Fairness of Google's Plan to Make the World's Collection of Books Searchable" (2006) 13 Mich. Telecomm. & Tech. L. Rev. 1; Matt Williams, "Recent Second Circuit Opinions Indicate that Google's Library Project is not Transformative" (2007) 24 Cardozo Arts & Ent. L.J. 303; and Vaidhyanathan, above note 2 at 1229.

6   17 U.S.C. § 107 [US *Copyright Act*].

of Novell) taking the reins at Google.[7] Even then the two founders retained the power to outvote the CEO. Whilst this might appear unremarkable now, it was certainly unorthodox when it was agreed to when Google was in its financing phase. Google is also reported to have taken the business model of a competitor.[8] In doing so Google faced, but apparently avoided, legal liability. In short, Google has proved to be a risk taker.

In late 2004 Google declared that it was going to engage in a partnership with a number of universities and libraries to create the largest repository of written works in digital form.[9] This was a bold step in the creation of the Google Print Project. There are currently two aspects to the Google Print Project. The first is termed the "Print Publishers Program," or "Partners Program." The Partners Program involves an agreement with publishers to digitize works and to share the revenues generated by advertising.[10] Under the Partners Program a user can search the text of a book and view a page that contains a particular search term and a few surrounding pages.[11] Importantly, the Print Publishers Program requires the consent of the publisher before a book can be scanned and made searchable on Google.

The second aspect is the GPLP. In establishing the GPLP, Google went beyond the Partners Program and entered into agreements with large libraries. The university libraries that Google engaged with were those of Harvard University, Oxford University, Stanford University, the University of Michigan, and the New York Public Library. None of these libraries or universities is a small commercial entity. Each would presumably be sophisticated enough to understand the ramifications of being found liable for copyright infringement.[12] Yet each entity has agreed to be involved in the GPLP.

It is important to understand what exactly the universities have agreed to with Google. It would appear that the agreements that are in place are

---

7   See, further, David Vise & Mark Malseed, *The Google Story* (New York: Bantam Dell, 2006) at 103.

8   Hetcher, above note 5 at 13.

9   See, further, Barbara Quint, "Google and Research Libraries Launch Massive Digitization Project" *NewsBreaks* (20 December 2004), online: http://newsbreaks. infotoday.com/nbreader.asp?ArticleID=16307; and Google Book Search, "Legal Analysis," online: http://books.google.com/googlebooks/newsviews/legal.html.

10   In this sense the GPLP is very similar to Grokster in that the revenue is generated from advertising.

11   For a more complete discussion of the Google Print Project, see further, Jonathan Band, "The Google Print Library Project: A Copyright Analysis," online: www. policybandwidth.com/doc/googleprint.pdf.

12   Potentially, the universities would be liable as secondary infringers under US law.

for the searching and browsing of public domain texts in their entirety. No legal liability attaches to this activity. Thus far, it appears that Oxford, Harvard, and the New York Public Library have consented only to the copying of public domain works.[13]

Both Michigan and Stanford have agreed to allow the scanning of copyright-protected works. However, where the books are in copyright they have been provided to Google. The books have then been scanned by Google in their entirety. Google then gives a digital copy to the library. Google makes the digital copy searchable on its website. However, what the user sees when they do a search is only a few brief sentences around the text of the search term.

Given the facts as they appear, there are four acts of copying that potentially give rise to legal liability. The first is the act of the libraries in providing copyright works to Google for the purpose of scanning. The second is the scanning of the full text of the books. The third is Google's act of supplying the scanned work to the libraries. The fourth is the search of the book on Google's website.

For the most part, Google and its advocates have blithely stated that their activities are covered by fair use. Further, in response to criticisms by publishers, Google declared in late 2005 that it would delay scanning until November of that year in order to give time to publishers to decide if they wanted to opt out of the project.[14] Google's opt-out policy runs directly in contradiction to the prevailing norms of copyright law. Normally Google, or any other potential user, would be required to approach the copyright owner or their collecting society for permission to copy their works.[15] In late 2005 both the Association of American University Presses (AAUP) and the Authors Guild filed suits against Google.[16]

The litigation between Google and the Authors Guild is ongoing. The matter is presently being conducted before Judge Sprizzo of the District Court of the Southern District of New York. At the time of writing it appears that the matter may finally be decided in 2009.

---

13   Jonathan Band, Office for Information Technology Policy Brief, "The Google Library Project: The Copyright Debate" (January 2006), online: www.policybandwidth.com/doc/googlepaper.pdf.

14   Band, *ibid.* at 2.

15   Band points out that the costs of approaching the owners would likely be prohibitive; see *ibid.* at 11.

16   *The Authors Guild, Inc. v. Google, Inc.*, No. 05 CV 8136 (S.D.N.Y., filed September 20, 2005); *The McGraw-Hill Cos., Inc. et al. v. Google, Inc.*, No.05 CV 8881 (S.D.N.Y., filed October 19, 2005).

Google retains some support from the legal fraternity for its project. For example, prominent Internet commentators such as Jonathan Band, William Patry, and Professor Lessig have all expressed the view that the Google Project constitutes fair use. Similarly, Fred Von Lohmann of Electronic Frontiers Foundation has also provided support for Google.[17] However, publishers and other industry groups have been openly critical of the way in which Google has conducted itself.[18]

The threat of liability and the worry of litigation must have unnerved Google. Tellingly, the GPLP was retitled as "Google Book Search." Despite the renaming, the fundamentals of the project remain and the issue of liability is still unclear.

C. GOOGLE BOOK SEARCH AND FAIR USE

The fair use doctrine is Google's primary line of defence.[19] But the fair use question with respect to the GBSP is much more complex than it seems. There is the possibility that the fair use doctrine needs to be applied to each and every book individually. However, this can be discounted at the outset of any legal analysis as other fair use cases involving mass copying focused on the process rather than the individual works themselves. For example, the *Sony Corporation of America v. Universal City Studios, Inc.*[20] and *American Geophysical Union v. Texaco Inc.*[21] cases both involved a number of copyrighted works being copied together. In both cases, the process of

---

17   Fred von Lohmann, "Authors Guide Sues Google" Electronic Frontier Foundation (20 September 2005), online: www.eff.org/deeplinks/2005/09/authors-guild-sues-google.

18   See, for example, Thomas Rubin, Associate General Counsel for Copyright, Trademark and Trade Secrets, Microsoft Corporation, "Searching for Principles: Online Services and Intellectual Property" (Speech to the Yale Club of New York, 6 March 2007) online: www.microsoft.com/presspass/exec/trubin/03-05-07AmericanPublishers.mspx.

19   Vaidhyanathan, above note 2 at 1210, states that "Google is exploiting the instability of the copyright system in a digital age. It hopes to rest a huge, ambitious, potentially revolutionary project on the most rickety, least understood, most provincial, most contested perch among the few remaining public interest provisions of American copyright: fair use." This very descriptive comment quite neatly summarizes the weakness in Google's legal position.

20   464 U.S. 417 (1984) [*Sony*].

21   60 F.3d 913 (2d Cir. 1994) [*Texaco*].

copying was relevant, not whether the copying of each individual program constituted a fair use.

Leaving aside the question of process, it is useful to clarify the issue of the number of fair use tests that need to be applied. Google has asserted that its use of the copyright protected books is fair use. Indeed, Google's advocates focus their fair use argument on the copy that is ultimately made available to others.[22] For example, noted Internet analyst Jonathan Band has analyzed Google's actions, and whilst acknowledging that there may be two processes that deserve fair use consideration, he focuses his analysis upon the excerpts that are made available to the user. Band's analysis does not engage deeply with the copy in Google's database or the digital copy that Google provides to the library.

There are still several different processes at play in the GBSP. Each of these needs to be considered in turn for there to be a comprehensive finding of fair use in either of the Google cases. Should Google actually fail with respect to any copying process, then the entire GBSP will be invalidated. Accordingly, the following acts require a fair use analysis: (i) the search of the books online on Google Book Search, (ii) the copying of books into Google's database, (iii) in the provision, by Google, of books in digital form to the libraries, and (iv) the supply of books to Google by the libraries.

D.   APPLYING THE FAIR USE TEST

The fair use doctrine is contained in section 107 of the US *Copyright Act*.[23] There are four elements to the fair use test and the defendant need only prevail on a majority of the factors. The first factor is concerned with the purpose and character of the use. The second factor considers the nature of the copyrighted work. The third factor regards the amount and substantiality of the portion used. The fourth factor considers the potential for market harm by the use of the copyright works.

E.   THE ONLINE GOOGLE BOOK SEARCH AND FAIR USE

The actual search conducted on Google's online Book Search stands a good chance of succeeding as a fair use. The user search on Google Book Search

---

22   See for example Band, above note 11. See also Lawrence Lessig, "Google Sued" (22 September 2005), online: http://lessig.org/blog/2005/09/google_sued.html.

23   *Supra* note 6, § 107.

is guided by the terms requested by the user and will reveal only a tiny portion of the book.

1) Purpose and Character of the Use

The two primary considerations under the first factor are whether the use is of a commercial nature and whether it is transformative.[24] The Google Book Search exists to aid users in seeking out information. However, the use is commercial—at least from Google's perspective.[25] Google's business model in this instance is very similar to that of *Grokster*.[26] As in *Grokster*, the copyrighted works are the draw to lure in the consumers, whilst the service provider receives income from advertising. The commerciality is not overt, but in the context of Google Book Search it is sufficient to colour the purpose and the character of the use as being commercial in nature. In essence, Google is a commercial enterprise, and the purpose of the Book Search is fundamentally commercial.

Whereas the commercial nature of Google Book Search weighs against a finding of fair use there is still the possibility that the use might be found to be transformative. The notion of transformative use is now synonymous with fair use.[27] The transformative use argument can be dealt with on both a legal and factual level.

As a purely factual matter, the way in which Google deals with the literary works should not be construed as transformative. Google might deliver the works to the public in a way that is different from the way in which it is normally delivered, but this does not rise to the level of being transformative. To be transformative the treatment of the copyrighted work must be such as to greatly change the original so as to make a new work. Another way of putting this in the Google context is that the search must render to the user something that is very different from the ordinary text.

This is in accord with the facts in *Campbell v. Acuff-Rose Music, Inc.*,[28] in which the bass and rhythm progressions of Roy Orbison's "Pretty Woman" were retained whilst the lyrics were greatly reworked and other elements

---

24   See, for example, *Campbell v. Acuff-Rose Music, Inc.*, below note 28.

25   *U.S. Copyright Act*, above note 6.

26   *Metro-Goldwyn-Mayer Studios Inc. v. Grokster, Ltd.*, 545 U.S. 913 (2005).

27   See Pierre N. Leval, "Toward a Fair Use Standard" (1990) 103 Harv. L. Rev. 1105. Leval's paper is widely credited as providing the impetus for the transformative use analysis in *Campbell*, below note 28.

28   510 U.S. 569 (1994) [*Campbell*].

were introduced. In this instance, Google does not rework the text, nor does it introduce other elements. Google simply limits the portion of the text that can be viewed on the basis of a user-generated search. The clear distinction between Google and *Campbell* was that in the latter the end product was substantially different from the original. Where Google is concerned, the end product is not something that is mostly or wholly new — it is simply a reduced version of the original.

In the alternative, Google might try to run a legal argument based on the decision in *Kelly v. Arriba Soft*.[29] In *Kelly*, the Ninth Circuit Court held that reducing images to thumbnail size to assist in the Internet search process was a transformative use. The Ninth Circuit applied the facts in *Kelly* to the test for transformative works derived from *Campbell*:

> The central purpose of [the first fair use factor] is to see . . . whether the new work merely supersedes the objects of the original creation, or instead adds something new, with a further purpose or different character, altering the first with new expression, meaning, or message; it asks, in other words, whether and to what extent the new work is transformative.[30]

Arguably, the Ninth Circuit Court erred in its decision in *Kelly*.[31] The test for transformative use stated by the Supreme Court in *Campbell*, if read strictly, requires that something new be added and that there is an alteration to the way in which the work is perceived. The facts in *Kelly* quite neatly fit the second part of this test. The reduction of the images to thumbnail size by Arriba Soft did alter the viewing of the work, making it functional in terms of the search, but not the aesthetic or entertainment value. But no new content was added. Similarly, with the Google Book Search the excerpts are provided for a different purpose because the book is not being read in a normal fashion. Indeed, the book cannot be read in its entirety. Again, however, no new content is added by Google.

It is difficult to say whether *Kelly* would actually be overturned.[32] On a policy basis the decision is very useful because it protects Internet searches from copyright liability. *Kelly* has been followed on the issue of transforma-

---

29   *Kelly v. Arriba Soft Corp.*, 336 F.3d 811 (9th Cir. 2003) [*Kelly*].

30   Above note 28 at 579.

31   See, for example, Williams, above note 5. Vaidhyanathan, above note 2, also suggests that *Kelly* may have been wrongly decided.

32   See, further, Cameron Westin, "Is *Kelly* Shifting Under Google's Feet? New Ninth Circuit Impact on the Google Library Project Litigation" (2007) Duke L. & Tech. Rev. 2. Westin argues that the decisions in *Perfect 10 v. Google Inc., et al.*, 416 F. Supp. 2d 828 (C.D. Cal. 2006) [*Perfect 10*] and *Field v. Google, Inc.*, 412 F. Supp.

tive works by subsequent decisions such as *Perfect 10 v. Google*[33] and *Bill Graham Archives v. Dorling Kindersley Ltd.*,[34] which suggests that it might again be followed. However, in *Bill Graham Archives*, the defendant added new biographical materials along with the copyrighted images. In contrast, Google is not adding new content. That said, as *Bill Graham Archives* follows the Kelly decision it can also be said to support Google.

The transformative-works issue will be vital to Google's fair use case. Google must at least succeed with a finding of fair use in relation to the online book search itself to have any chance of succeeding in the wider fair use battle. On balance, as the law stands it would appear that this factor will favour Google because the facts in the present matter fall within the parameters of the *Kelly* decision.

2) The Nature of the Copyrighted Work

The books that Google is copying from the libraries are both works of fiction and non-fiction. Whilst fictional works are closer to the core of copyright,[35] it should also be recognized that works of non-fiction often call upon substantial intellectual endeavour on the part of their authors. However, US copyright law has generally recognized that "the scope of fair use is greater with respect to factual than non-factual works."[36] It would appear that Google would be well-placed to succeed in relation to the second factor. Yet, it is worth noting the *obiter* remarks of the Supreme Court in *Feist Publications, Inc. v. Rural Telecommunications Service Company.*[37] The Supreme Court stated:

> In Harper & Row, for example, we explained that President Ford could not prevent others from copying bare historical facts from his autobiog-

---

1106 (D. Nev. 2006) can be read so as to suggest that the *Kelly* standard is being abandoned.

33   *Perfect 10, ibid.* at 849.

34   448 F.3d 605 (2d Cir. 2006) [*Bill Graham Archives*].

35   See, for example, Justice Souter in *Campbell*, above note 28 at 586. With regard to the second factor, Justice Souter noted the difference between fictional and factual works, stating that "[t]his factor calls for recognition that some works are closer to the core of intended copyright protection than others, with the consequence that fair use is more difficult to establish when the former works are copied."

36   *New Era Publications International v. Carol Publishing Group*, 904 F.2d 152 at 157 (2d Cir. 1990), Feinberg J. See also *Feist Publications, Inc. v. Rural Telephone Service Company*, below note 37.

37   499 U.S. 340 (1991) [*Feist*].

raphy, but that he could prevent others from copying his "subjective descriptions and portraits of public figures . . . This inevitably means that the copyright in a factual compilation is thin."[38]

This would suggest that, where a work of non-fiction required a great deal of subjective interpretation and analysis, the second factor (see section D above) might begin to weigh in favour of the author. At the same time it should be noted that in *Feist*, the Supreme Court decisively rejected the sweat of the brow doctrine.[39] This would preclude any reliance on the hard work and research that is often required to produce an academic or instructional text as a basis of denying fair use. Accordingly, this factor may favour Google.

3) The Amount and Substantiality of the Portion Used

The Google Book Search delivers only a small excerpt of a much larger text. As the Google searches are user-driven, it cannot be said that Google is delivering the creative heart of the work to the reader in every instance. In this regard, it is possible to distinguish the Google Book Search from the potentially unfavourable authority of *Harper & Row, Publishers, Inc. v. Nation Enterprises*.[40] In *Harper & Row* the defendants took portions of former US President Gerald Ford's unpublished autobiography and published them in an article in *The Nation* magazine. The fact that the portions selected were "among the most powerful passages in the book"[41] weighed against a finding of fair use. Further, Judge Learned Hand noted in *Sheldon v. Metro-Goldwyn Pictures Corp.* that, "no plagiarist can excuse the wrong by showing how much of his work he did not pirate."[42]

This is potentially awkward authority for Google. However, the facts in this instance favour Google. As the search is directed by the user, Google is not responsible for selecting the actual portion that is shown. Google can direct how much of the portion is made available, but once the full text is in the Google database the portion that is retrieved depends upon the particular search term. In this regard, provided that Google consistently delivers only a small portion of the copyrighted work, the third factor should favour Google.

---

38 *Ibid.* at para. 17.
39 *Ibid.* at para. 44.
40 471 U.S. 539 (1985) [*Harper & Row*].
41 *Ibid.* at 565, O'Connor J.
42 81 F.2d 49 at 56 (2d Cir. 1931).

4) Market Harm

The issue of market harm will require that Google resolve contradictory authorities. On the one hand, there is the Second Circuit Court decision in *Salinger v. Random House Inc.*,[43] which held that the publication of letters was not a fair use because it detracted from the ability of the author to sell his letters to the public.[44] In *Salinger*, the famous author J.D. Salinger had given his letters to the libraries of Harvard, Princeton, and the University of Texas. His biographer accessed the letters there and ultimately quoted them, in part, in a book. Salinger had vowed not to publish the letters. But the Second Circuit found that this statement did not diminish his right to change his mind.[45] In essence, the Second Circuit Court sought to preserve the potential market for Salinger's letters. The court followed a similar line of reasoning in the *Castle Rock Entertainment, Inc. v. Carol Publishing Group, Inc.* case.[46] In *Castle Rock* the publication of a Seinfeld trivia book was held not to be fair use because it infringed on the "creative and economic choice" of the copyright owner.[47] In that case the court again focused on the potential market available for the copyright owner.

To counter the adverse authorities of *Salinger* and *Castle Rock*, Google might again seek to rely on *Kelly*. The facts in the present matter are similar to those in *Kelly*, in that the excerpts are a reduction of the actual book just as the thumbnail images were a reduction of the full-size picture. Accordingly, if a reader wishes to read the book in its entirety they will need to either purchase a copy or borrow it from a library.

The publishers might argue that Google's actions prevent them from offering a product that is similar to the Google Book Search. This would be an arguable form of market harm. The publishers would have the necessary raw ingredients in terms of the copyright ownership of the books. However, for the publishers to offer a product that is actually similar to the

---

43   811 F.2d 90 (2d Cir. 1987) [*Salinger*].

44   *Ibid.*

45   *Ibid.* at para. 31.

46   150 F.3d 132 (2d Cir. 1998) [*Castle Rock*].

47   *Ibid.* at para. 38. Judge Walker stated, "Unlike parody, criticism, scholarship, news reporting, or other transformative uses, The SAT substitutes for a derivative market that a television program copyright owner such as Castle Rock 'would in general develop or license others to develop.' *Campbell*, 510 U.S. at 592. Because The SAT borrows exclusively from *Seinfeld* and not from any other television or entertainment programs, The SAT is likely to fill a market niche that Castle Rock would in general develop."

Google Book Search they would need to have Google's search function. As the publisher's do not have this capacity they might struggle to make out a market-harm argument. That said, this does not preclude the possibility that the publishers could have entered into a joint venture with another search engine company. Google's actions will likely have rendered this possibility null.

On balance, it would appear that Google will prevail with regard to the above four factors by a 3:1 margin in relation to fair use and the online book search. However, this margin should not disguise the fact that the fair use argument is reasonably evenly balanced.

F. THE COPYING OF BOOKS INTO GOOGLE'S DATABASE AND FAIR USE

Any fair use analysis of the copying of the books in their entirety is going to necessarily be coloured by the overall purpose of Google Book Search. As such, this is a very different type of fair use analysis.[48]

1) The Purpose and Character of the Use

The purpose of copying the book in its entirety into Google's database is to assist with the Google Book Search. Google will argue that this is a necessary step in the process of providing the Book Search service.[49] Jonathan Band, in his analysis of the GPLP, points out that the copying of the entire book is actually very similar to Google's ordinary search process.[50] Unless Google is able to copy materials, its search process, online or in the Book Search, cannot function properly. However, as Professor Hechter notes in his analysis of Google's intermediate copying, in Google's regular searches the materials are already online, whereas in this instance Google is required to digitize works that were not previously available electronically.[51] This is what makes Google so different to the facts in *Kelly*. The process at play in Google is one of analog to digital to online. Google is in effect exercising the copyright owner's right to decide whether the work should be digitized and available online.

---

48   In most fair use cases there are not three concurrent fair use tests running.
49   The type of copying at hand here is intermediate copying. See *Sega Enterprises Ltd. v. Accolade, Inc.*, 977 F.2d 1510 (9th Cir. 1992).
50   Band, above note 11.
51   Hetcher, above note 5 at 49.

A further consideration is that while the copying in this instance is not commercial *per se*, the overall process is commercial.[52] This will become a very difficult argument for Google. Logically, Google cannot seek the protection of the overall purpose when it suits for fair use reasons, and disavow it when it does not. For example, in this instance the copying of the book is not transformative because nothing is added and there is no new purpose.[53] Google cannot look to the transformative nature of the online search to cover the intermediate copy. Overall this factor must be decided against Google.

2) The Nature of the Copyrighted Work

This factor will again be subject to the same considerations as in the prior fair use analysis. It is likely that this might just marginally favour Google. However, this conclusion again rests on the possibility that a court might not give due weight to the depth of analytic work present in an academic text.

3) The Amount and Substantiality of the Portion Used

In this instance Google is copying the entire book. It has previously been held in the seminal case of *Sony* that the copying of a work in its entirety will not preclude a finding of fair use.[54] However, in *Sony* the copying of works in their entirety was permissible provided that works were not kept as library copies. In the present case the books are permanently stored in Google's database. Whilst the copying may be functionally necessary, the legal analysis must favour the copyright owners.

4) Market Harm

It would have been possible for Google to have purchased the books from the publishers. However, the cost of this would no doubt have been exorbitant. That said, there is clearly an available market. For example, Harper Collins has announced that it intended to digitize all of the 25,000 books in its catalogue.

Ultimately, the copyright owners would win the fair use argument in relation to Google's database on a 3:1 basis.

---

52   The intermediate step is still a necessary precondition for commerciality.

53   In contrast, in *Billy Graham Archives* new content in the form of biographical analysis was added.

54   Above note 20 at para. 46.

G. THE LIBRARY COPY AND FAIR USE

1) The Purpose and Character of the Use

This is an outright commercial exchange between Google and the libraries. Google is getting the vital raw materials that it needs in order to run a commercial project. In return, the libraries are getting something that would have cost them money to do themselves or to purchase from elsewhere. This factor favours the copyright owners.

2) The Nature of the Copyrighted Work

The reasoning in this instance is unchanged from the other fair use analyses. This might slightly favour Google.

3) The Amount and Substantiality of the Portion Used

As above, the book is provided in its entirety by Google. Furthermore, it is provided as a library copy. While the libraries do have some archival powers under section 108 of the US *Copyright Act*,[55] this is unlikely to cover this instance. This factor will favour the copyright owners.

4) Market Harm

An actual market for digitization exists because the publishers can sell e-books. There would also presumably be operators willing to scan and digitize the books with a licence to do so from the copyright owners. As such, Google has usurped a market of the copyright owners. This finding will favour the copyright owners.

In summary, the copyright owners would prevail under a fair use analysis in relation to the libraries copy on 3:1 basis.

H. FAIR USE

It does Google little good to win the fair use argument in relation to the online search but to lose it in relation to the database and the library copies. A defeat anywhere in the process renders the GBSP a legal impossibility. As can be seen from the analysis above, Google cannot prevail because ultim-

---

55   Above note 6, § 108.

ately the steps it needs to undertake in order to provide the Google Book Search are not covered by fair use.

I.   LIBRARIES' LIABILITY

Should Google be found to be liable for copyright infringement then the libraries would be liable under US copyright law as secondary infringers. There would be no need to engage in a legal analysis beyond the orthodox doctrines of secondary infringement. As such, the libraries could be cast as contributory or vicarious infringers. Contributory infringement requires (i) direct infringement by a primary infringer, (ii) knowledge of the infringement, and (iii) material contribution.[56] Similarly, vicarious liability requires (i) direct infringement, (ii) financial benefit, and (iii) the right and ability to supervise the infringing conduct.[57] It would be very simple to make out an argument for contributory infringement. Google is clearly a direct infringer, the libraries have actual and constructive knowledge, and, by providing the books, they have made a material contribution. Vicarious liability might be more difficult to make out because the libraries, depending on the licence agreements, most likely do not have the right or ability to supervise Google.

J.   GOOGLE BOOK SEARCH AND FAIR DEALING

In the remote chance that Google obtains some type of fair use clearance in the US,, there would still be the question of whether the Google Book Search can be validly available in Australia. Fortunately for Google, in this instance it need only be concerned with the online Book Search itself. As all the copying leading up to the book being available on the Internet takes place in either the UK or the US, the Australian analysis needs only to be concerned with the online Google Book Search process itself.[58]

Under Australian law, a dealing is considered fair if it is covered by one of the fair dealing exceptions in the *Copyright Act 1968*.[59] As the books are works, the appropriate part of the *Copyright Act* would be Part III, which

---

56   See *Metro-Goldwyn-Mayer Studios Inc., v. Grokster Ltd.*, 380 F.3d 1154 (9th Cir. 2004) [*Grokster*]. In *Grokster*, Thomas J. of the 9th Circuit identified the elements of contributory infringement but found that they could not apply to Grokster's peer-to-peer operation. On appeal the Supreme Court demurred upon this point, above note 26.

57   *Fonovisa, Inc. v. Cherry Auction, Inc.*, 76 F.3d 259 (9th Cir. 1996).

58   There is no indication as far as the author is aware that any Australian libraries are seeking to be a part of the Google Book Search process.

59   *Copyright Act 1968* (Cth.) [*Copyright Act*].

applies to literary works and other works. Under Part III, Google might be able to rely on section 40, which relates to fair dealing in relation to research or study.[60] The difficulty that Google would encounter under section 40 pertains to the authority in *De Garis v. Neville Jeffress Pidler Pty Ltd.*[61]

De Garis is problematic because in that case the Federal Court held that the benefit of the fair dealing exception would be available only to the user and not to an intermediary. Unfortunately, Google, as an intermediary, would not be entitled to the defence. However, *De Garis* is well and truly out of date as an authority because it precedes the emergence of the Internet and Australia's *Digital Agenda Amendment Act* copyright reforms.[62] The greatest benefit of the Internet is its functionality, and, importantly, the process of disintermediation, which allows so many transactions to take place online. It is possible that the High Court might reconsider *De Garis* if the appropriate case came along. However, as the law stands Google cannot succeed under the fair dealing exception.

K. AN EDEN OF KNOWLEDGE

If Google cannot succeed under the laws of the US or Australia, then it might be possible that a government could seek to do what Google cannot. In a sense, this is quite logical as it is usually one of the general functions of a government at a local or state level to provide library services. In doing so, a government might seek to go beyond the parameters of the Google Book Search and actually return to the notion of an online library.

On a policy level, the GPLP has some attractive features.[63] First, it removes private wealth, geography, and educational attainment as barriers to

---

60 *Ibid.*, s. 40.

61 (1990), 18 I.P.R. 292 [*De Garis*]. In *De Garis*, Beaumont J. noted that whilst the retrieval of material by Jeffress might have been complicated, it still did not mean that the purpose of Jeffress was that of research. Jeffress supplied photocopies of material for purely commercial reasons. Beaumont J. stated at 298 that, "The relevant purpose required by s. 40(1) is that of Jeffress, not that of its customer. That is to say, even if a customer were engaged in research, this would not assist Jeffress."

62 In 2000 Australia passed the *Copyright Amendment (Digital Agenda) Act 2000* (Cth.) in order to bring the *Copyright Act*, above note 59, into the digital era.

63 It begs the question of whether an exception should be made to allow the Print Library Project. For example, Proskine, above note 5 at 233–39 argues in favour of a legislative exception to assist Google. However, the obvious weakness would be that such a step would clearly favour a powerful company, and there would be no such exception for its rivals or smaller operators.

accessing information. This is not to say that there are no barriers to access the Google Library—one must still own a computer and have access to the Internet. But the Google Library clearly goes some way to levelling the playing field and allowing everybody to access written works. This would not be an insignificant achievement. For example, the Australian Government is still struggling to achieve equity in the education sector, and Internet and educational access in rural and remote Australia is still very much an ongoing public policy concern. So from this perspective the GPLP would help to solve some wider and more pressing concerns by allowing those in rural areas with Internet facilities to access materials that might otherwise be geographically remote.

Second, the Google Library offers a way to preserve, in digital form, almost every published work written by mankind. This is a concern that goes well beyond the narrow, economic confines of copyright law. An electronic repository of all the written works of human civilization is not a minor concern. Arguably, it is something that must be done at some stage. Otherwise all human knowledge will remain fragmented and there will be the danger that knowledge will be lost.

Third, libraries are already publicly available anyway. While publicly funded, libraries are free for their individual users. A digital library would merely supply an online service that is already physically available. The key differences would be non-rivalry in consumption and the absence of geographical boundaries.

As desirable as this sounds, any government that chose to supply an online library, or even something akin to the Google Book Search, would need to amend its copyright laws. In reality, such a process would be long, drawn-out, and contentious.[64] More importantly, the government would face serious obstacles in relation to its international obligations.

L. THE THREE-STEP TEST

The most difficult obligation, the one that would likely defeat any digital library, is the three-step test. The three-step test, which emerged from article 9(2) of the *Berne Convention for the Protection of Literary and Artistic Works*,[65]

---

64   See, for example, Kimberlee Weatherall, "Of Copyright Bureaucracies and Incoherence: Stepping Back from Australia's Recent Copyright Reforms" (2007) 31(3) Melbourne U.L. Rev. 967.

65   9 September 1886, as revised at Paris on 24 July 1971 and amended in 1979, S. Treaty Doc. No. 99-27 (1986) [The 1979 amended version does not appear in U.N.T.S. or I.L.M.] [*Berne Convention*].

can now also be found in the *Agreement on the Trade-Related Aspects of Intellectual Property Rights*,[66] the *WIPO Copyright Treaty*,[67] and the *WIPO Performances and Phonograms Treaty*.[68] For Australia, the three-step test is also contained in the *Australia-United States Free Trade Agreement*.[69] Even more remarkably, the Australian legislature decided in late 2006 to include the three-step test within the *Copyright Act*.[70]

The three-step test requires that exceptions to copyright owners' rights be limited to certain special cases that do not conflict with the normal exploitation of the work, and that do not unreasonably prejudice the legitimate interests of the author. The narrowness of the three-step test will likely preclude the GPLP, or any national imitator, from emerging. The problem is that if a nation, such as Australia, Canada, or the UK, ever tries to create a digital online library it would face the prospect of challenge by one of its trading partners.

Given the proliferation of the three-step test at an international level, it is now possible that the standard has become a part of customary international law. The continued application of the three-step test in relation to copyright exceptions in free trade agreements, and, in Australia's case, in domestic law, suggests that a customary rule has emerged or is emerging. This is a significant development for policy-makers because it binds their hands in terms of the policy schemes that they can develop. The danger for any nation is that if they act inconsistently with their international-trade-law commitments they may be subject to retaliation under the rules of the World Trade Organization or under other free trade agreements to which they may be a party.

M. CONCLUSION

Google's affirmative defence of fair use is incredibly flimsy and is unlikely to withstand challenge. Likewise, the question of whether Australian copyright law will ever accommodate anything as ambitious and challenging as the GPLP warrants a simple answer from a legal perspective—any lawyer with a fair degree of knowledge of the *Copyright Act* would have to respond

---

66   15 April 1994, Marrakesh Agreement Establishing the World Trade Organization, Annex 1C, 1869 U.N.T.S. 299; 33 I.L.M. 1197 (1994) [*TRIPS*].

67   20 December 1996, S. Treaty Doc. No. 105-17 (1997); 36 I.L.M. 65 (1997).

68   20 December 1996, S. Treaty Doc. No. 105-17 (1997); 36 I.L.M. 76 (1997).

69   Department of Foreign Affairs and Trade, *Australia-United States Free Trade Agreement*, online: www.dfat.gov.au/trade/negotiations/us_fta/final-text.

70   Above note 59, s. 200AB.

in the negative. Further, a negative answer would necessarily follow any question of whether a nation could provide an online library and still satisfy its treaty obligations. Yet copyright law has never been strictly about black-letter law to the exclusion of all other considerations. Those public policy concerns that underpin the laws of copyright make the Google question somewhat compelling. Indeed, Google might likely be defeated, but it has asked a question worth answering.

Third-party Copyright and Public Information Infrastructure/Registries: How Much Copyright Tax Must the Public Pay?

Brian Fitzgerald & Benedict Atkinson

A. INTRODUCTION: THE ISSUES IN QUESTION

In a case currently before the High Court of Australia (*Copyright Agency Limited (CAL) v. State of New South Wales*[1]) the fundamental question at issue is whether the owner (in this case, surveyors) of copyrighted material (in this case, land survey plans) that is submitted as part of a public register (in this case, the land titles registry), with all the benefits that entails, should nonetheless have the right to charge the government and end-users every time they reproduce or communicate that material to the public.

The counter argument is that:

1) The copyright owner, in submitting the material and receiving all the associated benefits (including land development), authorizes any further reuse in the public interest.
2) Not all uses are controlled by the copyright owner. Copyright law comprehends that outside the statutory exceptions certain uses may be unremunerated.
3) Constitutionally and in practice the power to make laws with respect to copyright has never been thought to allow copyright owners to claim remuneration for use of their material in a public registry, from which they gain benefits.
4) Copyright is not only about remuneration of the copyright owner but also about individual rights being bestowed for the public good.

---

1   [2008] HCA Trans 174 (AustLII) [*CAL*].

If the Copyright Agency Limited (CAL), on behalf of the surveyors, is successful in this case then, reasoning by analogy, use of any third-party copyright material submitted to a public register will be charged for (remunerable) every time the government, or an end-user (member of the public), reproduces or communicates it to the public.[2] In this article, we explain why such a result is not dictated by law, and would frustrate the important role copyright law now plays in the innovation system and productivity cycle of Australia.[3]

The focus of the argument has been on the plight of the surveyor as copyright owner, but this detaches the situation from the obvious fact that the plan is submitted to government to allow a land developer to make a profit. The people of New South Wales (NSW) should not expect to have to (nor should they ever let their government bargain for them to) pay for generations for this activity through a copyright royalty or levy. In anyone's terms, that would be regarded as an unacceptable state of affairs.

1)   CAL v. NSW[4]

The litigation currently before the High Court between the CAL and the state of NSW, as foreshadowed above, concerns copyright in survey plans.

CAL, which according to a decision of the Copyright Tribunal is a duly constituted collection agent for surveyors,[5] contends that survey plans of land, which in turn are part of, and underpin, the land titles registry in NSW and in every other state in the country, are the copyright (artistic) works of surveyors, and that government should pay a royalty for using them.

The litigation has raised a number of issues but the core issue to be resolved by the High Court is whether:

> 5. . . . in relation to any Relevant Plan, is the State, other than by operation of s. 183 of the *Copyright Act*, entitled to a licence to:
> (i)   reproduce that Relevant Plan; and

---

2   This would be subject to the operation of any exceptions or "free use" provisions in the *Copyright Act 1968* (Cth.) such as the fair dealing exceptions.

3   Brian Fitzgerald, "It's Vital to Sort out the Ownership of Ideas" *The Australian Higher Education* (27 February 2008), online: www.theaustralian.news.com.au/story/0,25197,23280526-25192,00.html.

4   *CAL*, above note 1; *Copyright Agency Limited v. New South Wales*, [2007] FCAFC 80, 240 A.L.R. 249 [*CAL FCAFC*].

5   *Reference by Australian Spatial Copyright Collections Ltd.*, [2004] ACopyT 1.

(ii) communicate that Relevant Plan to the public, within the meaning of the *Copyright Act*?[6]

On the basis of the litigation to this point, one can assume that the appeal will be argued on the basis that the survey plans are not first published by, or under the direction or control of, the Crown under section 177 of the *Copyright Act 1968*,[7] nor made by, or under the direction or control of, the Crown under section 176[8] — thereby copyright does not inhere in the Crown due to these special provisions in the Act.[9] It can also be assumed that although survey plans serve a largely functional role as the core infra-

---

6   *CAL FCAFC*, above note 4 at para. 8. Question 5 is one of eleven questions of law, or the "stated case," agreed to by the parties and referred by the Copyright Tribunal to the Full Federal Court for determination. In the appeal, the High Court was not required to consider all of the questions in the stated case and focused on Question 5, and to a lesser extent, Question 6.

7   Above note 2, s. 177:

> *Crown copyright in original works first published in Australia under direction of Crown*
>   Subject to this Part and to Part X, the Commonwealth or a State is the owner of the copyright in an original literary, dramatic, musical or artistic work first published in Australia if first published by, or under the direction or control of, the Commonwealth or the State, as the case may be.

Surprisingly, Mr. Catterns, Q.C. (Counsel for the Appellant CAL), in his argument before the High Court, appears to be saying that his fallback submission on publication before the Full Federal Court, which was ultimately adopted by that court, is no longer a persuasive submission (and that is one reason why his view of the application of s. 183 must prevail). He maintained that we "accepted our share of the blame" for making this submission: *CAL*, above note 1 at 17–18. Mr. Yates, S.C. (for NSW), on the other hand, said he was accepting of the decision of the Full Federal Court on this point: *ibid.* at 24.

8   *Ibid.*, s. 176

> *Crown copyright in original works made under direction of Crown*
>   (1) Where, apart from this section, copyright would not subsist in an original literary, dramatic, musical or artistic work made by, or under the direction or control of, the Commonwealth or a State, copyright subsists in the work by virtue of this subsection.
>
>   (2) The Commonwealth or a State is, subject to this Part and to Part X, the owner of the copyright in an original literary, dramatic, musical or artistic work made by, or under the direction or control of, the Commonwealth or the State, as the case may be.

9   Above note 2. See *CAL FCAFC*, above note 4.

structure of the Torrens system of title by registration, and can only be represented in one way,[10] they are the subject of copyright protection.

The rulings of the Full Federal Court on sections 176 and 177[11] of the *Copyright Act 1968* could be further argued and the Full Court seems to have missed an opportunity to have allowed an interpretation of these provisions exclusive of commissioned or contractual works. In other words, those provisions appear readily applicable to materials created pursuant to statutory requirements (as opposed to contractual arrangements) that come to form part of a public registry. Further, there are unresolved questions about how copyright law should protect functional works[12] and the extent to which anything like the US merger doctrine has application in Australia.

2) CAL's Argument

CAL is arguing that section 183 provides that the Crown (subject to some restrictions in section 183(11)) will never infringe copyright, yet the Crown must pay a reasonable fee for this copyright use. It appears to take the (very broad) view that all Crown use is remunerable, pursuant to section 183. There is conjecture as to whether, if pushed, CAL would argue that reliance by the Crown on fair-dealing provisions in the *Copyright Act 1968* is ousted by section 183, or at the very least that if those provisions can be used to

---

10   "For most Survey Plans, there is only one way of representing the division of a parcel of land. This means that if land is to be subdivided in a certain manner, the content and layout of the Survey Plan that accomplishes that division will inevitably be drafted in a prescribed way. If a surveyor repeats the work of a previous surveyor, the later surveyor should arrive at the same end result as the earlier surveyor and produce a Survey Plan that is of the same dimensions." *CAL FCAFC, ibid.* at 65, Emmett J. (Lindgren and Finkelstein JJ. concurring).

   Veeck v. Southern Building Code Congress International Inc., 293 F.3d 791 at para. 31 (5th Cir. 2002) (*en banc*): "If an idea is susceptible to only one form of expression, the merger doctrine applies and § 102(b) excludes the expression from the *Copyright Act 1968*. As the Supreme Court has explained it, this 'idea/expression dichotomy strike[s] a definitional balance between the First Amendment and the *Copyright Act* by permitting free communication of facts while still protecting an author's expression.' *Harper & Row v. Nation Enterprises*, 471 U.S. 539 at 556 (1985)."

11   The precursor of these provisions is s. 18 of the *Copyright Act 1911* (U.K.), 1 & 2 Geo. V, c. 46, which was expressed to have application in Australia through s. 8 of the *Copyright Act 1912* (Cth).

12   *Metricon Homes Pty. Ltd. v. Barrett Property Group Pty. Ltd.*, [2008] FCAFC 46.

avoid infringement, payment is still required under section 183.[13] The practice embodied in the current agreement between CAL and the Commonwealth governing remuneration for Crown copying appears to be that acts normally covered by fair-dealing exceptions are remunerable.[14] While CAL in both their oral submissions to the High Court and written submission in reply suggests that the "State might be able to avail itself of many other defences to infringement, such as making of backup copies of computer programs" they do not say such uses would be non remunerable.[15] Further, under the current agreement between CAL and the Commonwealth, one could only speculate how CAL would act in relation to Crown use of copyright materials embodied in a public register where the Commonwealth Parliament[16] has expressly said Crown use is not a copyright infringement.[17]

3) The Broader Dimension

The role and application of copyright in the digital networks of the information superhighway has been, and still is, a critical issue of our times. As many people use information technologies linked via the Internet to communicate with each other on a daily if not hourly basis, the notion of copyright has been embedded at the centre of our lives. In this context, to posit that every use of copyrighted material by people, industry, government, and educators must be licensed and remunerated, is a long way removed from the basic provisions of the *Statute of Anne*[18] — the first modern copyright

---

13   On this point, see, generally, Enid Campbell & Ann Monotti, "Immunities of Agents of Government from Liability for Infringement of Copyright" (2002) 30 Fed. L. Rev. 459; Austl., Commonwealth, Copyright Law Committee on Reprographic Reproduction, *Report of the Copyright Law Committee on Reprographic Reproduction* (Canberra: Australian Government Publishing Service, 1976) at para. 7.10 [Franki Report]. We acknowledge Mr. John Gilchrist for alerting us to these issues and resources.

14   Austl., Commonwealth, Attorney-General's Department, *Agreement between Copyright Agency Limited and the Commonwealth for Copying of Literary Works by the Commonwealth* (2003), online: www.ag.gov.au/www/agd/agd.nsf/Page/Copyright_IssuesandReviews_Governmentuseofcopyrightmaterial at 52 (Sch. 8, cl. 12).

15   Appellant's Submission in Reply S 595 of 2007 (18 April 2008) at para. 2. See also paras. 1–6 and *CAL*, above note 1 at 25.

16   It is suggested that the states cannot effectively do this due to the inevitable inconsistency with Commonwealth copyright law and the operation of s. 109 *Constitution Act 1900* (Cth.) [Constitution].

17   See, for example, *Petroleum (Submerged Lands) Act 1967* (Cth.), s. 150K.

18   *Copyright Act 1709* (U.K.), 8 Anne, c. 19.

statute—or the provisions of the Australian colonial copyright laws, or the first federal statutes in 1905 and 1912.[19]

Under those earlier statutes, would anyone have thought that drawing a plan of the boundaries of my property on my kitchen table to settle a dispute with my neighbour would have been an infringement of copyright, or that if a government officer had posted me a copy of a survey plan of my house block at marginal cost, that they would have been liable for copyright infringement?[20] The answer is a straightforward "no." The liberty to communicate in this space, and on these topics, would have been assured in true Diceyan fashion as an aspect of the rights and liberties that the law provides or does not take away. That kind of liberty is in serious jeopardy of being taken away.[21]

---

19   Ben Atkinson, *The True History of Copyright: The Australian Experience 1905–2005* (Sydney: Sydney University Press, 2007) cc. 1–3 [Atkinson].

20   It has been suggested by a Canadian scholar (somewhat contentiously, and the view is largely untested) that the Australian copyright legislation of 1905 and 1912 did not bind the Crown (on this notion, see *Australian Competition and Consumer Commission v. Baxter Healthcare Pty. Limited*, [2007] HCA 38) and therefore the Crown was not liable for copyright infringement up until the *Copyright Act 1968* entered into force. It is further suggested that infringement, in relation to unpublished copyrighted material (which survey plans would most likely have been considered), was actionable against the Crown at common law from late in the nineteenth century up until 1912 (remembering that there was no Crown copyright "by or under the direction or control of the Crown" style provision until 1912, and that unpublished copyright material was not dealt with exclusively by statute until 1912: *Pacific Film Laboratories Pty. Ltd. v Federal Commissioner of Taxation*, [1970] HCA 36, 121 C.L.R. 154 at 166–167); Jean-Pierre Blais, "Copyright and Compulsory Licences for the Services of the Crown: An Australia Model for Canadian Copyright Reform?" (1994) 5 A.I.P.J. 222 at 241–42. See also Austl., Commonwealth, Copyright Law Review Committee, *Report to Consider What Alterations are Desirable in the Copyright Law of the Commonwealth* by A.J. Arthur (Canberra: Commonwealth Government Printer, 1960) at para. 401 [Spicer Report]. It is unclear to what extent the introduction of the Crown copyright provision in the *Copyright Act 1912* (while dealing with copyright entitlement rather than infringement) contradicts this view. Nor does this analysis explore the possibility (up to 1968–69) of an agent or servant of the Crown being personally liable as an individual for copyright infringement whilst undertaking his duties: see, further, Peter Hogg & Patrick Monahan, *Liability of the Crown*, 3d ed. (Scarborough, ON: Carswell, 2000), especially cc. 6, 8, and 11 [Hogg & Monahan].

21   To so take away such a liberty in that time or today would require words of clear intent. It is settled law that a court should not impute to a legislature an intention either to abolish or to modify a common law right or privilege unless the relevant legislation makes such an intention unambiguously clear : *Coco v. The Queen* (1994),

4) What Is at Stake?

If CAL can establish that copyrighted material created by a non-government actor,[22] and required as a fundamental element of a public register and/or public record,[23] must be paid for every time the government reproduces or communicates it to the public, or the public later reproduces it, then the Australian government sector, the Australian taxpayer, and the Australian community more generally, will have a very significant levy to pay.[24] And more than likely the cost will be borne by everyday Australians. Anyone doing a basic conveyance that relies on the land titles register and the associated survey plan will no doubt be required to pay this extra cost. CAL acknowledged as much in argument before the High Court[25] but did not clarify that this would not necessarily be a one-off fee. Further copying by the end-user/consumer/new land owner of any survey plan would also potentially require permission and a copyright licence fee.[26] It would be unlikely that section 183 of the *Copyright Act 1968* would give the Crown the right to licence the end-user for this type of activity, or on a royalty free basis.

---

179 C.L.R. 427 at 437–38 and 446–47; *Baker v. Campbell* (1983), 153 C.L.R. 52 at 96, 116, and 123; *Daniels Corporation International Pty. Ltd. v. Australian Competition and Consumer Commission (ACCC)*, [2002] HCA 49, 213 C.L.R. 543 at 553; *Plaintiff S157/2002 v. Commonwealth*, [2003] HCA 2, 211 C.L.R. 476 at para. 30; *Coleman v. Power*, [2004] HCA 39, 220 C.L.R. 1 at paras. 185, 250, & 251; *Attorney-General (W.A.) v. Marquet*, [2003] HCA 67, 217 C.L.R. 545, 78 A.L.J.R. 105 at paras. 133 and 160; *Bropho v. Western Australia*, [1990] HCA 24, 171 C.L.R. 1 at 18; *Potter v. Minahan* (1908), 7 C.L.R. 277 at 304; *Corporate Affairs Commission of New South Wales v. Yuill* (1991), 172 C.L.R. 319; A. MacAdam & T. Smith, *Statutes: Rules and Examples*, 3d ed. (Sydney: Butterworths, 1993) at 262; *A. v. Boulton*, [2004] FCAFC 101; *Al-Kateb v. Godwin*, [2004] HCA 37, 219 C.L.R. 562 at paras. 19, 193, and 241; *Singh v. Commonwealth of Australia*, [2004] HCA 43 at para. 19; *Ruddock v. Taylor*, [2005] HCA 48, 221 A.L.R. 32 at 46; *Stevens v. Kabushiki Kaisha Sony Computer Entertainment*, [2005] HCA 58, 221 A.L.R. 448 at 497; *Thomas v. Mowbray*, [2007] HCA 33, 237 A.L.R. 194 at 300; *Chang v. Laidley Shire Council*, [2007] HCA 37, 237 A.L.R. 482 at 493.

22 The remuneration CAL would require for the use of copyright of the Crown in right of each state and the Commonwealth when used by each other in a public register is also unclear and a complicating factor.

23 On this notion, see *Conveyancing Act 1919* (N.S.W.), s. 199.

24 Compare *Patents Act 1990* (Cth.), s. 226.

25 *CAL*, above note 1 at 13.

26 One would also expect that a bank/mortgagee (or anyone with an interest in the land) would also need permission and have to pay a fee for any further copying and that this cost might be passed on to the landowner.

The ultimate question becomes whether Crown use of the plans is some form of unjust enrichment, or taking of value or property unfairly from actors engaged in providing commercial land surveying services, or whether it is the kind of use of the documents (which underpin land title and are guaranteed and endorsed by law) that a democratic society would never expect to be infringing or remunerated.

5) Further Implications

CAL is an agency that has been of great importance, but the advent of the digital age has seen it pursue new revenue streams that are far reaching. If Australia is to be a leader and innovator in the global economy, some leeway and some liberty to use copyrighted material—subject to international obligations—must exist, especially in the face of technology automates the potential for copyright infringement that every time it is used. Every time we use digital technologies they reproduce the material in question as part of their normal function or operation. The Australian schools sector under the PART VB statutory licence in the *Copyright Act 1968*[27] pays CAL remuneration for use of copyright material in schools. In 1999, they were paying some $9 million AUD and by 2007 this had risen to over $51 million AUD.[28] Our school level education system is by far and away the largest contributor to CAL, not industry, nor research institutions, and not even universities.[29] This dramatic rise in the amount we all pay CAL for school education—some might say this tax on knowledge[30]—is tied in with the way in which CAL seeks remuneration for a broad range of uses of copy-

---

27   Which Mr. Catterns, Q.C., in argument before the High Court, submitted has some similarities to the ss. 183 & 183A–D statutory licence: *CAL*, above note 1 at 10–11.

28   Delia Browne, "CC and Educators: A Marriage Made in Heaven?" (17 June 2007), online: http://icommons.org/articles/cc-and-educators-a-marriage-made-in-heaven [Browne].

29   The second reading speech of the 1980 *Copyright Amendment Act*, which created the educational statutory licence, stated that most educational copying would be fair dealing or otherwise fall within a statutory copyright exception. Parliament did not contemplate the possibility that the licence would come to function as a tax on all educational use, though the shadow attorney-general, Lionel Bowen, declared that the "users of copyright have been unjustifiably disadvantaged by this legislation.": see Atkinson, above note 19 at 360.

30   The Labor Senator Henry Givens introduced the phrase "tax on knowledge" into Australian political discourse in 1905 when attacking the thirty-year year posthumous term proposed in the *Copyright Bill 1905*: see Atkinson, *ibid.* at 39.

righted material, which is taken to new levels by the digital environment and the Internet.[31]

We move from that type of scenario to the one currently before the High Court. In this case the Crown will be obligated to pay CAL every time a survey plan of land is reproduced or communicated to the public. And what is more, the owner of the land will have no right to reproduce or communicate to the public the plan that is the bedrock of their very title to that land; so much for the notion of life, liberty, and estate. CAL argues that the surveyor holds copyright in the plan, and even though it is deposited into a public register (and is a public record), which in turn allows the developer of the land to reap financial benefit, we the people must, for the life of the surveyor plus seventy years, pay to CAL a fee whenever the government or citizen reproduces the plan, or communicates it to the public.

The prospect of such a scheme is alarming and one that the paying public, if apprised of the reasoning behind it, would regard as unconscionable — or, more bluntly, a "rip off." Such a scheme would also stifle access to government information surrounding land in an era where worldwide we are seeing the call for and implementation of policies to allow better access to government data and knowledge in the name of innovation — better decision making, accountability, health, education and services, and so on. In the words of Varian and Shapiro, we have moved to the view that we should "maximize value not protection" when it comes to management of government information.[32]

The CAL argument has an even broader prospect.[33] Think about how many public registers there are at the state and federal levels of government in Australia. Think about how much copyrighted material has been inputted into those registers covering things as foundational to commerce, research, and life as the record of births, deaths, and marriages. What of the copyrighted material that is inputted (by a doctor, nurse, parent, marriage celebrant or participant, relative, or funeral director) in each of these situations, usually in some standard government format — in much the same way a surveyor collects facts and puts them together in a standard form plan? Will any of that be reproduced or communicated to the public in the

---

31   For a detailed treatment of the history of CAL's collecting activities and its collecting philosophy see Atkinson, *ibid.* at 358–81.

32   H. Varian & C. Shapiro, *Information Rules: A Strategic Guide to the Network Economy* (Boston: Harvard Business School Press, 1999) at 5 [Varian & Shapiro].

33   To this extent, it is surprising that neither the Commonwealth nor any other state or territory has sought to intervene in this matter.

public register? The mining sector presents a key example. In that sector, most states will require mining reports to be submitted to the government, and many of these reports are made available in their original format as part of the mining register.[34] The obligation to input material, like the survey

---

34   See, for example, the *Mineral Resources Act 1989* (Qld.) [*MRA*]. The *MRA* establishes a data collection and management regime which features the following elements:

- the provision of reports (progress, relinquishment, and final), accompanied by maps, sections, charts, and other data such as full particulars and results of exploration programs and investigations, is made a condition of each of the various forms of tenure under the Act (exploration permits, mining claims, mineral development licences, and mining leases);
- the minister may "require" the holder of the tenure to provide such reports "when and in the way" the minister specifies (ss. 141(1) and 194(1)) or the tenure holder will provide prescribed reports, returns, documents, and statements "as prescribed" (s. 276(1)(f));
- the obligation to provide such reports is enforceable as the mining registrar may require the holder of a mining tenure to take all action necessary to rectify non-compliance with conditions of the tenure and deduct the cost of rectification from the security deposit lodged by the holder of the tenure.

The inclusion of a requirement to produce reports, etc., as and when required by the minister, as a standard condition of mining tenures, is illustrated by s. 141(1) of the *MRA*, which sets out the conditions attaching to all exploration permits. Section 141(1)(f) provides that each exploration permit shall be subject to various conditions, including that the holder must, when and how the minister requires, give to the minister progress, relinquishment, and final reports, accompanied by maps, sections, charts, and other data giving full particulars and results of the exploration program and investigations carried out on the area specified by the minister, including details of costs incurred for specified periods within the term of the exploration permit.

QDEX (online: https://qeri.dme.qld.gov.au/qeri/controller/Home) is an Internet-based digital document and data management system, managed by the Geological Survey of Queensland, which allows users to search, display, download, and lodge company exploration reports. QDEX contains more than 35,300 scanned copies of all open (that is, non-confidential) company reports filed with the government by mineral, coal, and petroleum explorers since the 1950s under mandatory reporting requirements. The collection commenced when the exploration permitting system was introduced in Queensland in the 1950s and continues to have several hundred reports added annually.

Since 1 January 2004, all reports lodged with the department (now the Department of Mines and Energy, but formerly the Department of Natural Resources, Mines and Energy) for work carried out on exploration permits, mineral development licences, and all petroleum tenures (including authorities to prospect) must be submitted digitally using the QDEX electronic lodgment system.

plan, is part of a mining company's cost of business (part of the cost of receiving the benefit of commercial development), and is used to augment knowledge so that we innovate downstream rather than reinvent the wheel.

More frightening is the complexity that such a development would bring to public administration, and the ability of people and industry to reuse the knowledge contained in public registries for all kinds of problem solving and innovation. If Australia was starting out on a strategy to improve its productivity, would it willingly embrace such a model as CAL is urging? The simple answer is "no" and we believe the law does not require such complexity and administrative mayhem to be imposed in our country.

6)   What Is to Be Done?

The Full Federal Court, by rejecting arguments based on sections 176 and 177 of the *Copyright Act 1968*, has in effect removed the assumed application of those provisions. When similar provisions were legislatively repealed in the UK in 1988, the UK parliament specifically enacted provisions that made it clear the Crown would retain rights to use copyright material in public registers royalty-free.[35]

In a nation state headed by the Queen of Australia (who is also the Queen of England), and significantly influenced by the English legal system, it would seem obvious that a similar sense of reasoning would apply. If third-party copyrighted documents (e.g., survey plans) are placed in a registry, and are not covered by the Crown copyright provisions, sections 176 and 177, then we need to articulate a rule of law, as was done legislatively in the UK, that reserves the right of the Crown to use the documents in the name of the public interest.

The Full Federal Court, by, for all intents and purposes, repealing the traditionally accepted view that these plans were covered by sections 176 and 177, has left a gap in the legal framework. The judges of the Full Court have filled the gap judicially (while in the UK it has been done legislatively) by the reasoning in their judgment — on the basis of authorization.

On the interpretation of the Full Federal Court in *CAL FCAFC*, above note 4, one might argue that these reports are first published when the consultant communicates them to the client (mining company) and therefore s. 177 of the *Copyright Act 1968*, above note 2, is not applicable. Likewise, there may be conjecture as to whether s. 176 applies.

35   *Copyright, Designs and Patents Act 1988* (U.K.), 1988, c. 48, ss. 47–50.

Further, while CAL has suggested the Crown will profit commercially from use of the plans (an issue raised in its submissions and argument to the High Court,[36] but not properly in issue in answering Question 5 of the stated case extracted above)—the international trend is to push for publicly funded research content and information to be provided in an open access[37], royalty-free, model. The notion, supported by the Australian Productivity Commission[38] and more recently the OECD,[39] is that allowing publicly funded

---

36   Above note 15 at paras.17 and 33; *CAL*, above note 1 at 7. In argument before the High Court Mr. Catterns, Q.C. said this went to the issue of whether an implied licence existed: "They are all done for the State but they are of a commercial character and we submit that is relevant to whether or not the surveyors are taken to have impliedly licensed what goes on."

37   On the definition of open access see: *The Bethesda Statement on Open Access Publishing* (2003), online: www.earlham.edu/~peters/fos/bethesda.htm; *The Berlin Declaration on Open Access to Knowledge in the Sciences and Humanities* (2003), online: www.zim.mpg.de/openaccess-berlin/berlindeclaration.html; *The Budapest Open Access Initiative* (2002), online: www.soros.org/openaccess/view.cfm;"Bermuda Principles" (1996), online: www.ornl.gov/sci/techresources/Human_Genome/research/bermuda.shtml; Neil Jacobs, ed., *Open Access: Key Strategic, Technical and Economic Aspects* (Oxford: Chandos, 2006); John Willinsky, *The Access Principle: The Case for Open Access to Research and Scholarship* (Cambridge, MA: MIT Press, 2006); The Hon. Kim Carr, Minister for Innovation, Industry, Science and Research, "There is More Than One Way to Innovate: Research for Discovery, Understanding and Application" (2008), online: www.go8.edu.au/storage/news/speeches/Go8/2008/Kim_Carr_speech_at_ANU_retreat_070208.pdf [Carr].

38   Austl., Commonwealth, Productivity Commission, *Cost Recovery by Government Agencies Inquiry Report* (Report No. 15) (Canberra: Commonwealth of Australia, 2001), online: www.pc.gov.au/projects/inquiry/costrecovery/docs/finalreport [*Cost Recovery Report*]. See also Office of Fair Trading, *Commercial Use of Public Information* (2006) online: www.oft.gov.uk/advice_and_resources/resource_base/market-studies/completed/public-information; David Newbery, Lionel Bently, & Rufus Pollock, *Models of Public Sector Information Provision via Trading Funds* (2008), online: www.berr.gov.uk/files/file45136.pdf [Pollock, Bently & Newbery]; John Houghton, Colin Steele, & Peter Sheehan, *Research Communication Costs in Australia: Emerging Opportunities and Benefits* (2006), online: www.dest.gov.au/NR/rdonlyres/0ACB271F-EA7D-4FAF-B3F7-0381F441B175/13935/DEST_Research_Communications_Cost_Report_Sept2006.pdf. [*Research Communication Costs*]; Aust., Commonwealth, Productivity Commission, *Public Support for Science and Innovation* (2007), online: www.pc.gov.au/__data/assets/pdf_file/0016/37123/science.pdf at 240 and 243.

39   The OECD has a draft set of principles on *Open Access to Public Sector Information* that will be considered for adoption at its ministerial conference in Korea in June 2008. See also OECD, *OECD Declaration on Principles and Guide-*

knowledge to flow freely will sponsor much greater innovation and productivity than locking it up and distributing it to a few. In the long run, it
will mean that much of the public information infrastructure, if it is not
already, will be provided to the public, including industry, free of charge
under liberal copyright licences. The business model of tomorrow, if it does
not already exist today, will be based, in much the same way as Google
operates, on providing search and value-added services for freely accessible
government material. It will not be based on charging for the copies of the
survey plan. The action of CAL in this case flows against this tide by seeking to place more barriers on open access to public registries.

In our view, the holding of the Full Federal Court should and must be
upheld for the following five reasons.

B. FIVE REASONS WHY THE HIGH COURT SHOULD REJECT CAL'S ARGUMENTS

1) The Crown use of the plans to create a public register and communicate
   their content to the public is authorized by the copyright owner as part
   of the bargain for the development of the land.
2) Not all uses of copyright material are remunerable and the use of plans
   by the Crown in order to establish a public register and communicate
   the contents of that register to the public is a non-remunerable act.
3) The acts of the Crown in using the survey plans to construct a public
   register and communicating that register to the public are not "any act
   comprised in the copyright" and therefore not an infringement under
   section 36(1) of the *Copyright Act 1968*.
4) The Crown use of the plans to create a public register and communicate
   their contents to the public is not an activity covered by the exclusive
   rights of the copyright owner as contemplated by the term "copyright"
   in the Constitution.[40]

---

lines for Access to Research Data from Public Funding (2004), online: www.
oecd.org/dataoecd/9/61/38500813.pdf and www.oecd.org/document/0,2340,
en_2649_34487_25998799_1_1_1_1,00.html. See also proceedings of a WPIE
Workshop on PSI, "The Socioeconomic Effects of Public Sector Information on Digital Networks: Toward a Better Understanding of Different Access and Reuse Policies" (2008), online: www.oecd.org/document/48/0,3343,
en_2649_34223_40046832_1_1_1_1,00.html.

40 Above note 16.

5) The acts of the Crown in using the survey plans to construct a public register and communicating that register to the public is fair dealing for the purpose of the public interest.

1) Argument 1 — Crown Use Is Authorized

The default rule in copyright is that you cannot reproduce or communicate to the public copyrighted material without the permission of the copyright owner. Permission, however, does not have to entail explicit written or verbal authorization. Nor does permission mean automatically that a royalty for copyright use is then payable. Section 183 is one form of obtaining that permission but it is not the only way. There is nothing stopping us from giving the Crown permission to reproduce this article without having to pay us any money or remuneration. To suggest otherwise in a democratic country like Australia would be mischievous.

In this instance, the surveyor has authorized (given permission through conduct) the Crown to use the plans in keeping a public register of land title, as part of the broader bargain of the developer gaining the right to develop, or further subdivide, existing land to their commercial advantage. The developer receives the imprimatur of the Crown and the benefit of ownership through registration of title, all based upon the functional nature and quality of the survey plan. This privilege is granted by the people of the state through their government, for a fee. The suggestion that the people of NSW should pay further for this development project through a royalty or levy on reproduction or communication to the public of the copyright material in question is contrary to policy and public expectation. By removing the issue of copyright in the plan from the broader context of the commercial development of land, we lose sight of the true bargain that is being struck between the citizens and the land and copyright holders.

Especially in a period of crisis concerning the affordability of housing in Australia, it would be folly to suggest that the people of NSW would agree to a commercial bargain that sees investing a land developer with the great privilege and commercial opportunity to develop land, yet they would have to pay a further fee to the developer or surveyor every time the public record of this is reproduced or communicated to them. The only common sense interpretation of the conduct in this case, as the Full Federal Court explained, is that the copyright owners have authorized the Crown to engage in the acts in question without seeking any further fee.

Justice Emmett (Lindgren and Finkelstein JJ. agreeing) explained:

There can be no doubt that the surveyor who was the maker of a Relevant Plan authorised the State to use the Relevant Plan in all of the ways described above. By assenting to the submission of the Relevant Plan for registration, the surveyor who made the Relevant Plan authorised the State to do everything that it was obliged to do in consequence of the registration of the Relevant Plan so as to become a registered plan. The consequence of registration is that the State was authorised to do the acts in question. It was an incident of each surveyor's assenting to the submission of a Relevant Plan to LPI, with the intention of its becoming a registered plan, that the surveyor authorised the State to do with the Relevant Plan all of the acts described above that might otherwise constitute an infringement of the copyright in the Relevant Plan.[41]

The argument advanced by CAL paints the state of NSW (and its people) as extremely naïve, not knowing how to structure a commercial bargain. It suggests they would sell off a valuable asset and then say to the purchaser and "what is more, we are happy to pay you (back) for generations, a royalty on the paperwork that could possibly exceed the amount of money you paid for the land in the first place." The reality is that in the situation at hand, the surveyor works with the developer and should seek remuneration from that commercial actor. In granting the privilege of land ownership (an estate in land) the Crown is not simply receiving (in return) the right to own one tangible plan, but more so the right to record the development plans in the public record as a part of an act of informing the public and bringing order to society.

In this bargain, as CAL envisages it, it seems odd that neither the ultimate (radical) title holder of the land (the Crown),[42] nor the everyday

---

41 *CAL FCAFC*, above note 4 at para. 155.
42 *Mabo v. Queensland (No. 2)*, [1992] HCA 23 at para. 7, 175 C.L.R. 1 at 80. There are many statements on the notion of radical title in this case. See, for example:

> The English common law principles relating to real property developed as the product of concepts shaped by the feudal system of medieval times. The basic tenet was that, consequent upon the Norman Conquest, the Crown was the owner of all land in the kingdom. A subject could hold land only as a tenant, directly or indirectly, of the Crown. By 1788, the combined effect of the *Statute Quia Emptores 1290* and the *Tenures Abolition Act 1660* had been largely to abolish the "pyramid of free tenants" (166) Gray, Elements of Land Law, (1987), p 57 which had emerged under the feudal system of tenure and to confine the practical significance of the basic tenet that all land was owned by the Crown to matters such as escheat and foreshore rights. The "estate" which a subject held in land as tenant was itself property which was the subject of "ownership" both

citizen that purchases the fee simple in good faith from the developer, ever obtains or reserves the right to make a copy of the survey plan. They require permission (statutory licence or otherwise) to do so. In this sense neither is ever sovereign in this aspect. Why the Crown, as the representative of the people of the state of NSW, would enter such a bargain is unfathomable. In broader thinking, it could be characterized as a breach of any fiduciary duty the Crown may hold to the public.

Justice Emmett (Lindgren and Finkelstein JJ. agreeing) explained that:

> The systems of land holding in New South Wales and the statutory and regulatory framework described above depend in no manner upon the existence of the *Copyright Act*. If s 183 did not exist, it is clear that there would be no utility whatsoever for a surveyor in submitting any of the Relevant Plans for registration unless, by doing so, or assenting to that being done, the surveyor authorised the State to do what it is obliged by the statutory and regulatory regime described above to do, as a consequence of registering the Relevant Plan. Whether or not s 183 has the effect that the doing of the acts, because they are done for the services of the State, are deemed not to be an infringement of copyright, a surveyor must be taken to have licensed and authorised the doing of the very acts that the surveyor was intending should be done as a consequence of the lodgement of the Relevant Plan for registration.[43]
>
> The whole purpose and object of the preparation and lodgement with LPI of the Relevant Plans was to obtain registration of them so as to become registered plans, with the intention of creating or affecting legal rights in, or with respect to, the land to which they relate, or to create or affect the capacity to create or affect legal rights in respect of that land. The purpose was that lots in the Relevant Plans, whether a plan of subdivision or a strata plan, would become separate and discrete parcels in the register of land holdings of the State. Those lots or parcels would

---

in law and in equity. The primary estate of a subject, the estate in fee simple, became, for almost all practical purposes, equivalent to full ownership of the land itself. Nonetheless, the underlying thesis of the English law of real property remained that the radical title to (or ultimate ownership of) all land was in the Crown and that the maximum interest which a subject could have in the land was ownership not of the land itself but of an estate in fee in it. The legal ownership of an estate in land was in the person or persons in whom the legal title to it was vested. Under the rules of equity, that legal estate could be held upon trust for some other person or persons or for some purpose.

43   *CAL FCAFC*, above note 4 at para. 156.

themselves become part of the cadastre of the State, by the infrastructure and mechanisms provided for under the *Real Property Act*, the *Conveyancing Act*, the *Strata Freehold Act*, the *Strata Leasehold Act* and the *Community Land Act*. The surveyors who prepared each of the Relevant Plans must be taken to have authorised the State to do, in relation to the Relevant Plans, everything that the State is obliged to do in consequence of their registration, quite apart from the coincidental effect of s 83(1).[44]

The notion of an implied licence is mentioned nowhere in the judgment of the Full Federal Court. This notion has been reintroduced by the appellant (CAL) in the special leave application and in its submission to the High Court.[45] The submission here is that there is express permission evidenced by the conduct of the parties. The bargain is not contractual in nature but rather it is a bargain evidenced by a series of statutory provisions. By acting in accordance with those statutory provisions the surveyor consented to the plan being used in the public register without further remuneration. This is the way it has always been.

The notion of an implied licence is a poor conceptual tool with which to underpin the reasons for the decision in this case. A more sophisticated approach is warranted, otherwise the implied licence established will simply be denied at the point of submission of the plan. The better view is that the state of NSW would only accept the plan for registration if it is authorized to reuse it in the way that public order requires. This raises no issues relating to "just terms"[46] nor would the state's refusal to register the plan be seen as an act inconsistent with the federal copyright law under section 109 of the Constitution as the Crown's need to hold appropriate user rights in building public registries has always been accepted even before the Constitution was enacted.

2) Argument 2 — Acts in Question Are Non-remunerable

Section 183 of the *Copyright Act 1968* only applies to remunerable uses and the use in question is not a remunerable use.[47] Copyright law is designed to provide an incentive for creators and makers to produce various types

---

44 *Ibid.* at para. 157.

45 Appellant's (CAL) Submissions (9 April 2008) at paras. 1 & 12.

46 See *CAL*, above note 1 at 4 and 22.

47 The statutory licence for Crown use of copyright material is broadly framed, but nothing in the report which recommended enactment of the statutory licence suggested a belief that *all* government uses were remunerable: Spicer Report, above note 20 at paras. 404–5. The function of a statutory licence is not taxation of uses made

of works and other subject matter.[48] In this instance, copyright confers no incentive on the surveyor. The surveyor's incentive to produce survey maps or plans is contractual: the payment of the surveyor by the land developer is the incentive to create the plans. There is no doubt that surveying business-es could, and in the past have, operated on the basis that they would receive no remuneration from the Crown for dealing with plans in the setting-up of a public register of land holding.[49]

The section 183 licence permits the government to use copyrighted material subject to payment of remuneration. Surprisingly, the parties to proceedings have focused most of their attention on the Crown's *rights* as user of copyright material, and paid no heed to the question of the surveyor's entitlement to *remuneration* for use. When the surveyor's assumed entitlement is examined, it can be seen that CAL's claim that the state must pay copyright fees for the use of survey plans is not consistent with policy. Statutory licences are instruments of public policy and their scope and ap-plication must be determined by reference to statutory language *and* policy.

When the elements of copyright policy are interrogated, including the policy of statutory licensing and the statutory exceptions, they reveal that:

- copyright does not confer a right of remuneration; and
- some copyrights are economically sterile.

---

by government purely in the public interest and without prejudice to the economic welfare of the copyright owner.

48 See *Welcome Real-Time SA v. Catuity Inc.*, [2001] FCA 445, (2000), 51 I.P.R. 327 at 354; *Mazer v. Stein*, 347 U.S. 201 (1954); Spicer Report, *ibid.* at para. 13; A. Fitzgerald & B. Fitzgerald, *Intellectual Property in Principle* (Sydney: Law Book Co., 2004) c. 1.

49 Arguments in this section focus on the content of legal rights, but it should be noted that legal policy, especially when dealing with economic rights, is informed by eco-nomics. Economic theory holds that if the copyright owner is permitted to impose fees on copyright use that exceed the return necessary for the owner to continue production, transaction costs increase, resulting in sub-optimal dissemination of information. In cases, such as the present one, where the copyright owner does not rely on the exclusive rights for economic reward, and copyright fees impose a public cost, the argument for policy-sanctioned taxation cannot be sustained on grounds of economic necessity. Compare *British Columbia Jockey Club v. Standen* (1985), 8 C.P.R. (3d) 283 (B.C.C.A.), Hutcheon J.A.: "The only thing that I would add is that there may be cases where the publication of material becomes part of the public domain either because of a statutory requirement to publish the material or because it is inherent in the circumstances that to recognize the claim to copyright would be contrary to public policy."

These propositions, and their relevance to the present case, are discussed below.

a)   No right of remuneration

The exclusive rights of copyright are commonly said to be economic rights. No exclusive right, however, confers a right of remuneration. The copyright enables the owner to bargain for payment. It does not confer a right to payment.[50] The exclusive rights are economic rights because they allow the owner to control the production and dissemination of copyright material, and the economic outcome of such control is usually payment for copyright use. In the case of statutory licensing, the government either imposes a bargain between the owner and user, or requires that a bargain be struck. But the exclusive rights in themselves do not entitle a copyright owner to remuneration for copyright use.[51]

If no right of remuneration exists, what is the scope of the copyright owner's economic entitlement? Within the boundaries of international law, (namely the three-step test)[52] this is, firstly, for government and legislature

---

50   In 1928, Sir Robert Garran, the secretary of the Attorney-General's Department, on behalf of the Attorney-General (the future Chief Justice) John Latham, informed a prominent licensee of the Australasian Performing Right Society (APRA) that APRA had "no right" to "demand" copyright fees. APRA could exercise its copyright to prosecute, prevent, or withhold permission for the public performance of music, and it could "name its price" for the public performance of music. But it could not compel payment: see Atkinson, above note 19 at 128.

51   For discussion of some questions of remuneration as they arose in Australian copyright legal history, see Atkinson, *ibid.*, cc. 4–8 generally (dealing with commercial disputes in Australia between the world wars centred around payment of performing right fees), and especially at 352–55, 359–63, and 428–30.

52   The three-step test, adopted in art. 9(2) of the *Berne Convention* [9 September 1886, as revised at Paris on 24 July 1971 and amended in 1979, S. Treaty Doc. No. 99-27 (1986)] in 1967, specified criteria for creating exceptions to the exclusive right of reproduction. The test is replicated in the WTO, *Agreement on Trade-Related Aspects of Intellectual Property Rights*, 15 April 1994, Marrakesh Agreement Establishing the World Trade Organization, Annex 1C, 1869 U.N.T.S. 299, art. 13 [*TRIPS Agreement*] (as the basis for creating copyright exceptions) and the *Australia-United States Free Trade Agreement*, 18 May 2004, [2005] ATS 1, art. 17.4.10(a) (also the *WIPO Copyright Treaty*, 20 December 1996, Article 10; EC, *Directive 96/9/EC of the European Parliament and of the Council of 11 March 1996 on the Legal Protection of Databases*, [1996] O.J. L 077; EC, *Directive 2001/29/EC of the European Parliament and of the Council of 22 May 2001 on the Harmonisation of Certain Aspects of Copyright and Re-*

to determine.[53] In the case of statutory licensing in Australia, policy has usually tied remuneration to copyright uses that prejudiced the owner's sales.[54] The compulsory licences in the 1912 *Copyright Act* provided that royalties were payable at a specified rate for each copy of records or books made for the purpose of sale.[55] The educational statutory licence passed into law in 1980 on the assumption that it would compensate the copyright owner for uses that prejudiced sales.[56]

---

lated Rights in the Information Society, [2001] O.J. L 167/10;and *WIPO Performances and Phonograms Treaty*, 20 December 1996).

53   Franki Report, above note 13 at para. 1.02. This report stated that the copyright owner's economic expectations should be balanced against public interest considerations: "There is, we believe, particularly in Australia, a very considerable public interest in ensuring a free flow of information in education and research, and the interests of individual copyright holders must be balanced against this element of public interest."

54   *Ibid.* at para. 1.52. The Franki Report recommended enactment of the educational licence for copying, and said: "However, in principle, we consider that multiple copying should not be carried out without remuneration to the copyright owner in any case where it represents a substantial use of his property or it could *prejudice sales* of his work, particularly if the work has specifically been written for use in schools." [emphasis added]. The remuneration policy of the s. 183 licence is less easy to discern, since neither s. 183 nor the related s. 183A were explained in second reading speeches. The Spicer Report, above note 20, which proposed the s. 183 licence, only sketchily outlined policy for the section. The Report recommended at para. 404, that "[t]he Commonwealth and the States should be empowered to use copyright material for any purposes of the Crown, subject to the payment of just . . . compensation." The Report did not, however, explain whether *all* Crown use demanded "just compensation."

55   The UK Parliament introduced the compulsory licences for sound recordings and books in the 1911 *Copyright Act* (incorporated in Australia's copyright legislation in 1912). The licences were consumer welfare measures although Parliament introduced the recording licence after extensive lobbying by the phonographic industry. The industry argued that unless a licence was introduced, a single phonographic company, or a combine, could purchase available music copyrights and establish monopoly or cartel control over the supply of music. Parliament intended both licences to compensate copyright owners for lost sales by the arbitrary fixing of royalty rates payable for each reproduction made under licence: see Atkinson, above note 19 at 47–53, 70–76, and 428–430.

56   Both the Franki Report and the second reading speech, which explained the 1980 legislation introducing the educational statutory licence, stated that the statutory licence was unlikely to apply to most copying by educational institutions. The Franki Report, above note 13 at para. 1.22 said: "The evidence we have shows that much of the photocopying that takes place is likely to be within the exceptions to the rights of the copyright owner established in the *Copyright Act*." The Franki Committee

To determine the scope of the section 183 licence, it is necessary to consider the policy of international, as well as domestic, copyright law. Neither can be said to posit that copyright use is, of itself, remunerable.[57] Analysis of the three-step test, which authorizes copyright exceptions in "certain special cases which do not conflict with a normal exploitation of the work and do not unreasonably prejudice the legitimate interests of the rightsholder," suggests that uses harmless to the copyright owner's economic interest may be free.[58] As discussed, it is possible to adduce from the history of statutory licensing in Australia the policy principle that a statutory licence compen-

---

earlier recognized that public welfare considerations played little part in copyright owners' arguments for remuneration: "The view that 'what is worth copying is worth protecting' has been put before us emphatically and persuasively. However what this usually means is 'what is worth copying is worth paying for.' Very few authors want restrictions for their own sake but rather as a means of securing remuneration." (Franki Report, *ibid.* at para. 1.20.)

57 See Franki Report, *ibid.* at para. 1.39: "We do not know of any proposal elsewhere that would require the payment of a royalty on all copies made, irrespective of the number of copies made and the purpose of the copying."

58 Note the approach of the Colombian Supreme Court (Cassation), which, in a judgment delivered on 30 April 2008, held that transferring music from vinyl to digital format did not constitute criminal infringement of the owner's reproductive right because, applying the three-step test, the use did not cause economic injury to the respondent: it was not profit-making, the appellant did not intend to cause economic injury, and the appellant did not cause economic injury. See the Spanish text of the judgment, online: www.karisma.org.co/carolina_publico/Sentencia%20CSJ.rtf. See the English summary, online: http://icommons.org/articles/colombian-ruling-on-copyright-without-profit-there-is-no-criminal-offence. Compare S. Ricketson, *The Three-Step Test, Deemed Quantities, Libraries and Closed Exceptions* (Strawberry Hill, NSW: Centre for Copyright Studies, 2002). Ricketson reasons tendentiously to propose an interpretation of the three-step test that would constrain fair use. His detailed discussion of considerations relevant to the application of the three-step test, including the proposition that a fair use must not place the user in "economic competition" with the owner, supplies insight into some of the treaty issues relevant to consideration of remunerable use. Discussing the meaning of "normal exploitation," Ricketson refers to guidance from a WTO Panel, which defined "exploitation" as activity "to extract economic value from their [copyright owners'] rights to those works." In proposing ways to determine whether a copyright owner could expect to receive compensation for a use, Ricketson suggests consideration of "potential, as well as current and actual, uses or modes of extracting value from a work." (Ricketson, *ibid.* at 32). It can be seen that even a partisan analysis of the three-step test must acknowledge that a use is not of itself remunerable, and remunerability must be related to economic or market analysis.

sates the owner for direct economic prejudice (that is, lost sales) caused by
the exercise of exclusive rights.

b) Sterile copyright

The exclusive rights enable the owner to bargain for payment for copyright
use. Do they do so in all cases? Or is it possible for a copyright to have no
economic potential? The answers to these questions lie in policy, and specifically in the policy of the statutory copyright exceptions. Although the
1911 UK *Copyright Act* specified six categories of non-infringing use, and the
subject aroused comment in Parliamentary debate, the policy origins of the
copyright exceptions are not altogether clear.[59] The logic of the exceptions,
however, is unambiguous. As stated in a relatively recent Australian government document, a copyright exception, "permits copyright material to be
used without authority or compensation."[60]

When analyzed, the elements of the three-step test, and the statutory
criteria for determining fair use or fair dealing, disclose a policy uniting
the copyright exceptions. This policy can be stated in the proposition that
if copyright use:

- does not unreasonably prejudice the economic or moral interests of
  the copyright owner, and
- is for a definable purpose consistent with public welfare, then
- the use is non-remunerable.

In the present case, the relevant question is whether copyright uses to
which the statutory exceptions *do not* apply may be non-remunerable. The
answer is yes—if it is agreed that the policy of the statutory exceptions is
as applicable to the state's copying and communication of survey plans as it
is to (for instance) copying and communication under the statutory library
exceptions. Recent scholarship has shown that parliaments in the US, UK,
and Australia traditionally tied remunerability of use to the copyright owner's
economic interests in a market. It may be inferred from this disposition on
the part of legislators and others that they would consider certain copyright
uses not governed by the statutory exceptions to be non-remunerable.[61]

59   Atkinson, above note 19 at 88–94.
60   Austl., Commonwealth, Attorney-General's Department, *Fair Use and Other Copy-
     right Exceptions: An Examination of Fair Use, Fair Dealing and Other Exceptions in
     the Digital Age* (Issues Paper) (Canberra: Australian Government Publishing Service,
     2005) at 8.
61   From the nineteenth century, copyright policy in the US, UK, and Australia con-
     sidered that the economic interests of the author defined the boundaries of copy-

It is therefore advisable to avoid the assumption that copyright uses to which the statutory exceptions do not apply must be remunerable. When parliaments created the exceptions they did not consider that these exceptions represented the totality of permitted uses that did not require consent of or payment to the copyright owner. They were just boundary markers along the way. However, owners then successfully created a public consensus, or more accurately a perception — that these markers mapped the entire perimeter of this type of permitted use. While the *Copyright Act 1968* states, in detail, rights and exceptions to those rights, the statute is *not* comprehensive. The *Copyright Act 1968* contains lacunae that may be falsely interpreted to misrepresent Parliament's intent.

The wide-reaching claims made by CAL that Crown use in this case must fall within section 183 is an example of false interpretation that misrepresents the will of the legislature. Such claims seek to remove any fabric of common sense or fairness from the statutory framework. To suggest that, outside of the exceptions stated in the *Copyright Act 1968*, all copyright uses are remunerable, is to propose that federal Parliament intended that surveyors would be entitled to tax government, and therefore the public, for copyright use that does no economic or moral harm to the surveyor and benefits the public. CAL's claims also distract attention from consideration of the purpose of a specific copyright use. Questions of remunerability, however, cannot logically be separated from consideration of purpose.

As discussed earlier, copyright does not confer a right of remuneration. A copyright's economic potency depends on whether it enables the owner to strike a bargain for reward. If the copyright owner is unable to rely on the copyright to bargain for reward, the copyright is economically sterile. Interpretation of the language and intent of the *Copyright Act 1968* shows, predict-

---

right. The author was not entitled to remuneration for uses that did not prejudice the author's economic interests. See Atkinson, above note 19 at 352–55 and 428–30. Among recent works published in the UK see, for example, Ronan Deazley, *Rethinking Copyright: History, Theory, Language* (Cheltenham, UK: Edward Elgar Publishing, 2006). Deazley suggests that nineteenth-century theorists helped to create a utilitarian concept of copyright's scope that informed twentieth-century copyright policy. Atkinson notes that policy makers and legislation never declared that the exclusive rights were underpinned by an implied "right of remuneration." See also earlier groundbreaking US scholarship on fair use. For example, L. Ray Patterson, "Free Speech, Copyright and Free Use" (1987) 40 Vand. L. Rev. 1, distinguished between the *purpose* and *function* of copyright. Hannibal Travis, "Pirates of the Information Infrastructure: Blackstonian Copyright and the First Amendment" (2000) 15 Berkeley Tech. L.J. 777, explained the exclusory effect of the fair use doctrine.

ably, that most copyrights are economically potent—the owner can, without restriction and consistent with policy, rely on the rights to bargain for reward.

While most copyrights are economically potent, in the present case the copyright in survey plans is economically sterile. Policy does not support the surveyor using the copyright to bargain for reward. Applying the policy of the statutory exceptions, the focus of analysis is not on the copyright but its use. A survey plan is used by the state in a way that does not unreasonably prejudice the surveyor's economic interests or moral rights. The use is not for the purpose of competing against the surveyor in a market; it is for public welfare.[62] The use does not negate the copyright but renders it eco-

---

62   This is not to say that government use undertaken for public welfare always maximizes public welfare. In the absence of clear government information protocols (compare *Cost Recovery Report*, above note 38) which stipulate that the government must disseminate certain types of copyright information to the public at marginal cost, the government may mistakenly assume that information distribution imposes costs that are more efficiently allocated to private third parties. If this is the case, third-party information brokers, commissioned to distribute some information to the public on the government's behalf, will do so at greater than marginal cost. It is important, however, when discussing the effect of government use on the economic potency of the surveyor's copyright, to distinguish between the government's failure to implement policy, and the merits of the policy itself. Sub-optimal dissemination by the government, which results directly from the failure to issue dissemination protocols that make mandatory the supply of certain types of material at marginal cost, in no way invalidates the policy that the information in survey plans should be disseminated to the public free of copyright imposts. Substantive elements of Ricketson's article, above note 58, lend weight to this proposition. Although the rights-based jurisprudence endorsed by authors like Ricketson seems delicately to suggest a sovereign role for the copyright owner in determination of what, under the *Berne Convention*, above note 52, art. 9(2)'s, "unreasonably prejudice[s]" the owner's "legitimate interests," discussion of the three-step test cannot escape the undertow of economic reality. Analyzing the term "normal exploitation" as it occurs in the language of the three-step test, Ricketson is unable to find a formula that allows the owner to entirely divorce the concept of normal exploitation, or utility of use, from considerations of economic utility. Thus, even adopting so limited a conception of free use as is evident in Ricketson's paper, it is apparent that, in the present case, the surveyor does not produce survey plans for a market purpose, but rather at the statutory behest of the state, which uses the plans *not* to compete in a market, but to disseminate information for public welfare. On the role of government in the digital age, see, generally, J. Stiglitz, P. Orszag, & J. Orszag, "The Role of Government in the Digital Age" (Computer and Communications Industry Association and Sebago Associates, Inc., October 2000); OECD, Directorate for Science, Technology and Industry Committee for Information, Computer and Communications and Policy, *Participative Web*

nomically sterile insofar as the particular use is concerned.[63]

It can be seen that in the absence of a right of remuneration, the copyright owner must use his copyright to bargain for reward (copyright fees), and policy determines the boundaries of his or her economic (bargaining) rights. In the present case, policy constrains the surveyor from bargaining for reward. The policy of the statutory exceptions, applied to the present circumstances, dictates that the state's use of survey plans is a non-remunerable use.[64] The surveyor's copyright in the survey plans is therefore economically sterile.

c) No right is absolute

The Report of the Copyright Law Committee on Reprographic Reproduction (Franki Report) of 1976 noted that:

---

and User-Created Content: Web 2.0, Wikis and Social Networking, Working Party on the Information Economy, Doc. No. DSTI/ICCP/IE(2006)7/FINAL (2007), online: www.oecd.org/dataoecd/57/14/38393115.pdf; UK, Cabinet Office, *The Power of Information* (Review) by E. Mayo & T. Steinberg (2007) (and UK Government response), online: www.cabinetoffice.gov.uk/reports/power_of_information.aspx; EC, *Web 2.0 in Government: Why and How?* (Luxembourg: EC, 2007). On protocols for managing Public Sector Information (PSI), see EC, *Directive 2003/98/EC of the European Parliament and of the Council of 17 November 2003 on the re-use of public sector information,* [2003] O.J. L 345/90, online: http://ec.europa.eu/information_society/policy/psi/docs/pdfs/directive/psi_directive_en.pdf; US, Office of Management and Budget, *Circular A-130 Revised or Management of Federal Information Resources (OMB Circular A-130),* online: www.whitehouse.gov/omb/circulars/a130/a130trans4.pdf; B. Fitzgerald *et al., Internet and E Commerce Law* (Pyrmont, NSW: Law Book Co., 2007) at 260–69 [Fitzgerald, "Internet"]; Queensland Spatial Information Council, *Government Information and Open Content Licensing: An Access and Use Strategy* (2006), online: www.qsic.qld.gov.au/QSIC/QSIC.nsf/0/F82522D9F23F6F1C4A2572EA007D57A6/$FILE/Stage%202%20Final%20Report%20-%20PDF%20Format.pdf?openelement; Austl., Commonwealth, Commonwealth Interdepartmental Committee on Spatial Data Access and Pricing, *A Proposal for a Commonwealth Policy on Spatial DataAccess and Pricing* (2001), online: www-ext.osdm.gov.au/osdm/policy/accessPricing/SDAP. pdf [*Policy on Spatial Data Access and Pricing*].

63 A "sterile" copyright may still be exercised by the author — the author may withhold consent to the use of the copyright — but the author is deprived of the right to receive remuneration for the use of the copyright.

64 Therefore s. 183 does not apply as it only applies to remunerable acts that require the permission of the copyright owner. In this case this use is allowed because the Crown has helped create and verify this document, the document was created for and has become part of a public register (a cornerstone of public administration and democratic governance) and thereby part of the public information infrastructure that underpins and brings order to the society and the economy.

The rights of the copyright owner have never been absolute, in the sense that no dealing with his work could ever take place without his consent. This is the position under the international conventions relating to copyright and the domestic laws of the countries where copyright is protected. The most universal exception is the right to copy minor or insubstantial parts of works. There is also widespread exclusion from the rights given to authors of various rights of copying of a fair dealing or public benefit nature by libraries, educational bodies, research establishments and individuals. In other words, it has always been the policy of the law that the monopoly granted to the author is of a limited nature. Historically therefore the author is not in a position to maintain his claim with regard to copying of published works from a position of absolute right.[65]

The Franki Report, at a later point, commented: "we are satisfied that *as a matter of principle* a measure of photocopying should be permitted without remuneration, for purposes such as private study, to an extent which at least falls within the present limits of 'fair dealing'."[66] The majority of the Copyright Law Review Committee, in its report titled the *Simplification of the* Copyright Act 1968 *PART 1 Exceptions to the Exclusive Rights of Copyright Owners (1998)*, agreed with the Franki Committee on this point.[67] They further explained:

> the Committee agrees with Kurtz, who stated that there is no "tax" in issue and copyright owners have never been entitled to an unlimited scope of rent[68] for their creations . . . . The preamble to the 1996 WCT sets out the international community's recognition of the need to ". . . maintain a balance between the rights of authors and the larger public interest, particularly education, research and access to information, as reflected in the Berne Convention . . . ."[69]

As well, this is not the first time the appellant in this case has sought to extend the exclusive rights of the copyright owner to cover wide-ranging activities, especially in the digital environment. In the recent litigation

---

65   Franki Report, above note 13 at para. 1.09.

66   *Ibid.* at para. 2.18 [emphasis added].

67   *Ibid.* at para. 6.24.

68   "In this context the Committee understands an economic rent to accrue when supply is restricted relative to demand. This situation may result from the absence of effective competition." (Austl., Commonwealth, Copyright Law Review Committee, *Simplification of the* Copyright Act 1968 (Canberra: Ausinfo, 1998) at 57, note 94.)

69   *Ibid.* at para. 6.27.

Copyright Agency Limited v. Queensland Department of Education,[70] CAL
had sought to include the action "[teachers] tell students to view" in the list
of questions used to survey the use of copyrighted materials by schools. The
purpose of the survey was to assess the amount of equitable remuneration
payable for the reproduction and communication of works in electronic
form under the educational statutory licence in Part VA of the *Copyright Act
1968*. CAL's argument was based on the assertion that when a student has
been directed to a website and clicks on a hyperlink or types a URL into
a browser window, the student is communicating the work to themselves.
Assuming that the student is a member of the copyright owner's public, it
follows that their action in accessing the website amounts to a communication to the public. Many people were surprised by such a far-reaching claim,
and ultimately the legislature moved to reject such an argument in the 2006
amendments.[71] The example provided in the explanatory note to this provision expressly states that a person who merely clicks on a hyperlink to gain
access to a website is not to be considered responsible for determining the
content of the communication and does not exercise the communication
right.[72] The point to be made is that not every act is or should be remunerable. Without common sense in the system every reproduction or communication to the public in the digital environment becomes a potential
infringement or cost and Australia's ability to engage in the Internet world
and digital life, culture, and economy is stifled. Mr. Catterns Q.C., counsel
for the appellant (CAL), conceded the existence of some leeway at the hearing of the special leave application by saying that "one lives with infringements around the edges whether they are impliedly licensed or not."[73]

3) Argument 3 — This is Not the Doing of "Any Act Comprised in the Copyright" under Section 36(1) or 183(5)

If the Crown use in question is not an infringement under section 36, then the
Copyright Act 1968 including section 183, is not in issue. Section 36(1) states:

> Subject to this Act, the copyright in a literary, dramatic, musical or art-
> istic work is infringed by a person who, not being the owner of the copy-
> right, and without the licence of the owner of the copyright, does in

---

70 [2006] ACopyT 1.
71 *Copyright Act 1968*, above note 2, s. 22(6A)
72 Fitzgerald, "Internet," above note 62 at 166.
73 *Copyright Agency Limited (CAL) v. New South Wales,* [2007] HCA Trans 700.

Australia, or authorizes the doing in Australia of, any act comprised in the copyright.

Section 183(5) states:

> Where an act comprised in a copyright has been done under subsection (1), the terms for the doing of the act are such terms as are, whether before or after the act is done, agreed between the Commonwealth or the State and the owner of the copyright or, in default of agreement, as are fixed by the Copyright Tribunal.

Section 13 provides:

> (1) A reference in this Act to an act comprised in the copyright in a work or other subject-matter shall be read as a reference to any act that, under this Act, the owner of the copyright has the exclusive right to do.
>
> (2) For the purposes of this Act, the exclusive right to do an act in relation to a work, an adaptation of a work or any other subject-matter includes the exclusive right to authorize a person to do that act in relation to that work, adaptation or other subject-matter.

Are the acts of the Crown, in using the survey plans to construct a public register and communicating that register to the public, acts comprised in the copyright? This question goes to the heart of the issues before the High Court. It leads directly to the deeper philosophical question: what is the content of copyright? Does copyright comprise a set of possessory entitlements (i.e., the exclusive rights) that are subject only to the limitations expressed in the statutory exceptions and exemptions stated in other legislation? Or are the possessory entitlements also subject to public policy that, while not made explicit in the *Copyright Act 1968*, is implicit in the exceptions, and logically applies to copyright uses not governed by the exceptions?

These questions have not been directly answered by a court before. The deep waters of copyright's purpose and scope have only partly been charted at common law. But the present case illustrates that increasingly questions of the statutory interpretation of demand an understanding of law and policy that goes beyond the simple proposition that copyright owners are entitled to demand payment for copyright uses irrespective of the purpose of the uses. It is a question of fact whether an "act is comprised in the copyright" in any given case.[74] No one case will be the same as the next. In this case the factual determination should be that this is not an act comprised in the copyright.

4) Argument 4 — This Is Not an Act Covered by the Rights of the Copyright Owner as Contemplated by the Constitution

The *Copyright Act 1968* has no constitutional basis to empower copyright owners to control the Crown use in question. It is almost inconceivable that in 1900 the word "copyright" as it appears in the Constitution would have been interpreted to allow the copyright owner to levy fees for the use of survey plans. The *Hansard* record of Parliamentary debates over the 1905 Copyright Bill, which became Australia's first federal copyright statute, show that the Senate (where substantive debate took place) was hostile to what senators considered commercial oppression by publishers and stressed the needs of the public in receiving access to copyrighted material.[75] In 1900, the building of the NSW land register, and the reproduction of material therein recorded, and its communication to the public, would not have been remunerable acts. No politician and no judge to this point have ever suggested that they were. It is not too presumptuous to state, on the basis of careful reading of the *Hansard* record of debates over the Commonwealth Copyright Bills of 1905 and 1912,[76] that not a single legislator would have supported CAL's contentions before either the Federal Court or the High Court.

The word "copyright" in the Constitution is not unbounded. For instance, copyright applies to expression, not ideas, and its term has some limit, it is not perpetual.[77] We would also suggest that in 1901 the Constitu-

---

74 *Network Ten Pty. Ltd. v. TCN Channel Nine Pty. Ltd.*, [2005] HCA Trans 842(Transcript of Proceedings); *Conkey & Sons Ltd. v. Miller* (1977), 16 A.L.R. 479, 51 A.L.J.R. 583 (H.C.A.); *University of New South Wales v. Moorhouse* (1975), 133 C.L.R. 1 at 12 and 21 (H.C.A.).

75 Atkinson, above note 19 at 37–41.

76 And also the *Copyright Bill of 1968*, in which many speakers focused on one or other aspect of the public interest in copyright.

77 In the last fifteen years, numerous scholars, including Rose, Feather, Bently, Sherman, and recently, Deazley, have examined the long-running debate in the United Kingdom over perpetual or common law copyright: J. Feather, *Publishing, Piracy and Politics: An Historical Study of Copyright in Britain* (London: Mansell, 1994); Ronan Deazley, *On The Origin of the Right to Copy* (Oxford: Hart, 2004); Mark Rose, *Authors and Owners: The Invention of Copyright* (Cambridge, MA: Harvard

tion did not allow, nor does it now, a copyright owner to control and seek remuneration for use of material created for use in a public register, which in turn brings a distinct commercial advantage to the material and associated activities, and is used to communicate fundamental knowledge about order in the society.

While it is acknowledged that the High Court has said that the notion of what falls within the term "copyright" can evolve over time, there is no reason to suspect that such a fundamental element of copyright law should have disappeared or changed.[78] We argue that the copyright head of power in 1901 did not permit the legislature to allow the copyright owner to limit the use of, or seek remuneration for, copyright material that was embedded in public registries. That was an established limit in much the same way as term limits and the expression/idea dichotomy. To the extent that section 183 seeks to override such a limit, our argument would be that it is beyond the power enumerated in section 51(18) of the Constitution, and to this extent is unconstitutional.

Put bluntly, prior to the enactment of section 183 in 1968 (effective from May 1969) it would have been inconceivable that a surveyor (or third-party copyright owner with material in any form of public registry) could have sought an injunction to restrain use of copyright material by the govern-

---

University Press, 1993); Brad Sherman & Lionel Bently, *The Making of Modern Intellectual Property Law: The British Experience, 1760–1911* (Cambridge: Cambridge University Press, 1999). See also C. Seville, *Literary Copyright Reform in Early Victorian England: The Framing of the 1842* Copyright Act (Cambridge: Cambridge University Press, 1999), and the recent précis of the issues by Atkinson, above note 19 at 31–37. In *Donaldson v. Beckett* (1774), 98 E.R. 257 (H.L.), the House of Lords declared that the *Statute of Anne 1709* extinguished so-called common law copyright, seemingly putting an end (in law) to the argument for perpetual copyright (at least in relation to published material; unpublished material being dealt with exclusively by statute since the British *Copyright Act 1911* and the Australian *Copyright Act 1912*). For a recent and detailed analysis of the different readings of the judgments, see R. Deazley, *On The Origin of the Right to Copy, ibid.* The famous satiric speech of Lord Macaulay in the House of Commons in debate over the 1842 Copyright Bill destroyed forever (or so it seemed) the continuing campaign for perpetual copyright. In 1905 in debate over the Australian Copyright Bill, Sir Josiah Symon, a leading Senator, strongly endorsed Macaulay's arguments. See also *Jefferys v. Boosey* (1854), 4 H.L.C. 815, 10 E.R. 681 (H.L.); *Grain Pool of Western Australia v. Commonwealth*, [2000] HCA 14, 202 C.L.R. 479 at para. 133, note 266.

78   On interpretation of the Constitution, above note 16, s. 51(18), see *Grain Pool of Western Australia v. Commonwealth, ibid.*; *Attorney General for New South Wales v. Brewery Employees Union of New South Wales* (1908), 6 C.L.R. 469 (H.C.A.).

ment[79] or the owner of the land in fee simple. This would not only be an "unbelievable" result, but it would undermine the very fabric of order in society including the economy. The enactment of section 183 in providing a statutory licence to the Crown does not paper over the fact that in history, we would never have allowed the function of government in creating public order (e.g., a functioning system for land title and transactions) to be at the discretion of or driven by a single private actor. Nor does it take away the same underlying issue of concern of having to be beholden to a private actor in relation to the operation of something as fundamental as the system of land title, through remuneration in the case of the Crown, and the requirement to seek permission and remunerate in the case of the current owner of the land in fee simple.

5) Argument 5 — Fair Dealing in the Public Interest for the Creation and Administration of Public Registries

The final argument is that the Crown use at issue is fair dealing for the purpose of the public interest. This doctrine, recognized by Mason J. (as he then was) in *Commonwealth v. John Fairfax and Sons Ltd.*,[80] is seen as a defence to copyright infringement:

> It has been accepted that the so-called common law defence of public interest applies to disclosure of confidential information. Although copyright is regulated by statute, public interest may also be a defence to infringement of copyright. Lord Denning M.R. considered that it is: see *Fraser v. Evans* (38), as did Ungoed-Thomas J. in *Beloff v. Pressdram Ltd.* (39); cf. *Hubbard v. Vosper* (40). Assuming the defence to be available in copyright cases, it is limited in scope. It makes legitimate the publication of confidential information or material in which copyright subsists so

---

79   See, generally, Atkinson, above note 19. On the narrowest reading of the law, only a copyright owner of unpublished copyrighted material could have taken such an action against the Crown at common law, and only from late in the nineteenth century up until 1912. After 1912, unpublished copyrighted material became the subject of statutory regulation and a Crown copyright provision was introduced: see Blais, "Copyright and Compulsory Licences for the Services of the Crown," above note 20. Individual servants of the Crown, on the other hand, were most likely subject to an action for infringement in relation to unpublished and published copyright material at any time up to 1968–69, after which the Crown was expressed to be bound by the new *Copyright Act 1968*: see Hogg & Monahan, above note 20, especially at 318–19.

80   (1980), 147 C.L.R. 39 at 56–57 [*Fairfax*]. See, further, *Ashdown v. Telegraph Group Ltd.*, [2001] EWCA Civ 1142.

as to protect the community from destruction, damage or harm. It has been acknowledged that the defence applies to disclosures of things done in breach of national security, in breach of the law (including fraud) and to disclosure of matters which involve danger to the public. So far there is no recorded instance of the defence having been raised in a case such as this where the suggestion is that the advice given by Australia's public servants, particularly its diplomats, should be ventilated, with a view to exposing what is alleged to have been the cynical pursuit of expedient goals, especially in relation to East Timor. To apply the defence to such a situation would break new ground.[81]

The contours of this defence are not fully understood,[82] although the existing decisions have sought to limit the application of the defence to specific circumstances.[83] The judgement of His Honour Justice Gummow in *Collier Constructions Pty. Ltd. v. Foskett Pty. Ltd.*[84] rejects such an imprecise notion in the face of a "complex of provisions, reflecting an accommodation by the legislature of a range of competing interests."[85]

While the *Copyright Act 1968* must be the starting point, we do not read His Honour to be suggesting that the legislation was born or remains in a vacuum. Its meaning must (to some extent) draw from its underlying assumptions and contextual setting.[86]

a) Assumptions

The Constitution (including section 51(18)) was created at a time and upon assumptions that a new nation, and government in particular, had a pri-

---

81   *Fairfax, ibid.* at 56.

82   There is conjecture as to whether the defence would meet the requirements of the *Berne Convention*, above note 52. However, arts. 2(4), 9, and 17 of the *Berne Convention* provide room for argument. In the instance at hand, public registries are a special case and, as explained above, the use proposed is not detrimental to the legitimate interest of the copyright owner.

83   See, generally, Robert Burrell & Allison Coleman, *Copyright Exceptions: The Digital Impact* (Cambridge: Cambridge University Press, 2005) c. 3.

84   [1990] FCA 392, 97 A.L.R. 460, 19 I.P.R. 44 at 54–57 [*Collier Constructions*]. See also *Corrs Pavey Whiting and Byrne v. Collector of Customs*, [1987] FCA 266, 10 I.P.R. 53; and *Smith Kline and French Laboratories (Australia) Ltd. v. Secretary to the Department of Community Services and Health* (1990), 17 F.S.R. 617 (F.C.A.).

85   *Collier Constructions, ibid.* at 55 (I.P.R.). Compare *Copyright, Designs and Patents Act 1988* (U.K.), 1988, c. 48, s. 171.

86   Compare *Collier Constructions, ibid.* at 56, Justice Gummow's reference to "fundamental principle."

mary role in creating order upon which commerce and success could build. The three federal copyright acts of the twentieth century, in 1905, 1912, and 1968, are based upon similar assumptions that are evidenced in the 1912 and 1968 legislation by the Crown copyright provisions, which, up until very recently, would have been regarded by all as allowing the Crown to deal (royalty-free) with survey plans in the public interest. CAL did not suggest otherwise.

b) Contextual setting

Furthermore, since the *Collier Constructions* judgment, much has changed. We now live in a world driven by information and computer technology fuelled by the Internet, technology that, by its very nature, reproduces content through mere use. In this context we have seen a greater appreciation of the need to properly define the boundaries of control a copyright owner can exert, especially over the general structure of social activity, and society more generally.[87] Despite the significant limits placed by international copyright law on exceptions to (or derogation from) the exclusive rights of the copyright owner, the content of the exclusive rights has yet to be fully explored and articulated by policy-makers and courts.

As part of its operation, copyright law must be able to accommodate such assumptions and contextual factors. Otherwise, its application will be artificial and therefore defeat its core purpose, which is to encourage creative endeavour in the name of the public interest. Every application of copyright law that exceeds that purpose comes at a cost to each and every Australian. That is why we argue that fair dealing in the public interest is a concept that must be considered when articulating the boundary of copyright law. It can either be expressed as an exception to the *Copyright Act 1968* or as a principle which a court should consider in interpreting provisions of the *Copyright Act 1968*.

i) *Fair dealing for the public interest (registries) as an exception or user right*[88]

We argue that in the case at hand the Crown holds the right to use (reproduce or communicate to the public) the plans (royalty-free) and that this is embodied in the Crown's power and obligation to establish registries in the

---

87   *Stevens v. Kabushiki Kaisha Sony Computer Entertainment*, above note 21.

88   On this notion see: *CCH Canadian Ltd. v. Law Society of Upper Canada*, 2004 SCC 13; Brian Fitzgerald, "Copyright 2010: The Future of Copyright" (2008) 30 Eur. I.P. Rev. 43, online: http://eprints.qut.edu.au/archive/00013305 .

name of public order (especially in relation to land). This is fair dealing for the public interest.[89] The existence of such a prerogative right or privilege is either guaranteed or informed by constitutional limits inherent in the copyright power, or is expressly preserved by section 8A of the *Copyright Act 1968*,[90] and can therefore be articulated as a stand-alone exception.[91] Section 183 does not purport to remove such a prerogative, rather it talks to the situation where the Crown would have "but for" section 183 infringing. As this kind of activity was never regarded as infringing, section 183 was not meant, or intended, to cover the activity, and, therefore, unless such a power has been removed by clear words it still remains.[92]

ii)   Fair dealing for the public interest (registries) as a principle underlying interpretation

If fair dealing for public interest is not an established defence to copyright infringement in Australia, as suggested by Justice Mason in *Fairfax,* then it should at very least be a fundamental principle that informs the construction of the *Copyright Act 1968,* and, in particular, section 36(1) and the words "any act comprised in the copyright." Ultimately, copyright law is not only about incentive for individual authors or publishers, but it is also about the benefit of such a law to the Australian community.

C.   SECTION 51(31): CONSTITUTIONAL — "ACQUISITION OF PROPERTY ON JUST TERMS" — ARGUMENTS

The impression that the Crown is able to use the copyright of a third party without paying for it, immediately raises the question of whether such use

---

89   It could be argued that such a prerogative is subject to a requirement of "acquisition on just terms": see H.V. Evatt, *The Royal Prerogative* (North Ryde, NSW: Law Book Company, 1987) at 249; *Attorney General v. De Keyser's Royal Hotel Ltd.*, [1920] A.C. 508 (H.L.); *Matthey v. Curling*, [1922] 2 A.C. 180 (H.L.); *Oxford and Cambridge (Universities of) v. Eyre & Spottiswoode Ltd.*, [1964] Ch. 736 [*Oxford and Cambridge*]. A reply to such claims is made more broadly below in relation to s. 51(31) of the Constitution, above note 16.

90   Above note 2, s. 8A(1) provides: "Subject to subsection (2), this Act does not affect any prerogative right or privilege of the Crown."

91   Such foundations, we submit, satisfy Justice Gummow's concern that "there is no legislative or other warrant for the introduction of such a concept into the law of this country": *Collier Constructions*, above note 84 at 57.

92   Nor do ss. 176 or 177 of the *Copyright Act 1968*, above note 2, purport to take away such a prerogative.

breaches the requirement of "acquisition of property on just terms" under section 51(31) of the Australian Constitution. This section, which enumerates legislative powers of the Commonwealth or federal Parliament, provides:

> The Parliament shall, subject to this Constitution, have power to make laws for the peace, order, and good government of the Commonwealth with respect to: (xxxi) the acquisition of property on just terms from any State or person for any purpose in respect of which the Parliament has power to make laws.

The provision has been seen as a guarantee (although not everyone would use this term) of the right to be compensated for acquisition of your property through a legislative enactment of the federal parliament.

Like similar provisions in constitutions throughout the world, this section is hard to define, especially in relation to intangible intellectual property. The jurisprudence of the High Court over the last fifteen years has appeared to move from a view that readjusting the scope of the exclusive rights of the copyright owner would not conflict with the section, to a view that readjusting the scope of exclusive rights of the copyright owner might need more scrutiny.

1) The Caselaw

A starting point is the case of *Australian Tape Manufacturers Association Ltd v. Commonwealth*[93] where the *Copyright Act 1968* was amended to provide for what the court ultimately decided was an unconstitutional "tax" on blank tapes. Another provision of the scheme provided that copying a sound recording on to a blank tape for private and domestic use would not be infringing activity. In relation to that provision Justices Dawson and Toohey (Mason C.J., Brennan, Deane, and Gaudron JJ. agreeing[94]) explained:

> Nor do we think that there is any force in the plaintiffs' second argument. Copyright consists of the exclusive right to do all or a number of acts with respect to the subject-matter of the copyright. For present purposes the most important is the right to make a reproduction or a copy. Copyright is capable of ownership and is designated by the Act as personal property which is transmissible by assignment, by will and by devolution by operation of law. There can be no doubt that copyright constitutes property

---

93   [1993] HCA 10, 176 C.L.R. 480 [*Australian Tape Manufacturers*].
94   *Ibid.* at 480.

within the scope of s. 51(xxxi) of the Constitution. Section 135ZZM(1) provides that copyright is not infringed by the copying of a sound recording on to a blank tape for private and domestic use. *The effect of that section is to diminish the exclusive rights conferred elsewhere in the Act by way of copyright but it does not result in the acquisition of property by any person. All that the section does is to confer a freedom generally to do something which previously constituted an infringement of another's proprietary right.* Moreover, s. 135ZZZA provides that despite any other provision of the Act, "the making of a copy of a sound recording that is not an infringement of copyright under [Pt VC], does not vest copyright in any work or other subject-matter in any person." Whilst the word "property" in s. 51(xxxi) is to be construed liberally so that it extends to "innominate and anomalous interests," for the paragraph to apply it must be possible to identify an acquisition of something of a proprietary nature. *The mere extinction or diminution of a proprietary right residing in one person does not necessarily result in the acquisition of a proprietary right by another.* Section 135ZZM(1) confers nothing upon any person which may be described as being of a proprietary nature. If the immunity which the section confers can correctly be described as a right, it is a right which is applicable to all but arises only on the occasions upon which copying takes place. It is not a right which is of a permanent character or capable of being assigned to third parties, those being usual characteristics of a right of property. It is not a right which can be described as being by way of copyright or of a licence under copyright since it entirely lacks exclusivity. It does not, in our view, amount to an interest in property. Section 135ZZM(1) is not, therefore, a law with respect to the acquisition of property.[95]

This decision was followed by a series of section 51(31) cases in the mid 1990s,[96] culminating in *Commonwealth of Australia v. WMC Resources*

---

95 *Ibid.* at 527–28 [footnotes omitted] [emphasis added].

96 *Nintendo Company Limited v. Centronics Systems Pty. Ltd.*, [1994] HCA 27, 181 C.L.R. 134; *Mutual Pools and Staff Pty. Ltd. v. The Commonwealth*, [1994] HCA 9, 179 C.L.R. 155; *Health Insurance Commission v. Peverill*, [1994] HCA 8, 179 C.L.R. 226; *Georgiadis v. Australian and Overseas Telecommunications Corporation*, [1994] HCA 6, 179 C.L.R. 297; *Re Director of Public Prosecutions; Ex Parte Lawler*, [1994] HCA 10, 179 C.L.R. 270; *Commonwealth v. Mewett*, [1997] HCA 29, 191 C.L.R. 471; *Newcrest Mining (WA) Limited v. Commonwealth*, [1997] HCA 38, 190 C.L.R. 513. See also Brian Fitzgerald, "Unjust Enrichment as a Principle of Australian Constitutionalism" (1995), online: http://eprints.qut.edu.au/archive/00007414 [Fitzgerald, "Unjust Enrichment"].

Ltd..[97] In that case Justice McHugh made forceful arguments that rights granted by legislation were necessarily subject to modification, and that this would not conflict with section 51(31).[98] An argument the current High Court (see below) is cautious not to overstate. Justice Gummow, in line with the *Tape Manufacturers Case*, explained:

> On the other hand, a law which reduces the content of the exclusive rights created by these statutes, for example, by providing that certain acts henceforth will not infringe those rights, will not attract s. 51(xxxi). Thus, as *Tape Manufacturers* decided, the immunity which the law in question conferred upon those who otherwise would have been infringers could not be described as proprietary in nature. For s. 51(xxxi) to apply, it would be necessary to identify an acquisition, whether by the Commonwealth or a third party, of something proprietary in nature. In *Tape Manufacturers*, this Court was concerned with the validity of Pt VC of the *Copyright Act* which was inserted by the *Copyright Amendment Act 1989* (Cth). The Court was particularly concerned with two provisions of that Part. Section 135ZZP imposed a "royalty" upon the first vendor of blank tape. Had it not been classified as a tax, the "royalty" would have constituted an "acquisition of property" to which s. 51(xxxi) applied. That provision is not of present concern. What is of present relevance is s. 135ZZM. This provided that copyright in a published sound recording, or in any work included in such a recording, was not infringed by certain copies made on blank tapes for private and domestic use. Section 135ZZM was held not to be a law with respect to the acquisition of the property in the respective copyrights. The present appeal does not involve reduction of the content of subsisting statutory exclusive rights, such as those of copy-

---

97   [1998] HCA 8, 152 A.L.R. 1 [*WMC Resources*]. The facts as summarized by Kirby J at para. 209 were:

> WMC Resources Ltd, formerly Western Mining Corporation Ltd (the respondent) was the holder of an interest in an exploration permit (the Permit) issued under federal legislation to permit and encourage exploration for petroleum in defined areas of the Australian continental shelf. Subsequently, the Commonwealth agreed with the Republic of Indonesia to establish a Zone of Cooperation (the Zone) in an area of the disputed seabed boundary between the Island of Timor and Australia known as the "Timor Gap." Some of the areas of exploration provided by the Permit fell within the Zone and by subsequent federal law were extinguished in order that new permits might be granted within the Zone by a joint authority constituted by Australia and Indonesia. [footnote omitted]

98   *Ibid.* at paras. 124–42.

right owners which were at stake in *Tape Manufacturers*, by the conferral upon third parties of immunity from infringement of those rights. The position of WMC is even weaker than that of the copyright owners and so is further removed from the application of s. 51(xxxi).[99]

It is interesting to compare the reasoning of Justice Gummow in the *WMC Case* with that of Gleeson C.J., Gummow, Hayne, and Crennan, JJ., in *Attorney-General for the Northern Territory v. Chaffey; Santos Limited v. Chaffey*[100] where their Honours explain:

> It is too broad a proposition, and one which neither party contended for in these appeals, that the contingency of subsequent legislative modification or extinguishment removes all statutory rights and interests from the scope of s. 51(xxxi). *Newcrest Mining (WA) Ltd v The Commonwealth* is an example to the contrary. That case concerned the use of statute to carve out mining interests from the radical title enjoyed by the Commonwealth upon the acceptance of the Territory pursuant to s. 111 of the Constitution. *Again, a law reducing the content of subsisting statutory exclusive rights, such as those of copyright and patent owners, would attract the operation of s. 51(xxxi).* On the other hand, the statutory licensing scheme for off-shore petroleum exploration the validity of which was upheld in the *Commonwealth v. WMC Resources* was constructed so as to subject the scope and incidents of licences to the form of the legislation from time to time. In *WMC*, as with Pt V of the *Work Health Act*, by express legislative stipulation in existence at the time of the creation of the statutory "right," its continued and fixed content depended upon the will from time to time of the legislature which created that "right."[101]

This reasoning, ten years on from the *WMC Resources*, shows the High Court (including Justice Gummow) being more circumspect in its approach to any universal rule on legislative modification, and, more specifically, rejecting the notion that reducing the content of subsisting exclusive rights of copyright and patent owners is not within the ambit of section 51(31).[102] In the latest pronouncement on section 51(31) by all current members of the High Court, we are provided with the starting point for our current

---

99   *Ibid.* at para. 185–87 [emphasis added].
100 [2007] HCA 34.
101 *Ibid.* at para. 24–25 [footnotes omitted] [emphasis added].
102 Compare Kirby J. in *WMC Resources*, above note 97 at para. 237.

discussion. In *Telstra Corporation Limited v. The Commonwealth*[103] Gleeson C.J., Gummow, Kirby, Hayne, Heydon, Crennan, and Kiefel JJ., state that

> Rather than begin from some constructed taxonomy of rule and excep-
> tions to a rule, it is necessary to begin by recognising the force of the
> observation by Brennan C.J., Toohey, Gaudron, McHugh and Gum-
> mow JJ. in *Victoria v. The Commonwealth* (*Industrial Relations Act Case*)
> that: "It is well established that the guarantee effected by s. 51(xxxi) of
> the Constitution extends to protect against the acquisition, other than
> on just terms, of *'every species of valuable right and interest* including . . . .
> choses in action'." (emphasis added) Further, references to statutory
> rights as being "inherently susceptible of change" must not be permitted
> to mask the fact that "[i]t is too broad a proposition . . . that the contin-
> gency of subsequent legislative modification or extinguishment removes
> all statutory rights and interests from the scope of s. 51(xxxi)." Instead,
> analysis of the constitutional issues must begin from an understanding
> of the practical and legal operation of the legislative provisions that are
> in issue."[104]

The starting point must now be the "practical and legal operation of the legislative provisions in issue" — reducing the content of a copyright owner's exclusive rights is no longer (if it ever were) a special category removed from the ambit of section 51(31).

2) Application to Our Arguments

Argument 1 that we have put forward above is based on authorization and, therefore, should not be subject to any claims that it requires the *Copyright Act 1968* to operate in conflict with section 51(31) of the Constitution, nor that any state legislation operates in a manner inconsistent with the *Copyright Act 1968* (as defined in section 109 Constitution).

Arguments 2–5 above, however, are likely to be challenged on the basis of section 51(31). This is confirmed by the fact that Justice Gummow alluded to section 51(31) in the hearing of argument before the High Court[105] and the approach of the current High Court in the *Telstra Case.*

We consider that any section 51(31) challenges to our arguments 2–5 can be countered on the basis that

---

103 [2008] HCA 7 [*Telstra*].
104 *Ibid.* at para. 49 [footnotes omitted].
105 *CAL*, above note 1 at 4 and 22.

a) The Crown use in question, as highlighted above, was anticipated when the Constitution was enacted;

b) The *Copyright Act 1968* interpreted as we suggest—"the practical and legal operation of the legislative provisions"—would not be a law with respect to the acquisition of property as

   i) there is no acquisition of property (in line with *Australian Tape Manufacturers*[106]);

   ii) the primary purpose of the legislation as interpreted is to allow the creation of a public register and instill order in the community, and any other impact on property is incidental;

   iii) in contrast to *Oxford and Cambridge (Universities Of) v. Eyre & Spottiswoode Ltd.*,[107] this is not expropriation of another's commercial interest in the exploitation of copyrighted material, but rather "use" of a plan created for a definable public purpose, in circumstances where the remuneration of the surveyor by the land developer is left intact and other commercial returns could not be expected;

   iv) there can be no acquisition where a "sterile" copyright (as explained above) is involved as nothing of value has been "subtracted" from the copyright owner;[108] and/or

   v) nothing is being acquired as the interpretation is simply an articulation of the rights of use already in place.

c) Copyright is a set of statutory entitlements and must be able to be recast as time goes on, a view reinforced by the fact that the *Berne Convention* in article 9 (see also *TRIPS Agreement*, article 13,[109] *Australia-United States Free Trade Agreement* article 17.4.10(a); *WIPO Copyright Treaty* Article 10;[110] *WIPO Performances and Phonograms Treaty* 1996[111]) permits exceptions and those types of exceptions must be able to exist and evolve in line with section 51(31) of the Constitution; in other words, unremunerated use in some form must be allowed and able to be implemented and adjusted in line with international law.

---

106 *Australian Tape Manufacturers*, above note 93 at 527–28.
107 *Oxford and Cambridge*, above note 89.
108 Fitzgerald, "Unjust Enrichment," above note 96.
109 Above note 52.
110 *Ibid.*
111 *Ibid.*

E. CONCLUSION: PUBLIC INFORMATION INFRASTRUCTURE AS THE BEDROCK OF BOTH ORDER AND PRODUCTIVITY — AT WHAT COST?

As outlined above, the case of *CAL* presents difficult questions for the High Court, yet common sense must prevail.

We should be mindful that in the UK, when Parliament chose to remove key aspects of Crown copyright, it legislated to keep in place long-held tradition by expressly allowing the Crown, and in certain circumstances the public, to deal royalty-free with third-party copyrighted material deposited in a public register. In Australia, surveyors have not until recent times requested any money from the government, presumably because they accepted that plans were made, or first published by, or under the direction or the control of the Crown. The Federal Court's decision concerning sections 176 and 177 has, like the UK legislation, removed what were thought to be key aspects of Crown copyright. In doing so, the court has left a gap in the law that should be filled by interpretations that will keep intact long-held traditions on Crown use, and will not fracture the fabric of government and order in Australia.[112]

The reach of copyright owners has grown exponentially over the last five years. As mentioned above, remuneration paid by Australian schools to CAL has skyrocketed from $9.6 million AUD in 1999 to $51 million AUD in 2006 (for the copying and communication of print and electronic works under the education statutory licenses in Part VB of the *Copyright Act 1968*).[113] In 1996, CAL's total annual revenue amounted to $18 million AUD. In 2006, annual revenue exceeded $100 million AUD, while expenditure remained below 15 percent of revenue.[114] As noted, the mere use of digital technologies automates the potential for copyright infringement. If common sense and basic logic cannot win the day in this case, then we layer another cost on the potential for innovation and building productivity.

The worldwide trend is for access to government information to be open (available under liberal copyright licences) and free (costed as close to zero as possible).[115] This is seen as a key innovation strategy that will fuel

---

112   Compare Brennan J. (as he then was) in *Mabo v. Queensland (No. 2)*, above note 42 at 29 and 43.

113   Browne, above note 28.

114   Atkinson, above note 19 at 374.

115   See, generally, *Cost Recovery Report*, above note 38; *Policy on Spatial Data Access and Pricing*, above note 62; Pollock, Bently, & Newbery, above note 38; ePSIplus, *Recommendations and Supporting Evidence to the EC's 2008 Review of the PSI Re-use Directive*

the activities of the research and business sector alike. Such a strategy aims to harness the great potential that information technology and the Internet can provide and promises to allow us the opportunity to find new ways of doing things and to solve key intergenerational issues of climate change, education, and health, to name a few. Information in public registries will be critical to this kind of activity.

In our view, developers and their commissioned surveyors, through the agency of CAL, should not be placed in a position to perpetuate the old charging-models of the past and, in effect, hold the public to ransom. The simplistic "user pays" copyright thesis advanced by CAL distorts the reality of cost allocation in the supply of information. Australian and international economists investigating the economics of intellectual property rights point to the consumer deficits caused by using legal rights to practice price discrimination (in the present case, meaning taxation of supply). The logic of economic arguments advanced by CAL, and other proponents of the copyright owner's entitlement to charge for use regardless of the purpose, crumbles in the face of current economic analysis.[116]

(2008), online: www.epsiplus.net/reports/epsiplus_recommendations_to_the_ ec_s_2008_review_of_the_psi_re_use_directive at 9 ["Economic Case"]; Brian Fitzgerald *et al.*, *Oak Law Project Report No. 1: Creating a Legal Framework for Copyright Management of Open Access within the Australian Academic and Research Sector*, online: http://eprints.qut.edu.au/archive/00006099/01/Printed_Oak_Law_Project_Report. pdf.; Fitzgerald "Internet," above note 62 at 260–69; *Research Communication Costs*, above note 38; Carr, above note 37; Peter Costello, "Australian Bureau of Statistics Centenary Celebration" (8 December 2005), online: www.treasurer.gov.au/Display-Docs.aspx?pageID=&doc=speeches/2005/019.htm&min=phc; N.Z., "Policy Framework for New Zealand Government-held Information" (1997), online: www.ssc.govt. nz/display/document.asp?DocID=4880; Varian & Shapiro, above note 32; OECD draft principles on *Open Access to Public Sector Information* that will be considered for adoption at its ministerial conference in Korea in June 2008. Compare *Convention on Access to Information, Public Participation in Decision-Making and Access to Justice in Environmental Matters* (1998), online: www.unece.org/env/pp/ctreaty.htm.

116   The economics of copyright have been increasingly investigated over the last twenty years. The interest of academic economists in the effectiveness or efficiency of copyright regulation is evidenced for example by the activities of the Society for Economic Research on Copyright Issues (SERCI). SERCI (online: www.serci.org) holds an annual congress to discuss research on the economics of copyright and a collection of congress papers were published in 2003 in Wendy J. Gordon & Richard Watt, eds., *The Economics of Copyright, Developments in Research and Analysis* (Cheltenham, UK: Edward Elgar Publishing, 2003). For a relatively brief summary of leading economists' studies of copyright regulation, see Atkinson, above note 19 at 3–9. It

Does a surveyor own copyright in an original artistic work in the form of a survey plan? The answer the High Court will most likely give is "yes." Should its use by government, land owners, or the public, when embedded as part of the most fundamental legal infrastructure in our society—land title—be remunerated? The answer of anyone looking to the future would surely be that such an impost will stifle innovation through the increased cost of the access to public information infrastructure. The next generation Australian will build wealth around information. Our submission to the High Court is that there is a persuasive interpretation of the law that will ensure the next generation will not be burdened with an outdated model of public sector information management. We need to ensure that Australians are not placed in a weaker position than other countries in the world.

As a general rule, people input copyrighted material into public registries to secure an entitlement to participate in a society in a particular way, and this in turn forms the bedrock of order and productivity. To unhinge this delicate balance with the complication that CAL's interpretation of the copyright law will introduce is both unnecessary and unwise.

The High Court should reject this appeal.

---

is clear from the literature that most significant analyses of the economic effects of copyright regulation adopt an equivocal view of the benefits of regulation that is at odds with the opinion—expressed by regulatory authorities and copyright organizations—that copyright monopoly deters free-riding and thus encourages production. Economists from Arnold Plant to the Nobel Laureates Ronald Coase and Kenneth Arrow accepted the necessity for property rights to encourage efficient production and dissemination, but also called into question the extent of regulation. Plant called for a compulsory licence in publishing five years after publication and Coase noted that over-regulation increased transaction costs causing social welfare deficits. Public choice theorists like James Buchanan and Gordon Tullock argued that collaborations between self-interested actors like copyright industries and government regulators distort regulation to the detriment of public welfare. Others, such as Edwin Hettinger, argued that much more empirical evidence is required before intellectual property laws can be declared to work efficiently. The US Supreme Court Justice Stephen Breyer has argued that regulation does not noticeably increase public welfare. It is evident from academic analysis that copyright regulation is an instrument of allocative inefficiency, precisely because laws were designed in accordance with the demands of vested interests—originally the proponents of authors' rights and later the representatives of copyright industries. To suggest that regulation promotes equity and efficiency is, in the words of Hettinger, "facile" (Edwin C. Hettinger, "Justifying Intellectual Property" (1989) 18 Philosophy and Public Affairs 31).

F. POSTSCRIPT

The High Court of Australia delivered its judgment in *Copyright Agency Limited v. State of New South Wales* on 6 August 2008.[117] The Court rejected the full Federal Court's finding that surveyors, by offering plans for registration, authorized the State to use the plans to fulfill its statutory obligations, an authorization that is not extinguished or limited by the section 183 licence for government copying. According to the High Court, the terms of the section 183 licence made clear that it applied to all government uses of copyright material, other than uses to which the statutory exceptions applied. With respect, we consider that the High Court's reasoning is deficient in scope. The Court dealt logically with the arguments put to it by the state's counsel but did not engage with any of the issues raised in this paper. Until higher courts consider deeply the legislative purpose that underlies statutory formulae, copyright law will continue to encroach on rights of access to information — rights that legislators have consistently considered a public entitlement. As we have argued, the principle uniting the statutory exceptions apply equally to any use of copyright material and not just the uses specified in statutory exceptions. This principle is that any use that does not cause economic harm to the owner, or injure the owner's moral rights, and that is consistent with an identifiable public interest, is non-remunerable. In such instances, the copyright is "sterile." If courts fail, at the decisive moments, to debate the question of copyright's purpose, an exercise that involves careful consideration of legislative history, copyright jurisprudence will lose itself in blind alleys and cul-de-sacs, to the continuing detriment of the public.

---

117   [2008] HCA 35.

CHAPTER 12

The Academic Authorship, Publishing Agreements, and Open Access Survey: An Australian Perspective

*Anthony Austin, Maree Heffernan, & Nikki David**

A. INTRODUCTION

In 2007 the Open Access to Knowledge (OAK) Law Project undertook an online survey, *Academic Authorship, Publishing Agreements and Open Access*, which was conducted from 2 October 2007 through to 9 November 2007. The survey attracted 509 participants.[1] The survey was designed to acquire empirical evidence relating to academic authors' perceptions of open access, copyright ownership, online repositories, open access journals, and publishing agreements. The survey also sought to obtain evidence on two specific themes. First, what have been the experiences of academic authors in negotiating and entering into publishing agreements with commercial publishers? Second, what motivates and what prevents academic authors from depositing their work into online repositories or publishing their work with open access journals?

---

* This chapter was derived from The OAK Law Project Report, *Academic Authorship, Publishing Agreements & Open Access: Survey Results* (2008) by Anthony Austin, Maree Heffernan, and Nikki David, with assistance from Professor Brian Fitzgerald, Paul Armbruster, Scott Kiel Chisholm, Professor Anne Fitzgerald, Lorraine Bell, Kylie Pappalardo, Paula Callan, Amanda Long, Derek Whitehead, Jill Rogers, Helen Demack, and Elliot Bledsoe.

1 See Anthony Austin, Maree Heffernan, & Nikki David, *Academic Authorship, Publishing Agreements & Open Access: Survey Results* (2008), online: http://eprints.qut. edu.au/archive/00013623/01/13623_3.pdf at 14 [*Academic Authorship*].

1)   What Does the Survey Tell Us?

The goal of the survey was to develop strategies to facilitate greater levels of open access depositing of author "items" and to balance and satisfy academic authors' concerns between open access and their commercial publishing interests. In the survey, "item" was defined as any periodical publication, journal article, research paper, conference paper, or book chapter.[2]

B.   SUPPORT FOR OPEN ACCESS AND END-USER RIGHTS

As evidenced in Figure 1, the majority of participants support the elements of open access. Over half of them stated that broader access to the results of publicly funded research, distribution of information freely and without cost, and the making of information available for reuse were "extremely important." The participants also stipulated which benefits of open access were of greatest relevance to them, being: increased accessibility to research outputs, easier access to material within specialized research field(s), and improved dissemination through broader circulation of research outputs.[3]

In addition, the majority of academic authors were happy to grant institutions a limited non-exclusive licence to place work in a non-commercial, publicly accessible, online institutional repository.[4] "Work" was defined by the survey as being any periodical publication, journal article, research paper, conference paper, or book chapter, but excluded any monographs or entire books.[5]

Despite the fact that authors regarded other elements of open access as being of greater relevance to them, Figure 2 shows that the majority of authors saw repositories as a "fairly," "very," and "extremely" important element of open access,[6] and nearly half of the survey participants (44 percent) had

---

2   But excluding monographs or entire books. *Ibid.* at 97.

3   The benefits of open access include increased accessibility to research outputs (61 percent strongly agreeing; *mean*=4.48), easier access to material within specialized research field(s) (56 percent strongly agreeing; *mean*=4.39), and improved dissemination through broader circulation of research outputs (52 percent strongly agreeing; *mean*=4.37). *Ibid.* at 53, Figure 21 "Benefits of Open Access."

4   Ninety-three percent of survey respondents are in favour. *Ibid.* at 47, Figure 19 "Use of Online Repositories."

5   *Ibid.* at 97, "Appendix B: Defined Terms in Survey." ("Work" was not defined in the appendix.)

6   Ninety-two percent. *Ibid.* at 53, Figure 21 "Benefits of Open Access."

placed a copy of their work in an institutional repository.[7] In addition, the majority of authors would like end-users to have rights to reuse work or to distribute to others on a non-commercial basis.[8]

Figure 1: The Benefits of Open Access[9]

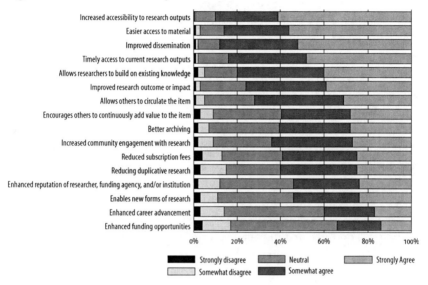

Figure 2: The Relative Importance of Elements of Open Access[10]

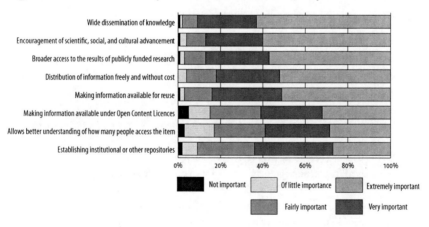

---

7   *Ibid.* at 60, Figure 22 "Frequency of Various Publishing Activities (Past Five Years)."
8   *Ibid.* at 63, Figure 24 "End-User Access Rights for Items Deposited into a Repository."
9   *Ibid.* at 53, Figure 21 "Benefits of Open Access."
10   See *Ibid.* at 50, Figure 20 "The Relative Importance of Elements of Open Access."

C. PUBLISHING DECISIONS AND DEPOSITING DECISIONS

In making a decision to publish, it seems that reputation, impact, and quality of peer review will be of greater relevance to an academic author's decision to publish than simply being able to deposit into an open access repository or to publish in an open access journal.[11]

In addition, the majority of authors have no preference between an assignment and a licence,[12] which may explain why the majority of authors have entered into assignment agreements with publishers.[13] Almost every second author did not understand the terms of a publishing agreement but signed it anyway, and they were unsure if they were allowed to deposit into a repository under either their previous publishing agreements or their most recent publishing agreements.[14] It is only the minority of academic authors who prefer assignments[15] or who prefer to retain rights of open access in their works through a licence.[16]

This habit of entering into assignments with publishers may be influenced by the fact that the majority of authors think that it is too much trouble to negotiate a licence with publishers.[17] Some survey participants stated that authors are not prepared to contest the assignment of their ownership rights to publishers if it may prejudice their chances of being published:

> Negotiating copyright conditions sounds like a good idea except that authors may not have their papers considered for publication if journals don't want to be bothered negotiating . . . the better journals hold all the cards . . . if you want to be published you need to accept their conditions.[18]

---

11   *Ibid.* at 25, Figure 8 "Relevant Factors Influencing Choice of Publication or Publisher."

12   According to 54 percent of respondents. *Ibid.* at 31, Figure 10 "Preference Regarding Assigning or Licensing Copyright."

13   Sixty-three percent of respondents. *Ibid.* at 31.

14   Over 50 percent of respondents. *Ibid.* at 33, Figure 12 "Deposit a Copy in A Repository."

15   Eight percent of respondents prefer assignments. *Ibid.* at 31. An assignment generally transfers all ownership rights in a work by an academic author to publisher, including the right to deposit that work into open access repositories.

16   Thirty-two percent prefer to retain rights of open access in their works through a licence. *Ibid.* A non-exclusive licence, however, will generally allow the author to retain ownership in that work and the right to deposit versions of that work into open access repositories, provided that the publisher is granted the exclusive right to publish the final version of the work.

17   Over 50 percent. *Ibid.* at 39.

18   *Ibid.* at 77.

By the time a journal article has been pushed through the peer review process we are always sick of it and will take any conditions on offer.[19]

... I am unhappy about the way publishers want copyright assigned to them and feel authors have little choice in the matter if we want our material published in particular journals.[20]

Despite that authors regarded the retention of rights to make and distribute copies for teaching and research as being of greater relevance to them, Figure 3 shows that the majority of authors saw the depositing of work into repositories as a "fairly," "very," and "extremely" important right for authors to retain in publishing agreements.[21]

Figure 3: Relevant Rights for an Author to Retain[22]

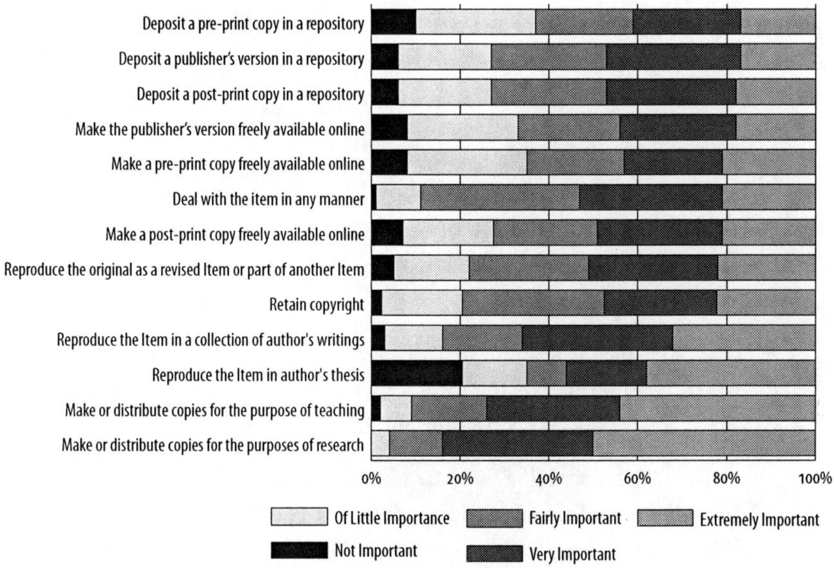

1) Reasons Not to Deposit or Publish in Open Access

When authors were queried about why they have chosen not to deposit work into repositories, it was either because of a lack of knowledge regarding

---

19   *Ibid.*

20   *Ibid.* at 78.

21   Sixty-three to seventy-three percent. *Ibid.* at 36, Figure 16 "Relevant Rights for Authors to Retain."

22   *Ibid.*

where to deposit their work,[23] their concern about publishers attitudes to the depositing of work into repositories,[24] the use and re-use of their works in repositories,[25] or because they were unsure how depositing would promote their work, profile, employment, or career[26] (See Figure 4).

Figure 4: Reasons for Not Depositing a Work into an Institutional or Other Repository[27]

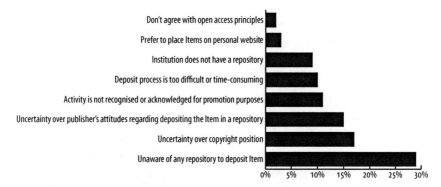

When authors were asked why they had not published with open access journals, they also cited factors such as funding restrictions, open access journal publishing fees, metrics, reputation, and impact as issues that influenced their decisions:

> Schemes like the RQF are a real disincentive to publish electronically ("open access" journals are not regarded as being as "serious," nor as prestigious as the traditional outlets for publishing research).[28]

> The main issue is that I don't see any significant advantages to me to publish outside the traditional journal paths and a significant disadvantage is that I have to pay to get published (which ARC and other agencies refuse to fund).[29]

---

23   Twenty-nine percent. *Ibid.* at 62, Figure 23 "Reasons for Not Depositing an Item into an Institutional or Other Repository."

24   *Ibid.*, 15 percent.

25   *Ibid.*, 17 percent.

26   *Ibid.*, 11 percent.

27   *Ibid.* at 62, Figure 23 "Reasons for Not Depositing an Item into an Institutional or Other Repository."

28   *Ibid.* at 103, Appendix C: Listing of Open-Ended Comments.

29   *Ibid.* at 76.

Open access journals in my area are not important publishers and do not attract citation counts. If they did, then that might change my and others attitude to open access publications.[30]

These newer (open access) journals are not yet established as high quality journals in my field of research. (i.e. no impact factor).[31]

D. END USERS OF OPEN ACCESS DEPOSITED OR PUBLISHED WORK

End users are those persons or organizations who access work that has been deposited or published online through repositories or open access journals. In the survey, almost three-quarters (72 percent) of authors indicated that they would like an end-user to have rights to view, print, and download an electronic copy when accessing their work in an institutional or other repository.

Over half (57 percent) of survey participants said that they would like a repository end-user to have rights to reuse the work for academic or non-commercial purposes, to distribute to others on a non-commercial basis (55 percent), or to place a link on another website to the work as deposited in the repository (54 percent)[32] (see Figure 5). As one author commented: "I'm happy with any non-commercial use that acknowledges the source of the material."[33]

Figure 5: Preferred End-User Access Rights for Work Deposited into a Repository[34]

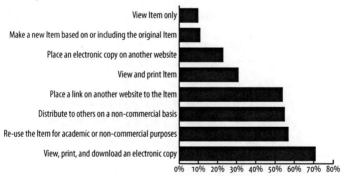

30   *Ibid.* at 77.
31   *Ibid.*
32   *Ibid.* at 65, Figure 25 "Preferred End-User Access Rights for Items Deposited into a Repository."
33   *Ibid.* at 66.
34   *Ibid.* at 65, Figure 25 "Preferred End-User Access Rights for Items Deposited into a Repository."

1)   What Does the Survey Tell Us About Open Access Journals?

For those participants who have published in an open access journal, most indicated that they did so because they either had an open access journal in their disciplinary area or because they desired to promote open access principles and ideals.[35] Participants made the following specific comments as to why they have published in an open access journal:

> To make my research more accessible and more widely recognized.[36]

> I have just submitted my first paper to an open access journal because I have come to understand its power to assist others to access regardless of financial circumstances.[37]

> For me one of the most important factors when choosing a journal is the reputation of that journal. So an open access journal also needs to have a good reputation (and good impact factors etc) to be considered. In my field there is one very good open access journal in which I have published a paper, and I would definitely consider them for future papers.[38]

However, more than half of the survey participants have never published in an open access journal.[39] Almost one-quarter indicated that they have not published in an open access journal because they were either unfamiliar with the process or they have no motivation to do so or because it is not adequately recognized or acknowledged for the purposes of promotion.[40] Academic authors specifically commented on dissuading factors such as publishing fees, metrics, reputation, and impact:

> The main issue is that I don't see any significant advantages to me to publish outside the traditional journal paths and a significant disadvantage is

---

35   Open access journal in their disciplinary area (45 percent); desire to promote open access principles and ideals (29 percent): *ibid.* at 73, Figure 28 "Reasons for Publishing in an Open Access Journal."

36   *Ibid.* at 75.

37   *Ibid.*

38   *Ibid.*

39   Fifty-nine percent of respondents have never published in an open access journal. *Ibid.* at 73.

40   Twenty-two percent of respondents indicated that they have not published in an open access journal because they were either unfamiliar with the process, they have no motivation to do so or it is not adequately recognized or acknowledged for the purposes of promotion. *Ibid* at 76, Figure 29 "Reasons that Prevented Authors from Publishing in an Open Access Journal."

that I have to pay to get published (which ARC and other agencies refuse to fund).[41]

Open access journals in my area are not important publishers and do not attract citation counts. If they did, then that might change my and others attitude to open access publications.[42]

My decisions about publication are based on journal impact factor, journal specialization, and likelihood of acceptance. Current open access journals do not tick enough of these boxes.[43]

In addition, participants were asked what things could be done to encourage publication in open access journals. Figure 6 shows that academic authors were in favour of there being a greater number of open access journals and receiving more information about open access opportunities and funding that covers author/publication costs in order to assist them to publish in open access journals.[44] Participants also suggested that issues regarding reputation, impact, publishing fees, and funding support need to be addressed:

Make the journals high impact—i.e., excellent reputation, high quality of peer review, excellent proofing.[45]

Make it free to publish in them.[46]

Positioning of the journals (impact factor and citation indexes) relative to other journals considered more prestigious to peers.[47]

Better ranking of these journals for NHMRC/other grant provider assessment.[48]

---

41 *Ibid.* at 76.

42 *Ibid.* at 77.

43 *Ibid.*

44 Forty-seven percent of academic authors would like more information about open access opportunities. Thirty-nine percent would like more open access journals. Thirty-six percent would like funding to cover author/publication costs to assist them to publish in open access journals. *Ibid.* at 78, Figure 30 "Ways to Encourage Publishing in an Open Access Journal."

45 *Ibid.* at 79.

46 *Ibid.*

47 *Ibid.*

48 *Ibid.*

Figure 6: Ways to Encourage Publishing in an Open Access Journal[49]

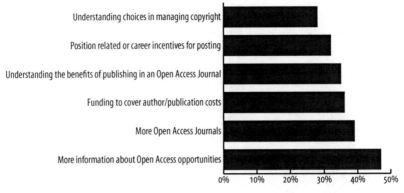

E. WHAT DOES THE SURVEY TELL US ABOUT ARTS AND SCIENCES?

The survey participants came from a diverse range of research fields. Approximately 57 percent of respondents indicated that their research was in the areas of Science and Technology and 43 percent of respondents indicated that their research was in the fields of the Arts and Social Sciences. Approximately 25 percent of participants identified medical, health, and epidemiology; 19 percent identified biology, chemistry and physics; 14 percent education; and 12 percent identified humanities as research fields in which they are involved.[50]

1) How Do the Arts and Sciences Differ?

Researchers in the field of Arts and Social Sciences (Arts) and researchers in the field of Science and Technology (Sciences) generally had similar views and experiences in relation to open access, copyright ownership, online repositories, open access journals, and publishing agreements, such as:

- Researchers in both Arts and Sciences publish with large commercial publishers[51]
- When choosing a publication or publisher, the quality of the peer review is important to both Arts and Sciences authors
- Both Arts and Sciences authors prefer end-users of repositories to have similar rights in relation to deposited works, namely: to view

---

49   *Ibid.* at 78, Figure 30 "Ways to Encourage Publishing in an Open Access Journal."

50   *Ibid.* at 18, Figure 2 "Main Disciplinary Area of Respondents."

51   *Ibid.* at 22–23.

only; to view and print; to view, print, and download; to distribute on a non-commercial basis; to reuse the work for academic or non-commercial purposes; and to make a new work based on or including the original work.[52]

The survey results also provide a number of examples where the Arts and Sciences disciplines gave different priorities to certain issues.

Arts

- Many principles of open access are of greater significance for Arts authors. They are more in favour of open access being a way to enable new forms of research, the establishment of institutional or other repositories, and encouraging a better understanding of how many people access work in repositories. [53]

- Arts authors are more likely to be active in searching for work within institutional repositories and to direct students to use repositories. Arts authors prefer that their institutions promote open access and that repositories give accurate information on work viewings and downloads.[54]

- Arts authors will give greater priority to Australian institutional publishers[55] and to publications that provide copy editing assistance and commissions or payments for publication.[56]

- In relation to publishing agreements, Arts authors are more likely to examine them before signature and to inform a publisher of any dissatisfaction they may have with its terms. They are more inclined to negotiate and amend publishing agreements[57] or to attach an author addendum.[58] When retaining rights in publishing agreements, Arts authors prefer to retain rights to the copyright in the work, to make or distribute copies for the purpose of teaching, and to reproduce the original as a revised work or part of another work.[59]

---

52   *Ibid.* at 64, Table 27 "End-User Access Rights for Items Deposited into a Repository by Disciplinary Area and Years Publishing."

53   *Ibid.* at 51, Table 19 "Mean Level of Relevance of Elements of Open Access by Research Area."

54   *Ibid.* at 48, Table 16 "Use of Online Repositories by Research Area."

55   *Ibid.* at 23, Table 1 "Type of Publisher by Area of Research."

56   *Ibid.* at 26, Table 4.

57   *Ibid.* at 41, Table 10 "Publishing Agreements by Research Area."

58   *Ibid.* at 61, Table 25 "Frequency of Various Publishing Activities (Past Five Years) by Disciplinary Area."

59   *Ibid.* at 37, Table 7 "Mean Level of Relevance of Rights for Authors to Retain by Research Area Organisation."

- Arts authors will not be inclined to deposit their work into any repository if a commercial publisher's attitude is against depositing or if they believe that the deposit process is too difficult or time-consuming. They will not deposit if they are uncertain about the copyright position in their work or if depositing is not recognized for promotion purposes.[60] In order to improve repository participation, Arts authors prefer that their institutions provide a service to answer author queries about depositing.[61]
- Although both Arts and Sciences authors prefer end-users of repositories to have similar rights, Arts is more likely to have deposited work into repositories where end-users can view, print, and download work, reuse the work for academic or non-commercial purposes, or be able to place a link on another website to the deposited work.[62]

Sciences
- Sciences authors are more likely to publish with international disciplinary societies,[63] and the reputation of a publication will be of greater significance for them when choosing a publisher or a publication.[64]
- When retaining rights in publishing agreements, Sciences authors prefer to retain the right to reproduce the work in the author's thesis over other rights.[65]
- Sciences authors are more likely to view publishing agreements as being hard to negotiate or to sign publishing agreements without examining its terms.[66]

Sciences authors will not be inclined to deposit their work into any repository if their institution does not have its own repository or if they prefer to

---

60   *Ibid.* at 62, Table 26 "Reasons for Not Depositing an Item into an Institutional or Other Repository by Disciplinary Area, Years Publishing and Employing Organisation."

61   *Ibid.* at 69, Table 29 "Mean Level of Relevance of University or Institutional Mechanisms to Improve Participation in Depositing Items in Institutional or other Repositories by Research Area."

62   *Ibid.* at 64, Table 27 "End-User Access Rights for Items Deposited into a Repository by Disciplinary Area and Years Publishing."

63   *Ibid.* at 23, Table 1 "Type of Publisher by Area of Research."

64   *Ibid.* at 26, Table 4.

65   *Ibid.* at 37, Table 7 "Mean Level of Relevance of Rights for Authors to Retain by Research Area Organisation."

66   *Ibid.* at 41, Table 10 "Publishing Agreements by Research Area."

place their work on a personal website.[67] They prefer that repository end-users only be allowed to view deposited work.[68]

F. WHAT DOES THE SURVEY TELL US ABOUT JUNIOR AND SENIOR ACADEMIC AUTHORS?

Approximately two-thirds (62 percent) of survey participants were actively involved in research for more than ten years (senior authors), 22 percent were actively involved in research between five and ten years, and 15 percent were involved for more than twelve months but less than five years (junior authors).[69]

1) How Do Junior and Senior Academic Authors Differ?

The survey results provide a number of examples where senior authors and junior authors differed in relation to issues of open access, copyright ownership, online repositories, open access journals, and publishing agreements.

Senior authors
- Senior authors are more likely to publish in open access journals in order to promote open access principles and ideals.[70]
- Senior authors are more likely to publish with large commercial publishers, international disciplinary societies, Australian institutional publishers, and Australian disciplinary societies,[71] and also if their work is commissioned.[72] Senior authors are more likely to inform a publisher of dissatisfaction with the terms of their standard publishing agreement and to negotiate and amend those terms.[73]
- Senior authors will not be inclined to deposit their work into a repository where they perceive depositing to be a difficult or time-

---

67 *Ibid.* at 62, Table 26 "Reasons for Not Depositing an Item into an Institutional or Other Repository by Disciplinary Area, Years Publishing and Employing Organisation."

68 *Ibid.* at 64, Table 27 "End-User Access Rights for Items Deposited into a Repository or Disciplinary Area and Years Publishing."

69 *Ibid.* at 19, Figure 3 "Length of Time Involved in Research."

70 *Ibid.* at 74, Table 33 "Reasons for Publishing in an Open Access Journal by Number of Years Publishing."

71 *Ibid.* at 23, Table 2 "Type of Publisher by Number of Years Publishing."

72 *Ibid.* at 27, Table 5 "Mean Level of Relevance of Factors Influencing Choice of Publication or Publisher by Number of Years Publishing."

73 *Ibid.* at 42, Table 11 "Publishing Agreements by Number of Years Publishing."

consuming process, or where they have uncertainty over publisher's attitudes towards depositing, or if they prefer to place their work on their personal website.[74]

- They prefer that repository end-users only be allowed to view and print deposited work.[75]

Junior authors
- Many principles of open access are of greater significance for junior authors. They are more in favour of the dissemination of knowledge through open access, broad access to the results of publicly funded research, the encouragement of scientific, social, and cultural advancement via open access, making information available for reuse through open access, making information available under open content licences, and encouraging a better understanding of how many people access work in repositories.[76]
- Junior authors prefer that open access provides them with the following benefits: easier access to material within specialized research field(s), new forms of research, increased research citation, timely access to current research outputs, enhanced career and funding opportunities, the enhancement of the reputation of the researcher, a reduction in subscription fees and duplicative research, and increased community engagement with research. They also prefer that open access allows researchers to build on existing knowledge and circulate works and encourages others to continuously add value to them.[77]
- Junior authors are more likely to be active in searching for work within institutional repositories[78] and they prefer to choose a publication or publisher that supports repository depositing. They also prefer publications or publishers that provide comments or feedback

74   *Ibid.* at 62, Table 26 "Reasons for Not Depositing an Item into an Institutional or Other Repository by Disciplinary Area, Years Publishing and Employing Organisation."
75   *Ibid.* at 65, Table 28 "Preferred End-user Access Rights for Items Deposited into a Repository."
76   *Ibid.* at 52, Table 20 "Mean Level of Relevance of Elements of Open Access by Number of Years Publishing."
77   *Ibid.* at 55, Table 23 "Benefits of Open Access by Number of Years Publishing (Mean Level of Agreement)."
78   *Ibid.* at 49, Table 17 "Use of Online Repositories by Number of Years Publishing."

from peer reviewers, but they are more likely to be influenced in this choice by the opinions of their own faculty or department.[79]

- When retaining rights in publishing agreements, junior authors prefer to retain the right to deal with the work in any manner they choose and to have the ability to retain copyright in the work. They prefer to retain the right to deposit a preprint copy of the work in an institutional or other repository, or to reproduce the original as a revised work or part of another work, and to reproduce the work in the author's thesis.[80] However, junior authors will not negotiate amendments to a publishing agreement if they feel that the need to publish for promotional purposes outweighs the risk of negotiating amendments.[81]

- Junior authors are more likely to deposit work into repositories that allow their end-users to view, print, and download works, distribute works on a non-commercial basis, and make new works based on or including the original work.[82] They also prefer repositories that allow end-users to place an electronic copy of or link to the work on another website.[83]

- In order to improve repository depositing,[84] junior authors would prefer that institutions link depositing to career advancement, provide assistance with cataloguing metadata, improve the searchability of repository works, conduct workshops for authors and end-users, and provide a service that answers author repository queries.[85]

- Practical aids such as template publishing agreements, copyright toolkits, template clauses, and template author addenda would be of greater benefit to junior authors in managing copyright in their works. They also preferred their institutions to provide them with

---

79 *Ibid.* at 27, Table 5 "Mean Level of Relevance of Factors Influencing Choice of Publication or Publisher by Number of Years Publishing."

80 *Ibid.* at 38, Table 8 "Mean Level of Relevance of Rights for Authors to Retain by Number of Years Publishing."

81 *Ibid.* at 42, Table 11 "Publishing Agreements by Number of Years Publishing."

82 *Ibid.* at 64, Table 27 "End-User Access Rights for Items Deposited into a Repository by Disciplinary Area and Years Publishing."

83 *Ibid.* at 65, Table 28 "Preferred End-user Access Rights for Items Deposited into a Repository."

84 *Ibid.* at 70.

85 *Ibid.*, Table 30 "Mean Level of Relevance of University or Institutional Mechanisms to Improve Participation in Depositing Items in Institutional or other Repositories by Number of Years Publishing."

an online advocacy centre and support from copyright or research offices for this purpose.[86]

- Institutional obligations and the availability of open access journals in a relevant disciplinary area are greater motivational factors for junior authors to publish in open access journals.[87]

G. UNIVERSITY AND NON-UNIVERSITY SECTORS

The majority of participants (89 percent, n=453) were employed by a university or a higher educational institution ("university"), with the remainder employed by government, industry, or other research bodies ("non-university"). The majority of respondents (80 percent) were employed by large organizations (i.e., organizations with 1,000 or more employees), with approximately 11 percent employed by organizations with between 500 and 1,000 employees. Almost 61 percent of respondents described their organizational role as "lecturer," 25 percent as "researcher," and 4 percent as "dean/head of school."[88]

University and non-university respondents were similar in terms of deciding who they choose to publish with,[89] and in the factors that influenced their choice of publication or publisher.[90] They also had similar strategies for managing copyright in work,[91] and similar ideas as to what could be done to improve their participation in depositing work in institutional or other repositories.[92]

1) How Do University and Non-University Sectors Differ?

Despite certain similarities, the survey results did raise a number of issues that the university and the non-university sectors gave different priorities and emphasis:

---

86   *Ibid.* at 46, Table 14 "Mean Level of Usefulness of Strategies to Better Manage Copyright of Items by Number of Years Publishing."

87   *Ibid.* at 74, Table 33 "Reasons for Publishing in an Open Access Journal by Number of Years Publishing."

88   *Ibid.* at 17.

89   *Ibid.* at 24, Table 3 "Type of Publisher by Employing Organisation."

90   *Ibid.* at 28, Table 6 "Mean Level of Relevance of Factors Influencing Choice of Publication or Publisher by Employing Organisation."

91   *Ibid.* at 39, Table 9 "Mean Level of Relevance of Rights for Authors to Retain by Employing Organisation."

92   *Ibid.* at 46, Table 15 "Mean Level of Usefulness of Strategies to Better Manage Copyright of Items by Employing Organisation."

University

- When retaining rights in publishing agreements, Universities prefer to retain the right to make a preprint copy of the work freely available online.[93]
- Establishing institutional or other repositories[94] and the depositing of work into repositories so that it is freely available online[95] is of great significance to universities.
- Universities will be inclined not to deposit work in a repository where they perceive depositing to be a difficult or time-consuming process, where they have uncertainty over the copyright position, or where depositing is not recognized for promotion purposes;[96]
- Being able to identify an open access journal in a disciplinary area was a greater motivating factor for universities to publish in open access journals.[97]

Non-university

- Non-universities want new forms of research to be enabled through the application of open access.[98]
- Publishing in an open access journal in order to promote open access principles is a significant motivator for non-universities.[99]
- When retaining rights in publishing agreements, non-universities prefer to deal with work in any manner they choose[100] and are more likely to amend a publication agreement.[101]

---

93   *Ibid.* at 39, Table 9 "Mean Level of Relevance of Rights for Authors to Retain by Employing Organisation."

94   *Ibid.* at 52, Table 21 "Mean Level of Relevance of Elements of Open Access by Employing Organisations."

95   *Ibid.*

96   *Ibid.* at 62, Table 26 "Reasons for Not Depositing an Item into an Institutional or Other Repository by Disciplinary Area, Years Publishing and Employing Organisation."

97   *Ibid.* at 74, Table 34 "Reasons for Publishing in an Open Access Journal by Employing Organisation."

98   *Ibid.* at 56, Table 24 "Benefits of Open Access by Employing Organisation (Mean Level of Agreement)."

99   *Ibid.* at 74, Table 34 "Reasons for Publishing in an Open Access Journal by Employing Organisation."

100   *Ibid.* at 39, Table 9 "Mean Level of Relevance of Rights for Authors to Retain by Employing Organisation."

101   *Ibid.* at 43, Table 12 "Publishing Agreements by Employing Organisation."

- Not being able to deposit in a repository because of uncertainty regarding publishers' attitudes was of greater impact for non-universities.[102]

H. SUPPORT FOR OPEN ACCESS

The majority of survey participants showed support for the elements of open access and broadly agreed as to the benefits of open access, particularly where open access would provide the benefits of access to another parties' information and research. They supported the depositing of work into a repository through a non-exclusive licence for non-commercial, publicly accessible online repositories, and giving end-users greater rights of access, reuse, and distribution of works on a non-commercial basis.

1) Factors that Impact Support for Open Access

Whilst there is support for open access, there are also impediments to that support. Most publishing agreements are not being negotiated or amended in order to retain rights for open access publication. This practice is exacerbated by assigning copyright ownership in works to publishers and a general lack of knowledge about ownership rights, publishing agreements, negotiating amendments, and understanding how open access publishing will affect career and reputation.

2) Education, Assistance, and Support

Academic authors need proactive assistance and education from institutions, repositories, open access journals, and funding bodies to ensure that support for open access publishing can continue. The benefits and disadvantages of open access publishing need to be addressed with authors. They need to know why depositing or publishing in open access should not prejudice their chances of publishing with commercial publishers and how it affects their career, particularly in the case of junior authors:

> I support open access as a principle but believe that the issue of impact factors reduces the usefulness of this avenue for publication. Unless OA

---

102 *Ibid.* at 62, Table 26 "Reasons for Not Depositing an Item into an Institutional or Other Repository by Disciplinary Area, Years Publishing and Employing Organisation."

publication is given a status as activity relevant to promotion there isn't much reward for the effort involved.[103]

Academic authors want to know how depositing or publishing with open access journals and repositories will benefit their careers. These facilities need to reassure authors that they can provide accurate and high-profile metrics, citation, and satisfy author requirements for reputation, impact, and quality peer review. As our survey participants commented:

> I am happy to submit articles to open access journals as long as they are of good quality. Some are already of good quality but others are not. Use of open access journals is increasing and will therefore pose stronger demands on the quality of the open access journals. However, the editors of open access journals should also impose strict demands on the quality of article submissions.[104]

> . . . I think institutions must spearhead the process of open access (if they support this) by (i) defraying the costs for their staff members; (ii) working to gain and recognize the quality of open access outlets (at this stage, the best journals in my field do not permit open access), (iii) advocating bibliometrics that would favour open access (for use by granting agencies, promotions committees). As academic research in Australian universities is owned by the university, the university has a responsibility to promote open access and not make this the responsibility of individual staff.[105]

Funding bodies may need to explain to authors whether they will support the depositing or publishing of funded work into repositories or open access journals:

> I believe in open access publishing whenever possible. The problem is that academic audit culture (e.g., RQF, journal impact factors) works in the other direction, forcing authors back to commercial publishers that want copyright licensed or assigned. Open access journals are lowly weighted in these exercises, even though they get read more often, generate more reputation (as measured through conference invitations, etc.), and at least in my field are at the cutting edge of advance.[106]

---

103 *Ibid.* at 113.
104 *Ibid.* at 58.
105 *Ibid.* at 59.
106 *Ibid.*

Different approaches and strategies will be needed to promote open access to different author groups.[107]

Ultimately, authors want active support from institutions regarding copyright issues,[108] as well as template clauses, publishing agreements, and addenda[109] (see Figure 7). Figure 8 shows that authors particularly wanted guidelines from their institutions which would instruct them on how to deposit work into repositories.[110] This could take the form of a practical guide for authors that would explain how to

- make informed decisions on depositing and publishing, and how to negotiate copyright with publishers; and
- identify assignments, exclusive licences, and non-exclusive licences in publishing agreements, and how ownership rights and their effect on retaining open access publication rights are dealt with in these various agreements.

Such a guide would also contain an author-friendly publishing agreement or author-friendly addenda that would license an author's work to publishers on a non-exclusive basis, without assigning ownership, and retain rights to deposit and disseminate the work for open access.

Figure 7: Relative Strategies to Assist in the Management of Copyright of Work[111]

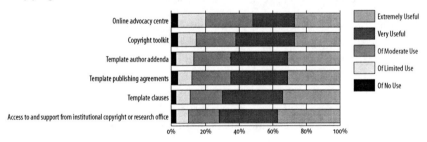

---

107 As demonstrated by the differences between junior and senior authors, arts and sciences authors, and university and non-university authors.

108 Seventy-two percent regarded this as "very" to "extremely" useful. See Figure 18 "Relative Strategies to Assist in the Management of Copyright of Items," *ibid.* at 44.

109 Sixty-five to seventy percent regard these as "very" to "extremely" useful.

110 Eighty-eight percent "somewhat agreed" or "strongly agreed" with this statement. *Ibid.* at 68, Figure 27, "University or Institutional Mechanisms to Improve Participation in Depositing Items in Institutional or Other Repositories."

111 *Ibid.* at 44, Figure 18 "Relative Strategies to Assist in the Management of Copyright of Items."

Figure 8: University or Institutional Mechanisms to Improve Participation in Depositing Work in Institutional or Other Repositories[112]

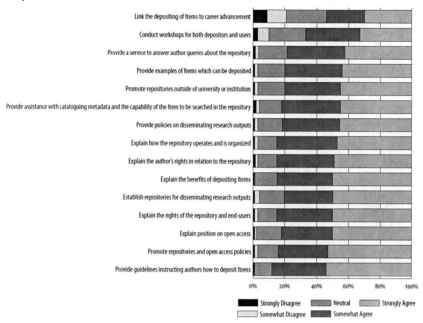

I. CONCLUSION

Whilst there is a growing trend for universities to introduce mandatory depositing into repositories in an effort to promote open access, they should also consider how such policies will be reconciled with academic authors' concerns regarding open access publishing. Will such mandates generate compliance or will they serve to prejudice the benefits of open access in the eyes of academic authors?

The survey has demonstrated that a majority of authors understand the value of open access and are willing to support it, but it also shows that there is a need to ensure that mechanisms are put in place that engage authors about open access and give them reassurance that they will not be disadvantaged by depositing or publishing in open access repositories or journals.

It is submitted that these concerns are not something that can be re-solved themselves by mandates. The survey participants have told us what

---

112 *Ibid.* at 68, Figure 27 "University or Institutional Mechanisms to Improve Participa-tion in Depositing Items in Institutional or other Repositories."

they want: the provision of education, support, and resources. Institutions, open access publishers, and funding bodies should take these requests into account when adopting policies to address open access publishing.

These suggestions are just small additions to the promising work that is already being done by the many dedicated universities, institutions, repositories, open access journals, funders, and other organizations that seek to promote the principles and benefits of open access.

CHAPTER 13

A Relational Theory of Authorship

Sampsung Xiaoxiang Shi & Brian Fitzgerald

A. INTRODUCTION

Over the years we have heard the debate as to whether authorship emanates solely from the individual or from the cultural context in which he inhabits. Writers such as Professors Woodmansee, Jaszi, and Cohen have asserted a cultural theory of authorship.[1] On the one hand, there is the liberal philosophy of autonomous creativity evidenced in the notion of a "romantic author" (after the period known as romanticism). On the other hand, we have more of a communitarian notion — that the author acts in a cultural context and authorship to some extent must be linked back to the social existence within which the author is situated.

This chapter argues that for too long we have privileged the notion of the romantic author so much so that it is hard to argue for any other approach to copyright than one that focuses primarily on the author and their assignees, such as publishers or associated commercializing agents, such as recording companies. Furthermore it suggests that this approach fits awkwardly with the burgeoning networked society fuelled by the Internet to the point where it threatens innovation and the potential for productivity. To this end the chapter argues that we should more explicitly acknowledge

---

1   See, generally, Peter Jaszi, "Towards a Theory of Copyright: The Metamorphoses of 'Authorship'" (1991) 2 Duke L.J. 455; Martha Woodmansee, "The Genius and the Copyright: Economic and Legal Conditions of the Emergence of the 'Author'" (1984) 17 Eighteenth-Century Studies 425; Julie E. Cohen, "Creativity and Culture in Copyright Theory" (2007) 40 U.C. Davis L. Rev. 1151 [Cohen, "Creativity and Culture"]; Carys J. Craig, "Reconstructing the Author-self: Some Feminist Lessons for Copyright Law" (2007) 15:2 Am. U.J. Gender Soc. Pol'y & L. 207.

the contribution of culture to authorship and, more so, the role of each and every individual in assisting and nurturing that authorship, as well as the contribution of users to creativity, through consumptive, productive, and transformative use of copyrighted works.

B. RECONCEPTUALIZE AUTHORSHIP

Since the birth of the modern copyright system, authors have been enshrined as people of individual genius whose "vivid sensation" and the "spontaneous overflow of powerful feelings" became the elements of creativity and thus authorship.[2] They have been seen as creating something entirely new and original.[3] By the middle of the eighteenth century this romantic conception of authors had become a "universal truth about art,"[4] and, furthermore, the doctrine of originality was "so orthodox that Samuel Johnson could state flatly that the highest praise of genius is original invention."[5]

However, this romantic notion on which the modern copyright regime was founded turns out to be more far-reaching than we could have imagined.[6] In recent years, it has been argued that the traditional concept of authorship, with its implications of individualism and authority over the interpretation of textual meaning, has been overthrown in theory, if not entirely in practice.[7] Since the romantic movement, literary definitions of "author" have changed a lot; however, the changes in literary definitions have not appreciably influenced legal definitions.[8]

---

2   Jacqueline Rhodes, "Copyright, Authorship, and the Professional Writer: The Case of William Wordsworth," online: www.cardiff.ac.uk/encap/journals/corvey/articles/cco8_no1.html.

3   See, further, Paul M. Zall, ed., *Literary Criticism of William Wordsworth* (Lincoln, NE: University of Nebraska Press, 1966) at 182.

4   James Boyle, *Shamans, Software, and Spleens: Law and the Construction of the Information Society* (Cambridge, MA: Harvard University Press, 1996) at 54.

5   Mark Rose, *Authors and Owners: the Invention of Copyright* (Cambridge: Harvard University Press, 1993) at 5.

6   For how this notion was invented and incorporated into the modern copyright laws, please see further Woodmansee, above note 1; Jessica Litman, *Digital Copyright* (Amherst, NY: Prometheus Books, 2001); Rose, *ibid.*

7   Jacques Derrida, *Of Grammatology* (Baltimore: Johns Hopkins University Press, 1976).

8   Martha Woodmansee & Peter Jaszi, "The Law of Texts: Copyright in the Academy" (1995) 57 College English 769 at 771. Woodmansee & Jaszi continued: ". . . while legal theory participated in the construction of the modern 'author,' it has yet to be affected by the structuralist and post-structuralist critique of authorship."

Romantic aesthetics emphasize that the author is the monarch of their writings; however, this proposition has been challenged since Roland Barthes' 1968 essay "The Death of the Author".[9] Barthes argues that a text cannot be attributed to any single author because "it is language which speaks, not the author."[10] This theory, labelled as "structuralism" or "post-structuralism," demonstrates that an author is not simply a "person" but a socially and historically constituted subject.

Michel Foucault argues in his 1969 essay "What Is an Author?" that all authors are writers, but not all writers are authors.[11] In Foucault's theory, an author exists only as a function of a written work, a part of its structure, but not necessarily as part of the interpretive process, although the author has been used as an anchor for interpreting a text. The author's name "indicates the status of the discourse within a society and culture."[12] In this approach the readers' importance is re-examined and more explicitly asserted in the construction of meaning.

Emerging notions of "hypertext" and "intertextuality" further highlight the need for the reconsideration of reader's position.[13] They disclose the evolutionary, modifiable, and open nature of the text and support the concept that the meaning of an artistic work does not reside in that work, but in the viewers.[14] More recent post-structuralist theory re-examines intertextuality as a production within texts, rather than as a series of relationships between different texts.[15]

Along with the critique of romantic authorship by literary theory, questions are also raised by emerging legal practices and theories.[16] Mod-

---

9   Roland Barthes, "The Death of the Author" in Roland Barthes, *Image, Music, Text*, trans. by Stephen Heath (London: Fontana, 1977).

10   *Ibid.*

11   Michel Foucault, "What Is an Author?" in Josué E. Harari, ed., *Textual Strategies: Perspectives in Post-Structuralist Criticism* (Ithaca, NY: Cornell University Press, 1979) 141.

12   *Ibid.*

13   Intertextuality is "the shaping of texts' meanings by other texts. It can refer to an author's borrowing and transformation of a prior text or to a reader's referencing of one text in reading another. The term 'intertextuality' has, itself, been borrowed and transformed many times since it was coined by post-structuralist Julia Kristeva in 1966." "Intertextuality," online: http://en.wikipedia.org/wiki/Intertextuality.

14   See, further, Barthes, *Image, Music, Text*, above note 9.

15   See, further, Daniela Caselli, *Beckett's Dantes: Intertextuality in the Fiction and Criticism* (Manchester: Manchester University Press, 2005).

16   The perception of the author as a "creative genius" possessing the "capacity to leap significantly beyond present knowledge and produce something new" is problematic

ern copyright law is an author-centred regime, and creativity in this model is "an individual activity, and the rights over its outcomes are clearly attached to the individual whose labour (mental creativity) is apparent in that outcome."[17] However, networked media technologies have presented the world with a completely different picture. The peer production of information and knowledge is a new creativity model; a decentralized innovation pattern. In this sense creativity is being recast as a collaborative activity rather than an individual activity.

The collaborative nature of literary and artistic creation has been pointed out by many scholars. As Jack Stillinger has explained in many cases, the singular authorship concept does not accord with the facts of literary production. He found that "numerous texts considered to be the work of single authorship turn out to be the product of many hands." Therefore, he asked: how many authors are being banished from a text or apotheosized in it?[18] It has also been argued that current copyright law fails to recognize the collective nature of authorial and artistic creations. Lior Zemer has complained that as a legal and social institution copyright rejects the very nature of copyright creation as a collectively imagined and produced activity, and denies the contribution of the public to the copyright creation process, imposing and maintaining an imbalance between private and public interests.[19]

Furthermore, some scholars have proposed that authorship is not at all a matter of heroic, individual creation but rather it is a social process. This proposition is composed of three aspects. First, there is collaboration, the fact that creative acts depend on interactive networks. Second, authorship is social in that it involves the recombination of existing symbolic materials from a historically deposited common stock. Third, social authorship is incremental in nature. Significant new developments result from many small innovations rather than major breakthroughs by single creators.[20]

---

to those challenging existing copyright standards. Lior Zemer, *The Idea of Authorship in Copyright* (Aldershot, UK: Ashgate, 2007) at 76.

17   James Leach, "Modes of Creativity and the Register of Ownership" in Rishab Aiyer Ghosh, ed., *CODE: Collaborative Ownership and the Digital Economy* (Cambridge: MIT Press, 2005) at 31.

18   See, further, Jack Stillinger, *Multiple Authorship and the Myth of Solitary Genius* (New York: Oxford University Press, 1991).

19   See, further, Zemer, above note 16.

20   See, further, Jason Toynbee, "Beyond Romance and Repression: Social Authorship in a Capitalist Age" *Open Democracy* (28 November 2002), online: www.opendemocracy.net/media-copyrightlaw/article_44.jsp.

To this end the "copyleft" movement can be seen as a better translation of the postmodern space of *creation* rather than *copyright*.[21] From open source to art, a radically new view of creation has been mapped out, within which not only the location of the author, but also the location of the work and of the user, have been shifted and reconfigured.[22]

In summary, over recent years the western world has witnessed the romantic notion of authorship being questioned both by literary critics and by legal scholars. The former argue that the work/text is a product of the author's cultural influences rather than her mere persona, and, furthermore, readers/audiences are as important as the author in the discourse process. The latter point out that the authors assemble, transform and adapt their works from the components of their cultural environment rather than make anew; therefore, the contribution of the public in this process should not be ignored.

C. THE SITUATED RELATIONAL AUTHORS

The existing definition of authorship embraces the presuppositions that individuals live in isolation from one another while ignoring "the individual's relationship with others within her community, family, ethnic group, religion — the very social relations out of which and for the benefit of whom the individual's limited monopoly rights are supposed to exist."[23] Accordingly, copyright as a legal institution based on this definition has "focused primarily on the relationships among those who write works of authorship and disseminate those works to the public."[24]

However, the growing public digital literacy and the rise of a "participative web"[25] have afforded a world of peer production and an age of mass

---

21   Severine Dusollier, "Open Source and Copyleft: Authorship Reconsidered?" (2003) 26 Colum. J.L. & Arts 281 at 288–89.

22   *Ibid.* at 288.

23   Shelley Wright, "A Feminist Exploration of the Legal Protection of Art" (1994) 7 C.J.W.L. 59 at 73.

24   Litman, above note 6 at 111.

25   "The use of the Internet is now characterised by increased participation and interaction of users to create, express themselves and communicate. The 'participative web' is the most common term and underlying concept used to describe the more extensive use of the Internet's capacities to expand creativity and communication. It is based on intelligent web services and new Internet-based software applications that enable users to collaborate and contribute to developing, extending, rating, commenting on and distributing digital and developing and customising Internet

participation.[26] The production of artistic and literary works is no longer considered a privilege and "the genius" of a social and cultural elite, but rather a daily engagement for a mass of individuals, which is enjoyable and provides for instance, communication, entertainment, creative play, and self-development.[27] In the new context, the creation of literary and artistic works is more than a process of creative expression. It is also a process of communication. The application of interactive information technology and participatory web infrastructure has given rise to an interactive information arena. If it continues to keep authors isolated and users irrelevant, copyright law will be in very real danger of becoming irrelevant. It has been suggested that authorship should be understood "within the context of cultural dialogue and participative processes, and in recognition of its audience and the public as a whole."[28] Carys Craig proposes to "re-imagine authorship as the formation of individual identity and the development of self and community through discourse,"[29] and that copyright should aim to "encourage meaningful relations of communication and participation with others."[30] Craig articulates a relational theory of authorship. A *relational author* is "always-already situated within, and constituted by, the communities in which she exists, and the texts and discourses by which she is surrounded."[31] Craig posits that "copyright must be understood in relational terms,"[32] and it "structures relationships between authors and users, allocating powers and responsibilities amongst members of cultural com-

---

applications." Graham Vickery & Sacha Wunsch-Vincent, *Participative Web and User-Created Content: Web 2.0, Wikis and Social Networking* (Paris: Organisation for Economic Co-operation and Development, 2007) at 17.

26   "In contrast to the Web 1.0 age, the Internet in the Web 2.0 age (the participatory media age) is not only 'characterised as a giant copying machine that facilitates widespread and undetectable copyright infringement,' it also enables a new creativity model and a new way for producing information and knowledge." See, further, Sampsung Xiaoxiang Shi, "Chinese Copyright Law, Peer Production, and the Participatory Media Age" in Brian Fitzgerald *et al.*, eds., *Copyright Law, Digital Content and the Internet in the Asia-Pacific* (Sydney: Sydney University Press, 2008) at 268–69 [Shi, "Chinese Copyright"].

27   Shi, "Chinese Copyright Law," *ibid.* at 262. See also Julie E. Cohen, "The Place of the User in Copyright Law" (2005) 74 Fordham L. Rev. 347; Cohen, "Creativity and Culture," above note 1.

28   Craig, above note 1 at 266.

29   *Ibid.* at 234.

30   *Ibid.*

31   *Ibid.* at 261.

32   *Ibid.*

munities, and establishing the rules of communication and exchange."[33] Moreover, "the importance of copyright lies in its capacity to structure relations of communication, and also to establish the power dynamics that will shape these relations. Its purpose is to maximize communication and exchange by putting in place incentives for the creation and dissemination of intellectual works."[34]

Instead of seeing authorship as commencing with the act of the individual who puts pen to paper or paint to canvas we should conceptualize authorship as being a product of the ecosystem in which it is born. This chapter furthers the arguments for a relational theory of authorship, looking at creativity "from a systematic perspective."[35] Relational authorship is a descriptive system that talks about cultural contributors rather than the solitary romantic author, and its subject focuses on the relational and multiple contributions. Grounded in the postmodernist social and cultural theory,[36] this theory perceives that the creative process and cultural progress is an open-ended and communication-oriented discourse and interpretation.

D. AUTHORIAL CULTURAL CONTRIBUTIONS

If we posit a creative act—let us call it the act of "first contribution" (FC)—as being preceded by culture, associated communication protocols, and markets, then we must somehow incorporate these contributions into our system of knowledge flows, usage, and ownership. This role that the culture plays prior to the FC could be labelled "pre-first contribution" (pre-FC); and the role that the fans/admirers, consumers, and users play following the FC could be "post-first contribution" (post-FC).

Therefore, the contributions to creativity and cultural innovation that raise the evolving culture could be mapped comprehensively by the following chart.

---

33 *Ibid.*

34 *Ibid.*

35 From a systematic perspective, "artistic and intellectual culture is most usefully understood not as a set of products, but rather as a set of interconnected, relational networks of actors, resources, and emergent creative practices." Cohen, "Creativity and Culture," above note 1 at 1183.

36 Social and cultural theories that emphasize the contingent, iterative, and performative development of knowledge are rooted in several philosophical traditions that liberalism has resisted, and of which copyright scholars have remained largely skeptical. *Ibid.* at 1166–67.

Figure 1

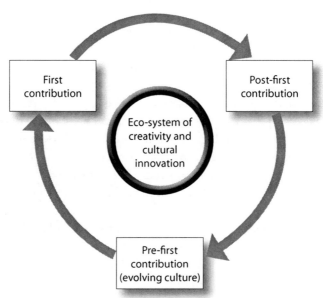

1)   Pre-FC and the Culture as Pre-FC Contributor

Culture as the pre-FC to creativity generated by the public (individuals and associated social groups and communities) is where the writer and artist are situated. Its role is evidenced in a small way in the limitations or exceptions found in copyright law, but these provisions are expressed and implemented in a manner that defers to the romantic notion of the author.

a)   The recognition of culture as a contributor to creativity

In the past few years, the affordance of the participative web has dramatic- ally challenged the copyright regime's arrogance towards the culture. The contribution of culture and cultural inhabitants to creativity has come to play a more obvious role in the processes of meaning-making and the progress of culture itself.

First of all, the advance of media technology has dramatically facili- tated the civic engagement in cultural creation that meanwhile increases the decentralization of creativity. On the other hand, the increasing civic engagement results in the diversity and complexity of relations between individuals and the exuberance of the species and amounts of social groups and communities. As Cohen has described, social groups "play a dual role in creative processes, functioning both as users and as immediate cultural environments for individual users";[37] and "within copyright law, the relative salience assigned to contributions of individuals and contributions of groups affects the designation of authorship."[38]

Additionally, the relatively low barriers to artistic and intellectual expression and civic engagement have increased the demands of intellectual commons as raw materials for individual development. From the perspective of the non-utilitarian, freedom is not simply defined as a function of the absence of restraint, but also depends critically on access to resources and on the availability of a sufficient variety of real opportunities.[39] Therefore, the access to extant cultural resources, characterized by Cohen as "cultural landscape,"[40] is playing a more and more important role in accommodating the fulfillment of human freedom. Moreover, open access to knowledge and information has become a worldwide movement, paving the way for a seamless access to culture and for a profound growth of the cultural landscape. The situated nature of creativity is becoming more and more prominent because of the evolution of cultural context. The relations between individuals, social groups, and the culture are more complicated and multiform. The creative process also becomes a more complex dynamic.

The popular culture paradigm has been undermined and replaced in more and more instances by distributed culture, which is spawned and incubated in a variety of distributed social groups and communities. Consequently, distributed cultural creativity is initiated, communicated, and appreciated within a specified community and particular cultural environment. However, in many cases, the particular distributed culture will not be meaningful outside of the community or the meaning must be understood as associated with its particular cultural context. The creative actors and creative outputs are more situated than when only popular culture prevails.

---

37   *Ibid.* at 1188.

38   *Ibid.*

39   *Ibid.* at 1159. See also Amartya Sen, *Inequality Reexamined* (Oxford: Clarendon Press, 1992); Amartya Sen, *Development as Freedom* (New York: Oxford University Press, 1999).

40   Cultural landscape is "neither geographically discrete nor composed entirely of resources that are publicly owned; therefore, it does not map neatly to the legal category of public domain expression. It is defined, instead, by the ways in which artistic and intellectual goods are accessible to individuals in the spaces where they live, and by the forms of interaction with preexisting expression that are possible and limited. The cultural landscape is what supplies the elements in culture that are experienced as common, regardless of their ownership status." *Ibid.* at 1180.

b) The pre-FC contributions

The pre-FC are multi-dimensional. For example, the culture contributes raw materials, context, markets, and environment to creativity. The accumulated cultural elements such as language, knowledge, texts, and conceptions of artistic and intellectual merit are raw materials for creativity. The cultural context within which the author is located and from which the author obtains his experiences, insights, values, education, and skills is another portion of contribution that should be attributed to the culture.

Additionally, individuals located in a given culture are social markets playing crucial roles, particularly in the new value chain approach to cultural production, in consuming, appreciating, and facilitating creativity.[41] Theorists believe that personal decisions about information consumption, under fair competition, will produce results that make sense,[42] especially in a networked information society of social markets.

Moreover, social groups and communities within which the author and creative practices are situated are immediate cultural environments contributed by the culture. The author is always related to many social groups such as family, ethnic, religion, local culture based communities. Although concrete creativity is always initiated and maintained by particular individual authors, their dynamic and complex interconnections with the groups or communities determine the overall path.

It is notable that such pre-FC are not authorial as it is unrealistic to acknowledge all individuals and associated culture as authors of a given piece of intellectual and artistic work. Copyright, even put in relational terms, could only be resident in individuals despite the fact that the individual contributors are already and always situated in particular relations with other individuals and associated culture. However, the recognition of the culture as a pre-FC to creativity would pave a way for a better, balanced

---

41   This new value chain approach to cultural production is as follows: (i) agents (who may be individuals or firms) are characterized by choice, decision-making, and learning (origination); (ii) social networks, both real and virtual adopt this choice; and (iii) market-based enterprise, organizations, and coordinating institutions retain these choices. John Hartley, "The Evolution of the Creative Industries — Creative Clusters, Creative Citizens and Social Network Markets" (Paper presented to the Creative Industries Conference, Asia-Pacific Forum, Berlin, 19 September 2007), online: http://eprints.qut.edu.au/archive/00012647/ at 19–20.

42   "The truest and most beautiful works will be the ones that appeals most strongly to the citizen's deliberative faculty, to the consumer's enlightened self-interest." Cohen, "Creativity and Culture," above note 1 at 1165.

copyright regime that sees the public within the relations of contributors of cultural innovation.

2) FC and the Initiating Contributor — The Initiator of a Dialogue and Communication

a) The process of authorship reconsidered

As has been suggested above, both authors and users are absolutely located within a particular cultural context and creative practice is substantially determined by this context. However, just as Cohen argued, recognizing the "situatedness" of creativity does not "require submerging the individual irretrievably within the social; creativity has 'internal' dimensions as well as 'external' ones."[43] Accordingly, the relational theory of authorship "recognizes the social dimension of the author, but also her duality: she encapsulates both our connectedness and our capacity for critical reflection."[44]

The romantic aesthetics saw the creative process as a result of the author's own genius. Of genius the only proof is "the act of doing well what is worthy to be done, and what was never done before . . . . Genius is the introduction of a new element into the intellectual universe."[45] This aesthetic view of intellectual creation entered the domain of law through the conceptualization of originality. Although the legal definition of "original" has significantly departed from the literary conception of the term,[46] the copyright regime built on the romantic conception authorship still primarily focuses on individual author with the perception that authorial process is an isolated individual phenomenon.

Instead of seeing authors as independent and unattached individuals, the relational theory conceptualizes one group of authors as the initiators of relatively new discourses, dialogues, and conversations, and another group of authors as consequential contributors who follow the initiating authors and take part in the discourse processes. In the process of authorship, the dialogues and conversations always begin from the cultural materials at hand. However, these materials of authorship are always both original and

---

43 *Ibid.* at 1178–79.
44 Craig, above note 1 at 261–62.
45 Zall, above note 3 at 184.
46 In *University of London Press Ltd. v. University Tutorial Press Ltd.*, [1916] 2 Ch. 601 at 608–10, Peterson J. stated: "the Act does not require that the expression must be in an original or novel form, but that the work must not be copied from another work — that it should originate with the author."

dependant.[47] The author creates from the given materials around them. It is a process of reinterpretation, recombination, and transformation.[48]

b)   The FC

Through the interpretation and reinterpretation of the culture and experiences, the initiating author opens a new dialogue and starts a new conversation. Such initiating contribution is a breakthrough or spore of the evolving culture and makes it possible to shift the existing cultural conversation to the next level and next dimension.

Accordingly, this initiating contribution could be called the FC to creativity. The contributor is first and foremost an initiator. In retrospect, her creative expression should be seen as an outcome of the entire human culture and should be attributed both to her intellectual labours and to the cultural context in which she is situated. The contribution of the initiating author is not in the sense of inventing an original thing *ex nihilo*, but nonetheless it is in the sense of initiating new directions bringing innovation to culture and society.

2)   Post-FC and the Ensuing Contributors

a)   The recognition of post-FC

From the perspective of the emergent and complex evolution of the culture, the initiating author's intellectual breakthrough is not an end; instead, it is a beginning. The initiating contribution would only be valuable in the context of attracting and captivating users, admirers, fans, followers, and responders.

The ensuing contributors are those who take part in and continue the conversation and discourse that were initiated by the FC. Such post-FC is also situated in a particular cultural context; however, it is directly and immediately derived from and dependent on the existing initiating contribution (the FC).

The continuous growth of culture is a product of a variety of post-FCs. The ensuing contributors play a key role in shaping meanings and

---

47   However, these materials are "always, and from the beginning, both given and created. They are given in that they are shaped by forces beyond any individual's control; they are created in that each new repetition of such cultural and personal artifacts is always a reinterpretation rather than merely a replication." Susan H. Williams, "A Feminist Reassessment of Civil Society" (1997) 72(2) Ind. L.J. 417 at 430.

48   Craig, above note 1 at 263.

sustaining the dynamic and conversational creative process and cultural progress. The post-FC is a dynamic process of appreciation, adaptation, derivation, translation, recombination, imitation, or transformation of the FCs and other pre-existing cultural materials.

b) Copyright monopoly reconsidered

Once a new discourse is initiated, the existing law awards copyright owners the monopoly power to control the ensuing conversation and dialogue with very limited and narrow exceptions. Copyright owners decide who can speak or take part in this conversation, how the participants should speak, and even what they should speak for. A copyright regime that merely focuses on a set of products without adequate rectification could be problematic, particularly in the networked information society. In the worst instances, it could be employed to depress and attack dissents, dissidences, and opponents.

In contrast, the relational authorship sees copyright in the light of a set of relational networks of actors and contextual culture. The post-FC, especially in the networked information environment, is recognized by the relational copyright as an authorial contribution and the ensuing contributors are relational authors. However, under existing law the creator of the post-FC will incur liability in most instances for engaging in copyright infringement.[49] We argue that no such liability should occur where the com-

---

49   It is a fundamental concept that copyright law "does not protect ideas, information or facts but instead protects the form in which those ideas, information or facts are expressed." Therefore as a general rule, if a creator's work is built on preexisting copyrighted works without authorization, the creator will incur liability for copyright infringement. Anne Fitzgerald & Brian Fitzgerald, *Intellectual Property in Principle* (Sydney: Lawbook, 2004) at 84. Additionally, the status of works/content unlawfully employing preexisting copyrighted material varies in different jurisdictions. For example, US copyright law refuses to recognize authorship of such works ("compilations" and "derivative works"). 17 U.S.C. § 103 provides that copyright protection does not extend to "any part of the work in which such material has been used unlawfully." House Report No. 94–1476 explains further that "the bill prevents an infringer from benefiting, through copyright protection, from committing an unlawful act, but preserves protection for those parts of the work that do not employ the preexisting work." Under Australian law, the creator will obtain authorship and copyright protection, but he will incur liability for unauthorized reproduction and communication. In *A-One Accessory Imports Pty Ltd., Noel Bruce Rogers and Stephen Arthur Bennett v. Off Road Imports Pty Ltd., Ross Bartley King and Julie Robyn King*, [1996] FCA 1353 at para. 46, Drummond J. concluded: "In my opinion, a work can be an original work in which copyright will subsist, even though it is itself an

mercial viability of the FC works is not destroyed. As part of the bargain for this immunity from liability, post-FC contributors should be granted a lower level of authorship and more limited rights and powers in relation to the post-FC work generated from their contribution. Additionally, benefits arising from commercial exploitation of the post-FC content should be shared between the initiating contributor (first author) and the post-FC contributor (ensuing author and secondary initiating author).

E. THEORIZING RELATIONAL AUTHORSHIP

We perceive creativity as a process of dialogue and communication. Copyright should be a legal institution aiming to structure relations of the participants in and contributors to this system.

In contrast to the romantic conception of authorship that focuses on the solitary romantic author and excludes any other cultural participants, relational authorship articulates an approach that includes and internalizes the evolving, emergent, and dynamic relations between the public, authors, and users/consumers. Therefore, this theory argues for an account of contributorship that supports a relational authorship, which in turn aims to "construct relationships of communication between authors, users, and the public by allocating powers and responsibilities."[50]

The naive acceptance of authorship as a predominantly individual and isolated act may foster authorial rights that are too broad or too powerful for the good of society.[51] A legal institution that was established upon the originality of text and the romantic notion of authorial creations is incapable of regulating how information and knowledge is actually produced in the networked information society. On the contrary, the relational theory of authorship will give rise to a responsive and flexible copyright regime.

---

infringement of the copyright in an earlier work because it is, in part, a copy of a substantial part of that copyright work. This will be the position provided the later work includes qualitatively significant changes to the copied material."

50   Craig, above note 1 at 267.

51   See further, Alan L. Durham, "Copyright and Information Theory: Toward an Alternative Model of 'Authorship'" (2004) 69 B.Y.U.L. Rev. 69.

1) Contributorship and Relational Authorship

a) The reconfigured author

The relational theory of authorship is constituted by the notion of contributorship. "Authors" are those who make contributions of some kind to a work instead of the one who creates the work. This analytical perspective on authorship is also in accordance with the findings of information theory.[52]

The decentring of creativity has "incorporated multiple contributing factors and made none primary."[53] Therefore, contributions of all sorts should be encouraged and valued. In the networked information society, any contribution including creation of new works, interpretation and re-interpretation of preexisting culture, and even combination and re-combination of copyright materials are crucial to the production of information and knowledge.

b) Contributors and the relational authors

Contributors are those who make contributions to creativity and the progress of culture and take part in the discourse process in whatever manner. Contribution is defined in a very broad way, disregarding its intellectual or artistic merit but emphasizing its substantial functional values for the free flow of information.

However, not all contributions are authorial and meanwhile not all contributors are authors.

---

52 The potential relationship between "originality" in copyright and "entropy" in information theory suggests at least two alternatives to the romantic model of authorship. The first alternative equates authorship with the addition of noise to a signal. The second proposes that authorship, like the addition of information to a message, reflects "freedom of choice" in the selection of one means of expression from a variety of available means. The second alternative is less disparaging of the talents of authors than the first, yet it is still "unromantic" enough to be more inclusive, and less dependent on the notion of genius or personality, than the traditional model. *Ibid.* at 145–58.

53 Cohen, "Creativity and Culture," above note 1 at 1177.

Figure 2

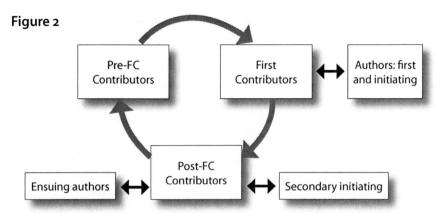

i)   Pre-FC contributors
In particular, the pre-FC is not authorial. The culture itself could not be attributed as the author, but its contributorship should be acknowledged unless the origin of the involved cultural elements is self-evident. For example, the Hollywood movie *Fa Mulan* should be attributed as "This movie is adapted from an old Chinese story." The contributorship of a work derived from a particular indigenous culture should be attributed to this indigenous group.

ii)   FC contributors = first/initiating author
All FCs are authorial and their contributors should be attributed as "initiating author" or "first author."

iii)   Post-FC contributors = ensuing authors + secondary initiating authors
In the networked information society, perhaps more than ever attention has been placed on the legal standing of the post-FC. Traditional approaches to copyright law have embodied the notion that creators act autonomously and independently, appropriating cultural elements to create works that are regarded as their own property. The role of downstream contributors is not well articulated. Contrast this approach to the practice apparent in networked society in which distributed cultural production and meaning-making are more dependent on each other. For example, creative practices such as fan fiction, remix, and mashup are not only built on but also highly dependent on the prevalence of their underlying works.

We argue that as a default rule post-FC should be encouraged and permitted and the contributorship/authorship of post-FC contributors should be accepted by copyright law. Consequently, we propose that copyright law should create space for them and treat them as another special kind of author. Such special authorship is different from the first/initiating authorship and will be vested with rights and powers of a different level.

Accordingly, we posit that all post-FCs are authorial but to varying degrees. If the works generated from post-FC are substantially composed of and highly dependent on existing FCs, the contributors would be attributed as "ensuing authors" as opposed to the first/initiating authors. In contrast, if the post-FC is substantially independent enough and it opens a new discourse and starts a new conversation, it would, to some extent, amount to an "initiating authorship" or "first authorship." In this case, the works generated from the post-FCs should be accepted as works that are independently recognized by copyright law (similar to derivative works under existing laws). This group of post-FC contributors should be attributed as "secondary initiating authors" who have a similar though not necessarily exactly the same status as the first/initiating authors.

2) What Status and Entitlements Should this Sponsor?

Generally speaking, the existing copyright legal framework has adopted a regulatory approach that forbids anyone, except the authors, from doing specific acts such as reproducing the works (making copies), publishing and distributing the copies to the public, performing the works in public, communicating the work to the public via information networks, and making adaptations of the works, unless such acts are expressly approved by the copyright owner or conducted for specific purposes such as personal use, study, research, criticism, review, and parody.

Historically, the acts controlled by the copyright owner were focused on commercial publication. This meant that in practice copyright law was not the focus of everyday life in that personal use, such as reading, was not an infringing act.

However, the advance of media technologies has continuously challenged this deliberate legal arrangement. The emergent information and communication technologies, in particular, afford more possibilities of acts that could be accomplished by individual users; and accordingly copyright law has successfully expanded to cover these possibilities with very few limitations. As a result, copyright has evolved from exceptional rules to general application; and meanwhile few usages could be realized without conducting the forbidden acts.

On the contrary, the relational theory articulates a "benefit sharing" scheme to structure and facilitate the relations of meaning-making among various contributors of creativity and to reconcile the interests arising from creativity. Therefore, the relational copyright adopts another approach by reversing the existing legal arrangement. In most occasions, the users have rights to conduct any acts in relation to copyright works, such as sharing, modifying, or copying, provided that such action would not unreasonably and immediately prejudice the commercial interests and other vested legal rights of copyright owners. Meanwhile, copyright owners are entitled to any commercial exploitation of copyright works unless the user rights are unreasonably restricted and undermined. To this end this chapter proposes the following scheme of status and entitlements that relational authorship could support to structure the above dynamic relations between authors, users, and the culture.

Figure 3: The Relational Copyright and the Evolving and Emergent Culture

Rights of first/initiating authors
» Right of attribution
» Right of commercial exploitation of FC
» Right of commercial exploitation of works of EA (limited)
» Right of sharing benefit of commercial exploitation of works of SIA

Rights of secondary initiating authors (SIA)	**Rights of Users**	**Rights of ensuing authors (EA)**
» Right of attribution » Right of commercial exploitation of post-FC contributions (limited)	» Right of personal use » Right of fair use/ dealing » Right of transformative use » Right of access to information	» Right of attribution » Right of sharing commercial benefit

a)   The rights of authors

The spectrum of the rights of authors should be in accordance with the varieties of the nature of their authorship. In particular, rights of commercial exploitation of post-FC works/content must be relative to specific authorial contribution. Where the post-First contribution is highly independent from existing FC works, the contributor (secondary initiating author) has the right to commercially exploit the works/content but has to share benefits with FC contributors (first authors). However, where the post-FC is not substantially independent enough, the first author of the underlying work, instead of the post-FC contributor (ensuing author), has the right of commercial exploitation. However, the first author should share benefits with the ensuing author depending on contribution.

i) The rights of first/initiating authors
The first/initiating authors should be awarded the most substantial power to harvest the benefits arising from creativity. However, their rights should not impede the occurrence of the post-FCs.

Therefore, the first/initiating authors should have the following rights: right of attribution of authorship/contributorship and right of commercial exploitation of works produced by them.

Additionally, the first/initiating authors should have the right to commercially exploit the works/content produced by the ensuing authors; however, commercial benefits arising from the commercial exploitation should be shared with the ensuing authors. The post-FCs made by the ensuing authors are the by-product of their creative play in daily life and are not substantially independent enough to initiate new discourses. Moreover, the works/content generated by such contributions is highly dependent on the prevalence of the first/initiating authors' works. The relational copyright does not require permission for the production of such works/content, however, it awards the first/initiating authors (not the ensuing authors) the right of commercial exploitation of such works/content.

Furthermore, the first/initiating authors should be entitled to share the commercial benefits arising from commercial exploitation of works generated by the secondary initiating authors. Although the post-FCs in this case are substantially independent from the underlying FCs, such works are, first and foremost, derivative. The relational copyright does not require permission for the creation of such works, however it would require that commercial benefits arising from the exploitation of such works be shared between the first/initiating authors *and* secondary initiating authors.

ii) The rights of the secondary initiating authors
The secondary initiating authors should enjoy the right of commercial exploitation of works of post-FCs (but commercial benefits generated must be shared with the first/initiating authors). The secondary initiating author should also enjoy the right of attribution.

iii) The rights of the ensuing authors
The only rights that the ensuing authors should enjoy are the right of attribution of their authorship/contributorship and the right to share commercial benefits arising from commercial exploitation of their contributions.

b) The rights of users

All of the individuals and associated social groups or communities of a culture—global or local—should have certain rights regarding the FC and the ensuing post-FCs. One example of how this might work is seen in the current law of limitations: fair use (fair dealing) and personal use. Those limitations are open to anyone who fits within their ambit, not just a selected few. This confirms the argument that individuals (not just a collective whole, such as society or culture) can be seen as bestowing a benefit on the creator of the FC and therefore they should be entitled to a "benefit share" in some defined context.

Personal use is not the same as fair use/dealing for research and study,[54] but it is notable that not all legislation differentiates between the two.[55] A personal use is the private use of a copyright work for one's own learning, enjoyment, or sharing with a colleague or friend—without any motive for profit.[56] Under current Australian copyright law, personal use includes "space shifting of recorded music, timeshifting television and radio programs and format shifting other types of material such as books, magazines or photographs."[57] However, fair use (under Australian copyright law, it is

---

54   As Patterson & Lindberg posit, it should be noted that "personal use by a consumer and fair use by competitor are two different concepts." L. Ray Patterson & Stanley W. Lindberg, *The Nature of Copyright: A Law of User's Right* (Athens, GA: University of Georgia Press, 1991) at 193.

55   For example, under Chinese copyright law, the concept of "personal use" is covered by "fair use"; see further, *Copyright Law of China*, art. 22 [adopted at the Fifteenth Session of the Standing Committee of the Seventh National People's Congress on 7 September 1990, and revised in accordance with the Decision on the Amendment of the Copyright Law of the People's Republic of China adopted at the 24th Session of the Standing Committee of the Ninth National People's Congress on 27 October 2001]. However, it is arguable that the rationale behind art. 11 is a little bit different from the concept of "fair use" in Western copyright acts. See further, Shi, "Chinese Copyright," above note 26 at 282.

56   The rule of personal use is: "An individual's use of a copyrighted work for his or her own private use is a personal use, not subject to fair-use restraints. Such use includes use by copying, provided that the copy is neither for public distribution or sale to others nor a functional substitute for a copyrighted work currently available on the market at a reasonable price." Patterson & Lindberg, above note 54 at 194.

57   The differences between fair dealing (fair use) and personal use are outlined as follows:

     Personal use:
     • You must own a copy of the material being reproduced;
     • Purpose of copying—for your own private use;
     • Works can be copied in full;

called "fair dealing" although the two concepts are not exactly the same) allows limited use of copyrighted material without requiring permission from the copyright owner, and it only applies to certain purposes such as research or study, criticism or review, parody or satire, reporting news, judicial proceedings, or professional advice.

Fair use and personal use unfortunately start from a position of weakness. They are subservient to or supplement the notion of the romantic author and its primary position in copyright law. By seeing the role of culture as bestowed by the individuals in a society as pre-dating authorship we are challenged to reassess such an approach.

This chapter posits that the pre-FC contribution should at very least give rise to certain user rights by the individuals. The user rights may include schemes such as a recalibrated fair use and personal use, and even may extend to transformative use and conductive use.[58] However, the user rights should not unreasonably prejudice the reconfigured rights of authors. In particular, the commercial value of copyrighted works should not be unreasonably and immediately undermined.

This proposition would provide a market for creativity through consumption, and in particular create possibilities for post-FC creativity through productive, transformative, and conductive use.

F. CONCLUSION

The participatory and collaborative production of knowledge and information is inherent to the very nature of creative process. As this chapter

---

- Copies cannot be lent or shared with anyone;
- The work being copied must be a legal (i.e. non-pirate) copy;
- Artistic works, sound recordings & films can be copied in full.

Fair dealing for research and study:
- You do not have to own a copy of the material being reproduced. The material can be held in, or borrowed from, a library, for example;
- Purpose of copying—must be for research or study;
- The amount copied is limited to 10 percent or 1 chapter whichever is greater. (More can be copied if it is considered "fair");
- Copies can be in the same format as the original (e.g. a photocopy of a book);
- The work being copied must be a legal (i.e. non-pirate) copy;
- Artistic works, sound recordings & films can only be copied if they satisfy the five factors for fairness.

See online: www.unimelb.edu.au/copyright/information/fastfind/personaluse.html.

58 See further, Shi, "Chinese Copyright," above note 26 at 291–93.

has narrated, the creative process is already situated in a particular cultural context and is always undertaken by a set of relational networks of actors, and they are characterized as contributors.

Instead of seeing the author as an isolated solitary genius, this chapter has articulated a relational theory of authorship, situating authors within a network of relations with other contributors, users, and the public. The mission of copyright law is to structure the relations of the contributors of creativity and cultural innovation through the allocation of rights and powers within the dynamics of creative processes that shape these relations.

The set of relational networks of creators and their contributions are summarized as dynamic relations between the pre-FC (pre-FC contributor, the culture), the FC (initiating contributor, the first author), and the post-FC (ensuing author and secondary initiating author).

This relational approach sponsors a more conversational and flexible copyright regime that is conscious of economic value. The public and consumers are entitled to more freedom and rights of using, sharing, and disseminating copyrighted works. Moreover, it allows individuals the freedom to make contributions to human culture and knowledge based on any existing intellectual materials in a more dynamic and accommodating context.

CHAPTER 14

Access to Digital Information:
Gift or Right?

*Margaret Ann Wilkinson**

A. INTRODUCTION

There are different factors involved in creating the intellectual property
environment within which digital information transactions take place in a
networked world. The most important is the attitude of the governments of
the various nation states in which aspects of the transactions occur. These
attitudes, in turn, shape, and are also shaped by, the second factor involved,
international agreements. The third factor is the activity of intellectual
property owners. Together these three create the environment within which
users experience both digital and non-digital information access to information. That environment, however, is not the same for each nation state, nor
does the environment necessarily remain static: for each nation state, the
copyright environment reflects a complex interplay between the three factors. This paper will explore the role of "open source" and "open access"
movements in Canada and in the United States within the context of the
three factors because the blend of the three in the two jurisdictions is different and therefore creates two different environments for access to digital
information.

The dominance, among the three factors, of the role of the governments of nation states has been clearly asserted in the Internet environment
as the Internet has developed and matured. Despite early notions that the

* Research assistance for this paper was provided by law students Vanessa Bacher
and Ann Chmielowski. An earlier version of this paper was delivered at the Digital
Copyright in a User-Generated World: Knowledge Policy for the Twenty-first Century Conference, held at The University of Western Ontario in April 2007.

law would be somehow different in the online environment than in the offline environment,[1] nation states have demonstrated their control in this new realm[2]—although, as in other areas of law where transactions cross jurisdictional boundaries, more than one state at a time can claim jurisdiction in a particular situation.[3] This paper will focus on copyright, a historic form of content control that has been virtually universally adopted by governments as appropriate for the digital telecommunications environment. Recalling that copyright laws give the owners of copyright interests certain legislated controls over uses of material that are defined as being "in copyright," it will become apparent from this paper that, while the open access movement, fuelled as it is by the decisions of copyright owners, appears to have an important and vigorous role to play in the American context, in Canada the role for the movement is much less obvious. The two different approaches, Canadian and American, in providing accessibility to digital content will be tested for "fit" in terms of the international obligations of the two states. Finally, it will be recommended that those copyright holders interested in providing free access to material in the Canadian context consider exploring the opportunity to create a collective.

B. THE DECISIONS OF COPYRIGHT OWNERS

The owner of a copyright interest in a work or other subject matter that is in copyright controls various uses of the work, sound recording, performer's performance, or broadcast and may therefore make any one of a number of decisions regarding further uses of that information. In the case of a work such as an article or a book, seven possibilities present themselves:

1)   Assign all the copyright interest to a "traditional" publisher.[4]

---

1   John Perry Barlow, "The Economy of Ideas: A Framework for Patents and Copyrights in the Digital Age (Everything You Know about Intellectual Property Is Wrong)" *Wired* (March 1994), online: www.wired.com/wired/archive/2.03/economy.ideas.html.

2   *Society of Composers, Authors and Music Publishers of Canada (SOCAN) v. Canadian Assn. of Internet Providers*, 2004 SCC 45 [*Tariff 22*].

3   *Tariff 22, ibid.*

4   A traditional publisher, in this context, means a publisher who, following the industrial model of publishing, requires the assignment of an author's copyright interest in return for giving that author access, through the publisher's machinery for publishing (originally the printing press itself), to readership.

2) Assign some aspects of the copyright interest to "non-traditional" pub-lishers—those publishers who will publish without insisting upon a full assignment of the copyright holder's interest in the work.

3) Retain copyright and grant permissions on a case-by-case basis as re-quested by potential users.

4) Retain copyright and grant certain permissions for use to all users or to certain classes of user.

5) Retain copyright and join with other copyright holders in arrange-ments of collective administration of rights.

6) Retain copyright and do not take any steps to enforce the interests.

7) Renounce copyright.

The first option was really the only option available to an author who wished to reach any audience up until the late twentieth century. The au-thor, in this historic industrial model, would have had no possibility of self-publishing, particularly to a large audience, because of the expense in-volved in owning and operating the machinery of reproduction. The pub-lisher would seek full assignment of the copyright in return for the high risk involved in expending the money to publish where the popularity of a pub-lication was usually unknown until the expenses had been incurred. The original industrial reasons for this model of publication have been eroded in the last quarter of the twentieth century, first by the spread of photo-copying and then by the spread of digital technology. However, traditional publishers continue to play a role in publishing—and in no small measure due to the value that users place upon the imprimatur of a known press as an indicator of quality. This first choice, therefore, is still a choice frequently made by authors and copyright holders.

The consequences of this first choice, and an environment in which it is entrenched for a number of reasons, can be seen in the academic sphere.[5] In Canada, copyright is generally taken to belong to professors when they create scholarly works.[6] During the period of the gestation and writing of

---

5   See Margaret Ann Wilkinson, "Copyright in the Context of Intellectual Property: A Survey of Canadian University Policies" (2000) 14:2 Intellectual Property Journal 141 [Wilkinson, "Survey of Canadian Policies].

6   In a case such as *Dolmage v. Erskine* (2003), 23 C.P.R. (4th) 495 (Ont. S.C.J.), involv-ing the parties at The University of Western Ontario, the capacity of professors (and not the university) to hold copyright was assumed. In Australia, however, faculty employed by the university, working within the scope of their employment, were found not to hold copyright; the university owned it: *Victoria University of Technol-ogy v. Wilson* (2004), 60 I.P.R. 392 (Vic. S.C.). In the Canadian context, it is difficult

the work, the university has borne the costs of the professor's scholarship. In order to be published in established peer-reviewed journals, it has been necessary, at least in the past, to assign the copyright in the work to the publisher of the academic journal.[7] Then, in order to bring the work back into the scholarly environment of the university, it has been necessary for the university, usually through its library system, to purchase a journal subscription from the publisher.[8]

The second option, partial transfer of copyright, for certain purposes, in exchange for publication, is an option for the copyright holder where the target publication makes this option available. It is slowly becoming more available in certain venues, for example, in university-level academic publishing.

The third option, retaining all copyright interests and giving permission on a case-by-case basis, is becoming more possible for copyright owners, particularly with the increased possibilities for self-publication fostered by the digital telecommunications environment—although, as will

---

to be certain what the outcome would be of litigation that put this assumption squarely to the test. Under s. 13(3) of the Canadian *Copyright Act*, R.S.C. 1985, c. C-42, as amended, copyright is first owned by the employer when the author is in an employment relationship. What is meant by "employment" is not further defined in the *Copyright Act*. Therefore, presumably, this would be determined with reference to labour law in Canada. Under the labour relations statutes of the various Canadian provinces, a group can only engage in collective bargaining where an employer-employee relationship exists. See Donald D. Carter *et al.*, *Labour Law in Canada* (NewYork: Kluwer Law International, 2002) at 44 and 250. Since over half of Canada's university faculty have unionized over the past several decades (64 universities out of roughly 78 in Canada (see online: www.caut.ca/pages.asp?page=128) (see "The Register of Post-Secondary and Adult Education Institutions," online: www.statcan. ca/cgi-bin/imdb/p2SV.pl?Function=getSurvey&SDDS=5075&lang=en&db=IMDB &dbg=f&adm=8&dis=2)), it would appear difficult to argue that Canadian university faculty are not employees, and if they are employees, copyright would be owned by the universities, absent contracts to the contrary.

7   The peer-review process that is an entrenched aspect of promotion and tenure in the university system has reinforced, traditionally, the power of the scholarly presses: the prestigious journals are sought-after by faculty for publication and these are often associated with presses that demand assignment of all copyright interests. Although this situation is slowly changing, particularly in science and medicine, there is still domination by traditional presses.

8   As will become evident below, universities in Canada pay a third time when they purchase licences for reprography from copyright collectives whose members are the publishers of the journals. See Wilkinson, "Survey of Canadian Policies," above note 5.

be discussed further, it is difficult and time-consuming to police copyright interests as an individual or corporation not usually engaged in publishing.

The fourth option, retaining all copyright interests and giving blanket permissions for certain uses or to certain classes of users, is the foundation for the Creative Commons licensing movement. It is also one option that governments can choose to create for their own creations. Although, as discussed below, it is not a choice available to many American governments, due to other policy decisions of the governments themselves, it is a choice available to Canadian governments. Canada's *Copyright Act*[9] contains special provisions for government creations but does affirm, at the same time, that governments in Canada hold copyright in works.[10] Various provincial governments have given blanket permissions for use of various copyrighted works held by them to be used.[11] The federal government, by regulation, has given the following permission:

- Anyone may, without charge or request for permission, reproduce
  » enactments,
  » consolidations of enactments,
  » decisions, or
  » reasons for decisions
- Provided
  » reasonable diligence is used in ensuring accuracy, and
  » no representation of the copy as official is made.[12]

This copyright permission is only for reproduction of certain works, not for other uses (such as translation) or for all works held in copyright by the Canadian federal government.

The fifth option for copyright holders is to retain their copyrights and join with others in collective administration of their copyrights. This option

---

9　*Copyright Act*, above note 6.

10　*Copyright Act*, *ibid.*, s. 12.

11　Neither is there uniformity across the provinces about what permissions are given or how they are given. Some, like the federal permission, are given in regulations — others, like Ontario, are in administrative manuals and are less permissions than they are instructions to employees not to enforce copyright interests in certain circumstances (see the sixth option discussed herein). See E. Prokopieva, "Crown Copyright Policy in Provinces and Territories of Canada" (2003, rev. 2007 by Ann Chmielowski) in Margaret Ann Wilkinson, ed., assisted by Vanessa Bacher, *Law 462: Cases and Materials on the Law of Intellectual Property, 2007–2008*, vol. 2 (London, ON: University of Western Ontario, Faculty of Law, 2007) at 267–73.

12　Paraphrased from S.I./97-5 (8 January 1997), C. Gaz. Part II, Vol. 131, No. 1.

is far more commonly selected by copyright holders in Canada[13] than it is by those in the US. The reasons for this difference between decisions of copyright holders in the two countries lie in choices made by the governments of Canada and the US that will be further discussed in the next section.

The sixth option, retaining copyright but not taking steps to enforce the interests is, in fact, a very frequently selected option by copyright holders: enforcing copyright can be time-consuming and expensive. However, this option is not one that can be relied upon by users, as will be further discussed below.

Copyright legislation does not provide for "renunciation" of copyright interests, but presumably someone who "gives up" their copyright would have no control over subsequent uses of the work[14] and could not exploit the potential of the copyright monopolies for economic value in the future—other than in competition with any others who have decided to exploit the work. The seventh option is also one that is unreliable from the point of view of *users*: it is not clear that a copyright holder's "renouncing" can be relied upon should that copyright holder subsequently change her or its mind and decide to enforce copyright against a particular user.

Meanwhile, concomitant with the decisions available to copyright holders, users of information can make any one of a series of decisions when faced with an environment involving copyright:

1) users can use materials that are not works covered by copyright;
2) users can make use of materials in ways not forming part of the copyright holders' rights bundle;
3) users can use materials in ways that do form part of the copyright holders' rights bundle but are excepted by governments from the purview of the copyright holders' exercise of their rights; and
4) users can use materials in ways that do form part of the copyright holders' rights bundle but for which they have been given permission by the copyright holders through
   i) copyright holders' collectives, or
   ii) permissions of copyright holders given in advance (open content licensing or Creative Commons), or
   iii) permissions negotiated directly, from time to time, with copyright holders.

---

13   The Copyright Board of Canada maintains a list of Canadian copyright collectives: see online: www.cb-cda.gc.ca/societies/index-e.html.

14   Other than through the exercise of moral rights.

It is only in the case of the fourth category of decision by *users* that the choices being made by the copyright holders, described above, become relevant to the availability of information for users. That is, where materials are not covered by copyright, or are not being used in ways governed by copyright, or are being used in ways permitted to users by law despite copyright interests, no action of a copyright holder can affect the activities of users.[15]

C. THE ROLE OF PHILANTHROPY IN NATIONAL LIFE

In any of the first four cases of decisions that can be made by *copyright holders*, as discussed above (assigning all the copyright, assigning part of the copyright, retaining the copyright but permitting certain uses on a case-by-case basis, and retaining the copyright but granting certain blanket permissions),[16] the copyright holder has a second decision to make: to seek compensation from users for the assignment or permission or to give it freely. If the copyright holder is not a government but is rather from the private sector, then a decision to give the copyright interest or permission away freely is a form of philanthropy—a gift to users.

Philanthropy plays a large role in many countries—and Canada and the US are no exception.[17] However, philanthropy is proportionately far more

---

15   As will be discussed further below, when governments enlarge the scope of any of the first three categories available to users, the opportunity of rightsholders to affect the environment of access for users is correspondingly diminished.

16   Where a copyright holder has chosen the fifth option, having a copyright collective administer the copyright holder's rights, the decision about whether to charge for uses or not is part of the administration of the collective and is no longer an individual decision of the rightsholder. Where a copyright holder has chosen the sixth course, to refrain from enforcing the copyright interest, that choice necessarily means the copyright holder will not be compensated for uses—and the implications are the same where the copyright holder attempts to renounce the copyright interest (the seventh option).

17   Both countries have a shared heritage based in the English tradition of philanthropy that developed in Tudor times, when it became standard for gentry to leave grand gifts to their communities. See David Owen, *English Philanthropy 1660–1960* (Cambridge, MA: Belknap Press of Harvard University Press, 1964). See also Peter Dobkin Hall, "Philanthropy (United States)" in John M. Herrick & Paul H. Stuart, eds., *Encyclopedia of Social Welfare History in North America* (Thousand Oaks, CA: Sage, 2005) at 272–74. In the early colonies that later comprised Canada, the British tradition of philanthropy held sway in Upper and Lower Canada (later, roughly, Ontario and Quebec) but the Maritime colonies took government action by enact-

important in the American context than in the Canadian.[18] Much that is created through philanthropy in the US is achieved through government action in Canada. As Michael Hall and Keith Banting point out, some distinctive features of Canadian experience do stand out. For example, the greater

> role that the state has played in the development of economic and social life throughout Canadian history, in comparison with the pattern south of the border [in the United States] and in many other countries, is clearly reflected in the sources of funding of the nonprofit sector.[19]

In the US, on the other hand, there is a deep-seated avoidance of government involvement in daily life.[20] Although the economic conditions of the twentieth century softened this anti-government stance to some degree,[21] there is still a national preference for philanthropy rather than government social assistance.[22]

It is perhaps not surprising that, given this history of philanthropic activity, the open source software movement began in the US during the 1970s.[23] The open source software movement followed upon the "revelation"

---

ing poor law legislation. See Janice Harvey, "Philanthropy (Canada)" in Herrick & Stuart, *ibid.* at 268–69.

18   Charities and nonprofit organizations in Canada rely much more heavily upon federal government funding than do comparable organizations in the United States, which rely much more on private philanthropy. See Michael Hall & Keith Banting, "The Nonprofit Sector in Canada: An Introduction" in Keith Banting, ed., *The Nonprofit Sector in Canada: Roles and Relationships* (Montreal: McGill-Queen's University Press, 2000) 1 at 2 [Hall & Banting].

19   Hall & Banting, *ibid* at 16.

20   After the American Civil War, support for the nonprofit sector became central to American conservative ideology—and it was thought that the problems of poverty and disadvantage could be solved completely by the private sector. See Lester Salamon, "The Nonprofit Sector at a Crossroads: The Case of America" (1999) 10:1 Voluntas: International Journal of Voluntary and Nonprofit Organizations 5.

21   The New Deal in 1932 was a turning point in the relationship between private and public life in the United States. Private philanthropy was joined by government in meeting the needs of the disadvantaged and social bureaucracy "mushroomed." See Judith Sealander, *Private Wealth and Public Life: Foundation Philanthropy and the Reshaping of American Social Policy from the Progressive Era to the New Deal* (Baltimore: Johns Hopkins University Press, 1997) at 244.

22   Waldemar A. Nielsen, *The Endangered Sector* (New York: Columbia University Press, 1979) at 25–48.

23   David Bretthauer, "Open Source Software: A History" (2002) 21:1 Information, Technology and Libraries 3. Richard Stallman, who worked in the Artificial Intel-

in law that software ownership and control lay within the sphere of intellectual property.[24] Once ownership of rights in software was established in law, a reaction began that saw creators develop a system of not-for-profit control in the software environment that "paralleled" the exploitation by the for-profit sector of software developments. As computers and telecommunications technology were increasingly able to handle content, it became apparent that intellectual property, with its attendant ownership controls, was following the importation of this content into the online and digital environment. This has led, in turn, to the genesis of the open access movement in the US.[25] One dominant form of the open access movement is the Creative Commons licensing system. That system has spread from the US into other jurisdictions, including Canada.[26] But will it be as successful at its objects outside the US, as it appears to be within? Is the open access ap-

---

ligence Lab at MIT during the 1970s and 1980s, does not actually identify himself with the Open Source movement but is, nonetheless, considered its originator.

24   In Canada, this "revelation" occurred when all levels of court hearing the case of *Apple Computer Inc. v. Mackintosh Computers Ltd.* found that software came within the existing definition of literary work in the *Copyright Act* and therefore was in copyright for the life of the author plus fifty years as soon as original software was written. See (1986), [1987] 1 F.C. 173 (T.D.), additional reasons (1987), 12 F.T.R. 287 (T.D.), var'd (1987), [1988] 1 F.C. 673, aff'd [1990] 2 S.C.R. 209. For further certainty, Parliament, during the course of the appeals in that litigation, added "computer programs" to the definition of "literary work" in s. 2 of the *Copyright Act*, above note 6, and further defined "computer program" in s. 2 as "a set of instructions or statements, expressed, fixed, embodied or stored in any manner, that is to be used directly, or indirectly in a computer in order to bring about a specific result" (*An Act to Amend the Copyright Act and to Amend other Acts in consequence thereof*, R.S.C. 1985 (4th Supp.), c. 10). In Canada, computer programs *per se* are not subject matter that is patentable (see *Schlumberger Ltd. v. Canada (Patent Commissioner)* (1981), [1982] 1 F.C. 845 (C.A.), leave to appeal to S.C.C. refused, [1981] 2 S.C.R. xi, although computerization can be a novel, unobvious, and useful invention or improvement in an "art, process, machine, manufacture or composition of matter" and therefore can be a material element in a patent (see, for example, *Re Motorola Inc. Patent Application No. 2,085,228* (1998), 86 C.P.R. (3d) 71 (Can. Pat. App. Bd. & Pat. Commr.)). In the US, however, software can be the subject of both copyright and patent, provided that the originality requirement is satisfied in the case of copyright and the other patentability tests for a patent are satisfied (see, for example, *State Street Bank & Trust Co. v. Signature Financial Group, Inc.*, 149 F.3d 1368, 47 U.S.P.Q.2d 1596 (U.S. Fed. Cir. 1998)).

25   The Creative Commons initiative started as an American nonprofit, registered in Massachusetts, in 2002. See online: http://creativecommons.org.

26   As at August, 2007, it offers licences in thirty-eight countries. See *ibid.*

proach, as developed through the Creative Commons approach, a good fit in all jurisdictions? Is it necessary, for example, in Canada? If there is a need in Canada, is open access the best way to fill this need?

D.   THE DECISIONS OF GOVERNMENTS

The scope and availability of the various choices for copyright holders just described are directly affected by the decisions of national governments in respect of copyright. Of course, the environment of access to information for users is also shaped by these decisions. A few years ago, American scholar Pamela Samuelson created a map of the public domain situated within the realm of intellectual property[27] and reflecting American intellectual property law, but a map drawn from the Canadian perspective, while similar, remains distinctly different.[28] The differences are created both by what is and is not included in copyright in each country and also, where there are copyright interests involved, by what exceptions or users' rights (to use the Canadian terminology) are available in each country.

In the first place, copyright is a creation of government. Without the statutory creation of copyright, copyright holders would not have a monopoly interest about which to make decisions. A prime example is the case of copyright interests and the governments themselves. In Canada, as mentioned above, crown copyright is recognized in the *Copyright Act*: the copyright legislation of the US, however, explicitly bars the American federal government from holding copyright in any of its creations.[29]

In the US, the *Digital Millennium Copyright Act* (*DMCA*)[30] considerably enlarged the scope of the American copyright. On the other hand, in Canada, not only has legislation modelled on the American *DMCA* not been passed by the legislature,[31] but also the courts have resisted the inclu-

---

27   Pam Samuelson, "Mapping the Digital Public Domain: Threats and Opportunities" (2003) 66 Law and Contemp. Probs. 147.

28   Margaret Ann Wilkinson, "National Treatment, National Interest, and the Public Domain" (2003–2004) 1 University of Ottawa Law and Technology Journal 23.

29   17 USC § 105. And many American states have followed suit—although these are examples of choice 7, discussed above (copyright holders renouncing their copyrights), since the state governments cannot legislate directly in the area of copyright (as the provincial governments in Canada cannot).

30   *Digital Millennium Copyright Act of 1998*, Pub. L. No. 105-304, 112 Stats. 2860. Section 1201 contains anti-circumvention provisions.

31   Databases are protected under the general copyright regime in Canada where the selection and arrangement of the material meets the originality requirement for

sion of data, facts, or ideas *per se* in copyright. In 2002, it was held that where the software for performance monitoring systems can only be created in one way in order to perform its function, then the expression of the idea of the software is merged with the idea itself and therefore the expression can have no protection in copyright. As the Ontario Court of Appeal put it,

> if an idea can be expressed in only one or in very limited number of ways, then copyright of that expression will be refused for it would give the originator of the idea a virtual monopoly on the idea. In such a case, it is said that the expression merges with the idea and thus is not copyrightable.[32]

Canada was the first country to legislate in the area of moral rights when they were first included in an international intellectual property instrument.[33] Since 1988, the moral rights in Canada have explicitly included the right of paternity (the right to be associated with the work as the author chooses, whether by name, pseudonym, or anonymously), the right of integrity in the work, and the right not to have the work associated with products, services, causes or institutions that would prejudice the author's honour or reputation.[34] In the US, on the other hand, there is no explicit mention of any moral rights protection in copyright legislation and the moral rights aspect of copyright is virtually ignored.[35]

---

copyright (see *Tele-Direct (Publications) Inc. v. American Business Information Inc.* (1997), [1998] 2 F.C. 22 (C.A.), leave to appeal to the S.C.C. refused, [1998] 1 S.C.R. xv) — and then only to the extent that the whole or a substantial portion of the selection or arrangement of the data is at issue in an infringement suit (see s. 3 of the Canadian *Copyright Act*, above note 6). There was an attempt to introduce American-style protections in Bill C-60, tabled 20 June 2005, particularly ss. 27 and 34, but that bill failed to pass before Parliament was dissolved. Bill C-61 of 2008, below note 85, similarly failed to pass.

32 The court of first instance had dismissed the claim of copyright infringement, *Delrina Corp. v. Triolet Systems Inc.* (1993), 47 C.P.R. (3d) 1 at 41 (Ont. Ct. Gen. Div.). The Court of Appeal refused to overturn the judgment: (2002), 156 O.A.C. 166 (C.A.), additional reasons [2002] O.J. No. 3729 (C.A.), leave to appeal to S.C.C. refused (2002), 305 N.R. 398n.

33 *Copyright Act Amendment Act, 1931,* 21–22 Geo. V., c. 8, s. 5.

34 See *Copyright Act,* above note 6, ss. 2, 14.1, 14.2, 28.1, and 28.2. For a discussion of the role of each of these in society and the relationship between each of them and the moral rights provisions of the *Berne Convention,* see Margaret Ann Wilkinson, "The Public Interest in Moral Rights Protection" (2006) 1 Michigan State L. Rev. 193.

35 Congress was somehow persuaded, on the eve of signing the *Berne Convention* in 1989, that American law generally already provided sufficient protection for moral rights and that there was no need to amend the copyright legislation. See Brian E.

In addition to these differences between the two countries in the scope of copyright, there are also important differences in the scope of the exceptions to the rights of rightsholders in intellectual property. In the US, one very important area of exception is the "fair use" provision.[36] Again, Canada has a similar but very different set of provisions in its copyright legislation — the fair dealing provisions.[37]

In Canada the fair dealing provisions, together with the other exceptions to the rights of copyright holders set out in the *Copyright Act*, have been described by the Supreme Court of Canada as embodying a set of "users' rights."[38] The Chief Justice, in the unanimous decision of the Court in *CCH v. Law Society of Upper Canada*, wrote:

> The language [of the fair dealing provision] is general. "Dealing" connotes not individual acts, but a practice or system. This comports with the purpose of the fair dealing exception, which is to ensure that users are not unduly restricted in their ability to use and disseminate copyrighted works.[39]

Moreover, wrote the Chief Justice, under the fair dealing sections of the *Copyright Act*, "Research must be given a large and liberal interpretation in order to ensure that users' rights are not unduly constrained."[40] Thus, through its judgments in copyright rendered between 2002 and 2006, the Supreme Court of Canada has come to the position that Canada's *Copyright Act*

1) permits agents for users who are exercising fair dealing rights and those agents can claim those fair dealing protections;
2) permits claims of fair dealing even where there are special-interest exceptions: not-for-profit "libraries, archives and museums" or "educational institutions";

Koeberle, "Play It Again, Samantha? Another Argument for US Adherence to Article *6bis* of the *Berne Convention*" (1989) 27 Duq. L. Rev. 609. Most commentators agree that moral rights protection is almost completely absent in the United States: see, for example, Edward J. Damich, "The Right of Personality: A Common-Law Basis for the Protection of Moral Rights of Authors" (1988) 23 Ga. L. Rev. 1; and David R. Grant, "Rights of Privacy: An Analytical Model for the Negative Rights of Attribution" (1992) Utah L. Rev. 529.

36   17 USC § 107.
37   *Copyright Act*, above note 6, ss. 29, 29.1, & 29.2.
38   *CCH Canadian Ltd. v. Law Society of Upper Canada*, 2004 SCC 13 at paras. 12 & 13 [*CCH v. Law Society*].
39   *CCH v. Law Society, ibid.* at para. 63.
40   *CCH v. Law Society, ibid.* at para. 51.

3) must be interpreted to embody research, private study, criticism, news reporting, review, and other provisions limiting the rights of rights-holders as representing rights for users;

4) does not cover information in records where there is not a demonstration of skill and judgment because such information does not lie within an expression included in copyright and therefore is not controlled by a copyright holder: mere copying of information does not create an original work; and

5) can encompass alternative means of compensating rightsholders through such mechanisms as the levy on blank tapes and the related private copying exemption.

Canada, therefore, finds itself in a position where many activities of users can be exempt from the copyright holder's control. For example, it is unlikely, but possible, that *every* act done with copyright material within an educational institution, which would otherwise fall within the purview of the copyright holder, will fall under a users' right (or exception): first, all educational institution employees can act as agents for their students and the students themselves have fair-dealing rights to private study, research, criticism, review, and news reporting (the latter three items with acknowledgement where possible); second, the employees of educational institutions themselves have fair-dealing rights for their *own* private study, research, criticism, review, and news reporting; and thirdly, activities by members of non-profit educational institutions (though not those of for profit educational institutions) that fall outside fair dealing may still be exempted under the exceptions provided for educational institutions in the Canadian *Copyright Act*.[41] Indeed, if not all, certainly the majority of the activities within an educational institution will be found to be exempt from the control of copyright holders.[42]

Another distinguishing feature of the Canadian copyright environment is the extent to which the Canadian legislation encourages the collective administration of copyrights. Beginning in 1988, the Canadian govern-

---

41 *Copyright Act*, above note 6, ss. 29.4–30.

42 See Margaret Ann Wilkinson, "Filtering the Flow from the Fountains of Knowledge: Access and Copyright in Education and Libraries" in Michael Geist, ed., *In the Public Interest: The Future of Canadian Copyright Law* (Toronto: Irwin Law, 2005) 331 [Wilkinson, "Filtering the Flow from the Fountains of Knowledge"]. This question is one with which the Canadian Copyright Board is currently wrestling in the proceeding concerning Access Copyright's Elementary and Secondary School Tariff 2005–2009.

ment has actively encouraged this approach by making extensive legislative provisions to smooth this avenue of connection between copyright holders and users: collectives of copyright holders[43] have been exempted from the purview of Canada's antitrust or anti-combines legislation[44] and the power of the Copyright Board of Canada to act as mediator for users and collectives has been increased.[45] These collectives for the holders of Canadian rights have, in turn, created reciprocal agreements with collectives in other countries, including the US. However, in general, American collective rights organizations do not represent the percentage of rightsholders that are represented by their Canadian counterparts.[46]

Canada's collective licensing regime has been strengthened by Parliament and adopted by a wide range of copyright owners to such an extent that it may now be the case that Canada should be classified as a country with an extended repertoire or extended licensing regime.[47] Under such a regime, collectives are deemed to represent all rightsholders of a given class,

---

43   It should be noted that the *Copyright Act*, above note 6, does not exempt collectives of copyright users from the purview of the *Competition Act*, R.S.C. 1985, c. C-34, as amended. This point has been fully investigated by Cathy Maskell, *Consortia Activity in Academic Libraries: Anti-competitive or in the Public Good?* (Ph.D. Dissertation, University of Western Ontario, 2006). See also Catherine A. Maskell, "Consortia: Anti-competitive or in the Public Good?" (2008) 26(2) Library Hi-Tech, 164–83.

44   *Copyright Act*, *ibid.*, s. 70.5 exempts collectives from the purview of the *Competition Act*, *ibid.*

45   *Copyright Act*, *ibid.*, s. 70.12ff.

46   See Glynn Lunney, "Copyright Collectives and Collecting Societies: The United States Experience," in Daniel Gervais, ed., *Collective Management of Copyright and Related Rights* (Alphen aan den Rijn, The Netherlands: Kluwer Law International, 2006) 311; where it is explained that collectives *per se* probably violate American antitrust legislation and the question is raised of how long the groups in the US that are organized as copyright collectives can last, given that reality. On the other hand, "collecting societies" such as the Copyright Clearance Centre in the US, where the copyright holders set their own terms and conditions for copyright permissions, but the administration is handled for them through the society, would seem to be compliant with antitrust requirements.

47   As pointed out by Daniel Gervais in "The Changing Role of Copyright Collectives," in Daniel Gervais, ed., *Collective Management of Copyright and Related Rights*, *ibid.*, c. 1. One indication in support of this position is the provision in s. 38.2 that a copyright holder not affiliated with a collective is limited, in an infringement lawsuit for unauthorized reprography against an educational institution or library, archive, or museum (as these institutions are defined in s. 2 of the *Copyright Act*, above note 6), to damages equal to the royalties that would have been payable by the infringer to the collective.

not just those who have chosen to actively become members of the collective. Users, where such a regime is in place, can then rely completely upon a licence from the collective. If Canada is not operating under such a regime, then users must be aware that permissions or licences from the collective will only be effective insofar as rightsholders are members of the collective or are members of collectives that have reciprocal arrangements with the licensing collective.

The Canadian environment surrounding open access initiatives thus differs from the American in at least five ways:

1) much of Canada's public information is held in crown copyright, whereas in the US, governments are frequently barred from holding copyright;
2) Canada has not enacted the same level of *sui generis* database and anti-circumvention legislation that the US Congress has;
3) Canada has actively legislated in the area of moral rights whereas the US has not;
4) Canada has strong language from its Supreme Court now characterizing as "users' rights" what are still regarded as "exceptions" to the rights of rightsholders in the American context (and clearly articulating an expansive scope for fair dealing in Canada); and
5) Canada has a well-developed system of collective rights administration for copyrights.

These differences put both users and copyright holders in Canada in different positions than their counterparts in the US. Thus the options available to both users and copyright holders in Canada differ from those available in the US. As will be further discussed, these differences would appear to make the selection of philanthropic donation by copyright holders, through participation in open access initiatives like the Creative Commons movement, less central to meeting the needs of users in Canadian society.

But first these differences observed between Canada and the United States must be placed in their constitutional and international contexts to see whether they are differences that are likely to linger, or differences that will be obliterated shortly by government action.

1) Nation States, Governments, and Constitutions

The composition of government in a particular sovereign state is determined by its constitution, whether written or otherwise. In the area of copyright, there is a significant difference between the US and Canada in constitutional terms. The US Congress made huge changes in copyright law toward the end of the twentieth century. Perhaps inevitably, this engendered constitutional challenge in the courts. Consequently, the US Supreme Court issued a landmark judgment articulating the constitutional position of copyright in the US. There has not been a similar judgment issued by the Supreme Court of Canada.

In the US Constitution, the power to legislate in the area of copyright is articulated as follows: "The Congress shall have power . . . to promote the progress of science and useful arts, by securing for limited times to authors and inventors the exclusive right to their respective writings and discoveries."[48]

Congress, during the last quarter of the twentieth century, extended the general term of copyright from twenty-eight years (with a possible renewal period of a further twenty-eight years) first to the life of the author of a work plus fifty years, and then to the life of the author plus seventy years. (It should be noted that, throughout this period and even still, the period of copyright in general in Canada has remained the life of the author plus fifty years.) In 2003, in the case of *Eldred v. Ashcroft*,[49] this second extension was challenged on constitutional grounds, invoking the American constitutional protection of freedom of speech, the First Amendment.[50] The US Supreme Court held that because of the particular wording of article 8 of the Constitution, Congress had been given wide powers to create an appropriate balance between access to information and the monopolies and controls inherent in copyright ownership. A majority of the Supreme Court held that the copyright extensions passed by Congress had not overstepped its constitutional capacity under this wide wording in article 8.[51]

In Canada, on the other hand, the constitutional ability of the federal government to legislate in the area of copyright is articulated in the one word "copyright."[52] Thus, the Canadian Supreme Court, were it ever to be

---

48   US Const., art. I, § 8, cl. 8.

49   537 U.S. 186, 123 S. Ct. 769 (2003), rehearing denied 538 U.S. 916, 123 S. Ct. 1505 (Mem. 2003).

50   US Const. amend. I.

51   Justice Ginsburg delivered the opinion of the court in which Rehnquist C.J., O'Connor, Scalia, Kennedy, Souter, and Thomas JJ., joined. Stevens and Breyer JJ. filed dissenting opinions. Justice Stevens was of the opinion that the impugned legislation improperly extended the lengths of existing copyrights. Justice Breyer would have read the Copyright Clause of the Constitution in light of the First Amendment and held the statute unconstitutional.

52   *Constitution Act, 1867* (U.K.), 30 & 31 Vict., c. 3, s. 91(23), reprinted in R.S.C. 1985, App.II, No.5.

faced with the same issue as came before the American courts in *Eldred v. Ashcroft*, would undertake an entirely different analysis than did its American counterpart in that case.

In a constitutional challenge involving Canada's freedom of speech constitutional provision, section 2(b) of the *Canadian Charter of Rights and Freedoms*,[53] and the Canadian federal government's enactments with respect to copyright,[54] Canada's Supreme Court would begin directly with analysis of the impugned legislation in terms of the section 2(b) right to freedom of expression, in light of section 1 of the *Charter* [55] (which has no direct counterpart in the US Constitution), which makes Canada's guaranteed rights and freedoms subject only to such reasonable limits prescribed by law as can be demonstrably justified in a free and democratic society.[56]

The point here is twofold: first, neither in Canada nor in the US is the legislative arm of government, which is responsible for copyright, beyond the oversight of the courts in terms of constitutional challenges; and, second, the US Congress has been adjudged by the US Supreme Court to have a greater latitude before the courts will interfere than would probably be the case should the Canadian courts review the Canadian situation. It is the first point that reinforces the claim made in this discussion — that the role of the nation state is the most important in determining the environment of copyright in the digital age. In Canada and in the US, as in all countries,[57] the law of the nation state will govern in any situation where

---

53 Part I of the *Constitution Act, 1982*, being Schedule B to the *Canada Act, 1982* (U.K.), 1982, c. 11 [*Charter*].

54 The Supreme Court of Canada, in *Harvard College v. Canada (Commissioner of Patents)*, 2002 SCC 76 at paras. 177–82 [the Harvard Mouse case in patent], Justice Bastarache for the majority, indicated a willingness to apply the *Charter* in an appropriate statutory intellectual property case.

55 *Charter*, above note 53, s. 1, states that the freedoms set out in the *Charter* are subject only to such reasonable limits prescribed by law as can demonstrably be justified in a free and democratic society. The "*Oakes* test" has become the accepted approach to analysis of this section. It involves three elements: the government measures restricting the freedom must be rationally connected to their objective(s); the measures should only impair the freedom minimally; and, the deleterious effects of the restriction must be proportional to the benefits of the legislation being challenged. See *R. v. Oakes*, [1986] 1 S.C.R.103.

56 *Charter*, *ibid.*

57 This point is especially clear for countries, like Canada and the US, where treaties and agreements are never self-executing in domestic law, but must be implemented through enabling legislation. Because of issues involving the division of power in federated states like Canada and the US, federated states usually cannot be among

there is conflict between international treaties or agreements to which the country has made itself signatory and the enactments or constitution of the nation state itself.

In the US, the government has dramatically enlarged the reach and the power of the copyright holder over the past quarter century, while the exceptions to the rights of copyright holders legislated by Congress have remained largely static. In Canada, on the other hand, there has been no comparable enlargement of the copyright holders rights, in part because the scope of copyright was larger throughout the first three-quarters of the twentieth century, but also because Canada has not taken copyright legislation as far as the US has in the last quarter of the twentieth century. Meanwhile, in Canada, there has been a very clear articulation of users' rights within the framework of the copyright legislation.[58]

2)   The International Context of Copyright

There has been an international dimension to copyright law since the earliest development of copyright itself. The two fundamental approaches to copyright developed in France[59] and in England[60] during a period of great international economic rivalry between the two states. Each system of national monopoly was designed to further the economic interests of its nation-state.[61] The decision of the US, for centuries, to legislate copyright in ways that differed markedly from the emerging international norm was a decision of economic positioning in the international environment for

---

the countries where treaties and agreements are self-executing. For example, in Canada, the federal government has most of the treaty-making capacity (see s. 132, taken together with the "peace, order and good government" language of s. 91 of *the Constitution Act, 1867*, above note 52), but, if it involves Canada in a treaty in an area where it has no constitutional ability to make law, implementation of that treaty must necessarily await the legislative decisions of each of the provinces.

58   Wilkinson, "Filtering the Flow from the Fountains of Knowledge," above note 42.

59   *Droit d'auteur* has been part of law in France since the French Revolution: see André Françon, *Le Droit d'auteur: aspects internationaux et comparatifs* (Cowansville, QC: Yvon Blais, 1993) at 121–22.

60   Copyright in England, beginning with the *Statute of Anne, 1709* (U.K.), 8 Anne, c. 19.

61   See Sam Ricketson, *The Berne Convention for the Protection of Literary and Artistic Works: 1886–1986* (London: Centre for Commercial Law Studies, Queen Mary College, 1987) at liii (in the Preface).

the emerging nation.[62] As noted by Justice Estey in the Supreme Court of Canada in 1979,

> The United States statutes have not been based upon the international copyright treaties of the nineteenth and twentieth centuries, being the *Berne Convention* of 1886 and the *Rome Copyright Convention* of 1928, as the United States of America did not become signatories thereto. Indeed, it was not until the adoption by that country in 1955 of the *Universal Copyright Convention* of 1952 that the United States participated in the field of international copyright law other than by a collection of bilateral agreements.[63]

However, in the nineteenth century, a number of international initiatives involving information exchange began on a large scale.[64] One of these, the *Berne Convention* of 1886,[65] focused on the coordination of copyright between countries. Countries were free to join the *Berne Convention*, or not, and, even after having joined, were free to adopt newer versions of the convention if they wished[66]—but they were also free not to do so. The US, for nearly a

---

62 See Edward Samuels, *The Illustrated Story of Copyright* (New York: Thomas Dunne Books/St. Martin's Press, 2000) at 7. The US created a form of copyright as early as 1790, but only for works created by Americans. It did not extend protection to foreign works until 1954, and even works by foreigners created in the US did not receive copyright protection until 1891.

63 *Compo Co. v. Blue Crest Music Inc.* (1979), [1980] 1 S.C.R. 357 at 367 [*Compo*].

64 The International Telegraph Union (1865, Paris, now the International Telecommunications Union, see online: www.ITU.int/aboutitu/overview/landmarks.html.); the Universal Postal Union (begun with the *Treaty of Berne*, 1874, see online: www.upu.int/about_us/en/history.html.); the *Paris Convention for the Protection of Industrial Property*, 1883; and, most important in this context, the *Berne Convention* on copyright, below note 65 (1886).

65 *Berne Convention for the Protection of Literary and Artistic Works*, 9 September 1886, 828 U.N.T.S. 221, as last revised 24 July 1971. See online: www.wipo.int/treaties/en/ip/berne/trtdocs_wo001.html. Canada adhered to this version on 26 June 1998 [*Berne Convention*].

66 Including the *Rome Convention of 1928*, to which Justice Estey referred in the *Compo* decision, quoted above note 53.

century, chose not to join the Berne Union. Canada chose to be a part of the Berne Union,[67] but to adhere to the convention at only the 1928 level.[68]

Meanwhile, in the context of international trade agreements, with the expansion of the *Free Trade Agreement* of 1989[69] into the *North American Free Trade Agreement* (*NAFTA*)[70] in 1994, Canada and the US first experienced the inclusion of intellectual property in a trade agreement with binding commitments reinforced through a dispute resolution process.[71] The intellectual property provisions of *NAFTA* were structured to include the *Berne Convention* by reference as the basis of the copyright provisions of the *NAFTA* and then make some additions in the text of *NAFTA* itself.[72] It was the most recent level of the *Berne Convention* that was included (from 1978).[73] Canada upgraded its legislation to reflect the 1978 version of the *Berne Convention* and eventually indicated its adherence to the later *Berne Convention*.[74] The US, for the first time, became a member of the Berne Union.[75]

---

67   Indeed, Britain was a founding member of the Berne Union and agreed to its obligations immediately (see the *International Copyright Act of 1886* (U.K.), 49 & 50 Vict., c. 33, which applied to Canada as a Dominion) and ratified the *Berne Convention* with effect from 5 December 1887.

68   Canada first became a signatory, in its own right, to the *Berne Convention* at the *Rome Copyright Convention of 1928*. The current *Copyright Act* was first passed by Parliament in 1921: S.C. 1921, c. 24. This Act was revised through *An Act Amending the Copyright Act, 1923* (13–14 Geo. V, c. 10), which came into force in Canada on 1 January 1924.

69   US and Canada, 22 December 1987, Can. T.S. 1989 No. 3 (entered into force 1 January 1989).

70   US, Canada, and Mexico, 17 December 1992, Can. T.S. 1994 No. 2 (entered into force 12 January 1994) [*NAFTA*].

71   Mexico, the third member of *NAFTA*, also, of course, had the same experience.

72   The basis of other intellectual property provisions was the *Paris Convention* which, from 1883, had existed in the industrial property environment of patent, trademark, and unfair competition.

73   The *Berne Convention* 1886, which came into force on 5 December 1887, was followed by the *Additional Act of Paris* 1896, which came into force 9 December 1897, the *Berlin Revision* 1908, which came into force 9 September 1910, and was concluded by the *Additional Protocol of Berne* in 1914, which came into force 20 April 1915, the *Rome Revision* 1928, which came into force 1 August 1931, the *Brussels Revision* 1948, which came into force 1 August 1951, the *Stockholm Revision* 1967, which, for its administrative sections only, came into force in 1970 but which, in terms of its substantive provisions, never came into force and was reviewed and replaced by the *Paris Revision* 1971, which came into force 10 October 1974.

74   *Berne Convention*, above note 65.

75   In 1989.

The intellectual property provisions of *NAFTA* were swiftly emulated in the huge, multilateral World Trade Organization (WTO), of which both Canada and the US were founding members. The *Trade Related Aspects of Intellectual Property Agreement* was a part of the WTO Agreement.[76] Like the *NAFTA*, as well as containing provisions dealing with various aspects of intellectual property itself, *TRIPS* also incorporated, by reference, virtually all of the text of the *Berne Convention*.[77] And, again, there is a binding dispute resolution process that forms part of the WTO.

The US lobbied successfully to ensure that *TRIPS* explicitly omits the requirement for adherence to article 6bis of the *Berne Convention*, but moral rights remain a part of the *Berne Convention* and *NAFTA*. The US, of course, is now signatory to the *Berne Convention* itself, but the *Berne Convention* has no sanctions against non-compliance such as exist in the international trade environment. Nevertheless, as described earlier, other countries, including Canada, make a much more robust effort to comply with the moral rights requirements of the *Berne Convention* than does the US.[78]

Both *NAFTA* and *TRIPS* tend to privilege copyright holders over users. Each contains a version of the "three-step test," which has become common in the international intellectual property environment recently.[79] Article 13 of *TRIPS* articulates the test as follows:[80]

Members [states] shall confine limitations or exceptions to exclusive rights

---

76 *Agreement on Trade-Related Aspects of Intellectual Property Rights* (1994), 33 I.L.M. 1144 [*TRIPS*].

77 Note that art. 6bis of the *Berne Convention*, on moral rights, which is, by reference, part of *NAFTA*, was deliberately omitted from *TRIPS*: see art. 9(1).

78 Since *NAFTA* incorporates by reference art. 6bis of the *Berne Convention* on moral rights and has a reasonably robust dispute resolution mechanism and enforcement process, it is possible that the US could lose a challenge from Canada or Mexico on moral rights grounds at some future date should occasion arise.

79 The "three-step test" originates in the *Berne Convention*—but there it appears only in connection with the right of reproduction (art. 9(2)). There is a version in *NAFTA*, art. 1709(6). A version also appears in the more recent *WIPO Copyright Treaty*, 20 December 1996, S. Treaty Doc. No. 105-17, 36 I.L.M. 65 (1997), art. 10, and the *WIPO Performances and Phonograms Treaty*, 20 December 1996, S. Treaty Doc. No. 105-17, 36 I.L.M. 76 (1997), art. 30.

80 See also *TRIPS*, above note 76, art. 30. Both *NAFTA* and *TRIPS* are discussed in this connection by Margaret Smith, "Patent Protection for Pharmaceutical Products under the World Trade Organization Agreements and the *North American Free Trade Agreement*" (1997), online: http://dsp-psd.pwgsc.gc.ca/Collection-R/LoPBdP/MR/mr145-e.htm#PROVISIONStxt.

- To certain special cases
- Which do not conflict with a normal exploitation of the work
- And do not unreasonably prejudice the legitimate interests of the right holder.

It may be noted that this language in the international instruments differs considerably from the language now prevalent in the Supreme Court of Canada with respect to copyright. Justice Binnie has written:

> The proper balance . . . lies not only in recognizing the creator's rights but in giving due weight to their limited nature. In crassly economic terms it would be as inefficient to overcompensate artists . . . as it would be self-defeating to undercompensate them . . . .[81]
>
> Excessive control . . . may unduly limit the ability of the public domain to incorporate and embellish creative innovation in the long-term interests of society as a whole, or create practical obstacles to proper utilization.[82]

And, in a case directly involving the digital environment, Justice Binnie wrote again, saying,

> Under the *Copyright Act*, the rights of the copyright owner and the limitations on those rights should be read together to give "the fair and balanced reading that befits remedial legislation" . . . .[83]
>
> [The exception to the rights of the copyright holder at issue] is not a loophole but an important element of the balance struck by the statutory copyright scheme.[84]

---

81 *Théberge v. Galerie d'Art du Petit Champlain inc.*, 2002 SCC 34 at para. 31.
82 *Ibid.* at para. 32.
83 *Tariff 22*, above note 2 at para. 88.
84 *Ibid.* at para. 89. Now it is true that by 2006, when the most recent copyright case, *Robertson v. Thomson Corp.*, 2006 SCC 43 [*Robertson v. Thomson*], was decided, the Supreme Court that had decided the earlier 2004 copyright decisions had changed in composition: Justices Iacobucci, Major, and Arbour have been replaced by Justices Abella, Charron, and Rothstein. Whereas the Court's decisions in *CCH v. Law Society*, above note 38, and *Tariff 22*, *ibid.*, were virtually unanimous (Justice LeBel wrote a separate judgment in *Tariff 22* in which he was the only justice to raise privacy concerns), the most recent decision in 2006 was a close 5:4 split decision. In *Robertson v. Thomson*, Justices LeBel and Fish wrote for the majority, with Justices Rothstein, Bastarache, and Deschamps joining. Justice Abella wrote for the minority, joined by Chief Justice McLachlin (the author of the unanimous judgment in *CCH v. Law Society*), and Justice Binnie (author of the majority judgments in the

The discrepancies between the kind of balancing language being used by the Supreme Court of Canada and the rightsholder-dominated language of the international trade agreements to which Canada is a party may soon place the Canadian government in a challenging position.

International agreements, once entered into, are perceived as limiting domestic national policy options, although public international law provides few effective sanctions where a nation state fails to live up to its international commitments. Certainly the migration of intellectual property into the international trade environment has upped the stakes for member nations, like Canada, since non-compliance puts a nation at risk of trade sanctions. Even so, international commitments are not binding on Canada's legislatures. On the other hand, if Canada's attempts to implement legislation to put it in compliance with its trade obligations run afoul of Canada's Constitution, the courts will strike down that legislation. International trade obligations are irrelevant to *Charter* concerns.

The use by Canada's Chief Justice of "rights" language in discussing the place of users in the copyright environment gives additional weight to concerns that further erosion of users' rights or exceptions to copyright holders' rights in Canada's copyright legislation will engender *Charter* scrutiny, focused on the right to freedom of expression, by the courts. Because of this, and despite grumbling from the foreign parties citing *TRIPS* or *NAFTA*, the users' rights currently in place in Canada's *Copyright Act* seem robust and likely to continue.[85]

Thus it seems likely that the differences between Canada and the US in terms of the copyright environment surrounding copyright holders and

---

2002 *Théberge* decision, above note 81 (a 4:3 split) and in the *Tariff 22* decision) and Justice Charron. The majority in *Robertson v. Thomson* says that the "process" is not important to its decision—just the "context" of the presentation of the works at issue, and in this way it distinguishes the approach of the earlier Supreme Court in *Tariff 22*. The minority in *Robertson v. Thomson* says the "process" approach should have been used. The issue in *Robertson v. Thomson* did not involve users' rights directly, although the public ultimately consumes the newspapers and online products that were at issue: the *lis* was between contributors to the newspaper and the newspaper publisher.

85   Bill C-60 of the previous Conservative administration fell when the government called the last election. There have been rumours of new copyright legislation for several years now but introduction of any bill has been long-delayed in the current minority government situation. There was a bill before the House of Commons, Bill C-61, *An Act to Amend the Copyright Bill*, 2nd Sess., 39th Parl., 2008 (first reading 17 June 2008), which also fell because of an election call.

users are likely to continue to exist, despite international pressures for conformity amongst nations, because of differences in constitutions and national character. Given that likelihood, what is the future for "open access" philanthropy in the two nations?

E.   OPEN ACCESS IN CANADA AND IN THE US

One problem that the open access movement has encountered as it has branched out from the US is that in most countries there is a second set of rights involved in the copyright environment—the moral rights. Moral rights do not necessarily lie with the holder of the economic rights in copyright. In some cases, the author of a work, who is the holder of the moral rights,[86] can frustrate the exercise of validly held economic rights in a work.[87] Thus, acting alone, the philanthropy of the holder of the economic rights in most countries may not be enough to secure for users the right to use the material.[88] In the US, however, since it is generally agreed that the moral rights are largely absent from the copyright environment,[89] when a copyright

---

86   The period of moral rights protection varies from country to country. In Canada the period of protection for the moral rights is the same as the period of protection for the economic rights. Thus, for the author's lifetime, the author is the owner of the moral rights—but for the fifty-year period following the death of the author, the author's heirs are the owners. In Canada, while the moral rights cannot be assigned, they can be waived (see *Copyright Act*, above note 6, s. 14.1(2)), but in other jurisdictions, waiver is not permitted (in France, for example, as in most European countries, moral rights are "perpetual, inalienable and imprescriptable," quoted by Charles R. Beitz from the *French Intellectual Property Code*, L121-1 found in *UNESCO Copyright Laws and Treaties of the World*, vol. 1, in "The Moral Rights of Creators of Artistic and Literary Works" (2005) 13(3) J. of Political Philosophy 330 at 332).

87   For example, the holder of the economic right to public display of an artwork could give permission for display of a work but the exercise by the author of her moral right to not have the work associated with products, services, causes, or institutions that would prejudice her honour or reputation could frustrate the efforts of a user to put together a public display which included that artwork.

88   This reality is explicitly acknowledged in the Canadian version of the Creative Commons licence: online, www.creativecommons.ca.

89   J.A.L. Sterling notes that the inclusion of moral rights protection in the *Berne Convention* after 1928 was one of the stumbling blocks for many years for the US (J.A.L. Sterling, *World Copyright Law: Protection of Authors' Works, Performances, Phonograms, Films, Video, Broadcasts and Published Editions in National, International and Regional Law* (London: Sweet & Maxwell, 1998) at 280). The US, since joining the Berne Union, has passed a very limited law in the moral rights area, providing a right of integrity to certain defined groups of artists: *Visual Artists' Rights Act of 1990*,

holder donates the economic interest to users, it is enough to permit the user to use the material as specified by the donor of the economic interest.[90]

Another challenge for the open-access movement in Canada is that the philanthropy of the copyright holder is unnecessary when either the material that is sought to be used does not attract copyright protection in Canada[91] or, in the case of material that is in copyright in Canada, users are guaranteed a right of access and certain uses of works pursuant to the users' rights aspects of the *Copyright Act*.

The final challenge for the open-access movement in Canada is the reach of the collective regime in Canada. If, as discussed above, Canada *is* operating under an extended repertoire or extended licence regime, the existence of a collective licence with an appropriate collective will protect any user from liability for infringement even from a non-member and will thus render redundant the efforts of copyright holders, such as those using the Creative Commons licence approach, to individually licence uses that are deemed to be administered by the recognized collectives. The open-access permissions would only be relevant for those users who did not have blanket licences in place.

If, on the other hand, Canada *is not* operating under an extended repertoire regime, then all users, even users with collective licences, will be able to breathe more easily about those rightsholders not represented by the collective, where it can be established that those "unrepresented" rightsholders have publicly "donated" their rights. In this event, the public access movement would still provide some value in the Canadian blanket-licence context.

In either case, whether Canada is an extended licensing regime or not, if enough rightsholders decide to be philanthropic and donate their rights,

---

Pub. L. No. 101-650, H.R. 5316, 17 U.S.C. § 106A. Even within this ambit of this law, however, the moral rights can be waived: see § 106A(e)(1).

90   Interestingly though, the American version of the Creative Commons licence, like others, including the Canadian, mentions moral rights toward the end of the contract and explicitly states that the licence does not cover them: see online: http://creativecommons.org/licenses/by_sa/3.0/US/.

91   Recall that all material in Canada, regardless of source or form, has a shorter term of protection than the life-plus-seventy-years term that is now the norm in the US. For any material being dealt with in Canada, the maximum possible term of protection is only the life of the author plus fifty years. Recall also that the courts in Canada have recognized the doctrine of merger and will not find a copyright interest where the expression of the idea is the only, or one of the only, ways to express a particular idea. And, finally, recall that Canada has not enacted legislation to protect databases and digital rights management as the United States has.

it would seem to be more efficient and better aligned with the Canadian copyright environment if those copyright holders formed a new collective of like-minded rightsholders that could be recognized under the Act.[92] This would be possible even where there are collectives representing rightsholders in a particular market (since more than one organization can be recognized in a particular market).[93] In the electronic rights environment there is not at present a collective in place for literary works,[94] for example. In the music environment there is.[95] In either case there would be room and a role for a philanthropically based collective of rightsholders.

---

92   A "collective society" is defined in s. 2 of the Canadian *Copyright Act*, above note 6, as

> a society, association or corporation that carries on the business of collective administration of copyright. . . for the benefit of those who, by assignment, grant of licence, appointment of it as their agent or otherwise, authorize it to act on their behalf in relation to that collective administration, and (a) operates a licensing scheme, applicable in relation to a repertoire of works . . . of more than one author . . . pursuant to which the society, association or corporation sets out classes of uses that it agrees to authorize under this Act, and the royalties and terms and conditions on which it agrees to authorize those classes of uses . . . .

This definition was added to the *Copyright Act* in 1997, see S.C. 1997, c. 24. There are at least four different systems of administration in relation to collective societies legislated in the Canadian *Copyright Act*. For administration of rights in works generally s. 70.1 addresses

> a collective society that operates (a) a licensing scheme, applicable in relation to a repertoire of works of more than one author, pursuant to which the society sets out the classes of uses for which and the royalties and terms and conditions on which it agrees to authorize the doing of an act mentioned in section 3 in respect of those works . . . .

Such a collective does not need to have its tariff set by the Board. In the case of the philanthropic collective proposed here, the collective could set its royalties at $0 and, pursuant to s. 70.12, "for the purpose of setting out by licence the royalties and terms and conditions relating to classes of uses . . . (b) enter into agreements with users."

93   Although the Copyright Board frowns upon this practice, it is obviously contemplated by the legislation: see, for example, *ibid.*, s. 38.2(2) which assumes the possibility of multiple reprographic societies. See also Mario Bouchard, "Collective Management in Commonwealth Jurisdictions: Comparing Canada with Australia" in Daniel Gervais, ed., *Collective Management of Copyright and Related Rights*, above note 46, 283 at 286.

94   Thus, for the moment, a user must locate and approach each individual rightsholder in order, for example, to get permission to post materials in copyright in Canada to the Internet.

95   SOCAN administers this right on behalf of its members: see *Tariff 22*, above note 2.

The "philanthropic" collective would become part of the dominant landscape of copyright ownership in Canada and be visible in that connection to users, as well as recognizable to policy-makers and administrators in government.[96] Moreover, in an adjudication involving tariffs, the existence of the "philanthropic" collective that was donating its permissions and licences would be squarely before the Copyright Board of Canada as it set the "fair" tariff for any other collective in a particular sector.

Even if those interested in pursuing the philanthropic approach in Canada do not create a collective, at the very least, in order to affect the economics of the copyright environment in Canada, when the Copyright Board is considering any tariff where there is active open access activity in the sector, evidence of the rate of participation in the open access movement (such as numbers of Creative Commons licences issued in Canada for a particular sector represented otherwise by the applicant collective) should be made available to the Copyright Board to take into account when establishing the tariff for the corresponding collective.

F. CONCLUSION

Although there has long been an international dimension to copyright, it is, at the end of the day, a matter for the jurisdiction of individual nation states. Governments within those nation states will find themselves bounded in copyright decision making by a number of factors: their na-

---

96 As the legislative environment in Canada continues to evolve, such a philanthropic collective would be able to take advantage of all the provisions of the *Copyright Act* provided for collectives and users holding licences from it would also receive all the statutory benefits flowing to those with relationships with collectives. For example, in the current *Copyright Act*, educational institutions who have licences from reprographic collectives receive the benefit of s. 30.3 whereas others do not (although that particular benefit is probably rendered moot by the interpretation of the fair dealing provisions by the Supreme Court in *CCH v. Law Society*, above note 38: see Margaret Ann Wilkinson, "Filtering the Flow from the Fountains of Knowledge," above note 42). It has also become common practice for copyright collectives to routinely register the interests of their rightsholders in the Copyright Register (although registration is not required, it does have some evidentiary advantages under the *Copyright Act*). Should the proposed philanthropic collective take up this practice, or at least make information about its repertoire available to users, it would help users by providing an increased collection of information about the state of copyright in Canada.

tional histories and traditions, their international agreements, but, perhaps most controlling in many circumstances, their constitutions.

Although Canada and the US now have similar international commitments in the copyright area, their national histories and traditions are dissimilar (and, most especially to this analysis, dissimilar in the realm of copyright) and their constitutions differ with respect to copyright. These differences mean that the role that copyright holders play by philanthropically participating in the open access movement is different in the two countries.

Although providing access to users through the philanthropic activities of copyright holders fits well within the context of the current international trade environment for copyright, it does not guarantee users permanent, free, and universal access to information in the way that legislated users' rights provide those guarantees.

Canada's current copyright environment is more balanced than the current American situation, explicitly providing three sets of rights: for copyright holders, for moral rightsholders, and for users. The American environment has become dramatically tipped toward control by copyright holders over the past twenty years. Given the balance of interests represented in the Canadian legal environment, there is less of a role for copyright holders' philanthropy. This is consistent with Canada's historic nature and probably best in line with its constitutional priorities. On the other hand, the US Supreme Court has already ruled that Congress has latitude to establish the copyright environment in the US and that measures taken by the US (exceeding even the copyright-holder-dominated requirements of the current international trade agreements) are constitutional. In the American environment, then, the copyright-holder-based philanthropy of the open access movement is critical to user access and it is indeed fortunate that philanthropy has such a strong and enduring presence in American society.

In Canada, it is suggested that those copyright holders interested in philanthropic aims explore the option of creating a collective, rather than simply adopting open access initiatives generated from the US. Because of the impact of collectives in Canada and the enlarged regime of legislated users' rights, individual philanthropic gestures through open source licensing using, for example, the Creative Commons licence will be lost, or at least diminished, in the Canadian context. A philanthropically based collective in the Canadian context, on the other hand, could have a greater impact on the copyright environment for Canadian users.

CHAPTER 15

Creating a Legal Framework for Copyright Management of Open Access within the Australian Academic and Research Sector*

Brian Fitzgerald, Anne Fitzgerald, Mark Perry, Scott Kiel-Chisholm, Erin Driscoll, Dilan Thampapillai, & Jessica Coates

A. INTRODUCTION

There is an increasing recognition, in Australia and internationally, that access to knowledge is a key driver of social, cultural, and economic development. The argument for greater access to, and reuse of, research outputs is reinforced by the fact that much research in Australia is funded by public money and, consequently, that there is a public benefit to be served by allowing citizens to access the outputs they have funded.[1] This recognition poses both legal and policy challenges, in terms of existing legal frameworks such as copyright law and traditional business models.

---

*   This chapter is derived from Brian Fitzgerald *et al., Oak Law Report No. 1—Creating a Legal Framework for Copyright Management of Open Access within the Australian Academic and Research Sector* (Brisbane: Department of Education Science and Training, 2006). Special thanks to Kylie Pappalardo for her assistance.

1   Markus Buchhorn & Paul McNamara, "Sustainability Issues for Australian Research Data: The Report of the Australian e-Research Sustainability Survey Project" (Canberra: ASPR, 2006), online: http://dspace.anu.edu.au/handle/1885/44304, or www.apsr.edu.au/aeres/ [Buchhorn & McNamara, *Issues for Research Data*]. At page 26 the report states that in 2002–2003, 45 percent of the $12.25 billion expended on research and development in Australia was funded by government and in 2004, 90 percent of the $4.3 billion expended on research and development by higher education institutions was funded by government.

With the rise of networked digital technologies, our knowledge landscape and innovation systems are becoming more and more reliant on best-practice copyright management strategies and there is a need to accommodate both the demands for open sharing of knowledge and traditional commercialization models. As a result, new business models that support and promote open innovation are rapidly emerging.

This chapter analyzes the copyright law framework needed to ensure open access to outputs of the Australian academic and research sector such as journal articles and theses. It overviews the new-knowledge landscape, the principles of copyright law, the concept of open access to knowledge, the recently developed open content models of copyright licensing, and the challenges faced in providing greater access to knowledge and research outputs.

B. THE NEW KNOWLEDGE LANDSCAPE

There have been fundamental changes in the framework within which knowledge is generated, accessed, disseminated, and reused. The digital, networked environment and, in particular, the widespread availability of broadband Internet access, is democratizing creativity and innovation and has made it possible to process and construct knowledge in ways that were unimaginable only two years ago.

These changes have provided researchers and the general community with enormous possibilities for new forms of collaborative and serendipitous innovation. It is now in the hands of millions of people to readily produce and disseminate their own creative works; research groups can share information and develop collaborative synergies in ways that were not previously feasible.[2] For example, blogs (web logs), wikis, VoIP (Voice over Internet Protocol), podcasts, and vodcasts are now commonplace, as are digital repositories.[3] There has also been a rise in collaborative projects such

---

2   See Eric Von Hippel, *Democratizing Innovation* (Cambridge: MIT Press, 2005), online: http://web.mit.edu/evhippel/www/democi.htm.

3   Neil Jacobs believes that technologies such as blogs, wikis, and peer-to-peer repositories often come into universities and colleges "under the radar."

    The PROWE project (online: www.prowe.ac.uk) is asking whether blogs and wikis in particular can be used to support the huge distributed networks of tutors associated with the Open and Leicester Universities. The SPIRE project (http://spire.conted.ox.ac.uk/) is installing the secure Lionshare (http://lionshare.its.psu.edu/main/) peer-to-peer system, to explore its potential in teaching and learning and, in part, to dispel the

as Wikipedia—an online peer-produced encyclopedia also available on CD—which now contains more than 4 million articles in 229 languages.

The legal challenges to this evolving landscape rest in the fact that while much of this research output can be presented at the click of a button, it is often subject to copyright law and can only be used with permission of the copyright owner or on the basis of some other authorizing principle or provision. The great challenge for this evolving knowledge landscape is, therefore, to build more efficient copyright ownership, management, and licensing models that can be used to allow access to knowledge and prosper the research sector.

C. OVERVIEW OF THE PRINCIPLES OF COPYRIGHT LAW

Providing better access to research and knowledge through best-practice copyright management can only be achieved by appreciating and understanding the scope and limitations of copyright law.

1) What Is Copyright?

Copyright is a type of intellectual property founded on a person's creative skill and labour. It allows the copyright owner to control certain acts (such as copying) and to prevent others from using protected material without permission, unless an exception applies. A copyright owner has the right to take action for copyright infringement in the event that a person uses all, or a "substantial part," of their copyright material in one of the ways exclusively controlled by the copyright owner, without their express or implied permission and where no defence or exception to infringement applies.

A person or an organization can also be liable for copyright infringement if they have authorized someone else to infringe copyright to the extent that they sanction, approve, or countenance the infringing conduct. For example, allowing Ph.D. students to provide online access to a thesis knowing that the student has not obtained the prior permission of all the underlying rightsholders (such as owners of copyright in pictures, graphics included in the thesis, or accompanying audiovisual material) to digitize

---

mistaken notion that peer-to-peer equals Napster equals insecure and probably illegal activity.

Neil Jacobs, "Digital Repositories in UK Universities and Colleges" (2006) 200 FreePint 13 at 15, online: http://web.freepint.com/go/newsletter/200#feature [Jacobs, "Digital Repositories"].

and communicate the work could potentially result in a university being held liable for authorizing copyright infringement.

2)   What Type of Material Does Copyright Protect?

For copyright to subsist material must fall within a category recognized under the *Copyright Act 1968* (Cth.)[4]: namely, original literary, dramatic, musical, and artistic works, as well as sound recordings, films, sound and television broadcasts, and published editions. Therefore, copyright protects not only written material (such as books, theses, and reports) and creative works such as photographs, paintings, and multimedia works, but also scientific and technical creations (for example, computer software and datasets).

3)   What Rights Does Copyright Protect?

The exact nature of the rights granted to copyright owners will depend on the nature of the material being protected. However, in general they will include the exclusive right of reproduction, publication, performance, communication, and adaptation. As with all intellectual property rights, the exclusive rights provided by copyright are intangible in nature, generally granted for a limited time (for example, either seventy years from the death of the creator of a work or seventy years from first publication of a film or sound recording), and are distinct from the physical property in which protected material is embodied.

4)   Balancing the Interests of Copyright Owners and Users—Exceptions to Copyright

Most copyright laws have been structured to provide a balance between the provision of incentives in the area of innovation and creativity, and achieving the public interest goal of encouraging education, research, the free flow of information, and freedom of expression,[5] while also being careful not to restrict competition in the marketplace. To give effect to this balance,

---

4   *Copyright Act 1968* (Cth.) [*Copyright Act*].
5   Australia, Copyright Law Review Committee, *Copyright and Contract* by James Lahore (Canberra: The Committee 2002), online: www.clrc.gov.au/www/agd/agd.nsf/Page/Copyright_CopyrightLawReviewCommittee_CLRCReports_Copyrightand-Contract_CopyrightandContract at 24.

the *Copyright Act* contains a range of "free use" or "blanket" exceptions to copyright infringement which allow material to be used without the permission of, or a licence from, the copyright owner, together with a range of statutory licences that allow the making and communication of multiple reproductions of certain works for a set licence fee, thereby reducing overall administration and transactional costs.

The copyright exceptions of relevance to the education and research sector include the fair dealing exceptions for research and study, criticism, review, and reporting the news. These exceptions are necessarily limited in that the dealing must have been performed for one of these four purposes, and it must be considered to be "fair." Thus, there is no open defence such as "general fair dealing" or "fair use" under Australian copyright law.

The statutory licences for the education sector enable educational institutions to copy television and radio programs off-air and to reproduce and communicate print copyright works and electronic versions of literary, dramatic, artistic, and musical works for educational purposes, in return for payment to declared collecting societies.

5) Rights Related to Copyright—Moral Rights and Performers' Rights

In addition to the traditional economic rights discussed above, the *Copyright Act* also bestows certain moral rights and performers' rights.

Australian copyright law grants performers both economic[6] and personal rights over audio (but not audiovisual) recordings of their performances. These rights consist of:

- the right to authorize the recording and communication of live performances (and distributions of recordings of live performances);[7]
- copyright in sound recordings;[8] and

---

6   The economic rights for performers in sound recordings became effective from 1 January 2005. Section 22(3A) of the *Copyright Act*, above note 4, provides that the performer and the owner of any sound recording of the performance own the copyright jointly, subject to any agreement to the contrary. Commissioned sound recordings for which the performer is paid a fee, or those made under an employment contract, are owned by the commissioner or employer (s. 97(3)).

7   See *Copyright Act, ibid.*, s. XIA.

8   *Ibid.*, s. 22(3A). This right is subject to any agreement to the contrary, and does not apply to commissioned performances or performances conducted in the course of employment: s. 97(3).

- moral rights in performances.[9]

The first two of these rights only apply to performances that took place after 1 October 1989. A performer's rights to authorize recording and communication of their performances or the reproduction or performance of recordings last for fifty years from the date of the performance. Rights to authorize communication of recordings or the use of a recording in a soundtrack last for twenty years from the date of recording.[10]

Individual creators of literary, dramatic, musical and artistic works, and films[11] have the following moral rights in relation to works or films they have created: the right to be attributed (credited) for their work; the right not to have their work falsely attributed; and the right not to have their work treated in a derogatory way.

Performers also have moral rights in relation to live performance, so far as the performance consists of sounds, or a sound recording of a live performance. These rights apply to live performances as defined in the *Copyright Act*, which include expressions of folklore and musical, dramatic, and dance performances.[12] The moral rights granted to performers mirror the moral rights in traditional works. Generally, they will last for the duration of the copyright in the sound recording, although the right of integrity in a recorded performance only lasts until the performer's death.[13] The same reasonableness exemptions that apply to traditional moral rights also apply to performers' moral rights.[14] Furthermore, to make the authorization process efficient for performances involving multiple performers, the *Copyright Act* permits an agent acting for a group of performers to grant permission to reproduce any sound recordings.[15]

6)   Technological Protection of Copyright Material

Digital technology has made it possible to easily reproduce and communicate copyright material in near perfect form. Copyright owners have, there-

---

9   *Ibid.*, ss. 195AXA, 195AXB, & 195AXC.
10 *Ibid.*, ss. 248CA(3), 248G(1), & (2).
11 In relation to a film, the director, producer, and screenwriter all separately own moral rights in relation to a film, and where there are multiple directors, it is only the principal director, screenwriter, and producer who hold moral rights.
12 *Copyright Act*, above note 4, s. 22(7).
13 *Ibid.*, s. 195ANA.
14 *Ibid.*, ss. 195AXD and 195AXE.
15 *Ibid.*, ss. 113A and 191B.

fore, sought — as an alternative to traditional forms of legal protection — to rely on technology to prevent others from using their work without their permission. However, the *Copyright Act* also provides legal recognition for new mechanisms for copyright owners to protect and enforce their rights. For example, the *Copyright Act* provides legal protection for the use of Electronic Rights Management Information (ERMI) (such as digital watermarks) to described, identify, monitor, and track digital copyright material. These rights, in effect, potentially enable a copyright owner to monitor every access and use of their copyright material.

The *Copyright Act* also contains specific provisions that reinforce the use of technology, in the form of digital locks (known as Technological Protection Measures (TPMs)) to regulate access and further copying of copyright material. It is a civil infringement and/or a criminal offence (the level of liability depending on the circumstances of the infringement) under sections 116AO, 116AP, 132APD, and 132APE of the *Copyright Act* to deal in circumvention devices or services, including the manufacturing, importing, distribution (including online), provision, and offering to the public of circumvention devices and services. Under section 116AN(1) of the *Copyright Act*, a copyright owner or exclusive licensee of copyright in a work or other subject matter may bring an action against a person who does an act resulting in the circumvention of a TPM protecting the work or other subject matter, where that person knows or ought reasonably to know that their act would result in circumvention of the TPM. Criminal penalties may also apply under section 132APC(1), where the circumvention was done with the intention of obtaining a commercial advantage or profit. The *Copyright Act* contains a set of exceptions that allow the circumvention of TPMs for certain permitted purposes (such as security testing or error correction).

7) Copyright Licensing

Despite legal recognition of copyright owners' rights to embrace technology and better control access to and use and dissemination of copyright material in the digital environment, general principles of copyright law, through mechanisms such as licensing, can also support open access to knowledge.

While it is possible to either sell or give away copyright via either an assignment, transfer, or through a bequest, it is equally possible for copyright owners to share copyright between themselves and third parties under a licence. A licence is a "permission" or form of authorization from the copyright owner to use the copyright material in one or more of the ways that falls within the copyright owner's exclusive rights. A licence can be exclusive, non-exclusive, or implied.

Under an exclusive licence the licensee (in other words, the recipient of the licence) is the only person who can use the works in the way or ways covered by the licence (even to the exclusion of the copyright owner). A non-exclusive licence merely provides a user/third party with the right to exercise one or more of the copyright owner's rights in the work but not to the exclusion of the copyright owner or other licensees. Therefore, a copyright owner may grant multiple and simultaneous non-exclusive licence.

It is also important to note that with both assignments and licence, copyright can be divided in a number of ways, including by territory, time, and type of use. For example, a licence can give a person permission to reproduce a work, without giving permission to publish or communicate the work. Similarly, a licence may give a publisher the right to publish the material only in Australia, or only until a certain date. The various licensing models for managing access to research findings are outlined in "Open Access," below in Section E and "Open Content Licensing," below in Section F(1)

D. THE LEGAL PROTECTION OF DATABASES—A SPECIAL CASE

Open access can be pursued not only in relation to academic and research output in traditional forms (such as, research proposals, project plans, summaries of research results, conference papers, journal articles, and books in published form), but also in relation to new forms of output such as data files, complex databases involving compilations of datasets, and embedded software and multimedia works.

In developing systems designed to promote open access to knowledge in the Australian academic and research sector, and to data in particular, academics and researchers need to consider

- the copyright status of the database and whether the data is protected by copyright;
- whether third-party copyright is affected by making a database available to the public; and
- the type of legal or technological measures that can be used to protect a database.

1) Whether Databases Are Protected by Copyright

As a general principle, copyright law protects the expression of an idea and not the idea itself. To this end, data, without more, is not protected by copyright law. The compilation of data, however, is protected to varying degrees by copyright law in different jurisdictions throughout the world. In the US and the EU, data compilation—selection and arrangement of the data—is protected where there is an element of intellectual creation. In addition to copyright protection available for databases, Europe also has a *sui generis* database right that may protect non-original databases that do not attract copyright protection but are nevertheless valuable and have required substantial economic investment.[16]

In Australia, databases may attract copyright protection if the creation of the database has involved sufficient expenditure of time, money, skill, or effort to satisfy the threshold level of originality required in order for copyright to subsist in a literary work. In the recent case of *Desktop Marketing Systems Pty Ltd v. Telstra Corporation Limited*,[17] the Full Court of the Federal Court held that the mere arrangement of names in alphabetical order in a phone book was sufficient to found copyright protection. As a result, the standard of originality for copyright protection in Australia is considerably lower than in other jurisdictions.[18] Thus, it is the case that where facts are compiled through industrious labour (in other words, where the intellectual effort is very low or non-existent) they will receive a higher degree of protection in Australia than in other jurisdictions.

In addition to the broad scope of protection available for databases in Australia, the very narrowly defined nature of the fair dealing exceptions (as explained in "Overview of the Principles of Copyright Law," above in Section C) confers further control for owners of copyright in databases.

2) Practical Measures for Database Compilers to Protect Their Copyright

From a practical standpoint, database compilers need to identify the uses of their database that they wish to allow. They then need to put in place the relevant agreements to facilitate those uses. This involves identifying and, where necessary, obtaining copyright permissions from third-party

---

16   On Europe, see the European Union Database Directive, online: http://ec.europa. eu/internal_market/copyright/prot-databases/prot-databases_en.htm.

17   [2002] FCAFC 112 [*Desktop Marketing*].

18   See also *Nine Network Australia Pty Ltd. v. IceTV Pty Ltd.*, [2008] FCAFC 71.

copyright owners. It also involves preparing agreements that clearly set out the conditions of use of the database. In addition database owners could employ TPMs to regulate the use of a database, or they could seek to adopt a range of licensing models such as open content licensing like Creative Commons licence.

3) Third-party Content

When researchers develop databases containing information from a range of sources, copyright in some of the materials selected for inclusion will belong to third parties (in other words, commercial publishers, governments, individual authors, and research institutes).

However, when the researcher makes the database available for access by other researchers, it will be necessary to ensure that the researcher has the legal authority to do so, either under a recognized exception or through a licence.

Where a licence is used to obtain permissions by third-party owners of copyright material included in the database, the licence should sufficiently permit the researcher to authorize other persons to use the material in the way in which the database compiler and database users wish to use the material. If the licence does not do so, release of copyright material owned by third parties will infringe their copyright.

E. OPEN ACCESS

With the growth of the new digital and virtual knowledge landscape, we have seen the potential for greater control over access and usage by copyright owners. The rising costs of subscriptions to key academic journals, in large part made possible by, and implemented through, the first generation of digital distribution and licensing models, has motivated a frustrated research community into finding new ways to disseminate knowledge. Faced with the enormous potential of the Internet and the increasing limitations presented by traditional journal licensing, researchers worldwide have united in the open access movement, which aims to disseminate knowledge broadly and freely across the Internet in a timely fashion (especially that which is publicly funded).[19] User-led movements such as open access and Free/Libre and Open Source Software (FLOSS)[20] have sought to utilize the great advances in information and communication technologies to make research outputs more easily and immediately accessible and to promote a collaborative and participatory knowledge paradigm. This has resulted in the development of a worldwide network of institutional and disciplinary repositories containing numerous research outputs that use advanced Internet computing and Grid technologies to enable direct and shared collaboration amongst researchers in the form of e-Research. In Australia there are initiatives like E-Print and Digital Theses Repositories and large supercomputing projects based around bio-informatics and geo-spatial data.[21]

1) Open Access Movement

a) Core principles of open access
The core principle of open access is to open access up to research and scholarship, especially that which is publicly funded. This principle has been endorsed and further developed in the following declarations: *Budapest Open Access Initiative* (2002),[22] the *Berlin Declaration on Open Access to Knowledge in the Sciences and Humanities* (2003),[23] and the *Bethesda Statement on Open Access Publishing* (2003).[24]

---

19   In 1991, the first free scientific online archive, arXiv, was created at Los Alamos, but it is now hosted by Cornell University. The fields covered include physics, mathematics, non-linear science, computer science, and quantitative biology. See online: www.lib.mtu.edu/eresources/eresearch/searchresults.aspx?publisherid=240 and http://arxiv.org.

20   See further, Glyn Moody, *Rebel Code: The Inside Story of Linux and the Open Source Revolution* (Cambridge, MA: Perseus, 2001). See also, Lawrence Lessig, *The Future of Ideas: The Fate of the Commons in a Connected World* (New York: Random House, 2001) at 50*ff.*; Sam Williams, *Free as in Freedom: Richard Stallman's Crusade for Free Software* (Sebastopol, CA: O'Reilly, 2002); Eric Raymond, *The Cathedral and the Bazaar* (Cambridge, MA: O'Reilly, 2001), online: www.catb.org/~esr/writings/cathedral-bazaar; Brian Fitzgerald & Nic Suzor, "Legal Issues For the Use of Free and Open Source Software in Government" (2005) 29 Melbourne U.L. Rev. 412.

21   The Australian Partnership for Advanced Computing (APAC) has been a key player in building this framework over the last six years. See online: www.apac.edu.au.

22   See online: www.soros.org/openaccess [BOAI].

23   See online: www.zim.mpg.de/openaccess-berlin/berlindeclaration.html [*Berlin Declaration*].

24   See online: www.earlham.edu/~peters/fos/bethesda.htm [*Bethesda Statement*].

The *Berlin Declaration*'s definition of open access contribution mirrors the definitions drafted in the *BOAI* and *Bethesda Statement*:

There are three main essentials: free accessibility, further distribution, and proper archiving:

Open access is real open access if:

(1) The article is universally and freely accessible, at no cost to the reader, via the Internet or otherwise, without embargo

(2) The author or copyright owner irrevocably grants to any third party, in advance and in perpetuity, the right to use, copy, or disseminate the article, provided that correct citation details are given

(3) The article is deposited, immediately, in full and in a suitable electronic form, in at least one widely and internationally recognized open access repository committed to open access and long-term preservation for posterity.[25]

Another significant document representing a major international step forward in promoting open access to knowledge, and more broadly the sharing of knowledge, is the *Draft Treaty on Access to Knowledge*.[26]

The *A2K Treaty* is largely a result of the work of Brazil and Argentina who, in August 2004, discussed a possible treaty concerning access to knowledge as part of the development agenda for the World Intellectual Property Organization (WIPO).[27] Amongst many purposes and objectives, the *A2K Treaty* is seeking to enhance the sharing of the benefits of scientific advancement and to promote new incentives to create and share knowledge resources without restrictions on access.[28] Article 1–1 of the *A2K Treaty* provides that the main objectives of the treaty are to protect and enhance access to knowledge and to facilitate the transfer of technology to developing countries. Key areas that the *A2K Treaty* covers are provisions regarding limitations and exceptions to copyright and related rights; patents; expanding and enhancing the knowledge commons; the promotion

---

25   Johannes Velterop, *Open Access Publishing and Scholarly Societies: A Guide* (New York: Open Society Institute, 2005), online: www.soros.org/openaccess/scholarly_guide.shtml.

26   "Why We Need a Treaty on Access to Knowledge," online: www.cptech.org/a2k/ [*A2K Treaty*].

27   *Ibid.*

28   *Ibid.*, preamble.

of open standards; the control of anti-competitive practices; authors' and performers' rights; and the transfer of technology to developing countries.

2) Access to Knowledge as a Human Right

The principle of open access can also find a legal basis in international human rights laws, some of which clearly provide that people should have the right to hold private property, including intellectual property rights. For example, the clearest enunciation of the right to hold private property is found in article 27(2) of the *Universal Declaration of Human Rights (UDHR)*.[29] However, this obligation is not absolute and must be read in the context of international human rights law that supports access to knowledge; for example:

- article 17 of the *Convention on the Rights of the Child*[30]
- article 19 of the *Universal Declaration of Human Rights*[31]
- article 13 of the *International Covenant on Economic, Social and Cultural Rights*[32]
- article 1.1 of the *International Convention on Cultural and Political Rights*.[33]

International declarations, conventions and covenants are important in that they may also act as an interpretative guide when courts are called on to define the ambit of intellectual property rights.[34]

---

29 *Universal Declaration of Human Rights*, online: www.un.org/en/documents/udhr/. Article 27(2) provides: "Everyone has the right to the protection of the moral and material interests resulting from any scientific, literary or artistic production of which he is the author."

30 See online: www.unicef.org/crc/.

31 See above note 29.

32 See online: www2.ohchr.org/english/law/cescr.htm.

33 See online: www2.ohchr.org/english/law/ccpr.htm.

34 *Minister of State for Immigration and Ethnic Affairs v. Ah Hin Teoh* (1995), 183 C.L.R. 273 at 25–26 (H.C.A.) As at 27 June 2006, this case has been applied in thirty-four subsequent decisions. See also *Kruger v.Commonwealth* (1997), 190 C.L.R. 1 (H.C.A.); *Horta v. Commonwealth* (1994), 181 C.L.R. 183 (H.C.A.); *Newcrest Mining (WA) Ltd.v. Commonwealth* (1997), 190 C.L.R. 513 (H.C.A.); *Kartinyeri v. Commonwealth*, [1998] HCA 22, 195 C.L.R. 337. See also Bryan Horrigan & Brian Fitzgerald, "International & Transnational Influences on Law & Policy Affecting Government" in Bryan Horrigan, ed., *Government Law and Policy: Commercial Aspects* (Leichhardt, NSW: Federation Press, 1998) 2; Brian Fitzgerald, "International Human Rights and the High Court of Australia" (1994) 1 J.C.U.L. Rev. 78.

3) Key Features of Open Access

Peter Suber of Earlham College, states that the open access movement:

- proposes that authors electronically publish (or archive) pre-prints of their papers, in a manner analogous to "Departmental Working Papers" series of bygone days;
- recommends the establishment of E-Prints Archives by universities and other research institutions (to provide a manageably small number of persistent, professionally managed, and readily discoverable locations, rather than tens of thousands of ephemeral, personal websites);
- publishes software that enables such E-Prints Archives to be managed;
- recommends use of the Open Archive Initiative metadata standard, in order to support cross-discovery services;
- approaches journal publishers to sanction author self-archival (already with great success); and
- communicates with governments, with a view to ensuring that government policy and amendments to copyright law support and not undermine open access to authors' pre-prints.[35]

4) Support for Open Access

There has been significant support for the open access movement at the international level. As at 8 July 2008, 250 organizations around the world have signed the *Berlin Declaration*.[36] At the local level, various organizations have endorsed the principles of open access through developing organization-specific declarations or policies on the topic. For example, some tertiary institutions recommend (or even mandate) that staff deposit their papers in the institutional repositories and many tertiary institutions make the submission of post-graduate research papers and Ph.D. theses into the institutional repository mandatory. For example, the world's two largest funders of medical researchers, the UK's Wellcome Trust[37] and the US' Na-

---

35   Roger Clarke, "A Proposal for an Open Content Licence for Research Paper (Pr) ePrint" (2005) 10:8 First Monday, online: http://firstmonday.org/htbin/cgiwrap/bin/ojs/index.php/fm/article/view/1262/1182.

36   See online: http://oa.mpg.de/openaccess-berlin/signatories.html.

37   See Wellcome Trust, online: www.wellcome.ac.uk and http://en.wikipedia.org/wiki/Wellcome_Trust.

tional Institutes of Health,[38] adopted, in 2005 and 2008 respectively, policies with a requirement to provide open access to the results of successful grantees. Such support of open access arguably benefits society by enabling access to medical research that can be used to save lives or enhance the quality of life.

F. NEW LICENSING MODELS

One of the most significant responses to the technological advances that have revolutionized the creation and distribution of copyright materials during the last decade has been the development of new systems for licensing (or authorizing) others to obtain access to, and make use of, the protected material. These new forms of licences—usually referred to as "open content"—are founded upon an acknowledgement of the existence of copyright in materials embodying knowledge and information. As mentioned in "Overview of the Principles of Copyright Law," above in Section C, copyright law makes it unlawful to reproduce and communicate copyright material unless the permission of the copyright owner or some other form of authorization has been obtained. Therefore, while I might place an article in an institutional repository, if I say nothing more, the "all rights reserved" default position will most likely apply, meaning that the end user's rights to engage in reproduction or communication of the material as an act of reuse will be unclear. Users may be able to read the material online or print a copy, but can they post an enhanced version on another website, or make thirty copies for their students in a class? In order to deal with these questions and to provide greater legal certainty and fluidity to the act of sharing knowledge, we have seen the rise of Open Content Licenses (OCLs). Running with the copyright material to which they are attached, OCLs identify materials that are available for reuse and grant permissive rights to users, thereby facilitating access and dissemination. In comparison to licences commonly used before the advent of the digital era, they are standardized, conceptually interoperable with other OCLs, machine (computer) enabled, and they eliminate (or at least minimize) transaction costs (as they are automated). The best known of the open content licensing systems are those developed by the Creative Commons project and its associated Science Commons project.[39] Another project employing open content

---

38 See National Institutes of Health, online: www.nih.gov.
39 See online: http://creativecommons.org and http://sciencecommons.org.

licensing models include AEShareNet,[40] a collaborative system designed to streamline copyright licensing to enable the more efficient development, sharing, and adaptation of Australian educational materials.[41]

1)   Open Content Licensing

OCLs are essentially voluntary intellectual property licensing agreements designed to provide an effective model for managing copyright in digital content. These agreements call on intellectual propety owners to consider sharing knowledge with the world through a legal mechanism that will allow a broad ambit of reuse. While open access aims to have research disseminated rapidly through the Internet, open content licensing aims to ensure that downstream user rights are clear. Therefore, OCL is not anti-copyright— it uses copyright as the basis for structuring open access.

A range of OCLs exist, including:

- Creative Commons licences;[42]
- AEShareNet Instant Licences;[43]
- Design Science Licences;[44]
- GNU Free Documentation Licences;[45]
- Open Content Licences;[46]
- Open Directory Project Licences[47] used by the Open Directory Project;[48]
- Open Game Licences[49]—licences of the Open Gaming Foundation,[50] as drafted by Wizards of the Coast;[51]

---

40   See online: www.aesharenet.com.au/.

41   See further Intrallect Ltd. (Ed Barker & Charles Duncan) and AHRC Research Centre (Andres Guadamuz, Jordan Hatcher, & Charlotte Waelde) *Final Report to the Common Information Environment Members of a Study on the Applicability of Creative Commons Licenses* (2005), online: www.intrallect.com/cie-study/ at c. 3.6.

42   See online: http://creativecommons.org.

43   See online: www.aesharenet.com.au/coreBusiness/#Instant.

44   See online: http://en.wikipedia.org/wiki/Design_Science_License.

45   See online: http://en.wikipedia.org/wiki/GNU_Free_Documentation_License.

46   See online: http://en.wikipedia.org/wiki/Open_Content_License and http://open-content.org/opl.shtml.

47   See online: http://en.wikipedia.org/wiki/Open_Directory_Project_License.

48   See online: http://en.wikipedia.org/wiki/Open_Directory_Project.

49   See online: http://en.wikipedia.org/wiki/Open_Game_License.

50   See online: http://en.wikipedia.org/wiki/Open_Gaming_Foundation.

51   See online: http://en.wikipedia.org/wiki/Wizards_of_the_Coast.

- Open Publication Licences[52]—a licence for the Open Content Project;[53] and
- the Commonwealth of Australia, represented by the Office of Spatial Data Management (OSDM), Spatial Data License used by Geoscience Australia.[54]

As well as providing an effective model for managing copyright in digital content, open content licensing also has the added benefit of making copyright more active in the sense of enabling copyright material left inactive in archives (such as, in government or public film, or television authorities and museums) to be "licensed out" and reused in an inexpensive and generic manner.

OCLs can also be seen to promote sustainable business models as they commonly adopt a dual licensing approach—in the sense that an OCL provides open access for non-commercial purposes but restricts reuse for commercial purposes. For example, the Creative Commons licences referred to above provide that anyone can use the content subject to providing *attribution* to the author (BY) and any one or a number of the following optional conditions:[55]

- *non-commercial* distribution (NC);
- that *no derivative* materials based on the licensed material are made (in other words, all copies are verbatim) (ND); and
- *share and share alike* (others may distribute derivative materials based on the licensed material under a licence identical to that which covers the licensed material) (SA).

Therefore, if a person writes an article on the legal aspects of downloading MP3s off the Internet, she might put that up on her website with an OCL such as a Creative Commons licence allowing the user to reproduce, recast, and communicate the content so long as they provide attribution (BY), do not use it for a commercial purpose (NC), and share their innovations with the people of the world (SA). Thus a person can give permission in advance for their content to be used for non-commercial purposes before it can be used commercially.

---

52   See online: http://en.wikipedia.org/wiki/Open_Publication_License.
53   See online: http://en.wikipedia.org/wiki/Open_Content_Project.
54   See online: www.osdm.gov.au/OSDM/Policies+and+Guidelines/
     Spatial+Data+Access+and+Pricing/OSDM+Licence/default.aspx.
55   Note that the ND and SA terms are mutually exclusive.

G. CREATING LEGAL FRAMEWORKS FOR OPEN ACCESS TO ACADEMIC AND RESEARCH MATERIALS

As discussed throughout this chapter, there is increasing interest in ensuring that the output of publicly funded academic and research work is accessible and widely disseminated through open access channels.

It is essential to appreciate at the outset that, from the legal perspective, it is not possible to establish any kind of open access system simply by default. Rather, development of an open access system can only successfully occur through deliberate construction and active management.[56]

In establishing the legal framework for a system of open access to academic and research materials, it is necessary for the key institutional players to:

- determine the degree of "openness" required in relation to those materials;[57]
- understand the roles of, and relationships among, the relevant parties involved in funding, creating, publishing, distributing, and using academic and research materials; and
- consider how best to manage the often complex inter-relationships among the various parties, especially with respect to their copyright interests in the materials, so that the relationships and copyright

---

56   This point is reflected in Principle 1 of the Zwolle Principles which states:

> (1) Achievement of [the overall objective] requires the optimal management of copyright in scholarly works to secure clear allocation of rights that balance the interests of all stakeholders.

See online: http://copyright.surf.nl/copyright/zwolle_principles.php [Zwolle Principles].

57   There are various statements/declarations on open access in the context of academic materials, including: the *Bethesda Statement*, above note 24; *the Berlin Declaration*, above note 23; the Zwolle Principles, *ibid.*; and the Bermuda Principles (1996), online: http://en.wikipedia.org/wiki/Bermuda_Principles. In addition to the numerous articles and blogs dealing with open access, there is now an emerging literature. Recently published books include: Richard Jones, Theo Andrew, & John MacColl, *The Institutional Repository* (Oxford: Chandos, 2006) [Jones, Andrew, & MacColl]; Neil Jacobs, ed., *Open Access: Key Strategic, Technical and Economic Aspects* (Oxford: Chandos, 2006) (most of the chapters are self-archived online: www.earlham.edu/~peters/fos/2006_07_16_fosblogarchive.html#115325936391251995); John Willinsky, *The Access Principle: The Case for Open Access to Research and Scholarship* (Cambridge, MA: MIT Press, 2006), available in part online: http://mitpress.mit.edu/catalog/item/default.asp?tid=10611&ttype=2.

interests can be effectively managed to achieve the desired degree of open access in the system.

1) Developing and Publishing a Policy on Open Access

Before implementing a copyright management policy for the provision of access to and reuse of research outputs, each institution should develop and publish its policy on open access, clearly enunciating its objectives and interests in providing materials by this means.[58] This involves clearly identifying, articulating, and observing the following:

- the categories of materials that are to be made available by open access, and
- the scope of open access which is to be afforded, in terms of the classes of persons who are to be allowed access and the extent of rights granted to access and reuse the materials.

Each institution should formally allocate responsibility to a suitability experienced and resourced office within the institution for implementation of the open access policy and for periodically reviewing its operation.

2) Mapping the Network of Legal Relationships

To ascertain who is permitted to use academic materials (that are available in a repository) and the extent of the permitted use of such materials, it is necessary to identify the various stakeholders and their respective roles, describe the legal relationships among them, and understand how copyright interests are allocated.[59]

---

58   For example, the Zwolle Principles state the overall objective as follows:

> To assist stakeholders—including authors, publishers, librarians, universities and the public—to achieve maximum access to scholarship without compromising quality or academic freedom and without denying aspects of costs and rewards involved.

See "Zwolle Principles," *ibid.*

59   This point is reflected in principle 5 of the Zwolle Principles, which states: "Copyright Management should strive to respect the interests of all stakeholders involved in the use and management of scholarly works; those interests may at times diverge, but will in many cases coincide." See Zwolle Principles, *ibid.*

To date, much of the literature and research on copyright issues in open access systems has failed to adopt a sufficiently broad perspective that encompasses not only the full range of stakeholders involved, but also the way the legal relationships among them impact upon the rights of repositories and end users. In particular, in considering rights to use materials deposited in repositories, much of the discussion has been overly focused on the author-publisher relationship, as defined in the publishing agreement. Further, this already narrow focus has been channelled even more narrowly by the fact that much of the discussion has considered only those situations where copyright is assigned (or exclusively licensed) by the copyright owner (usually the author) to the publisher. The broader range of possible arrangements in relation to copyright ownership— including retention of copyright by the author— has received insufficient attention. To fail to adopt a broader perspective on the relationships among all of the relevant stakeholders means a loss of the opportunity to achieve the most efficient and effective open access system by leveraging all the factors that can be brought to bear in pursuit of the open access objective.

The key stakeholders and relationships that will come into play in the structuring of an open access system are:

- **Funding organization–author**: The relationship between the organization providing grants of funding for research and the author of outputs (such as academic articles and research reports) of the funded research project, or the author's university or research institution [*funding agreement*].
- **Author–employer**: The relationship between the author of academic or research outputs and his employer (such as a university or research institution) [*employment agreement and IP policy*].
- **Author–publisher**: The relationship between the author (or another party who owns copyright in works produced by the author, such as the author's employer) and the publisher [*publishing agreement*].
- **Author–digital repository**: The relationship between the author (or another party who owns copyright in the author's works, such as the author's employer or the publisher) and the digital repository in which a copy of the author's article is deposited [*repository deposit licence*].
- **Digital repository–end users**: The relationship between the digital repository in which the author's article is deposited and persons who are authorized to access it (which may be the public at large or may

be restricted to a particular group with defined access rights) [*repository distribution (end user) agreement*].

- **Author/publisher–end users**: The relationship between the author/ publisher (or other owner of copyright, such as, the author's employer) and end users (in other words, persons authorized to access and use the material) [*distribution agreement*].

- **Copyright collecting society–digital repository and end users**: Much of the administration of copyright in the educational context in Australia occurs pursuant to statutory licences administered by copyright collecting societies such as the Copyright Agency Limited (CAL), which collect fees from educational institutions as compensation for educational use of copyright materials. In establishing a system to enable access to academic and research materials in online repositories, it is necessary to consider how such materials will be treated under the statutory licence for reproduction and communication of works in electronic form under Division 2A of Part VB (ss 135ZMA to 135ZME of the *Copyright Act*) [*educational statutory licence*].

Each of these relationships and the particular copyright management issues they raise are considered, in turn, below.

a) Funding organization–author / research institution (funding agreement)

Where research is being funded by an external source, that organization may impose conditions on the researcher or recipient institution in relation to how the output of the funded research will be made available. For example, it would not be unusual for a funding organization to impose requirements relating to protection and/or ownership of intellectual property in a research output and how the research output is to be disseminated.

The Australian Government now provides more than $5 billion annually in funding science and innovation.[60] In some fields (for example, human health-related biotechnology), virtually all research carried out in Australia (whether in universities, research institutes, or government departments or agencies) is funded by the Australian Government. The government understands that "access is a critical issue in the drive to optimize Australia's

---

60   Australia, Productivity Commission, *Terms of Reference for Economic, Social and Environmental Returns on Public Support for Science and Innovation in Australia* (Melbourne: Commonwealth of Australia, 2007), online: www.treasurer.gov.au/DisplayDocs.aspx?pageID=&doc=pressreleases/2006/010.htm&min=phc.

research infrastructure."[61] The Australian Government, Department of Education, Science and Training's (DEST) *National Collaborative Research Infrastructure Framework—Strategic Roadmap*[62] states:

> Consistent with the NCRIS principles, the Roadmap identifies those capabilities that will provide the most strategic impact in terms of delivering national benefit, producing world-class excellence in both discovery and application driven research, and/or enhancing the overall capacity of the research and innovation system by providing enabling research platforms and promoting accessibility and collaboration.[63]

A critical issue is how to strike the appropriate balance between commercialization and increased access.[64] It follows that research funding bodies need to review the terms of their funding agreements to ensure that the objective of providing open access to research results is not contradicted by obligations on funding recipients to protect and commercialize intellectual property that is developed in funded projects.

i)   Promoting self-archiving in open access repositories

According to Stevan Harnad:

> Articles made open access by self-archiving them on the web are cited twice as much, but only 15 percent of articles are being spontaneously self-archived. The only institutions approaching 100 percent self-archiving are those that mandate it. Surveys show that 95 percent of authors

---

61   Australian Government, Department of Education, Science and Training, *National Collaborative Research Infrastructure Strategy — Strategic Roadmap* (February 2006) 3, online: http://ncris.innovation.gov.au/Documents/2006_Roadmap.pdf [*NCRIS Roadmap*]. For a more recent indication of government policy see: Hon. Kim Carr, Minister for Industry Innovation Science and Research, "There is More than One Way to Innovate" (7 February 2008), online: http://minister.innovation.gov.au/carr/Pages/THEREISMORETHANONEWAYTOINNOVATERESEARCHFORDISCOVERY,UNDERSTANDING,ANDAPPLICATION.aspx.

62   *NCRIS Roadmap*, *ibid.*

63   *Ibid.* at 4.

64   See generally, Australian Government, Department of Education, Science and Training, *Knowledge Transfer and Australian Universities and Publicly Funded Research Agencies* (Canberra: Department of Education, Science and Training, 2006), online: www.dest.gov.au/NR/rdonlyres/36818C20-9918-4729-A150-464B662644B3/12630/Knowtran_FinalCompilation_005_web1.pdf.

will comply with a self-archiving mandate; the actual experience of institutions with mandates has confirmed this.[65]

Since surveys indicate that a majority of researchers favour research funding bodies mandating self-archiving[66] and, as 95 percent of authors say they would comply with a self-archiving mandate,[67] it has been proposed that institutions and funding bodies should mandate that the author's final draft[68] must be deposited into the institutional repository immediately upon acceptance for publication.[69]

In recent years, research funding bodies in the US, the UK, and Germany have adopted open access policies and guidelines calling upon researchers to publish in open access journals and to deposit materials resulting from funded research in an open access repository.[70]

---

65 Stevan Harnad, "Monitoring Research Impact through Institutional and National Open-access Self-archiving Mandates" in Keith Jeffrey, ed., *Proceedings of CRIS 2006. Current Research Information Systems: Open Access Institutional Repositories* (2006) at 1, online: http://eprints.ecs.soton.ac.uk/12093 [Harnad, "Monitoring Research"]; An example is CERN, online:http://public.web.cern.ch/Public/Welcome.html, which has an institutional self-archiving mandate and is close to providing open access to 100 percent of its own current published research-article output in its institutional repository, see online: http://cdsweb.cern.ch.

66 Sue Sparks, "JISC Disciplinary Differences Report" (London: Rightscom, 2005) at 7, online: www.jisc.ac.uk/uploaded_documents/Disciplinary%20Differences%20 and%20Needs.doc. For a survey of public attitudes to access to publicly funded research output, see Alliance for Taxpayer Access, Press Release, "Americans Support Free Access to Research" (31 May 2006), online: http://old.arl.org/ata/media/Release06-0531.html.

67 Alma Swan & Sheridan Brown, *Open Access Self-archiving: An Author Study* (Truro: Key Perspectives, 2005) at Tables 30 and 64.

68 That is, the version that is commonly referred to as the "PostPrint."

69 For the best up-to-date overview of the open access policies applied or being developed by funding bodies in the US, UK, Canada, South Africa, and several European countries (including Sweden, France, and Germany), focusing on whether open access is mandated or merely encouraged, see Peter Suber, "Ten Lessons from the Funding Agency Open Access Policies" *SPARC Open Access Newsletter*, #100 (2 August 2006), online: www.earlham.edu/%7Epeters/fos/newsletter/08-02-06.htm. See also Stevan Harnad, "Monitoring Research," above note 65; Stevan Harnad, "Opening Access by Overcoming Zeno's Paralysis" in Neil Jacobs, ed., *Open Access: Key Strategic, Technical and Economic Aspects* (Oxford: Chandos, 2006) c. 8, self-archived 19 March 2006, online: http://eprints.ecs.soton.ac.uk/12094.

70 For an overview of research funding bodies' policies on open access, see the European Commission, Open Access: Opportunities and Challenges—A Handbook (Luxembourg: Office for Official Publications of the European Communities, 2008).

In the US, in February 2005 the National Institutes of Health (NIH), the world's largest non-military research funder, "prodded by federal departments and Congressional committees," adopted an open access policy[71] with the aim of increasing the availability of the research that it funds. The policy requested all NIH-funded investigators to submit, from 2 May 2005, an electronic version of the author's final, peer-reviewed manuscripts to the PubMed Central[72] database, the NIH's free digital archive of journal literature in the biomedical and life sciences, upon acceptance for publication. The policy applied to any journal articles resulting from research supported wholly or partially with direct funds from NIH. However, in a survey conducted by Janice Hopkins Tanne in 2006,[73] it was found that less than 5 percent of NIH-funded researchers were acting in accordance with the NIH's policy.[74] On 11 January 2008, NIH announced a revision to its open access policy that made its application mandatory rather than voluntary for all peer-reviewed articles arising in whole or in part from direct costs funded by NIH, or from NIH staff, that are accepted for publication on or after 7 April 2008.[75] Funded researchers/institutions were given the responsibility for ensuring that any publishing or copyright agreements concerning submitted articles fully complied with the NIH open access policy.[76]

The Research Councils UK's (RCUK) revised *Position Statement on Access to Research Outputs* of 28 June 2006[77] endorsed the following principles:

- Ideas and knowledge derived from publicly-funded research must be made available and accessible for public examination as rapidly as practicable.

---

71   National Institutes of Health, Office of Extramural Research, "Policy on Enhancing Public Access to Archived Publications Resulting from NIH-funded Research," online: http://publicaccess.nih.gov/ and http://publicaccess.nih.gov/policy.htm.

72   See online: www.pubmedcentral.nih.gov.

73   Janice Hopkins Tanne, "Researchers Funded by NIH Are Failing To Make Data Available" (2006) 332 B.M.J. 684.

74   Peter Suber, "Thursday, March 9 2006" Open Access News, online: www.earlham.edu/~peters/fos/2006_03_19_fosblogarchive.html.

75   See Peter Suber, "The Mandates of January" in *SPARC Open Access Newsletter*, Issue #118 (2 February 2008), online: www.earlham.edu/~peters/fos/newsletter/02-02-08.htm; see also the NIH Public Access online: http://publicaccess.nih.gov/.

76   *Ibid.*; see also Kylie Pappalardo, *Understanding Open Access in the Academic Environment: A Guide for Authors* (Brisbane: ePrints, 2008) [Pappalardo, *Understanding Open Access*], OAK Law Project, online: http://eprints.qut.edu.au/13935/2/13935.pdf.

77   RCUK, "Research Council UK Updated Position Statement on Access to Research Outputs" online: www.rcuk.ac.uk/research/outputs/access/default.htm.

- Published research outputs should be effectively peer-reviewed.
- Models and mechanisms for publication and access must be an efficient and cost-effective use of public funds.
- Outputs must be preserved and remain accessible for future generations.[78]

While each of the eight Research Councils (representing diverse research disciplines)[79] were not directly required to mandate open access archiving for all RCUK-funded research, each were encouraged to develop specific guidelines for the communities it funded, relating to access to research outputs in the particular field/s of research. The intention was to ensure that each discipline was able to respond in ways that are best-suited to its own needs. To date, all but one of the Research Councils have adopted a mandate requiring deposit of peer-reviewed research outputs in an open access repository.[80] The access policies of the RCUK, along with the policies of research funding bodies in other countries (such as Germany and the US), are included in the Juliet website established by SHERPA.[81]

Similarly, in Europe, the European Research Council (ERC) requires that all peer-reviewed publications resulting from funded research be deposited in an openly accessible repository within six months of publication.[82]

---

78   RCUK, News Release (28 June 2006), online: www.rcuk.ac.uk/
     news/20060628openaccess.htm.

79   There were originally eight Research Councils: Arts & Humanities Research
     Council (AHRC); Biotechnology & Biological Sciences Research Council (BBSRC);
     Council for the Central Laboratory of the Research Councils (CCLRC); Economic
     & Social Research Council (ESRC); Engineering & Physical Sciences Research
     Council (EPSRC); Medical Research Council (MRC); Natural Environment
     Research Council (NERC); and Particle Physics & Astronomy Research Council
     (PPARC). On 1 April 2007, PPARC and CCLRC merged to become the Science and
     Technology Facilities Council (STFC): see online: http://en.wikipedia.org/wiki/Par-
     ticle_Physics_and_Astronomy_Research_Council.

80   Each of the Research Councils, except the Engineering & Physical Sciences Re-
     search Council (EPSRC), has adopted open access mandates: see SHERPA-JULIET
     online, Research funders' open access policies: www.sherpa.ac.uk/juliet/.

81   *Ibid.*

82   Policy accessed via SHERPA-JULIET, *ibid.*; see also European Research Council,
     "ERC Scientific Council Guidelines for Open Access" (17 December 2007), online:
     http://erc.europa.eu/pdf/ScC_Guidelines_Open_Access_revised_Dec07_FINAL.
     pdf.

In Australia, while 90 percent of the $4.3 billion expended on research and development by higher education institutions in 2004 was funded by government,[83] there is not as yet a policy mandating the archiving/depositing of researching articles in open access repositories. However, Australia's primary funding bodies, the Australian Research Council (ARC) and the National Health and Medical Research Council (NHRMC), moved in 2007 to encourage funded researchers to deposit their research results in open access repositories.[84] The ARC also requires researchers who are not intending to deposit their research publications in an open access repository to explain their reasons for refraining. This places a greater emphasis on researchers to consider the reasons for their decision and whether those reasons are justifiable.

Government reports by the Australian Law Reform Commission (ALRC: *Genes and Ingenuity: Gene Patenting and Human Health*,[85] DEST: *Review of Closer Collaboration between Universities and Major Publicly Funded Research Agencies*,[86] and *Analysis of the Legal Framework for Patent Ownership in Publicly Funded Research Institutions*)[87] while not focusing directly on the question of imposition of conditions regarding open access to publications and other outputs resulting from funded research projects are significant in that they demonstrate that the issue of attaching conditions to funding grants to ensure that the project outputs is dealt with in the desired manner and, in particular, is consistent with the funding body's public-benefit objectives.

---

83   Buchhorn & McNamara, *Issues for Research Data*, above note 1 at 26.

84   Australian Research Council (ARC), "Discovery Projects Funding Rules for Funding Commencing in 2009" at 13, online: www.arc.gov.au/ncgp/dp/dp_fundingrules. htm.

85   Australian Law Reform Commission, "Genes and Ingenuity: Gene Patenting and Human Health," (2004) ALRC Report No. 99, online: www.austlii.edu.au/au/other/ alrc/publications/reports/99/.

86   Department of Education, Science and Training, "Review of Closer Collaboration between Universities and Major Publicly Funded Research Agencies" (Canberra: Commonwealth of Australia, 2004) online: www.dest.gov.au/NR/ rdonlyres/327F4C1D-99CC-4F93-91FB-1A2DEA8F299E/3623/pub.pdf.

87   Department of Education, Science and Training, "Analysis of the Legal Framework for Patent Ownership in Publicly Funded Research Institutions" by Andrew Christie *et al.*, (Canberra: Commonwealth of Australia, 2003), online: www.dest.gov.au/ sectors/research_sector/publications_resources/other_publications/patent_owner- ship_in_publicly_funded_research_institutions.htm#6._Recommendations_for_ Australia.

A 2006 report to DEST titled *Research Communication Costs in Australia— Emerging Opportunities and Benefits* recognizes the importance of conditioning grants in promoting access to research results:

> Research evaluation is the primary point of leverage, influencing strongly the scholarly communication and dissemination choices of researchers and their institutions. A related secondary point of leverage is funding, and the conditions funding bodies put upon it. To attain the goals of accessibility articulated in the Accessibility Framework (Appendix III) and elsewhere, and realise the potential benefits of enhanced access, it will be essential to ensure that funding and grant assessment, research evaluation and reward take account of emerging possibilities and opportunities, and build in open access options.[88]

The Accessibility Framework referred to is the "Quality and Accessibility Frameworks for Publicly Funded Research" proposed by the Australian Government in May 2004 as part of "Backing Australia's Ability— Building our Future through Science and Innovation."[89] The Accessibility Framework is intended to provide a strategic framework to improve access to research information, outputs and infrastructure.[90]

As part of the policy development process, universities and research funders need to closely consider the benefits of open access to knowledge. The Open Access to Knowledge (OAK) Law Project, funded by DEST under the Systemic Infrastructure Initiative, is seeking to provide institutions and research funders with assistance in identifying these benefits and guidance to promote the adoption of effective and cutting-edge copyright management frameworks.[91]

---

88   John Houghton, Colin Steele, & Peter Sheehan, *Research Communication Costs in Australia: Emerging Opportunities and Benefits* (Melbourne: Centre for Strategic Economic Studies, Victoria University, 2006) at 7, online: www.dest.gov.au/NR/rdonlyres/oACB271F-EA7D-4FAF-B3F7-0381F441B175/13935/DEST_Research_Communications_Cost_Report_Sept2006.pdf [Houghton, Steele, & Sheehan, *Research Communication Costs*].

89   See online: www.backingaustraliasfuture.gov.au/default.htm.

90   Houghton, Steele & Sheehan, *Research Communication Costs*, above note 88 at 132.

91   See Brian Fitzgerald et al., *Oak Law Report No. 1—Creating a Legal Framework for Copyright Management of Open Access within the Australian Academic and Research Sector* (Brisbane: Department of Education Science and Training, 2006).

b) Author–employer (employment agreement and intellectual property policy)

Universities and research institutes may require their academic and research staff to make their academic and research output available through open access institutional[92] or disciplinary (or subject-based)[93] repositories. The legal context in which this outcome is secured is the relationship between the university or research institute as an employer and the academic- or research-project author as an employee.[94]

Since the mid-1990s, the majority of Australian universities have developed intellectual property policies that address ownership of intellectual property (patents, copyright, confidential information, etc.) generated in the course of academic or research activities performed within the scope of the employment relationship. Intellectual property policies are often part of the formal regulations approved by the governing body of the university for its administration and are generally published in the university handbook and on the institutional website. Such policies may also be incorporated by reference into employment contracts between the university and its employees.

A range of approaches to the question of copyright ownership can be found in university intellectual property policies. Most policies seek to balance the interests of the parties by reserving certain rights to the party that does not own copyright. In a review of university copyright policies, the Zwolle project identified the following three approaches taken by UK universities:[95]

---

92   See Harvard University Faculty of Arts and Sciences, *Faculty of Arts and Sciences Agenda* (February 2008) at 3, online: www.fas.harvard.edu/~secfas/February_2008_Agenda.pdf. Institutional repositories assist in raising the profile of institutions, making their research output more visible and accessible.

93   Disciplinary, or subject-based, archives provide efficient and centralized access to full-text articles in specific domains. Eight disciplines have successfully set up E-Print archives: high-energy physics and mathematics (arXiv), economics (RePEc), cognitive science (CogPrints), astronomy, astrophysics, and geophysics (NTRS and ADS), and computer science (NCSTRL).

94   For caselaw addressing the issue of whether an institution can enforce university policies (in the context of patent ownership) through a faculty member's employment contract (by reference, either specific or general, to the policies in the employment contract) see: *Victoria University of Technology v. Wilson and Others*, [2004] VSC 33; *University of Western Australia v. Gray (No 20)*, [2008] FCA 498.

95   Frederick J. Friend, "Copyright Policies And Agreements: Implementing The Zwolle Principles" (2003), online: http://copyright.surf.nl/copyright/files/implem_Zwolle_principles.pdf.

Scenario A: individuals own copyright with a licence to the institution

University College London, UK: "UCL recognises the rights of its staff to ownership of copyright in research publications, books and other similar academic publications in all formats . . . UCL will seek to secure, free, unconditional and perpetual, non-exclusive licence to use academic and teaching materials in all formats which are generated by members of staff arising out of employment by UCL."[96]

Scenario B: institution owns copyright but university agrees not to benefit from individuals' work

University of Bristol, UK: "University policy adopts and imposes UK Statute [*Copyright, Designs and Patents Act 1988*]. University policy is set out in the Standing Orders of Council e.g. section 12.3 of the Standing Orders of Council governing the appointment of members of the Non-professorial Academic Staff. Normally, therefore, the University is the first owner of IP and IP rights generated by its employees . . . The University will not in normal circumstances seek to benefit from any rights it may have as employer in the academic publications of members of the Academic Staff."[97]

Scenario C: institution owns intellectual property rights but publications excepted or rights waived

University of Oxford, UK: "The University claims ownership of all IP . . . devised, made or created . . . by persons employed by the University in the course of their employment . . . Notwithstanding section 6 of this statute, the University will not assert any claim to the ownership of copyright in . . . artistic works, books, articles, plays, lyrics, scores, or lectures, apart from those specifically commissioned by the university."[98]

The intellectual property policies adopted by Australian universities typically vest ownership of copyright in some materials (e.g., course guides and handbooks) in the university while providing for copyright in a wide range of other materials (including published journal articles, books and reports) to be owned or controlled by the employee author/s.[99] This splitting

96   University College London, *ibid.* at 1.
97   University of Bristol, *ibid.* at 2.
98   University of Oxford, *ibid.*
99   For a comprehensive overview of the intellectual property policies of Australian universities, see Anne Louise Monotti & Sam Ricketson, *Universities and Intel-*

of copyright according to the nature and purpose of the material is apparent in many university intellectual property policies.

An example is Charles Sturt University's intellectual property policy,[100] which states that the university owns all intellectual property created by an employee-author in pursuance of the author's duties under a contract of employment, including copyright in "courseware (books, print, videos, CD-ROMs, manuals, audiovisual recordings, computer software or other materials) created specifically for use in, or in connection with, a course, subject, or unit offered by the university."[101] On the other hand, employee-authors own intellectual property in copyright works "the subject matter of which is primarily concerned with scholarship, research, artistic expression, creativity or academic debate," including "books, articles or other similar works, whether in written or any other form, . . . artistic works created by researchers in fine art or design . . . [and] any other professional work" created by an employee author.[102] The policy expressly excludes from employee-copyright ownership materials that "were prepared for CSU course work and teaching, . . . were created using intellectual property owned by CSU . . . [or if CSU] . . . has made a specific and significant contribution of funding, resources, facilities or apparatus which led to the creation of [the] works."[103]

For those materials in which the intellectual property policy vests copyright ownership in the university, no problems arise. The university, as copyright owner, can exercise all the rights required to make the material available through its own institutional open access repository or an external disciplinary repository. By contrast, where the terms of the intellectual property policy vest copyright ownership in the employee, the situation is more complex and needs to be carefully managed by the university if it is to ensure that its employees do not, by exercising their rights as copyright owners, limit the university's ability to implement its policy on open access to academic and research output. In particular, in the absence of

lectual Property: Ownership and Exploitation (Oxford: Oxford University Press, 2003) [Monotti & Ricketson]. The intellectual property policies of many Australian universities are set out on SURF, online: http://copyright.surf.nl/copyright/implementing_principles/university_copyright_policies/examples.php.

100 Charles Sturt University, "Intellectual Property Policy," Version 4.0, adopted 1997, last modified August 2007, online: www.csu.edu.au/adminman/tec/Policyon-IntellectualProperty.pdf.

101 *Ibid.*, Clause 6.1.

102 *Ibid.*, Clause 6.2 at paras. (a)–(d).

103 *Ibid.*, Clause 6.2 at paras. (e)–(h).

any restriction imposed by the university (whether through its intellectual property policy or express terms of the employment contract) there is nothing to prevent employed academics and researchers who own copyright in their academic and research output from assigning copyright or granting an exclusive licence to a third party (such as a publisher), without reference to the university. In the typical case, where the assignment is of the whole of the copyright (for example, in the traditional publishing agreement), the university will not be in a position to require the material to be made available in an institutional or disciplinary repository once the transfer has been effected.

Where a university is seeking to develop a comprehensive open access institutional repository containing the academic and research output of its employees, it should review the terms of its employment contracts and intellectual property policy to ensure consistency between the institution's policies regarding open access to academic and research output and the obligations imposed on academic and research staff. To address the problems arising from copyright transfer by employees, it may be appropriate for universities to include in their intellectual property policies a requirement that before transferring copyright ownership to a third party the employee must first grant the university all the rights required to enable it to make the material available in an open access repository. Such a grant of rights may take the form of an assignment of part of the copyright to the university or it may be in the form of an irrevocable, non-exclusive licence in favour of the university. In either case, it should expressly state the rights granted to the university and should be in writing, signed by the employee.

The first Australian university to implement a formal requirement for academic authors to deposit all academic and research output was the Queensland University of Technology (QUT), under "Policy F/1.3 E-print repository for research output at QUT,"[104] adopted in 2003.[105] The QUT E-Prints policy states that deposit of materials is subject to "any necessary agreement with the publisher" and advises that "guidance on copyright arrangements and standards for publishers is available from the University Copyright Officer." The deposit policies of all other Australian universi-

---

104 (Brisbane: QUT, 1991–), online: www.mopp.qut.edu.au/F/F_01_03.jsp.

105 Since that time, Charles Sturt University has implemented a mandatory deposit policy for all staff (in January 2008). The University of Tasmania has been implementing a university-wide deposit mandate in a "patchwork" fashion—department by department. The School of Computing at University of Tasmania has had a deposit mandate in place since 2006.

ties (except Charles Sturt University and the University of Tasmania) are based on voluntary submission by academic and research staff. Professor Arthur Sale surveyed the proportion of DEST-funded research output deposited in institutional repositories. It was found that no Australian university with a voluntary policy collects significantly more than 15 percent of DEST-reportable content, and in most cases the amount was considerably less. This finding was comparable with international surveys that have also found 15 percent to be the average deposit level achieved voluntarily.[106] In comparison, QUT achieved deposit rates 2.5 times higher than its nearest competitor in 2004 and 5 times higher in 2005, with estimated deposit rates of 60 percent for 2005 and 80 percent for 2006.[107] Sale attributes the difference between the high deposit levels being achieved by QUT as compared to those observed at other Australian universities to "the deposit policy coupled with good author support practices,"[108] a finding consistent with a major international study by Swan and Brown in 2005.[109] Sale drew the following conclusion:

> A requirement to deposit research output into a repository coupled with effective author support policies works in Australia and results in high deposit rates . . . . Authors are willing to comply with a requirement to deposit. Voluntary deposit policies do not result in significant content, regardless of any author support . . . . [110]

It should also be noted that recent developments, most notably at Harvard University, have seen university academics vote to subject themselves to a requirement to provide their university with permission to make their scholarly articles available in an institutional open access repository. The Harvard Faculty of Arts and Sciences adopted such a policy on 12 February 2008.[111]

---

106 A. Sale, "Comparison of Content Policies for Institutional Repositories in Australia" (2005) 11:4 *First Monday*, online: http://firstmonday.org/htbin/cgiwrap/bin/ojs/ index.php/fm/article/view/1324/1244 [Sale, "Comparison of Content Policies"].

107 *Ibid.*

108 *Ibid.*

109 Alma Swan & Sheridan Brown, *Open Access Self-Archiving: An Author Study* (Truro, UK: Key Perspectives, 2005), online: http://eprints.ecs.soton.ac.uk/10999.

110 Sale, "Comparison of Content Policies," above note 106.

111 See above note 92 at 3; for more information about the Harvard Faculty of Arts and Sciences policy, see Peter Suber, "The Open Access Mandate at Harvard" *SPARC Open Access Newsletter*, Issue #199 (2 March 2008), online: www.earlham.

c)   Author–publisher (publishing agreement)

The degree of control that an academic author is able to exercise in respect of a published article, in terms of the use that the author can personally make of it or authorize others to make of it, depends on the scope of the rights (if any) that the author has in the published article. This, in turn is largely dictated by the legal relationship between the author and publisher, as established by the publishing agreement. The extent to which authors of published articles can continue to reproduce, distribute, or provide access to the article, for example, by self-archiving it or depositing it with an institutional or disciplinary repository, depends on the scope of the rights (if any) retained by the author.

Even though the author has written the article, if they have assigned copyright to the publisher and have not obtained a licence back from the publisher permitting them to continue reproducing and distributing the article, their actions in doing so will be every bit as much an infringement of copyright as if the acts were done by a completely unrelated third party. Likewise, if academic writers are to permit third parties to use their published articles, they must have the authority to be able to grant that permission. In particular, academic authors who wish to submit copies of their published articles to digital repositories from which they can be viewed and reproduced by the public at large or by members of a qualified community, must be able to warrant to the repository manager (custodian) that they have the rights to authorize the repository to make the copyright material available to those who access the repository. That is, they have the rights to reproduce, first publish, and communicate the copyright material to the public electronically (in other words, by making the material available on a website or by transmitting the material in digital form).

Much of the discussion of the allocation of rights between publishers and authors in the academic context has started from the assumption that copyright is assigned in its entirety from the author to the publisher at the time the publishing arrangements are agreed. There has also been little discussion of the importance of identifying the actual owner of copyright in a published article. Too often, discussion of authors' rights in relation to ongoing use of their published articles has been based upon assumptions that do not necessarily apply across the board. There has been a tendency to assume that the author has, prior to publication, assigned copyright to the publisher. The focus on the publisher as controlling the ongoing use of

---

edu/~peters/fos/newsletter/03-02-08.htm#harvard; see also Pappalardo, *Understanding Open Access*, above note 76.

published articles has tended to put alternative models of rights management into the shadows, which involves a lesser ceding of control by the author (e.g., through a partial transfer of copyright or merely granting the publisher a licence to publish). If the participants in the discussion were to shift their focus, they would find that the increased emphasis on open access has been accompanied by a shift away from the dominant model in favour of one in which copyright is retained by the author, the publisher is granted a licence to publish, and the author retains rights over further reuse of the material.

The range of models of copyright management in the author–publisher relationship, can be seen along a continuum of control, with maximum control by the author at one extremity and maximum control by the publisher at the other. At the one end of the spectrum the author retains copyright (and thereby maximum control) and merely licenses the publisher to publish the article, on an exclusive, sole, or non-exclusive basis. At the other end of the spectrum, the publisher obtains a full assignment of copyright from the author (and thereby maximum control) and does not permit the author to self-archive the article (either in its draft pre-print form or the published post-print form) or further distribute it (although the author may purchase hard copy reprints). In retaining copyright the author has control of further distribution of the article (including the right to self-publish, self-archive, or deposit it in a repository).

Points along the continuum from maximum author control to maximum publisher control can be identified, in broad terms, as follows:

(i)   Author retains copyright and controls distribution (which may include self-publishing, self-archiving, or depositing the output in a repository).

(ii) Author retains copyright and grants a licence (exclusive, sole, or non-exclusive) to the publisher to publish the article.

Ultimately in developing any licensing model for managing the author-publisher relationship, the scope of the rights granted to the publisher will be determined by how the licence deals with a range of issues, including:

- whether the licence granted is exclusive, sole, or non-exclusive;
- the period of time for which the licence is granted;
- the territory covered by the licence;
- whether any restrictions are imposed on the commercial use of the material (or whether it can be used only for non-commercial purposes); and

- the conditions applying to any further distribution of the material.

(i)   Author assigns copyright partially to publisher, retaining (reserving) ownership of part of the copyright.

(ii) Author assigns copyright to publisher but obtains an express licence back from publisher to further reproduce and distribute on terms determined by the publisher.

(iii) Author assigns copyright entirely to the publisher, with an implied licence to self-archive or deposit the article into an institutional or disciplinary repository.

(iv) Author assigns copyright entirely to the publisher.

Recent surveys of authors have clearly indicated a preference for a copyright model under which the author retains copyright and continues to be able to exercise rights over reuse of the material for educational, academic, or commercial purposes.[112] In *The Institutional Repository*, Jones, Andrew and MacColl comment that they have "noted that the major difficulties with clearing permission arise when dealing with materials that are not owned by the submitting author [and] advocate that [generally speaking] authors should retain as much of their rights as possible."[113]

i)   *Examples of rights management models under the author-publisher relationship*

aa) Author retains copyright and grants a licence (exclusive, sole, or non-exclusive) to the publisher to publish the article

This is the model favoured by the Open Access Law Program established by Lawrence Lessig (Stanford Law School), Michael Carroll (Villanova Law School), and Dan Hunter (New York Law School) under the umbrella of the Science Commons project.[114] It encourages authors to negotiate indi-

---

112   See Maurits van der Graaf & Esther Hoorn, "Towards Good Practices of Copyright in Open Access Journals" (Amsterdam: Pleaide Management Consultancy, 2005), the first output of the JISC-SURF partnering on copyright project, online: www.lboro.ac.uk/departments/ls/disresearch/poc/pages/jou-report.html; see also Anthony Austin, Maree Heffernan, & Nikki David, "Academic Authorship, Publishing Agreements & Open Access: Survey Results" OAK Law Project (May 2008) online: http://eprints.qut.edu.au/13623/.

113   Jones, Andrew, & MacColl, above note 57 at 54–155.

114   See online: http://sciencecommons.org/resources/readingroom/.

vidually with the journals in which they publish, to retain ownership of copyright, and to retain the right to deposit their material in open access repositories. The program has developed the following resources to promote open access in legal publishing, including:

- *The Open Access Law (OAL) Journal Principles*: The OAL program encourages law journals to commit to a set of OAL journal principles. These principles require that a journal: (i) take only a limited term licence, (ii) provide a citable copy of the final version of the article, and (iii) provide public access to the journal's standard publishing contract. In return, the author promises to attribute first publication to the journal.[115] (See http://sciencecommons.org/literature/oalawjournal).
- *The Open Access Law Author Pledge*: For authors wishing to commit publicly to open access ideals, OAL has established the OAL author pledge. This pledge commits authors to only publish law review articles in journals that adhere to a minimum OAL commitment.
- *The Open Access Model Publishing Agreement*: The OAL program also provides a model agreement that embodies the OAL journal principles in a fair and neutral contract that is easy for both authors and law reviews to adopt. It also provides for an easy mechanism for authors and journals to adopt Creative Commons (CC) licences to make their work more easily available.[116]

bb) Author assigns copyright partially to publisher, retaining (reserving) ownership of part of the copyright

Under this model, based on the splitting of copyright interests among the parties, the author assigns copyright partially to the publisher but retains (or "reserves") certain key rights required to enable them to control certain uses of the article (e.g., to enable the author to self-archive the article or to deposit it in a digital repository).

This model underlies the so-called SPARC author addendum (or simply, SPARC addendum),[117] developed by Professor Michael Carroll for the Scholarly Publishing and Academic Resources Coalition (SPARC).[118] The SPARC Addendum is a set of clauses intended for inclusion by an author

---

115   *Ibid.*
116   *Ibid.*
117   Version 3.0 of the SPARC Author Addendum, online: www.arl.org/sparc/author/AuthorsAddendum2_1.shtml.
118   See online: www.arl.org/sparc.

in a standard publication agreement in which copyright is assigned to the publisher, in order to limit what would otherwise be a general transfer of copyright, by excluding from the transfer certain distribution rights that are reserved to the author. In particular, the SPARC Addendum reserves to authors certain key rights; in particular, the right to post their articles in digital repositories.[119]

cc) Author assigns copyright to the publisher but obtains an express licence back from the publisher to further reproduce and distribute, on terms determined by publisher

The prevalence of the copyright assignment model is apparent from the survey of publishers conducted by the UK SHERPA (Securing a Hybrid Environment for Research Preservation and Access) project. The information about publishers' practices on the SHERPA website[120] shows that the majority obtained a transfer of copyright from the author. The SHERPA website provides a useful overview of publishers' practices, with a primary focus on whether or not they permit authors to self-archive or further distribute pre-prints and post-prints.

In formulating the SHERPA categorization (green/blue/yellow/white), much emphasis was placed on the policies issued by publishers. Such policies represent to the public at large the publisher's practices. In some cases, for example, where the publisher's policy states that authors are permitted to self-archive, or make the published article available in an institutional or disciplinary repository, the publisher may be going beyond what has been expressly stated in their standard, written publishing agreements which provide for assignment of copyright by the author but are silent as to any rights the author may have to further use or distribute the published article. In this case, the question arises as to whether the general statement of policy can be regarded as unilaterally varying the express terms of the existing publishing agreements with authors. The more likely situation is that the publishers' policy statements are merely a representation which, if acted on by authors, cannot be disavowed by publishers (doctrine of estoppel). Essentially, the publisher is indicating that it will not enforce its rights as copyright owner if the author makes use of the published article in the manner described by the publisher in its policy statement.

---

119 See SPARC, "Author Rights: Using the SPARC Author Addendum to Secure Your Rights as the Author of a Journal Article," online: www.arl.org/sparc/author/addendum.shtml.

120 See online: www.sherpa.ac.uk.

While the publishers' policy statements have retrospective effect in relation to existing contracts, it would be expected that new contracts would be drafted to expressly reflect the published policy.

dd) Author assigns copyright entirely to the publisher, with an implied licence to self-archive or deposit the article into an institutional or disciplinary repository

Many publishers require the author to assign copyright and, while the question of the author's rights to self-archive or deposit the article (in pre-or post-print version) is not expressly addressed in the publishing agreement, the circumstances may give rise to an implied licence to the author to use the article in this way. While there may be circumstances that can be relied upon to support the existence of an implied licence, there will inevitably be uncertainty about the terms and extent of any such licence.

ee) Author assigns copyright entirely to the publisher

Under the traditional model of academic publishing, the author assigns the whole copyright to the publisher in exchange for having the article or work published. Few, if any rights are licensed back to the author.

In the context of pursuit of open access objectives, this option is the least suitable. It minimizes the author's control over the published article, while maximizing the publisher's ability to prohibit or impose restrictions on further distribution and educational uses of the published work without consulting the author.

d) Author–digital repository (repository deposit licence)[121]

The relationship between the author (or another party who owns copyright in the work, such as the author's employer or the publisher to which copyright has been assigned) and the digital repository in which a copy of the article is deposited is governed by the terms of the repository deposit licence between the parties.

The repository deposit licence will be entered into by the administrator of the digital repository and the author, the author's employer, or the publisher.

---

121 See further, Kylie Pappalardo & Anne Fitzgerald, *A Guide to Developing Open Access Through Your Digital Repository, OAK Law Project* (Brisbane: Oak Law Project, QUT, 2007), online: http://eprints.qut.edu.au/archive/00009671/01/9671.pdf. Includes a sample repository deposit licence [Pappalardo & Fitzgerald].

If the repository is an institutional repository or disciplinary repository established by the author's employing institution, the parties to the repository deposit licence will be the author and their employer.

Surprisingly, many E-Print repositories do not enter into formal agreements with authors who deposit their works because such agreements are thought to discourage authors from depositing. In a 2000 survey of E-Print repository practices, the Rights MEtadata for Open Archiving (RoMEO) project found that about 32 percent of respondents took it on trust that the author had the right to deposit the work without explicitly asking them to confirm that they held all necessary rights.[122] However, a 2005 report commissioned by SHERPA on deposit licences for E-Prints emphasized the value of such licences in establishing a formal relationship between the repository and authors depositing their works. It concluded that:

> [d]eposit agreements should be considered an essential part of an e-print repository's operation . . . . For the repository, it provides a formal framework that defines what the repository can and cannot do, making it easier to manage the e-print in the long-term while helping to reduce its legal liabilities. For the author, it provides reassurance that the repository is not taking ownership of their work, and makes them aware of what type of service the repository is providing.[123]

It is necessary for a digital repository to determine the basis on which repository content may be accessed and reused by end users. The repository deposit licence between the author (or publisher) and the repository should address the extent to which the deposited material can be made available to other users and institutions and should grant an express licence to the repository to enable the repository to do all acts required to make the material available for access, use, and/or further distribution by end users.

In particular, the matters addressed in the repository deposit licence may include:

- permissions granted by the author (or other copyright owner) to the digital repository, which may include:
  - grant of a non-exclusive licence to the digital repository

---

122 The RoMEO study is referred to in Gareth Knight, *Report on a Deposit Licence for E-Prints*, online: http://ahds.ac.uk/about/projects/sherpa/report.htm.

123 *Ibid.*

- extent of rights granted to digital repository, for example, to reproduce and distribute the deposited material (including the abstract) worldwide in print and electronic format in any medium
- retention by author of rights to make use of the current and future (revised) versions of the deposited work
- rights granted to digital repository to translate the deposited work (without changing the content) to any medium or format for the purpose of preservation
- the requirement for citation to the published version to be included and clearly visible
- author's rights to provide updated versions of the work
- conditions under which the repository administrators can remove the deposited work
- rights granted to digital repository to copy the deposited work for purposes of security, back-up, and preservation
- access to work by other parties
  - basis on which work is to be made available to other users and institutions
  - rights of other parties to access, use and further distribute the work
- representations and warranties by the author (or copyright owner) to repository administrators
  - representation by the author of authority to enter into the repository deposit licence
  - representation by the author of the right to grant the rights to the digital repository as stated in the repository deposit licence
  - where the deposited work has been sponsored or supported by another organization, a representation by the author that obligations required by the agreement with such sponsor regarding use of the work have been fulfilled
  - warranty by the author that the work is original, and, to the best of his knowledge, does not infringe any other party's copyright
  - representation that, where the deposited work contains material for which the author does not hold copyright, the author has obtained the unrestricted permission of the copyright owner to grant the digital repository administrator the rights required by the repository deposit licence and that any third-party-owned material is clearly identified and acknowledged within the text or content of the deposited work
- responsibility for enforcement of intellectual property

· whether the administrators of the digital repository have any obligations to take legal action on behalf of the author (or copyright holder) in the event of breach of intellectual property rights in the deposited work

e) Digital repository–end users[124]

The repository distribution (end user) agreement grants rights to end users, to access and reuse deposited material, that are consistent with (and do not extend beyond) the licence granted to the repository by the author (or publisher) under the repository deposit licence.

End users may be individual members of the public or members of a specific academic community with defined access rights. The terms and conditions governing access to and use of material in the repository should be clearly displayed on the repository website and brought to the attention of end users so they understand that their use of the repository and materials in it is subject to those terms and conditions. In particular, any limits on the rights of end users to copy and further distribute the material in the repository should be stated.

Where it is essential to obtain assent by end users to comply with restrictions on access and use, the click-wrap format should be used for the repository distribution (end user) agreement.[125] A click-wrap website agreement involves end users first viewing the terms and conditions governing access to and use of the materials in the repository, and clicking an "I accept" or "I agree" button or icon to indicate that they assent to those conditions before they are able to obtain access to and use articles in the repository. Where restrictions apply and the repository will not permit access unless end users have agreed to be bound by the terms and conditions of access and use, end users who do not accept the terms and conditions should be given the opportunity of declining (by clicking a "I decline" or "I do not agree/accept" button), in which case they will not be permitted to continue to access the repository or download material from it.

In cases where few, if any, restrictions are imposed on access to and use of the materials in the repository, it will suffice if the repository distribution (end user) agreement is in browse-wrap form or if the terms and conditions

---

124 See further, Pappalardo & Anne Fitzgerald, above note 121, sample repository deposit licence.

125 A similar approach to that described in this paragraph is advocated by Richard Jones, Theo Andrew, & John MacColl, *The Institutional Repository* (Oxford: Chandos, 2006) at 152–54.

are available by clicking on hypertext links at the bottom of the reposi-tory website pages. In the browse-wrap form of agreement, the end user is required to view the terms and conditions but is not required to click on a button to indicate assent.

f)   Author/publisher–end users

Where the article is distributed by the author or publisher (or another copy-right holder), the rights of end users are governed by the terms of the distri-bution agreement. If the author has assigned copyright to a publisher, the rights of end users will be determined by the terms of the licence granted to end users by the publisher. However, in cases where the author has retained copyright wholly or partially, it may be the author who directly authorizes end users to use the article (author distribution agreement).

An example of an author-end user agreement is the SCRIPT-ed Open License,[126] used by the SCRIPT-ed online law journal, which takes the form of a non-exclusive licence granted by the author to users.[127] Users are given the right to disseminate the original and unmodified work, provided it is not done for commercial purposes.[128]

g)   Copyright collecting society–digital repository and end users

In establishing a system to enable access to academic and research materials in online repositories, it is necessary to consider how such materials will be treated under the statutory licence for reproduction and communication of works in electronic form under Division 2A of Part VB of the *Copyright Act.*

The question is whether the obligation to pay remuneration to a col-lecting society for the use of the copyright work still remains when a licence to use the work is granted expressly or impliedly by the copyright owner. If the obligation to pay remuneration continues in force unless expressly excluded by the terms of the licence to archive the material, this will have implications for the drafting of publication agreements.

---

126   See SCRIPT-ed Open License (SOL), online: www.worldlii.org/int/other/ PubRL/2009/52.html.

127   "User" is defined as "the person who reads, copies, issues copies of the work, translates, displays, performs or broadcasts the Work" in "Definitions," Clause 1 of the SCRIPT-ed Open License (SOL), *ibid.*

128   *Ibid.* Clause 4 deals with modifications and Clause 5 deals with adaptations.

H. COPYRIGHT MANAGEMENT ISSUES FOR ELECTRONIC THESES AND DISSERTATIONS

The electronic distribution of theses also raises many copyright issues.

1) Ownership Principles—The Legal Status of Theses

a) Copyright

Theses and dissertations will automatically be protected by copyright as a literary work, with the rights vesting in the author who has created them. It should also be noted that a thesis may consist of more than literary work or dramatic, musical, or artistic work.[129] For example, sound recordings and cinematograph films are now common in theses in some disciplines and these materials may also contain more than one layer of copyright. For example, the underlying rights in the script or any sound recording may co-exist alongside the copyright in the film.

b) Ownership of copyright in theses

Subject to any express agreement to the contrary (such as an agreement assigning copyright to the university or a third party), Ph.D. students will own copyright in the original expressions in their theses.

Where a student is receiving a scholarship or there has been a significant investment made towards the student's thesis, the investor may seek to obtain ownership of copyright in the thesis.[130]

c) Performers and moral rights

Performers' rights may be relevant for theses and dissertations, in particular theses in the area of creative industries and performing arts. In addition to having the personal right to prevent the making, copying, or public performance of an unauthorized recording or communication of a live performance (as outlined in "Overview of the Principles of Copyright Law," above in Section C), performers also have new economic rights to the extent that the performer and the person who, at the time of the recording, owned the record (being the person who owned the master recording on which the record was made) are now co-owners of the copyright in equal shares in the sound recording of the live performance.[131] These rights are relatively new,

---

129 *Copyright Act*, above note 4, s. 31.
130 Monotti & Ricketson, above note 99, c. 7
131 *Copyright Act*, above note 4, s. 97(2A). See also ss. 100AA–100AH.

following amendments to the *Copyright Act*[132] arising out of the *Australia-United States Free Trade Agreement.*[133] Performers may assign their share of the copyright to the original copyright owner in the sound recording or to a third party. The normal employment provisions under the *Copyright Act* will also apply— for example, copyright in a performance done in the course of employment will be owned by the employer.

Ph.D. students and researchers could also have moral rights in their theses, including the right to be attributed/ cited as the author of a work in third-party papers and publications reproducing parts of their theses. In addition, the moral right of integrity may be relevant for theses in the creative industries, such as film-making or sound production, where the remixing and reuse of aspects of a work (such as in a pastiche or multimedia work) could potentially subject the work to derogatory treatment in a way that demeans the creator's reputation if done without the consent of the creator—thereby infringing their moral right of integrity.

2)   A History of the Distribution of Theses

a)   The pre-digitization of theses

Prior to the digitization of theses, the thesis service that libraries could provide was necessarily limited. Theses were predominantly distributed in hard-copy form, usually a bound copy, which would then be deposited in the library of the degree-awarding institution, and perhaps that of the external assessor's institution. The core problem prior to digitization of theses was that, in the majority of cases theses were not published on a commercial basis. This made it extremely difficult to locate and access theses in many cases, as they were held at the library of the institution where the degree was awarded, with access limited to personal inspection of the hard copy within the library.

In some cases, copies of theses and dissertations are also held in the various state libraries and the National Library of Australia (NLA). However, as the NLA currently does not receive a copy of every thesis awarded by an Australian university it recommends that the relevant institution

---

132   *Ibid.*, s. 22(3A). See ss. 22(3B)–(3C).

133   Online: www.dfat.gov.au/trade/negotiations/us_fta/final-text/.

where the thesis was completed be consulted in order to obtain access to the required theses or dissertations.[134]

In contrast to Australia, the British Library provides a thesis service, which is known as the British Thesis Service, comprising:[135]

- Full text access to over 170, 000 doctoral theses dating from the 1970s to today, with most UK universities making their students' theses available on the service.
- This collection of theses is held in either paper bound copies or on microfilm. The service also makes available for sale the majority of theses in the collection, through either microfilm copies or bound paper copies.

b) The digitization of theses

With the growth of computer usage over the last twenty years we have seen the gradual development of the notion of submitting a thesis or dissertation in digital form into an electronic or digital repository.

For example, the Australasian Digital Theses Program (ADT Program) was established in order to improve access to, and enhance the transfer of, research data contained in theses through the provision of full text theses available on the Internet. It establishes a distributed database of digital versions of theses produced by postgraduate students at all Australian universities, which is made available on the Internet. The aim behind the ADT Program is to provide access to, and to promote, Australian research to the international community through the reproduction of theses on the ADT database.

Given that it is the responsibility of each individual institution to maintain an archived copy of the theses, every member of the ADT Program is required to host their own theses on a server located within the university. However, every member uses an identical database configuration, standards, and metadata, ensuring compatibility with all electronic theses contained in the ADT Program.

---

134 National Library of Australia, eResources, "Theses," online: www.nla.gov.au/apps/eresources/action/item?id=1484&loaditem=true.
135 The British Library, "British Thesis Service," online: www.bl.uk/britishthesis.

3)   Copyright Management Issues for Electronic Theses and Dissertations

With the increasing trend towards the promulgation of research findings electronically, there has been a concomitant increase in the number of Australian academic institutions that have "put online" electronic versions of dissertations and theses. Accordingly, there is a need for comprehensive protocols for managing the copyright issues in providing access to Electronic Theses and Dissertations (ETDs).

To build protocols for managing the legal aspects involved in making ETD available online, it is necessary to consider the issues from the perspective of each of the following four distinct stakeholders:

(1)   The student. As the contributor of original material, the submitting student will have intellectual property rights in most, if not all of the content. This will include copyright, but may also have patent issues arising (for example, containment of pre-patent disclosure).[136]

(2)   The supervisor. Depending on the discipline, there may be some content of the thesis that is directly or co-contributed by the student's supervisor. This may give intellectual property rights to the supervisor and/or the supervisor's employer (i.e., the relevant academic institution).

(3)   University, granting agency, and industrial partner. Universities, granting agencies, and industrial partners typically have intellectual property agreements and policies that may govern some of the ETD content.

(4)   ETD disseminating institution (Repository). Institutions that have a repository of ETD need clarification of intellectual property rights ownership. What is the status of the repository? (Is it a publisher?); what are the permissions required for cited materials; and are there any exemptions available (such as fair dealing for research or study, or criticism or review)? There may also be tortious issues arising in rare circumstances (such as defamation or passing off).

---

136   Publication prior to the filing of a patent will usually result in the inability to get the patent, as the invention would no longer be "novel." There are now some provisions for grace periods.

Adopting the perspective of each of these stakeholders, the management of intellectual property rights in ETD needs to be considered at a fine level of granularity. Taking this approach, numerous questions arise, including:

(1) How to manage licensing of distribution?

(2) How is the whole work in the thesis and dissertation to be regarded (in other words, is it entirely an original work of the student or does it contain third party or other contributions)?

(3) Is this discipline dependent?

(4) How to manage cited materials?

(5) How to manage contributions by others? (for example, technical photos, cite charts etc.)

(6) How to manage derivative works?

(7) How to manage confidential information (for example, pre-patent materials)?

(8) Liability and risk management?

(9) What protocols should be adopted?

The key objective of copyright management in this context is to ensure that the ETD repository has appropriate authorization to be able to legally carry out all the acts involved in putting the ETD online. In other words, the ETD repository must be granted a licence (preferably in written form) by the copyright owner—usually by the author of the thesis—authorizing the ETD repository to reproduce and communicate or otherwise disseminate the thesis via the Internet. Where third-party copyright material is included in the ETD, it will be necessary to ensure that appropriate "clearances" (in other words, permissions) have been obtained to use that material in the ETD, unless permission is not required under law.

4) Status of the Repository: Is it a "Publisher"?

Copyright issues facing ETD repositories may include whether the repository is a publisher or a "re-publisher" of the thesis for the purposes of copyright, defamation, confidential information, (trade secrets) and privacy issues.

In terms of copyright, where a hard copy of a thesis in the form of a literary, dramatic, musical, or artistic work is digitized and made available online in an ETD repository where it can be accessed and downloaded by members of the academic and research community, it is arguable that it would be deemed to have been published on the basis of the operation of section 29(1)(a) of the *Copyright Act*. However, the deemed publication provision has a much narrower scope of operation in relation to cinematograph films (section 29(1)(b)) than for "works." Publication is only deemed to occur if copies of the cinematograph film have been sold, hired, or offered or exposed for sale or hire to the public. While it is arguable that copies of film-based ETD are supplied to the public when they are made available for access in an ETD repository, the absence of any commercial dealings in the way of sale or hire, for example, means that it is not possible to rely on the deemed publication provision.[137] Since ETD consisting of moving images (and attracting copyright protection as cinematograph films) will not have the benefit of the deeming provision, it will be necessary to consider whether non-commercial distribution of film ETD from ETD repositories, where they can be accessed by members of the academic and research community, can amount to publication.

5)   Converting Paper Theses to Digital Theses

Where any paper thesis is converted to a digital thesis a number of copyright issues may arise. These include scanning the thesis without permission of the copyright owner, which will breach copyright as it involves the exercise of the copyright owner's rights of reproduction.[138]

Furthermore, in retroactively distributing electronic versions of paper-based theses (especially older theses) there is the difficulty in getting the permission of the author. Obtaining such permissions would be expensive both in terms of time and actual fees. One suggested option is to adopt a risk-management approach and engage in the digitization and digital ar-

---

137   *Copyright Act*, above note 4, s. 29(1)(b).

138   *Ibid.*, ss. 31 and 101. See also ss. 51 and 53. Section 51(2) applies to a manuscript or a reproduction of an unpublished thesis or other similar literary work that is kept in a library or a university or other similar institution. It provides that copyright in the thesis or other work is not infringed by the making or communication of a reproduction of the thesis or other work by or on behalf of the officer in charge of the library if the reproduction is supplied (whether by communication or otherwise) to a person who satisfies an authorized officer of the library that she requires the reproduction for the purposes of research or study. Section 53 extends the application of s. 51 to illustrations accompanying the thesis or other work. See further, Emily Hudson & Andrew Kenyon, *Copyright and Cultural Institutions: Guidelines for Digitisation* (Parkville, Australia: CMCL, 2005) at 129 [Hudson & Kenyon].

chiving process anyhow, given that the risk of copyright infringement proceedings commencing is low.[139]

Another problem with older theses is that even if the author is located, it is unlikely that the author will invest much time or money in establishing that use of any third-party content copied is permitted or, indeed, engage in resolving any of the issues that may arise. Therefore, considerable caution needs to be taken when dealing with the authors of paper-based theses and a more specialized licence agreement may be needed.

6) Third-party Copyright in Electronic Theses and Dissertations

A high proportion of ETD will contain third-party materials in the form of quotes of text passages, drawings, photographs, reproductions of paintings, video and sound clips, and so on. It is essential for ETD repositories to develop and implement strategies to avoid incurring liability (whether through an action for copyright infringement or through a request for payment of equitable remuneration to a copyright collecting society) due to the unauthorized use of any third-party copyright materials included in ETD.

If the copyright owner of the third-party content has given permission for the work to be used, repositories must ensure that the terms of such permission are not only confined to use in the original theses or dissertation but extend to reproducing or communicating the content for the purposes of digitization and public access via the repository. The use of third-party copyright materials in ETD will typically involve acts within the scope of the copyright owner's exclusive rights to reproduce[140] or make a copy[141] and to communicate to the public.[142]

---

139 See Hudson & Kenyon, *ibid.* at 50. Arguably, authors of theses would be happy to have theirs distributed. The greatest risk of copyright infringement would arise if the student assigned the copyright in their thesis to a third party, such as a publisher, and the publisher sought to take action against the repository for breach of their reproduction and communication rights.

140 *Copyright Act*, above note 4, Part III "Copyright in Original Literary, Dramatic, Musical And Artistic Works."

141 *Ibid.*, Part IV "Copyright In Subject-Matter Other Than Works."

142 "Communicate" is defined in s. 10(1) of the *Copyright Act, ibid.*, as meaning to "make available online or electronically transmit (whether over a path, or a combination of paths, provided by a material substance or otherwise)."

a) Exercise of the reproduction/copying right

Incorporation of third-party materials into the new copyright work created by the student (in other words, the ETD) whether in the form of a quote of a passage of text from a literary work, inclusion of a diagram, or samples of digital images or sounds, will involve the exercise of the reproduction or copying right. Where an ETD is born digital, it will be the student (rather than the university) who does the initial reproduction and copying of the third-party material although the consequences of any further reproduction or copying made by the repository need to be considered. Note that, in the case of a thesis submitted by the student in hard copy, the reproduction right will be exercised by the university when it converts the work from hard copy into digital format.[143]

b) Exercise of the communication right

Making an ETD available on a repository website where it can be accessed by users involves an exercise of the communication right, which encompasses making copyright material available online or electronically transmitting it.[144] In a system that is designed so that the ETD is uploaded to the repository directly by the student, it may be that only the student engages in an act of communication. However, in the situation where the student provides the repository with the ETD and authorizes the repository to make the ETD available online but all further steps required to make the ETD available online at the repository's website are carried out by the repository, it is likely to be the case that the act of communication is done by the repository.

The only guidance provided by the *Copyright Act* is found in section 22(6), which states that "a communication . . . is taken to have been made by the person responsible for determining the content of the communication." The question that arises is whether it is the repository or the student who is the person responsible for determining the content of the communication.[145]

Due to the intimate connection the university has with the inception, completion, and subsequent uploading of a thesis, there is strong argument that it has either undertaken an act of communication or authorized such

---

143   *Ibid.*, s. 21(1A).
144   *Ibid.*, s. 10(1).
145   See further *Universal Music Australia Pty Ltd. v. Cooper*, [2005] FCA 972 at paras. 70–76 [*Universal Music*].

an act.[146] If the university has undertaken the primary act of infringement (in other words, if it actually undertook the infringing act of communication) then liability accrues regardless of fault, subject to the exceptions already highlighted. If the university has merely authorized the act of communication then a number of "fault-based" factors will need to be considered, including the power to prevent the act, the relationship between the university and the infringer (student), and whether the university took reasonable steps to avoid the act (including complying with any industry codes of practice). Regardless of which argument is correct, due to the university's close connection with the thesis, its risk of liability for communicating the thesis must be carefully managed.

There are a number of options available to a repository in order to mitigate the risk of copyright infringement in relation to third-party content for born digital theses and dissertations.

These include:

(1) Ensuring that ETD candidates are provided with sufficiently extensive information and, if necessary, practical training on the basic principles of copyright law, so they understand when they can use third-party content in their thesis without permission (in other words, an insubstantial part or a substantial part that can be used because of the operation of fair dealing or another exception to infringement) and when they will need to obtain permission (clearance) from the copyright owner to use third-party content and how to obtain permission.

(2) Requiring the ETD candidate to be responsible for identifying all third-party content included in the thesis, determining what third-party content they require permission to use, and obtaining all necessary licences (typically a non-exclusive, perpetual licence) from the owners of such third-party content, which must be broad enough to permit the thesis containing the third-party material to be reproduced and communicated via the Internet (whether by the student, the university or the disciplinary repository).

---

146 For this reason it would seem unlikely that the university could rely on ss. 39B and 112E of the *Copyright Act*, above note 4, which state that merely providing facilities to make or facilitate the making of a communication is not, without more, an authorization of copyright infringement: *Universal Music, ibid.* at paras. 97–99; *Universal Music Australia Pty Ltd. v. Sharman License Holdings Ltd.*, [2005] FCA 1242 at para. 418. In relation to moral rights see *Copyright Act, ibid.*, s. 195AVB.

(3) Requiring the ETD candidate to "self manage" any third party con-
     tent that is not authorized for digital distribution.

Copyright law does not require permissions where an insubstantial
amount of a third-party copyright work is involved or where an exception
such as fair dealing applies. However the operation of both these doctrines
is very fact-specific. The best that can be done is to provide ETD candidates
with clear examples of what the courts have decided in the past so they
have a practical understanding of what material they can use and when
they should seek permission. For example, in *TCN Channel Nine Pty Ltd.
v. Network Ten Pty Ltd. (No. 2)*[147] it was held that whether a part taken is a
substantial part or not involves an assessment of the importance of the part
taken to the work as a whole.[148]

As discussed in "Overview of the Principles of Copyright Law," above
in Section C, copyright is not infringed by dealings with copyright materials that are considered to be "fair" and provided the dealing falls within one
of the following five classes of purpose in the *Copyright Act*:

(1) research or study (sections 40 and 103C)
(2) criticism or review (sections 41 and 103A)
(3) reporting news (sections 42 and 103B)
(4) judicial proceedings or professional advice (sectionss 43 and 104)
(5) parody or satire (sectionss 41A and 103AA).

Once it is established that the purpose for using the third-party copyright
material fits into one of these categories, the next step is to consider whether
the use made of that material for that purpose is fair.

In the context of ETD, the most relevant of the fair dealing provisions
are those that are exempt from infringement dealings with copyright materials for the purposes of "research or study" and "criticism or review."[149]
The terms "research" or "study" are not defined in the *Copyright Act*. However, in *De Garis v. Neville Jeffress Pidler* Beaumont J. held that term "re-

---

147 [2005] FCAFC 53 at para. 52 (Sundberg, Finkelstein, and Hely JJ., 26 May 2005)
     [*TCN Channel Nine Pty Ltd. (No. 2)*].
148 *Network Ten Pty Ltd. v. TCN Channel Nine Pty Ltd.* (2004), 78 A.L.J.R. 585 at
     589 and 605 (H.C.A.); *TCN Channel Nine Pty Ltd. (No. 2)*, *ibid.* at paras. 12 and
     50–52; *Network Ten Pty Ltd. v. TCN Channel Nine Pty Ltd.*, [2005] HCA Trans 842,
     McHugh & Kirby JJ. See also *Haines v. Copyright Agency Ltd* (1982), 42 A.L.R. 549
     (H.C.A.).
149 *Copyright Act*, above note 4, ss. 40–43, 103A, 103B, 103C, and 104.

search," within the meaning of section 40 of the *Copyright Act*, is intended to have its ordinary dictionary meaning:

> According to the Macquarie Dictionary, "research" may be defined as
>
> "1. diligent and systematic enquiry or investigation into a subject in order to discover facts or principles: research in nuclear physics . . . ."[150]

Similarly, the Copyright Act does not define "criticism" or "review," although it has been held that the words are of "wide and indefinite scope which should be interpreted literally."[151] In Warner Entertainment Co. Ltd. v. Channel 4 Television Corp. PLC Henry L.J. stated that the question to be answered in assessing whether a dealing is fair or not is: "is the [work] incorporating the infringing material a genuine piece of criticism or review, or is it something else, such as an attempt to dress up the infringement of another's copyright in the guise of criticism."[152]

It is clear from the judicial consideration of the meaning of these terms[153] that an individual student engaged in activities involving the use of third-party copyright material in the course of researching and writing a thesis would be able to establish that their acts are for the purposes of "research or study" or "criticism or review." It is also clear from the wording of sections 40 and 41 of the *Copyright Act* that the fair dealing provisions can be raised as a defence to copyright infringement in relation to an act of communication. Furthermore, there does not seem to be any doubt that a student can rely on the fair dealing provisions to communicate copyright material for the purposes of "research or study" or "criticism or review." The only doubt raised here is whether any act of communication[154] by the university can be regarded as being for the purposes of "research or study" or "criticism or review."[155] This is explored in the following two arguments.

---

150 *De Garis v. Neville Jeffress Pidler* (1990), 18 I.P.R. 292 at para. 25 [*De Garis*].

151 *TCN Channel Nine Pty Ltd v Network Ten Pty Ltd.*, [2001] FCA 108 at para. 66 [*TCN Channel*, FCA].

152 (1993), 28 I.P.R. 459 at 468 [*Warner Entertainment*].

153 *De Garis*, above note 151 at 298; *CCH Canadian Ltd. v. Law Society of Upper Canada*, [2004] 1 S.C.R. 339 [*CCH Canadian*]; *Warner Entertainment*, *ibid.*; *TCN Channel*, FCA, above note 151 at paras. 16–17 and 66; see also *TCN Channel Nine Pty Ltd. v. Network Ten Pty Limited*, [2002] FCAFC 146 [*TCN Channel*, FCAFC].

154 If the university is not regarded as undertaking an act of communication but rather authorizing an act of communication, then the issue will stand or fall on the basis of the student's ability to rely on the defence.

155 See, generally, *De Garis*, above note 150; compare with *CCH Canadian*, above note 153.

Argument 1: The student's act of research or study or criticism or review includes dissemination of the end product and the university communicating that the ETD is part of that process.

If the university can successfully argue that it is simply a part of or an extension of the student's activities and merely a conduit for dissemination then it is more likely that a court will accept an argument that the university, in communicating the ETD, is doing so for the purpose of "research or study" or "criticism or review." For what other purposes is the university engaging in this activity? Is it to promote the university as a commercial entity, or is it to disseminate a product of research or review?

In the old hard-copy world the student reproduced copies of the thesis usually through a copying service, supplied them to the university, and they were placed on the library shelf. History tells us that no one in the hard-copy world has ever questioned the role of the thesis copying service in terms of copyright infringement and the applicability of the fair dealing provisions. If anyone had successfully argued that the thesis copying service could not rely on the fair dealing provisions then the thesis would never have been copied or made available for others to read. It seems odd that a similar activity cannot be undertaken with the same degree of legal certainty in the digital environment, especially when technological neutrality is seen to be a key part of our legal framework.[156]

Thus, the university could argue that the student's act of "research or study" or "criticism or review" includes dissemination of the end product and the university in communicating that the ETD is part of that process. In *CCH Canadian*[157] the Supreme Court of Canada explained that when library staff made copies of legal materials they did so for the purpose of research: "although the retrieval and photocopying of the legal works are not research in and of themselves, they are necessary conditions of research and thus part of the research process."[158] Dissemination of research is very much

---

156   Consider *Electronic Transactions Act 1999* (Cth.), ss. 11(6) and 12(6).

157   Above note 153.

158   *Ibid.* at para. 64. See also TCN Channel, FCAFC, above note 153 at para. 101:

> Ten engaged Working Dog Pty Ltd (Working Dog), referred to by the
> primary judge as "its contracted production team," to produce for it
> a television programme which would, amongst other things, involve
> criticism and review and the reporting of news events. The purpose of
> Working Dog in the production of these programmes was the purpose
> of Ten. Consistently with the decisions of the UK Court of Appeal

part of the modern research process and the university is merely helping this to happen. As the Supreme Court explained, a restrictive interpretation of the fair dealing provisions "could result in undue restriction of users' rights."[159]

If this argument for the university, based on its function as a conduit for dissemination, cannot be sustained then the argument for the operation of the fair dealing provisions must focus solely on the nature of the activity being undertaken by the university. In particular, it is unlikely that the university would be able to avail itself of the fair dealing defence for purposes of criticism or review, although such a purpose may well underlie the student's use of the third-party material. However, it is arguable that current concepts of "research" (and, possibly, "study") are sufficiently broad to encompass the dissemination of research outputs by means such as making ETD available for access through web-based repositories. In a recent report, The British Academy stated the following in relation to the broader meaning of research:

> UK law has always provided for exemption from copyright for fair dealing in the course of research. There is, however, no statutory definition of research, or clarity on what differentiates the use of otherwise copyright material in research from its use in private study, or in criticism, or in review. Research involves the production of new ideas, whereas private study might represent only the consideration of existing ones. But this is a fine line indeed, and not one that it would seem appropriate for a publisher, or a court, to draw . . . But research without the publication of the results is barely if at all distinguishable from private study, and there is little or no public benefit in the production of new ideas unless they are made publicly available.[160]

. . .

---

earlier referred to, the "purpose" referred to in sections 103A and 103B is to be ascertained objectively, and it was neither necessary nor appropriate for officers of Ten or of Working Dog to give evidence that they had a sincere belief that he or she was criticising a work or an audio-visual item or reporting news.

159 *CCH Canadian*, above note 153 at para. 54.
160 British Academy, *Copyright and Research in the Humanities and Social Sciences* (London: British Academy, 2006) at 9, online: www.britac.ac.uk/reports/copyright/index.html.

In the absence of clarity in either statute or case law, we focus on what we believe the position should be. We consider that the research exemption must extend to the publication of research. The exemption would be largely nugatory and the consequences seriously inimical to scholarship if it did not do so. We also consider that the distinction between non-commercial and commercial research should relate to the purpose of the research, rather than the purpose of the publication of the research.[161]

To restrict the concepts of "research" and "study" to the narrow range of activities associated with collecting, reading, summarizing and extracting parts of the material may unjustifiably limit the operation of this fair dealing provision. In the digital networked environment in which research and study now occur and in which research and teaching processes are iterative and collaborative, communicating research findings to an online audience of colleagues and commentators is considered an integral part of the research and teaching process.

Argument 2: In communicating the ETD, the university is engaged in an act of research, broadly defined as an intermediary.

As explained, the university is either engaged in the act of communicating the ETD or in assisting such communication. Amendments to the *Copyright Act* introduced as a result of the *AUSFTA* limit the liability (by way of limiting remedies available) for certain acts performed by intermediaries.[162] These provisions apply to "carriage service providers" and provide for a "safe harbour" from liability in defined circumstances. They are commonly called the "ISP safe harbour provisions" and are modelled on similar provisions in the US *Digital Millennium Copyright Act of 1998*.[163] These new provisions limit the remedies available against carriage service providers for copyright infringements that occur on their systems, as long as they comply with certain conditions.

There is currently some uncertainty as to whether universities may take advantage of this scheme. This uncertainty relates primarily to whether universities fall within the definition of "carriage service provider," which, for the purpose of the safe harbour provisions, is drawn from the highly technical definition provided by the *Telecommunications Act*.[164] From 1997 to 2001 a determination by the then Minister for Communications, In-

---

161   *Ibid.* at 10.

162   *Copyright Act*, above note 4, ss. 116AA–AJ, Part V, Division 2AA.

163   *Digital Millennium Copyright Act*, 17 U.S.C. §§ 101–22 (1998).

164   *Telecommunications Act 1997* (Cth.) [*Telecommunications Act*].

formation Technology, and the Arts, Mr. Richard Alston, under section 95 of the *Telecommunications Act*, effectively excluded universities from being carriage service providers by stating that services provided by tertiary education institutions in connection with their research, educational, and administrative functions were not carriage services. Since this determination was allowed to lapse, the general opinion seems be that universities are nevertheless excluded from being carriage service providers because they do not provide their services "to the public," as required by section 88 of the *Telecommunications Act*.[165] In late 2005 the Attorney General's Department commenced a review of the scope of the safe harbour scheme that, among other things, sought comments on this issue. In making a submission to that review the Australian Vice-Chancellor's Committee (AVCC) explained:

> As the regime currently stands, only carriage service providers (within the meaning of the *Telecommunications Act*) can obtain the protection of the safe harbour regime. As most universities are not engaged in supplying a carriage service to the public but rather to their immediate circle (as that term applies under the *Telecommunications Act*) they do not qualify to take advantage of the safe harbour regime.[166]

The government has yet to announce the findings of this review. Until that point in time we must assume that universities, even if they could satisfy the condition for enlivening the safe harbour provisions, cannot take advantage of them because they are not carriage service providers.

One other suggestion is that any potential infringement of third-party content by the university in the ETD process could be covered by the statu-

---

165 See, generally, Australian Government, Department of Education, Science and Training, "Limitation on Remedies Available against Carriage Service Providers under Part V Division 2AA of the *Copyright Act*," submission by the Department of Education, Science and Training to the Attorney General's Review, October 2005.

166 AVCC, "Safe Harbour Regime: Review of the Scope of Part V Division 2AA of the Copyright Act," submission by the AVCC to the Attorney General's Review, October 2005, online: www.universitiesaustralia.edu.au/documents/publications/policy/submissions/AVCC-SafeHarbourSubmission-OCT05.pdf. It seems commonly accepted that the University of Queensland is the only Australian university that currently falls within the definition of "carriage service provider": AVCC, "University IT Systems: Managing Liability for Transmitting, Caching, Hosting and Linking to Copyright Material" (March 2007) at 2, online: www.acu.edu.au/__data/assets/word_doc/0007/44548/Copyright_AVCC_Resource_paper_IT_Systems_Mar_07.DOC.

398 Brian Fitzgerald *et al.*

tory educational licences, which allow certain acts on the basis of equitable remuneration. Whether or not this is the case, it raises a number of difficult legal questions that deserve close consideration. However, it is important to keep in mind that the statutory licences do not require remuneration where there is a fair dealing or use of an insubstantial part and as such close scrutiny of the material is the sensible starting point.

7)   Protocols for the Practical Handling of ETD[167]

In light of the foregoing analysis it is clear that universities are subject to the risk of copyright liability for the communication of ETD and as such need to put in place workable and effective compliance mechanism. The sensible way to approach these steps is to have the ETD-candidate self manage the process from the very first day of their candidature. That is, the student would be asked to record all third-party copyright materials included in the thesis, to make an assessment of the copyright status of these materials, and to note this in their copyright compliance table on a continuous basis. In managing these situations the following steps are suggested:

(1)   Identify all third-party copyright materials included in the ETD.

(2)   Is there a substantial part? Examine each item of third-party copyright content included in the ETD to assess if its inclusion involves the exercise of acts (for example, reproduction or adaptation) in relation to a substantial part of the third-party copyright content; where only an insubstantial part of any item of third-party content is used, there is no need to take further steps as use of an insubstantial part is not an infringement and does not need to be authorized by the copyright owner. Establishing guidelines for what is a substantial part is integral to the risk management process. It is not possible to provide absolute and firm guidelines for all situations, but it must be understood that any figures stated in the guidelines will essentially become the de facto rule.

---

167   See further, Damien O'Brien & Anne Fitzgerald, "Copyright Guide for Research Students: What You Need to Know about Copyright before Depositing Your Electronic Thesis in an Online Repository," OAK Law Project (Brisbane: QUT, 2007), including copyright compliance table and model third party copyright permission requests available online: www.oaklaw.qut.edu.au/files/Copyright%20Guide%20 for%20Research%20Students.pdf.

(3) Is there a fair dealing? If a substantial part of an item of third-party copyright content is included in the ETD, consider whether use of that part is justified under one or more of the fair dealing provisions.

(4) Does any other exception to copyright infringement apply? For example it is not an infringement of copyright to take a photo of a sculpture or work of artistic craftsmanship that is on permanent public display,168 so if a student includes an image of such a work in a public place there is no need to obtain permission from the owner of copyright in the publicly displayed work. A list of these kinds of miscellaneous exceptions which are relevant to the education sector should be compiled. A dated but useful starting point for understanding these exceptions is found in the Copyright Law Review Committee's reports, Simplification of the Copyright Act 1968 Part 1169 and Copyright and Contract.170

(5) Should permission be requested? If after going through these steps there is still uncertainty about whether the use of the third-party content in the thesis is authorized, a request should be sent to the copyright owner specifying the third-party materials that are to be included in the thesis and the use to be made of that material, and seeking express permission for such use; any licence obtained for the use of third-party content must be broad enough to permit the thesis to be reproduced in digital form and communicated online (whether by the student, the university, or a disciplinary repository). Since there will be doubt about whether the reproduction and communication of some materials included in theses is permissible, in some cases there will be no option but to seek express permission.

a) Adopting appropriate licences

In general, repositories will be seeking to rely on non-exclusive licences from owners of copyright in theses that they seek to place in the repository. The four types of licences listed below should be considered in relation to licensing issues for ETD.

(1) Deposit licence: Between the owner of copyright in the ETD and the ETD-repository in order give certainty to repositories in terms of

---

168 *Copyright Act*, above note 4, s. 65.

169 See Copyright Law Review Committee, *Simplification of the Copyright Act 1968 Part 1* (Canberra: The Committee, 1998), online: www.clrc.gov.au/agd/WWW/clrHome. nsf/Page/Overview_Reports_Simplification_of_the_Copyright_Act:_Part_1.

170 Lahore, *Copyright and Contract*, above note 5.

what rights they have to store, manage, and organize the ETD stored within the repository. The licence could also contain terms that reduce repository liability through disclaimers and indemnities.171

(2) End user licence: The end user, should be clearly informed about the specific activities of use and reuse that are permitted under what is termed an "end user licence." For example, this would typically include activities such as browsing (reading on screen); downloading and printing; or possibly downloading and distributing copies in class. To ensure that end users are clearly informed of the uses they are permitted to make of ETD, it is recommended that a standard—though flexible—protocol be adopted for end user licensing. For example, a straightforward approach would be for the ETD holder to license end users under one of the standard open content licences such as the Creative Commons (CC)172 or AEShareNet licence.173

(3) Third party licence: As explained at length above, where third party copyright content is included in the ETD it is necessary to confirm that rights to use the content have been granted by the third-party copyright owner (in the absence of any exemption or exclusion from copyright infringement).

(4) Publisher licence: A licence between the publisher and the ETD repository will be crucial where an ETD candidate has already assigned the copyright in all or part of their thesis, such as where they have had an article published prior to submitting the electronic thesis and dissertation.

I.   CONCLUSION

The challenge for knowledge management lies in harnessing the enormous power of networked digital technologies. At the heart of this issue is best practice copyright management. What we have shown in this article is that

---

171   Examples of current deposit licences include Swinburne University of Technology, "Access to Thesis," online: www.swin.edu.au/research/postgrad.htm; the National Library of Canada, "Theses Non-Exclusive License," online: www.nlc-bnc.ca/obj/s4/f2/frm-nl59-2.pdf.

172   See, for example, Oleg Evnin's CC-licensed doctoral thesis, *On Quantum Interacting Embedded Geometrical Objects of Various Dimensions* (Ph.D. Thesis, California Institute of Technology, 2006) online: http://resolver.caltech.edu/caltechetd:etd-06072006-174745.

173   See online: www.aesharenet.com.au.

to achieve this, institutions and people have to appreciate the variety of copyright management models that are emerging and how to employ them. If open access is a value we wish to promote for social, economic, and cultural reasons, institutions must articulate their commitment in clear policies. From this touchstone an effective copyright management framework can be built. At the end of the day, we must realize that better copyright management will provide us with more choices (including open access)—but it will not happen by default. It must be structured and managed. That is the challenge and the path forward.

CHAPTER 16

Digital Copyright Reform in New Zealand: An Own-Interest Approach for a Small Market Economy

Susy Frankel*

A. ABSTRACT

It is often stated that one of the underlying rationales for copyright protection is to encourage the creation and proliferation of copyrighted works. How much protection is needed to actually encourage the creation of copyrighted works is frequently debated. The basic contention is that over-protection may in fact have the opposite effect to encouraging creativity. In the digital age the battle over what is the appropriate level of copyright protection has become a worldwide debate. Some countries maintain that a high level of protection is a benefit not only for their own economies, but also for the world economy. Others regard lower levels of protection as necessary to foster growth and, in some instances, copyright-related technology transfer. A small market economy, such as New Zealand, finds itself in the middle ground in this debate. With interests in common with both the developed and the developing world, New Zealand has created an own-interest approach to digital copyright protection. This chapter discusses that approach.

B. RECENT HISTORY OF NEW ZEALAND COPYRIGHT LAW

New Zealand has historically adopted the United Kingdom's copyright law either without alteration or with minor alterations to the substantive law.[1]

---

*   Many thanks to Mark Perry and Brian Fitzgerald who organized the conference at which an earlier version of this paper was presented.

1   *Copyright Act 1962* (N.Z.), 1962/33, repealed, for example, is much the same as the *Copyright Act 1956* (U.K.), 4 & 5 Eliz. 2, c. 74, repealed.

A digital copyright bill was introduced to the New Zealand Parliament in 2006 and was passed as an *Amendment Act* to the *Copyright Act 1994.*[2] This chapter discusses the approach of that *Amendment Act* and the circumstances and policy objectives that led to it.

In 1994 New Zealand's copyright law was substantially updated to reflect the developments similar to those that had been enacted in UK law some several years earlier.[3] The 1994 Act was almost entirely drafted and conceived with a pre-digital technology mindset. It contains a prohibition on interfering with technological protection mechanisms,[4] but in other respects was essentially "digital free." The 1994 Act, for example, continued to define communication rights in terms of broadcasts and cable programs. It would appear that the legislature took the view that as there was no treaty directly addressing digital copyright, it need not be considered in the 1994 reforms. This view was perhaps short-sighted as the diplomatic negotiations around digital technology and copyright were well underway at the World Intellectual Property Organization (WIPO), and the resulting copyright treaty, known as the *WCT*,[5] arising from that series of WIPO negotiations came to fruition less than two years later. In any event, New Zealand is not a member of the *WCT* and the current law reform process does not make it clear that it will become a signatory of that treaty.[6]

Once a bill is introduced it is read in the House of Representatives (the House) and then it goes to a select committee process where it is discussed

---

2   N.Z., Bill 102-3, *Copyright (New Technologies and Performers' Rights) Amendment Bill*, 48th Parl., 2008 (assented to 11 April 2008), online: www.parliament.nz/en-NZ/PB/ Legislation/Bills/b/2/a/ooDBHOH_BILL7735_1-Copyright-New-Technologies-and-Performers-Rights.htm [*Copyright Bill*] and *Copyright (New Technologies) Amendment Act 2008* (N.Z.), 2008/27 [*Amendment Act*].

3   Many of the provisions of the *Copyright Act 1994* (N.Z.), 1994/143 [*Copyright Act 1994*], are adopted from the *Copyright, Designs and Patents Act 1988* (U.K.), 1988, c. 48.

4   *Copyright Act 1994, ibid.*, s. 226.

5   *WIPO Copyright Treaty*, 20 December 1996, S. Treaty Doc. No. 105-17 (1997), 36 I.L.M. 65 [*WCT*].

6   *Copyright Bill*, above note 2. The *Copyright Bill* stated in its opening commentary that "the bill takes into account international developments in copyright law, and incorporates many aspects of the two treaties negotiated by the members of the World Intellectual Property Organization (WIPO) — the *WIPO Copyright Treaty* and *WIPO Performances and Phonograms Treaty*." Even though New Zealand is not a member of the *WCT* it does, however, in some of its free trade agreements, agree to meet the standards of the *WCT*.

and public submissions are called for.[7] Submissions were made and the select committee reported back to the House recommending a number of changes. Bills that have returned to the House from the select committee process are voted on in Parliament at what is known as the third reading.[8] Although delay and further amendment often occur at the third-reading stage, bills can equally often occur with reasonable speed, particularly as the debate on the third reading is limited to two hours.[9] The copyright bill did not speedily progress and debate was halted in late 2007. At that stage it looked like the law would not pass in a hurry, however, in April 2008 it was passed.

C. POLICY AS STATED IN THE *COPYRIGHT (NEW TECHNOLOGIES) ACT*[10]

Objectives and policies of the reform process were set out in the *Copyright Bill*. A statement of purpose of legislation is a standard procedure for New Zealand bills, but when the bill becomes an Act they are not necessarily included in the Act. Among the objectives stated were:[11]

a) to clarify the application of existing rights and exceptions in the digital environment;

b) to create a technologically neutral framework to the *Copyright Act 1994*; and

c) to maintain the balance between creators, owners, and users in the digital world.

The need for clarification of existing rights and exceptions in the digital environment arises, in part, because the *Copyright Act 1994* was potentially ambiguous. Like many pre-digital copyright laws, it has the potential to

---

7   Public submissions were also called for at the policy discussion paper stage which precedes the drafting of the bill.

8   For discussion of New Zealand legislative process, see Geoffrey Palmer & Matthew Palmer, *Bridled Power: New Zealand's Constitution and Government*, 4th ed. (South Melbourne: Oxford University Press, 2004).

9   *Ibid.* at 196.

10   The bill was originally entitled the *Copyright (New Technologies and Performers' Rights) Amendment Act*, but the select committee recommended the shortening of the title because "[a]lthough the bill does amend some provisions concerning performers' rights, all these amendments relate only to making these provisions technologically neutral." See *Copyright Bill*, above note 2 at 2.

11   *Ibid.* at 1.

capture as infringements some digital world activities that arguably ought not to be infringements, such as functional transient copies, which might be made in order to view a website.[12]

The desire for a technologically neutral framework is laudable. In relation to infringement this is achieved by the inclusion of a right to communicate to the public, replacing the right tied to the technology of broadcasting and cable programming.[13] In many respects the *Amendment Act* is potentially technologically constrained; for example, it provides copyright protection for specific technologies such as technological protection mechanisms (TPMs) and circumscribed permitted acts that are based primarily around known and technologically specific modes of communication.[14]

Additionally, the general policy statement that was included with the bill when it was first read provided: "[t]he key principle that guides copyright reform in New Zealand is the enhancement of the public interest — copyright law must benefit New Zealand as a whole and contribute to overall growth and development."[15] This policy principle, with its focus on growth and development, suggests that the most important goal of the reform is the maximizing of economic benefits. The use of "overall" to qualify growth and development seems to suggest that the relevant growth and development is not necessarily confined to copyright-related businesses and industries. One would hope that the interests of copyright owners are primarily relevant. Notably, however, the traditional copyright justifications of protecting the authors and creators of copyrighted works have been subsumed into the contribution to overall growth and development. This focus on growth and development is consistent with the stated objectives of the ministry responsible for intellectual property policy: the Ministry of Economic Development.[16]

---

12 Such transient copies would have to be an infringement because s. 2 of the *Copyright Act 1994* states that copying means "in relation to any description of work, reproducing or recording the work in any material form." It was therefore possible to argue that something that is transient is not material, but such an argument is not clear-cut and has not been tested before the New Zealand courts.

13 *Copyright Bill*, above note 2, provides for a technology-neutral right to communicate to the public and a category of "communication work" which means "a transmission, or the making available by a communication technology, of sounds, visual images, or other information, or a combination of any of those, for reception by members of the public, and includes a broadcast or a cable programme."

14 Discussed below note 50.

15 *Copyright Bill*, above note 2, s. 102-1.

16 For information regarding the Ministry of Economic Development see their website, online: www.med.govt.nz.

Of note is that growth and development of New Zealand culture, whatever that may be, is not expressly excluded from the principle.

Defining the scope of a copyright law that would contribute to New Zealand's growth and development is a potentially complex matter. New Zealand is a developed country and therefore it might be expected to follow the lead of many developed countries and have strong copyright protection. Indeed, that has been the position of New Zealand's copyright policy in the twentieth century. However, New Zealand does not have a large economy and although copyright is important for many domestic interests, New Zealand is often described as a net-user of copyrighted works. In effect this means that New Zealand imports more copyrighted works than it makes for the domestic market or exports. This so-called net-user status suggests that the best way for copyright law to contribute to growth and development is to ensure that the law protects the interests of users.[17] It can be argued that it is in the users' interest to protect copyright so that users benefit from the creation of copyrighted works. Alternatively, it can be argued that overly protective copyright laws do not encourage innovation and creation and place unduly high costs on users of copyrighted works.

The objective, set out above, to maintain the balance between owners and users in the digital world suggests maintaining the current balance. Why the current balance is the appropriate balance was not explained in the *Copyright Bill* or in any of the policy papers that preceded it.[18] This policy objective does implicitly acknowledge that the balance is different in the digital world and the balance should not be shifted towards either owners or users. New Zealand's current copyright law purports to achieve balance through the framework, familiar in countries whose copyright law comes directly from the UK, of giving copyright owner's rights and addressing certain categories of user needs through a series of statutorily defined permitted acts.[19] The copyright law does not give "rights" to users. Users are required to show that their otherwise infringing use is justified under one of some forty-plus detailed provisions. The *Amendment Act* continues this approach of per-

---

17   Difficulties arise with the concept of being a net-user as not all uses of copyrighted works are the same. In small developed countries in particular, there may be net-users of some works and net-owners of others suggesting that net-user/net-owner status is not necessary clean-cut.

18   The policy papers leading up to the drafting of the bill can be found on the Ministry of Economic Development's website, "Policy/Discussion Papers," online: www.consumeraffairs.govt.nz/publications/index.html#policy.

19   For owners' exclusive rights, see *Copyright Act 1994*, above note 3, s. 16 and for users' permitted acts, see ss. 40–91.

mitted acts for users by drafting additional permitted acts to the existing framework.

I submitted to the *Copyright Bill* select committee that increasing copyright protection in the digital world, including protecting technological protection mechanisms, tips the balance in favour of owners, and it is only because of that tipping of the balance that the need for some of the new detailed permitted acts arises. I also submitted that the need for New Zealand to consider permitted acts as equal in status to copyright-exclusive rights is crucial in the digital age. Recognizing not only the rights of owners, but also the rights of users, is more likely to achieve the bill's stated aim of balancing the interests of users and owners. Users' interests are inevitably secondary to owners' rights if the terms of their use are always defined as permitted acts (i.e., "an exception" to owners' rights). Treating users as having rights puts users and owners on a more even footing.

New Zealand copyright law has, particularly since 1994, been framed around the approach that copyright is a property right and that permitted acts are somehow taking away from that property right. An approach that would better reflect the balance of rights is to define the boundaries of the property right—that is, what a copyright owner has the exclusive right to do—as being delineated in part by what others may do. In this sense, users' rights do not take a bite out of the property owners' apple, but users' rights define the shape of that apple in the first place. Such an approach could be thought of as more aligned to the US's "fair use" approach and the rights of users.[20] The historical basis for copyright permitted acts in New Zealand is not the same as the "fair use" approach, but the broad policy objective to achieve a balance of users and owners rights is not different.

In reality, however, New Zealand's position in copyright law is now primarily driven by its trading interests. New Zealand is highly dependent on international trade, particularly trade in agricultural products. In this trading context the Government of New Zealand does not treat intellectual property as a matter of purely domestic policy, but as an area of law that is directly linked to concerns of the World Trade Organization.[21]

---

20   For a discussion of fair use in the digital context see Jane C. Ginsburg, "Legal Protection of Technological Measures Protecting Works of Authorship: International Obligations and the U.S. Experience" (2005) 29 Colum. J.L & Arts 11 at 30 [Ginsburg].

21   In particular, WTO, *Agreement on Trade-Related Aspects of Intellectual Property Rights*, 15 April 1994, Marrakesh Agreement Establishing the World Trade Organization, Annex 1C, 1869 U.N.T.S. 299, 33 I.L.M. 1197 [*TRIPS Agreement*].

It is clear that some types of digital copyright reform might be beneficial for economies that are larger and have a greater volume of copyright industries than New Zealand. That does not necessarily mean, however, that a high level of copyright protection is problematic for an economy such as New Zealand's. However, it may very well be that New Zealand would be prepared to entertain high-level copyright protection, of the kind found in the US free trade agreement with Australia,[22] in order to obtain other gains, particularly in relation to market access for agricultural products. So copyright law may not necessarily contribute to the growth and development of local copyright industries, but it might indirectly contribute to the growth and development of agriculturally based industries. Such growth and development may be difficult to measure, particularly in the short term.

The above statements of policy objectives in the reform process are the tests by which some of the proposed reforms are measured in this chapter. The next section discusses some of the key reforms in the *Amendment Act*.

D. THE APPROACH OF THE AMENDMENT ACT

In this section the *Amendment Act*'s approach to certain key digital copyright concepts is outlined.

1) Communication to the Public and Communication Work

The *Amendment Act* provides for copyright owners to have the exclusive right to communicate works to the public.[23] In addition to providing a right to communicate, the *Amendment Act* introduces a category of work: "the communication work." A communication work would include a broadcast, a cable program, and any combination of those two, as well as other methods of communication with the public.[24]

The communication work and the communication right are together framed in a technologically neutral way. Like the *WCT*, the means of making the work available to the public is not technologically specified. "Communicate" is defined as "to transmit or make available by means of communication technology, including by means of a telecommunications

---

22   *Australia-United States Free Trade Agreement*, Australia and United States, 1 January 2001, [2005] ATS 1, c. 21, online: www.dfat.gov.au/trade/negotiations/us_fta/final-text [*AUSFTA*].

23   *Amendment Act*, above note 2, s. 18, substituting a new s. 33.

24   *Ibid.*, s. 3.

system or electronic retrieval system . . . ."[25] Like in the *WCT*, "public" is not defined.[26] Courts interpreting this are likely to look at the interpretation of "public" under other provisions of the 1994 Act, which include small as well as larger audiences.[27]

2) Permitted Act of Transient Copying

The *Amendment Act* provides a new permitted act of transient copying. It provides that a copy is not an infringement of copyright if the reproduction is

(a) transient or incidental; and
(b) is an integral and essential[28] part of a technological process for—
   (i) making or receiving a communication that does not infringe copyright; or
   (ii) enabling the lawful use of, or lawful dealing in, the work; and
(c) has no independent economic significance.[29]

There is no express guidance as to what "independent economic significance" means. The exception seems to suggest that transient copying is not an infringement because the copies have no independent economic value from the copyrighted work itself. It is clearly possible that a transient copy does not have an economic value that is attributable to copyright, but it seems quite probable that the communications system that creates the transient or incidental copy has an economic value independent of the copyrighted work. The phrase in that sense is not clear.

3) Copying a Sound Recording for Personal Use

A person can copy a sound recording for personal use provided certain conditions are met.[30] The select committee report refers to this provision as "format shifting." The draft provision does not, however, expressly require

---

25 *Ibid.*
26 See discussion in Sam Ricketson & Jane Ginsburg, *International Copyright and Neighbouring Rights: The Berne Convention and Beyond*, 2d ed. (New York: Oxford University Press, 2006) at 12.58.
27 See Susy Frankel & Geoff McLay, *Intellectual Property in New Zealand* (Wellington: LexisNexis Butterworths, 2002) at 5.11.4.
28 "Integral and essential" was substituted in the select committee process for "a necessary," see *Amendment Act*, above note 2, s. 23, inserting a new s. 43A(b).
29 *Amendment Act, ibid.*, inserting s. 43A.
30 *Ibid.*, s. 81A.

that the format be changed.[31] Therefore, a person can copy a CD for use in an MP3 player or copy a CD so that she has two CDs—perhaps one for each CD player she owns. Such copying is only permissible provided that the conditions of the section are met.[32] The conditions include that the sound recording is not itself an infringing copy[33] or cannot be borrowed or hired;[34] only one copy can be made for each device;[35] and the owner of the sound recording must be the owner of any copy and retain ownership of the sound recording.[36]

In the first reading of the *Copyright Bill* the format-shifting provision had a sunset clause so that it expired two years after the date on which it came into force, but it may have been extended for further periods of two years. During the select committee process this sunset clause was removed.[37] The select committee report on the bill stated that it was removed because its inclusion "would create uncertainty to whether purchasers of sound recordings on older technology would be allowed to continue format-shifting those recordings for private and domestic use in the future."[38]

The select committee report notes that the reason for the proposed enactment of this permitted act is in recognition "that format shifting of music for private and domestic use is widespread."[39] This recognition of reality is also used to reject a submission that format shifting be extended to other forms of media, such as DVDs. The committee was of the view that format shifting of other media is not widespread.[40] Such reasoning is predicated on a view of technology that is not forward-looking. It is highly possible that technology will develop so that format shifting of other media does become widespread. It is difficult to see that copyright law has a sensible policy basis if it amends itself simply because everyone commits an infringement anyway. Surely, the real question is whether other types of format shifting for personal use could be legitimate under the *Copyright Act 1994*.

---

31   *Ibid.*

32   *Ibid.*, s. 81A(1).

33   *Ibid.*, s. 81A(1)(b).

34   *Ibid.*, s. 81A(1)(c).

35   *Ibid.*, s. 81A(1)(g).

36   *Ibid.*, ss. 81A(1)(d) & (h).

37   *Copyright Bill*, above note 2, clause 44(3) struck out.

38   *Ibid.*, commentary at 5.

39   *Ibid.*

40   *Ibid.*

The provision also requires that the copy is for the owner of the sound recording or a member of that owner's household.[41] The person who makes the copy has to retain ownership of it. So, presumably, if it is given to a member of the household and that member leaves, then the person who made the copy must be sure to get it back. There is an obvious unreality and impracticality to such a requirement. If one teenage member of the household copies a song for his elder sibling who then moves away to university, the younger sibling must make sure that this copy of the sound recording, perhaps made a few years ago, does not leave for university also. Further, copying for friends is perhaps as widespread, if not more so, than it is for members of a household.

Additionally, the select committee process recommended that another condition be added; that "the sound recording is not a communication work or part of a communication work."[42] The exact meaning of this phrase is not clear. Infringing copies are not permitted to be copied under the format-shifting provision in any event. Therefore, if a communication work is illegitimately recorded it cannot be format shifted. The intention of this additional condition seems to be to exclude communication works from being unduly copied. However, the wording does not clearly reflect that intention. A sound recording once made from a communication work is no longer categorized, in copyright terms, as a communication work, rather it is a sound recording. There can of course be a sound recording and a communication work, or indeed several of each, of the same musical work, but that is a different point. The sound recording and the communication work are two separate works. Where a communication work is recorded, the recording cannot be both a communication work and a sound recording at the same time.[43] This is not simply a problem of semantics, but could lead to confusion. An example of potential confusion is illustrative. Suppose a person legitimately makes a sound recording of a communication work such as a radio broadcast. Under the *Amendment Act*, and the *Copyright Act 1994*, this kind of reproduction might be permitted if the purpose of the recording was to listen to the broadcast at a more convenient time.[44] This is known as time-shifting. Say the sound recording is made on a CD

---

41   *Amendment Act*, above note 2, s. 44, inserting s. 81A(1)(f).

42   *Ibid.*, s. 81A(1)(a).

43   The converse is not true: a sound recording can be communicated, and both works exist simultaneously at the time of communication.

44   See *Copyright Act 1994*, above note 3, s. 84 and *Amendment Act*, above note 2, s. 45, inserting s. 84.

but "A" wants to listen to it on his MP3 player. Then, in order to do so, "A" can format-shift the work. Under the format-shifting provision "A" must keep the original sound recording, but under the time-shifting provision "A" must destroy the copy made within a reasonable time after viewing it. It seems likely therefore that the intention of the legislature is that in such a situation both copies are destroyed. That intention, however, has not been made clear. The solution to this particular scenario is to amend the condition to: "the sound recording is not made from or is not a recording of a communication work." This scenario illustrates the difficulties with drafting this kind of very specific permitted act. The policy of the permitted act can be lost in the detail and circumvented in the wake of unforeseen technological developments. In such a way the policy of copyright law is lost in a sea of statutory detail and the big-picture policy of copyright law becomes unfortunately indiscernible. But perhaps the icing on the cake of the permitted format-shifting act is the ultimate elevation of owners' rights above users' interests. The *Amendment Act* also makes it clear that the owner of copyright in a sound recording can contract out of this provision.[45]

4) TPM Protection and Related Permitted Acts

Under the existing 1994 copyright law, copyright owners may take action against anyone who supplies or manufactures devices, or provides the means or information specifically designed to circumvent TPMs for the purpose of infringing copying.[46] The *Amendment Act* also extends this to prohibit conduct that involves obtaining a device to circumvent a TPM in order to infringe copyright.[47] In contrast to other jurisdictions, such as the US and Australia, there is no liability for the act of circumvention.[48] Broadly, the policy behind the provisions is that access controls can be circumvented but not copy controls.[49] Thus, the definition of TPM states:

> for the avoidance of doubt, [TPM] does not include a process, treatment, mechanism, device, or system to the extent that, in the normal course of operation, it only controls any access to a work for non-infringing purposes (for example, it does not include a process, treatment, mechanism, devise, or system to the extent that it controls geographic market

45   *Amendment Act, ibid.*, s. 81A(2).
46   *Copyright Act 1994*, above note 3, s. 226.
47   *Amendment Act*, above note 2, s. 89, inserting s. 226A(1).
48   See Ginsburg, above note 20.
49   *Copyright Bill*, above note 2, commentary at 8.

segmentation by preventing the playback in New Zealand of a non-infringing copy of a work.[50]

This is consistent with other parts of copyright law which allow for parallel importation of copyrighted works.[51] It would defeat New Zealand's parallel importation regime if a parallel import of a DVD, for example, was rendered ineffectual because regional coding prevented its playback.[52]

Before the select committee process, the *Copyright Bill* contained a definition of the term "TPM spoiling device"; the term was amended to "TPM circumvention device" to remove the implication that circumvention was necessarily "spoiling."[53]

Under the *Amendment Act* it is not permitted to sell[54] a TPM circumvention device if the seller knows or has reason to believe that it will be used to infringe copyright in a TPM-protected work. The person who has the rights in relation to the TPM is described as the "issuer" of the TPM rather than the owner of the TPM.[55] That person has the same rights of delivery in civil and criminal proceedings as a copyright owner would in respect of infringement of copyright.[56]

The select committee report stated that the TPM provisions "are necessary to manage the risk of piracy of copyrighted works in a digital environment, and that they strike the correct balance between the interests of copyright owners and those of copyright users."[57] This policy, to maintain the balance between owners and users, is given effect by allowing the circumvention of TPMs in order to perform a permitted act.[58] Where this legitimate circumvention is not possible because of, for example, digital lock-up, the person seeking to perform a permitted act may seek assistance from a "qualified person" to effect the circumvention.[59] This elite group, of the so-called qualified includes educational establishments, prescribed

---

50   *Amendment Act*, above note 2, s. 89, inserting s. 226.
51   *Copyright Act 1994*, above note 3, s. 12.
52   Most DVD players sold in New Zealand play DVDs with any region code.
53   *Amendment Act*, above note 2, s. 89, inserting s. 226.
54   The provision makes it a prohibited act to "make, import, sell, distribute, let for hire, offer or expose for sale or hire, or advertise for sale or hire" a TPM circumvention device, *Amendment Act*, *ibid.*, s. 89, inserting s. 226A.
55   *Ibid.*, s. 226B.
56   *Ibid.*, s. 226B(3).
57   *Copyright Bill*, above note 2, commentary 8.
58   *Amendment Act*, above note 2, s. 89, inserting s. 226D(2)(a).
59   *Ibid.*, s. 226D(2).

libraries, and archives.[60] Although allowing circumvention for permitted acts is a starting point to balancing the interests of users and owners, the requirement that the permitted act may only be done by a select group shifts the balance back the other way. The *Amendment Act* then addresses a user's options if the user is prevented from exercising a permitted act because of a TPM.[61] A person wanting to exercise the permitted act can either a) apply to the copyright owner to do so, or b) engage a statutorily deemed, qualified person.[62] The qualified person is limited to only charging the total "cost of the provision of the service and a reasonable contribution to [their] general expenses."[63] This is unlikely to produce a boom in the business of being qualified to circumvent TPMs, but this attempt to control the price is, quite obviously, subject to potential dispute over what a reasonable fee is.

The *Amendment Act* purports to effect balance, but the moment TPMs are protected in their own right the balance shifts in favour of owners and it is very difficult to "unshift." It is interesting that New Zealand should now protect TPMs in this way when TPM protection has been in place for the better part of a decade in the US and the EU. Even some of its initial supporters now question the need for such protection. Most notably, however, in the ten years or more that TPM protection of this sort has not been in force, there is no New Zealand-based evidence that the failure to protect TPMs has led to any increase in piracy.

5) Decompilation of Software

The *Amendment Act* allows for decompilation of computer programs under certain conditions.[64] The primary condition is that the decompilation is for the purpose of creating an independent but interoperable program.[65] Decompile means

(a) to convert a computer program expressed in a low level language into a version expressed in a higher level language; or

(b) to copy the program as a necessary incident of converting it into that version.[66]

---

60 *Ibid.*, s. 226D(3)
61 *Ibid.*, s. 226E.
62 *Ibid.*, s. 226E(2)
63 *Ibid.*, s. 226E(4).
64 *Ibid.*, s. 43, inserting s. 80A.
65 *Ibid.*, s. 80A(2)(a).
66 *Ibid.*, s. 80A(4).

A further subsection provides that decompilation is not permitted if the "lawful user" of a copy of the computer program uses "the information obtained from decompiling the computer program to create a program that is substantially similar in its expression to the program that has been decompiled."[67] The select committee report urged the Ministry of Economic Development to monitor the effect of this provision to ensure that it is not used to restrict competition in the software market.[68] An agreement that attempts to prohibit or restrict this "permitted" decompilation shall have no effect.[69] Some submissions to the select committee process were concerned that this would mean that suppliers of computer software would not license New Zealand use.[70] Other submissions suggested that software contracts would apply foreign law to avoid this permitted act. This reasoning misunderstands the role of contract law and copyright law. This provision has the effect of making this a mandatory requirement of copyright law. Copyright is applied on a territorial basis so that even if an agreement between a New Zealand and, for example, a US software supplier purports to apply US law, New Zealand law and not US law will apply to the copyright, even though US law applies to the contract.

Other provisions allow for copying of a computer program to lawfully use the program. The section gives the example of copying to correct an error.[71] It is also not an infringement to observe, study, or test a computer program to "determine the ideas and principles that underlie any element of the program."[72] Unlike the permitted decompilation act, the *Amendment Act* does not expressly provide that this permitted act cannot be contracted out of. The absence of express provisions regarding the other permitted acts in relation to computer programs suggests that they can be contracted out of. The drafters of the *Amendment Act* seem to assume that permitted acts can be contracted out of. This is consistent with the notion of permitted acts being exceptions, but the legitimacy of contracting out of permitted acts has not been tested in New Zealand law. Given the stated policy that permitted acts are designed to effect a balance between users and owners, it

---

67 *Ibid.*, s. 80A(3)(d).

68 *Copyright Bill*, above note 2, commentary 10.

69 *Amendment Act*, above note 2, inserting s. 80D.

70 New Zealand Law Society Submission, online: www.parliament.nz/NR/rdonlyres/ CF21D3BE-051E-463E-9E50-6F2820474270/56459/NewZealandLawSociety3.pdf at para. 20.

71 *Amendment Act*, above note 2, inserting s. 80B. This permitted use cannot be contracted out of, see s. 80C.

72 *Ibid.*, s. 80C.

is questionable as to why it should be presumed, without further analysis, that these acts can be contracted out of.

6) Internet Service Provider Liability

Internet service providers (ISPs)[73] are not liable for infringing copyright or authorizing infringement if a person uses the services of an ISP when infringing copyright.[74] This exemption from liability is, however, subject to a copyright owner's right to injunctive relief.[75]

For an ISP, storing (but not modification) of infringing material is not an infringement unless the ISP knows that the material stored is infringing or has reason to believe that it is infringing.[76] The *Amendment Act* implements a notice and takedown procedure. An ISP that "knows or has reason to believe that the material infringes copyright" must delete the material or prevent access to the material "as soon as possible after becoming aware of the infringing material."[77] A court, when deciding if an ISP "knows or has reason to believe that material infringes copyright," must take into account if the ISP has received a notice of infringement.[78]

Submissions were made that a notice and notice procedure should be adopted, rather than a notice and takedown procedure.[79] A notice and notice procedure requires the ISP to notify its client of a copyright owner's complaint of infringement, but that notice alone does not require them to take down material. The suggestion of a notice and notice procedure was not adopted. Also, an ISP is not liable for copyright infringement in certain instances of caching material.[80]

---

73   ISPs are defined to include those who provide "transmission, routing or providing of connections for digital online communications, between or among points specified by a user" and hosting services. *Ibid.*, s. 4.

74   *Ibid.*, s. 92B.

75   *Ibid.*, s. 92B(2)(a) and in relation to exclusion from liability for storing infringing material s. 92B(3) provides "However, nothing in this section limits the right of the copyright owner to injunctive relief in relation to [a user's] infringement or any infringement by the Internet service provider."

76   *Ibid.*, s. 92C(2).

77   *Ibid.*, s. 92C(2)(a).

78   *Ibid.*, s. 92C(3).

79   See InternetNZ, "Submission on the *Copyright Amendment Bill 2007*" (9 March 2007), online: www.internetnz.net.nz/issues/submissions/archive/2007/copyright/view.

80   *Amendment Act*, above note 2, new s. 92D.

E. THE OVERALL APPROACH TO PERMITTED ACTS

The policy to maintain the balance between users and owners in the digital world is difficult to achieve. Copyright protection of TPMs inevitably favours owners. Even though the policy is to maintain the existing balance the reforms beg the question of whether the balance is correct in the first place.

As discussed above, the distinctions between approaches to fair use and permitted acts are set in sharp relief in the digital age because permitted acts become harder and harder to exercise when copyright protection is given to technologies like TPMs. New Zealand's approach of permitted acts needs to be looked at carefully.[81] While the proposals to allow circumvention of TPMs to undertake permitted acts and introducing the permitted acts of decompilation of computer programs, format shifting, and additional educational[82] and archival[83] exceptions and the like are for the benefit of users, there is an overarching difficulty with this approach. In the digital environment, it is not clear that this sort of tinkering with permitted acts actually will achieve the policy objectives that the *Amendment Act* intended to implement. It is questionable whether rearranging and increasing permitted acts does enough to benefit those New Zealanders who are users. New Zealand, like Canada, has a fair dealing approach to copyright law specifying specific categories of permitted acts and requiring certain criteria to be met. Like Canada, New Zealand does not have a broad "fair use," US-style provision. Unlike Canada, the New Zealand courts, and it would seem copyright owners in practice, have not interpreted the law in the broad terms similar to that of the Canadian Supreme Court.[84] New Zealand has a fairly restrictive approach to permitted acts. It is questionable whether it is desirable or indeed necessary to retain that restrictiveness in the digital environment.

Neither the *Copyright Act 1994* nor the *Amendment Act* as a whole decisively demonstrates any overarching guiding principles of the scope of permitted acts. Such overall guiding principles are important so as not to eliminate permitted acts because of unforeseen technological or business

---

81 Others have suggested that the whole *Copyright Act 1994* needs to be overhauled. There appears to be reluctance at the Ministry of Economic Development to do this as it is not a priority, given that the whole Act was overhauled in 1994. However, as that was a pre-digital Act the reluctance is not really justified.

82 *Amendment Act*, above note 2, s. 44A.

83 *Ibid.*, ss. 30–36.

84 See *CCH Canadian Ltd. v. Law Society of Upper Canada*, 2004 SCC 13.

nuances. I submitted to the select committee that guiding permitted-act principles be included in the *Amendment Act*. In the 1994 Act these general principles of guidance, which resemble US law, can be found as part of the general provision allowing fair dealing for research and private study in some circumstances. The relevant part of that provides:

> In determining, for the purposes of subsection (1) of this section, whether copying, by means of a reprographic process or by any other means, constitutes fair dealing for the purposes of research or private study, a court shall have regard to —
>
> a) The purpose of the copying; and
> b) The nature of the work copied; and
> c) Whether the work could have been obtained within a reasonable time at an ordinary commercial price; and
> d) The effect of the copying on the potential market for, or value of, the work; and
> e) Where part of a work is copied, the amount and substantiality of the part copied taken in relation to the whole work.[85]

These principles, or similar ones, should be elevated to be guiding principles for all permitted acts. This will enable courts and other interpreters of legislation to capture the meaning behind the exceptions and to achieve the Act's stated aim of maintaining a balance between users and owners of copyright protected matter.

F.   CONCLUSION

The approach of drafting provisions specifically for New Zealand's interests is an important step towards developing a sound intellectual property law for New Zealand.[86] The disappointment with the *Amendment Act* is that it is not preceded by a full economic or social analysis of which approach to digital copyright protection would benefit New Zealand. The *Amendment Act* adopts the approach that digital copyright protection measures "are necessary to manage the risk of piracy of copyrighted works in the digital environment."[87] There is no conclusive evidence that in the last ten years

---

85   *Copyright Act 1994*, above note 3, s. 43(3).

86   I have argued elsewhere that development of a New Zealand intellectual property law for New Zealand is important. See Susy Frankel, "Towards a Sound New Zealand Intellectual Property Law" (2001) 32 V.U.W.L.R. 47.

87   *Copyright Bill*, above note 2, commentary 8.

of the digital environment the balance has been tilted in the wrong direction in New Zealand. The opening passages of the select committee report indicate that the legislation will be reviewed in five years' time "to ensure that copyright legislation in New Zealand keeps pace with technological advances."[88]

---

88   *Ibid.*, commentary 1.

Contributors

Mark Perry is Associate Dean Research, Graduate Studies and Operations at The University of Western Ontario. He is internationally renowned for his research into the interface between law and new technologies, in particular in intellectual property and software licensing. He has published in this field in Australia, Canada, Germany, Japan, New Zealand, the UK, and the US. He has addressed audiences in these and other countries, usually as an invited speaker. Recent publications, not listed below, include a new chapter on Technology Law for the reference work Butterworths' looseleaf *Electronic Business Law*. He is a Barrister and Solicitor of the Law Society of Upper Canada, a Faculty Fellow at IBM's Center for Advanced Studies, a correspondent for the *Computer Law & Security Report*, and a member of the International Association for the Advancement of Teaching and Research in Intellectual Property, the Institute of Electrical and Electronics Engineers, the Intellectual Property Institute of Canada, and the Association of Computer Machinery (ACM) and a committee member of the ACM Special Interest Group of Computers in Society. He is a reviewer for multiple granting societies and associations.

By focusing on the nexus of law and science, and the area of autonomic computing system development, combined with his experience developing software, Professor Perry has a unique perspective on researching and teaching in the FLOSS license area. He is also researching the legal ramifications of technological developments in biotechnology innovation.

Brian Fitzgerald is an internationally recognized scholar specializing in Intellectual Property and Cyberlaw. He holds post-graduate degrees in law from Oxford University and Harvard University and his recent publications include *Cyberlaw: Cases and Materials on the Internet, Digital Intellectual Property and E-commerce* (2002); *Jurisdiction and the Internet* (2004); *Intellectual Property in Principle* (2004), and *Internet and E-commerce Law* (2007). Over the past ten years, Brian has delivered seminars on Information Technology, Internet, and Intellectual Property Law in Australia, Canada, China, Brazil, New Zealand, US, Nepal, India, Japan, Malaysia, Singapore, Norway, Croatia, France, Thailand, Slovakia, and the Netherlands. Brian is a Chief Investigator and Program Leader for Law in the Australian Research Council Centre of Excellence on Creative Industries and Innovation and is Project Leader for the Australian government-funded Open Access to Knowledge Law Project (OAK Law) (see: www.oaklaw.qut. edu.au) and Legal Framework for e-Research Project. He is also a Program Leader for the Cooperative Research Centre for Spatial Information. His current projects include work on intellectual property issues across the areas of copyright, digital content and the Internet, copyright and the creative industries in China, open content licensing and the Creative Commons, Free/Libre Open Source Software, research use of patents, patent transparency, science commons, e-research, licensing of digital entertainment, and anti-circumvention law. From 1998–2002 Brian was Head of the School of Law and Justice at Southern Cross University in New South Wales, Australia, and from January 2002 – January 2007 he was Head of the School of Law at QUT in Brisbane. He is currently a specialist Research Professor in Intellectual Property and Innovation at QUT. He is also a Barrister of the High Court of Australia. See further information here www.law.qut.edu. au/staff/lsstaff/fitzgerald.jsp and here www.ip.qut.edu.au.

Benedict Atkinson is the author of *The True History of Copyright: The Australian Experience 1905–2005* (Sydney University Press, 2007), which tests the incentive theory of intellectual property regulation by examining the origins and development of copyright law. He has practised as a lawyer and worked in government contracting and legislative policy. He helped to implement the Commonwealth's digital agenda reform program and his recommendations led to reform of the New South Wales Government's administration of copyright policy. He is co-author with Professor Brian Fitzgerald of two articles interpreting copyright law. One is reproduced in this volume and discusses limits on the copyright owner's control of copyright use: "Third Party Copyright and Public Information Infrastructure/ Registries: How Much Copyright Tax Must the Public Pay?" Ben is a Research Fellow, Faculty of Law, QUT, and Australian Research Council Centre of Excellence for Creative Innovation. He graduated B.A. (Hons.) LL.M. (Hons. 1) from Sydney University.

Anthony Austin is a research officer for the OAK Law Project and the Legal Framework for e-Research Project at the Queensland University of Technology, Brisbane, Australia. Anthony worked as a solicitor for ten years in private practice before joining the OAK Law Project, primarily in intellectual property and commercial law. Anthony completed his Masters of Law degree at Queensland University of Technology in 2007 and has worked and advised on numerous OAK Law and Legal Framework for e-Research publications including *The Queensland University of Technology and ARC Centre of Excellence for Creative Industries and Innovation Guide: CCI Blog, Podcast, Vodcast and Wiki Legal Guide for Australia 2008.*

Marcus Bornfreund B.A., LL.B., LL.M. (Law & Technology), of the Bar of Ontario, is the founding project lead for Creative Commons Canada and a member of the Law Society of Upper Canada. A steadfast supporter of strong civil liberties, Marcus is committed to using computer technology and royalty-free copyright licensing to facilitate access to legal information and services. You can download the LawShare (ILE) Browser at http://lawshare.ca/resources.htm.

Emma Carroll is a research assistant with the Creative Commons Clinic, a project of the Australian Research Council Centre of Excellence of Creative Industries and Innovation, based at QUT in Brisbane, Australia. Prior to completing a Bachelor of Laws at QUT in 2008, Emma earned a Bachelor of Music with First Class Honours in Music Technology at the Queensland Conservatorium. She is a freelance audio engineer, musician, university lecturer, and project officer for the Queensland Conservatorium's Music Technology Work Integrated Learning program. Emma has also worked in theatre, radio, festival production, music retail, and commercial law and has travelled and lived abroad extensively. In 2009 Emma will work as a trainee solicitor for Blake Dawson and hopes to specialize in Intellectual Property law.

Jessica Coates is the Project Manager of Creative Commons Australia and the Creative Commons Clinic, a program of the Australian Research Council Centre of Excellence for Creative Innovation at QUT. The clinic aims to further the implementation of the international open content licensing movement, Creative Commons, through the promotion of Creative Commons research and usage in Australia.

Jessica's main areas of research are copyright, open content licensing, and Internet law. She presents regularly at national and international conferences and workshops, runs an undergraduate research unit, and is a principle author of a number of books and reports, including *Open Content Licensing: Cultivating the Creative Commons* (http://creativecommons.org.au/ocl), *Unlocking the Potential Through Creative Commons* (http://creativecommons.org.au/unlockingthepotential), and *Legal Aspects of Web 2.0* (www.ip.qut.edu.au/files/Queensland%20Government%20Report%20-%20reformat.pdf).

In her role as Project Manager of the Creative Commons Clinic, Jessica also regularly participates in industry and community-based events, with the clinic being a major partner in projects such as Open Channel Screen Resource Centre's "Video Slam" (http://blog.apc.org.au/category/projects/video-slam), Melbourne Fringe Festival's "Digital Fringe" (http://digital-fringe.com.au), and the Australia Council funded "Remix My Lit" (http://www.remixmylit.com).

Prior to working for the clinic, Jessica spent most of the last decade as a copyright and communications policy officer with the Commonwealth Department of Communications, Information Technology and the Arts (DCITA), where she worked on major legislative reforms such as the Digital Agenda Review and the Australia-US Free Trade Agreement. She has a Bachelor of Laws and a Bachelor of Arts (English Hons.) from the Australian National University.

Erin Driscoll has significant expertise in copyright law and policy, and has previously worked for the Attorney-General's Department, the National Museum of Australia, and the Australia Film Commission. She was also a member of the secretariat supporting the Copyright Law Review Committee in its inquiry into the relationship between copyright and contract in 2002.

Since 2003 Erin has also chaired the Copyright in Cultural Institutions Group (CICI), which is a working group of copyright and intellectual property managers across Australia, with membership including the Australian Digital Alliance, Australian Film Commission, National Museum of Australia, National Archives of Australia, and National Gallery of Australia.

Anne Fitzgerald is Professor of Law at QUT and a recognized expert in the field of Intellectual Property Law, which is demonstrated through her outstanding contributions to research, publication, training, teaching, and professional practice. Anne has specialized for the past fifteen years in Intellectual Property Law, in particular its application to information technology. During this time she has gained extensive practical experience in intellectual property and technology contracting and recent hands-on experience negotiating, drafting, and advising on information technology and biotechnology contracts for the Queensland Government.

Anne has conducted extensive research in these fields, resulting in the publication of several books, articles, and chapters on Intellectual Property Law (particularly as it applies to digital technologies), and e-commerce law. Since 1991, she has taught courses in the areas of Intellectual Property and e-Commerce Law to students in Law, Biotechnology, Information Technology, Multimedia, and e-Commerce courses, as well as to IT professionals, writers, and designers. Each year since 2003 she has taught the Intellectual Property Law course offered by Macquarie University's School of Law as a summer intensive and, since 2004, she has been the co-coordinator (with John Stonier) of the Patents and Commercialization course in the Master of Laws program at QUT Law School. Anne teaches in the undergraduate Internet Law and e-Commerce Law and Technology Contracts courses offered at QUT Law School and has taught in the Cyberlaw course in Southern Cross University's summer law school program since 1998.

Anne was an initiator of the *Going Digital* series of seminars on legal aspects of e-commerce, multimedia, and the Internet that were held in Brisbane, Melbourne, and Hobart in 1997 and 1998 in association with QANTM Australia Co-operative Multimedia Centre. The project culminated in the publication of *Going Digital: Legal Issues for Electronic Commerce, Multimedia and the Internet* (Prospect Media, now LexisNexis/ Butterworths) in August 1998. A second, completely revised edition of the book, *Going Digital 2000: Legal Issues for e-Commerce, Software and the Internet* was published in February 2000.

Susy Frankel is a Professor of Law at Victoria University of Wellington, New Zealand. She is the author of many articles in the field of intellectual property and co-author of *Intellectual Property in New Zealand* (Butterworths, LexisNexis, 2002). She is a member of the Editorial Board of the *Journal of World Intellectual Property Law*, Co-Director of the New Zealand Centre of International Economic Law, a mediator and arbitrator for the World Intellectual Property Organization, a Hearings Officer for the Intellectual Property Office of New Zealand, and Chair of the New Zealand Copyright Tribunal.

Maree Heffernan works for the Queensland Government and was formerly a research officer with the Legal Framework for e-Research Project and a senior research officer with the Centre for Social Change Research at Queensland University of Technology. Graduating from the University of

Queensland with a first class honours in psychology in the late 1990s, she is currently completing a Ph.D. in the School of Humanities & Human Services at QUT. The focus of her research is the human element in the uptake of new technologies, and she has broader interests in the areas of social justice and marginalization. In the Legal Framework for e-Research project, Maree has worked with the project team to develop an online survey regarding legal and project agreement issues in collaboration and e-Research and has been responsible for the statistical analyses of survey data. Maree is also working with the OAK Law team on another online survey of Australian authors regarding publishing agreements. These projects build on a number of projects Maree has initiated, including: digital storytelling as a qualitative research methodology, collaborative research frameworks (including working with Indigenous communities), and the use of geographic information systems in the context of human service provision.

Scott Kiel-Chisholm completed his articles of clerkship with Blake Dawson Waldron Lawyers in 2001, after working in the insurance, projects, intellectual property, and communications and corporate advisory practice groups. He then travelled to Silicon Valley in California, and upon his return, Scott commenced work in the litigation practice group of McInnes Wilson Lawyers, concentrating on the defence of professional indemnity claims. In 2004, Scott joined the commercial litigation practice group of Home Wilkinson Lowry Lawyers which provided broader litigation experience in project management contracting, retailing, construction, manufacturing, and franchising. In an effort to progress a career in intellectual property law, Scott commenced work with Colavitti Lillas Lawyers before becoming project manager of the OAK Law Project in November 2005. In September 2006 Scott also became the project manager of the Legal Framework for e-Research Project and has been involved in the development of two online surveys and two international conferences and the production of numerous reports and guides. In December 2007, Scott was awarded a Master of Laws specializing in intellectual property law from the University of Queensland.

Matt Norwood is an American lawyer and Free Software advocate. He lives and works in Toronto. He previously served as Legal Counsel at the Software Freedom Law Center in New York City.

Damien O'Brien holds a Bachelor of Laws from QUT, a graduate certificate in International Studies (International Relations) from the University of Queensland, a graduate diploma in Legal Practice from QUT, and a Master of Laws (Intellectual Property and Technology Law) from the National University of Singapore. He is admitted as a Solicitor of the Supreme Court of Queensland, Australia, and is currently practising as a foreign lawyer in the Intellectual Property and Technology Law practice of one of the leading law firms in Singapore. Damien has published numerous articles and book chapters on topics such as blogs and the law, search engine liability for copyright infringement, digital music law, and digital copyright law.

Rami M. Olwan (LL.B., LL.M. (Intellectual Property Law), LL.M. (Internet Law)) is an Australian government Ph.D. scholarship candidate at QUT. He graduated from the University of Yarmouk Faculty of Law (Jordan) with an LL.B. in 1997, and obtained an LL.M. from Buckingham University Law School (UK) in 2000. Mr. Olwan obtained a scholarship from the Berkman Center for Internet and Society at Harvard Law School to attend the Internet Law program in Rio de Janeiro, Brazil, in March 2003. He also obtained an LL.M. from Columbia University Law School in 2007 on a scholarship from Open Society Institute.

Prior to joining QUT, Mr. Olwan was working as a legal consultant in e-Commerce Law in Jordan, United Arab Emirates, and the Sultanate of Oman from 2000 to 2005. He specializes in domain names and digital copyright issues. Mr. Olwan interned with the World Intellectual Property Organization in New York in 2007. Mr. Olwan has published articles in various journals, including the *Kuwait Law Journal* and the *United Arab Emirates University Law Journal*. He has been a member of the Jordanian Bar since 2001 and he is fluent in Arabic and English.

Joseph Potvin is a senior economist with the Information Technology Division, Chief Information Officer Branch, Treasury Board of Canada Secretariat. For five years he has coordinated planning towards the creation of Intellectual Resources Canada (Ressources Intellectuelles Canada), a forthcoming inter-departmental and inter-sectoral initiative for any community engaged in the joint creation and evolution of data, information, or knowledge that helps government carry out its mandate and achieve its objectives. He also coordinates the Government of Canada's IT expenditure reporting, for which he initiated the ITERation Project for automated expenditure data assembly, management, statistical analysis, and reporting. Mr. Potvin joined the federal government in 1999, first with the International Development Research Centre where he served as the lead architect and Project Manager of one of the Canadian Government's first Free/Libre Open Source Software (FLOSS) releases, a full-featured grants and contributions management system for the Online Proposal Appraisal (OPA). Eight years later OPA is still in use in numerous organizations, it continues to run the largest international development research grants initiative of the World Bank, and is on the way to version 3 with the participation of Treasury Board of Canada Secretariat. He is co-founder and an active participant in GOSLING (Getting Open Source Logic INto Governments), a voluntary, informal learning, and knowledge-sharing community of practice, involving civil servants and other citizens who actively assist the engagement of FLOSS methods and software solutions in government operations.

During the decade prior to his involvement with IT systems, he worked internationally as an ecological economist, with assignments for six different divisions of the World Bank including the Global Environment Facility, and he was on the core drafting team for Canada's Green Plan in 1990. Today he volunteers as a leading organizer on community projects in Canada's national capital region to advance agro-residential development, rail, and cycling transportation infrastructure, sport-ecology synthesis, and municipal water pollution reduction. He is also active in formative work on two free/libre/open macroeconomic software projects: "The Earth-Reserve Resources Exchange (TERRE)" system, and the "Resource and Ecosystems Degradation (RED) Tax" system.

Sampsung Xiaoxiang Shi is a researcher at the Australian Research Council Centre of Excellence for Creative Industries and Innovation (CCI) and Ph.D. candidate at the Faculty of Law, QUT. His Ph.D. research focuses on copyright law and innovation in the networked information economy in Australia and China. His research interests cover the laws of copyright, media, entertainment, and especially the social and legal implications of the Internet and ICT. Sampsung was accepted into the annual Summer Doctoral Programme (SDP) run by the Oxford Internet Institute in partnership with The Berkman Center for Internet and Society at Harvard Law School in 2007. Sampsung received a Bachelor in Law (2003) and a Master in Civil and Commercial Law (2006) from the East China University of Political Science and Law (ECUPL). From 2003 to 2006, he was a research assistant to Professor Fuping Gao, Dean of the Intellectual Property School of ECUPL, and co-authored several research reports for the Shanghai government.

Richard Stallman launched the development of the GNU operating system (see www.gnu.org) in 1984. GNU is free software: everyone has the freedom to copy it and redistribute it, as well as to make changes either large or small. The GNU/Linux system, basically the GNU operating system with Linux added, is used on tens of millions of computers today. Stallman has received the ACM Grace Hopper Award, a MacArthur Foundation fellowship, the Electronic Frontier Foundation's Pioneer award, and the Takeda Award for Social/Economic Betterment, as well as several honorary doctorates.

Phil Surette (B.Sc., M.Sc., LL.B.) has an LL.B. from the University of Ottawa, a Master's in Computer Science from UWO, and a Bachelor's degree in Cognitive Science from the University of Toronto. Phil is interested in improving access to law and legal research through open source software. He is currently working as a software developer in Ottawa and can be reached at philsurette@yahoo.com.

Nic Suzor is an Institute for Creative Industries and Innovation Ph.D. researcher in the Law School at QUT, exploring constitutional principles for the governance of virtual communities. His background is in both Law and Computer Science, holding undergraduate degrees in Law and IT from QUT, and having worked as a computer programmer before moving to legal research. He has published on issues including copyright law, free software licences, parody and other copyright exceptions, new media regulation, and legal issues around the development and participation in computer games. He holds a Masters of Laws (research), and his thesis examined the transformative use of copyright material in Australia. He is involved in several research projects including Creative Commons Australia, research into legal issues of Free and Open source Software, computer games (with particular reference to massive multiplayer online environments), and commons-based peer production.

Nic is also a board member of Electronic Frontiers Australia, and teaches in QUT Law School's undergraduate and post-graduate programs.

Peter P. Swire is the C. William O'Neill Professor of Law at the Moritz College of Law of Ohio State University and a Senior Fellow at the Center for American Progress.

From 1999 to early 2001 he served as the Clinton Administration's Chief Counselor for Privacy in the US Office of Management and Budget. In that position, he coordinated administration policy on the use of personal information in the public and private sectors, and served as point of contact with privacy and data protection officials in other countries. He was White House coordinator for the proposed and final *Health Insurance Portability and Accountability Act* medical privacy rules, and played a leading role on topics including financial privacy, Internet privacy, encryption, public records and privacy, e-commerce policy, and computer security and privacy.

Professor Swire has published extensively, testifies regularly before the Congress, and is quoted frequently in national and international press. He is faculty editor of "The Privacy Year in Review," published by *IS, A Journal of Law and Policy for the Information Age*, which is distributed to all members of the International Association of Privacy Professionals. He is lead author of *Information Privacy: Official Reference for the Certified Information Privacy Professional*. Many of his writings appear at www.peterswire.net.

Professor Swire graduated summa cum laude from Princeton University and in law school was a Senior Editor of the Yale Law Journal.

Dilan Thampapillai is a Lecturer with the School of Law of Victoria University in Australia. Dilan has an LL.B. from the Australian National University, a Master of Commerce from the University of Sydney, and a Master of Laws from Cornell University. Dilan has also been a visiting student at Harvard University and the National University of Singapore. Dilan is currently undertaking a Ph.D. at the University of Melbourne. Prior to joining Victoria University, Dilan was a lawyer with the Attorney-General's Department and the Australian Government Solicitor. Dilan specializes in Intellectual Property Law. Dilan researches in the areas of Intellectual Property Law, International Trade Law, and International Law.

Dr. Margaret Ann Wilkinson is Professor in the Faculty of Law at UWO and Director of the Area of Concentration in Intellectual Property, Information, and Technology Law. For fifteen years, she held a joint appointment in the Faculty of Law and the Faculty of Information and Media Studies at UWO and continues to supervise graduate students in both faculties. She has also held visiting positions at Dalhousie University and Newcastle University. She also holds an Adjunct position at the Richard Ivey School of Business at UWO (currently in their Health Sector program). Dr. Wilkinson has written widely on copyright and moral rights, personal data protection and privacy, and other areas of Intellectual Property and Information Law, as well as on management and professional ethics.

CPSIA information can be obtained at www.ICGtesting.com
Printed in the USA
LVOW081231101211

258686LV00006B/2/P